✠

LIVES OF THE BIGAMISTS

mil, setecientos, sesenta, y ocho años en vista de lo declarado
y ratificado por el Liz.do D.n Manuel Joseph Rosales,
pase el presente Notario al Registro de los Libros de Informaciones, y Casamientos copiar de la información de Andres Grisalva, y su casamiento al pie de la letra cuya diligencia se
pondrá authorisada con su concuerda, assi su Merced
mandó y firmó.

Manuel Jph Chacon   Por mandado de su merced

                                          Thomas Chacon
                                          Notario.

Incontinenti Yo el infrascripto Notario pasé al Registro de Libros,
por mandado de su Merced el S.or Comissionado D.n Manuel Joseph Chacon, y en el Libro de informaciones à foxas ciento,
y tres buelta la información siguiente. = En esta Yglesia Parro-
quial del S.r S.to Domingo de Ysq.a en quinze dias del Mes
de Junio de mil setecientos sesenta, y dos con licencia Parrochi.l
Ante mi D.n Manuel Joseph Rosales, se presentó Andres Grisalva crioyo de Juriapa, hijo de Pasqual Grisalva, y de Ysabel
de Aguilar con Paula Salazar hija de Juan de Dios de Salazar, y de Jacinta de Obando, à fin de contraer Matrimonio,
y para su información presentaron por testigos del hombre,
à Matheo Hernandes, y à Xroval Manuel crioyos de Juriapa, y de la muger Gregorio, Maris Ypolito Joseph Manuel,
y Joseph truxillo dichos testigos Mayores de edad, de quienes
recivi Juramento el que hizieron por Dios N.ro S.or y una se-
ñal de la S.ta Cruz so cuio cargo prometieron decir verdad
en todo lo que supieran, y les fuere preguntado. Y siendolo por
mi bien instruido en la gravedad del Juramento, y las penas del perjuro declararon siendo preguntados segun el tor-
den del S.to Consilio de Trento, despues de vastantes pregunt.s
que no tenian impedimento los pretendientes que esta es la
verdad del Juram.to que fecho tienen en que se afirmaron,
y ratifican, y declararon no tocarles las generales de la ley,
y puesto cada uno de los pretendientes en su libertad dixe-
ron que de su libre, y expontanea voluntad se querian
casar, y en vista delas informaciones por las Clausulas conte-
nidas fechas por dichos testigos lo que no firmaron por no
ver Mande se hamonestasen segun el orden S.ta à fin
... en su resulta prover lo que mas combenga, y por ...

Andres Grisalva con ... ... firmé. = Manuel Joseph Rosales =
... Paula Salazar. del mes de Julio de mil setecientos sesenta, y dos en esta Yglesia Parro-

RICHARD BOYER

Lives of the Bigamists

MARRIAGE, FAMILY, AND COMMUNITY

IN COLONIAL MEXICO

University of New Mexico Press ✢ *Albuquerque*

FOR MY FAMILY

Josette, Nicolas, Thomas, and Christophe

Library of Congress Cataloging-in-Publication Data

Boyer, Richard E.
    Lives of the bigamists : marriage, family, and community in
colonial Mexico / Richard Boyer.
        p.   cm.
    Includes bibliographical references and index.
    ISBN 0-8263-1571-2
        1. Bigamy—Mexico—History.   2. Marriage—Mexico—History.
3. Family—Mexico—History.   I. Title.
HQ561.B69   1995
364.1′83′0972—dc20   94-38576
                                                          CIP

Frontispiece: Inquisition document concerned with a case of bigamy
Illustrations reproduced courtesy of Editorial Patria, Mexico City.
Design by Stephanie Jurs

Contents

Tables and Map

✠

✠

Acknowledgments

✛ THE TWO HUNDRED or so bigamists of this book have been fascinating companions over the years. Collectively, I view them as representative of colonial Mexico's plebeian world; individually, I see them as fashioning their worlds in distinctive ways. Trying to understand them has been a demanding task and, on taking leave of them now, I am all too aware that much about them can never be recovered. Readers interested in their stories, dispersed in the chapters, may use the index to keep the following in view more directly: Antonio de Azevedo, Gerónimo Benavides, Marcos de la Cruz, Mateo de la Cruz, Juan Gómez Franco, Agustín Hoz Espinosa, Juan Lorenzo del Castillo, Bárbara Martina, Pedro Mateo, Mariana Monroy, Joseph Múñoz de Sanabria, Juan Antonio Ramírez, Felipe Rodriguez, Francisco Rodriguez, and Manuel Romano.

But I have tried. And where I have faltered, it will not be for lack of encouragement and support from friends and colleagues. I hope that they will understand that the brief listing that follows, probably with too many omissions, cannot show how deeply I appreciate their comments, advice, and suggestions. Without implying that any of them is responsible for the book's errors and shortcomings, I warmly thank Asunción Lavrin, Solange Alberro, Cathy Duke, Sergio Ortega Noriega, Leda Torres, Murdo MacLeod, Dolores Enciso, Catherine LeGrand, Geof Spurling, Jean-Pierre Dedieu, William French, James Lockhart, Michelle McFarlane, Doris Ladd, Douglas Cole, Brad Benedict, Jorge García, David Barnhill, Steve Stern, María Urquidi, the late Richard Sullivan, Hugh M. Hamill, Jr., Steve Peterson, Ben Metcalfe, Paul DeGrace and former students, now colleagues, Jim Boothroyd, Jennifer Asp and Jacqueline Holler. Throughout I relied on Peter Gerhard's published work to track the movements of bigamists and to regularize the spellings of place names.

I owe special thanks to several colleagues who read and commented on the entire manuscript: Michael Fellman, Edward Ingram, and Woodrow Borah fought their way through the thicket of a preliminary draft—more preliminary than I realized when I passed it to them—and managed to express their enthusiasm even as they pointed out that much remained to be done. Lyman Johnson, Jacqueline Holler, Philip Amos, and Ann Twinam took the time to make painstakingly detailed comments on a subsequent draft. Paul Edward Dutton gave invaluable suggestions for a late and all-important shift in the structure of the manuscript, and William B. Taylor for final revisions. My wife Josette Salles read various versions as I wrote and rewrote them. Her concern that I moderate my fascination with the particular by a more developed framing of it led to a great deal of cutting and revising, a decidedly ego-bruising business, but the result, I hope, is a more reasonable balance between trees and forest.

I acknowledge with gratitude the financial support of the Social Sciences and Humanities Research Council of Canada which allowed me to carry out most of the archival research for this project. From Simon Fraser University, travel grants and a President's Research Grant supported supplementary research, and a University Publications Grant, the production of a map and the index. My thanks go to the University of Nebraska Press and to the Universidad Nacional Autónoma de México for allowing me to publish, in somewhat different form, parts of essays that appeared in Asunción Lavrin, ed., *Sexuality and Marriage in Colonial Latin America*, and in Ricardo Sánchez, Eric Van Young, and Gisela von Wobeser, eds., *La ciudad y el campo en la historia de México: Memoria de la VII Reunión de Historiadores Mexicanos y Norteamericanos*. I am also grateful to the Huntington Library for permission to quote from a document in their Mexican Inquisition collection.

When reading Inquisition records at the Archivo General de la Nación during a year's residence in Mexico, the director, Leonor Ortiz Monasterio, and the staff of that remarkable institution extended many professional courtesies for which I thank them. At my home institution, Simon Fraser University, my work was assisted by the attentive assistance of the interlibrary loans office of the W. A. C. Bennet library. In my own department of history, while juggling the demands of teaching, committee work, and the work to complete this project, Joan MacDonald, Maylene Leong, Joanna Koczwarski, and Jennifer Alexander helped in dozens of ways. Anita Mahony, the word-processing expert in the office of the Dean of Arts, formatted the completed manuscript. Finally, my special thanks to David Holtby, *patrón editorial* of the University of New Mexico Press, for taking an active interest in the project and guiding it through to publication.

January 1994
Simon Fraser University

✠

LIVES OF THE BIGAMISTS

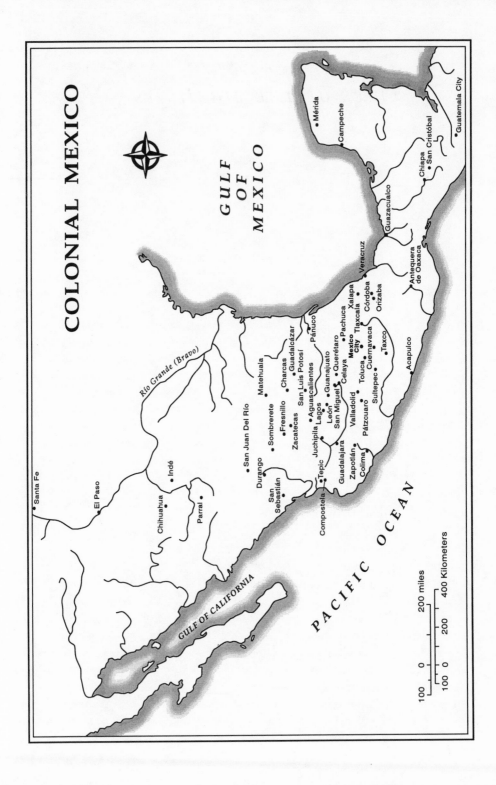

INTRODUCTION

✢ THIS BOOK IS about family, marriage, and community in colonial Mexico from the mid-sixteenth to the mid-eighteenth century. It treats individuals as actors and protagonists, mostly in the ordinary situations of everyday living, by looking at their actions and their representations. It also treats them as social beings whose networks range outwardly from the hearth to circles of relatives, neighbors, friends, work associates, and clienteles. These were the "friends and relatives" of the mass who for hundreds of years remained at the center of Catholic social and ritual life.[1] Charity, just as protection from one's enemies, came from the close circles of conviviality and support that enclosed the routines of everyday life.[2] It is my view that these clusters, more than the formal institutions of church and state, did most to shape daily life in colonial Mexico.[3]

As a group the people I shall be discussing come mostly from the laboring classes, but they did not see themselves in class terms. I have therefore used other terminology—plebeians, lower orders, ordinary people, and the like—when speaking of them collectively. This reflects more accurately, I think, that the groupings of the lower orders came as family and clientage networks, within neighborhoods, as coworkers. Yet in a sense, *class* is an appropriate term for introducing the bigamists as a group, for it characterizes, broadly speaking, how they made their livings, how well they lived, and where they stood in a hierarchical society. As we shall see, they were mainly not administrators, professionals, large merchants, or estate owners, but people selling their labor, working seasonally and short-term, and wandering the countryside to find work or escape debt. That they exercised considerable initiative and some choice in day-to-day existence must not obscure their overall place in their society. They were people dependent on employers, masters, and patrons more than reliant on their own tools, land, and capital to earn a living. In this they were gradually, but more rapidly from the second half of the eighteenth century (a period mainly outside the scope of this study), being drawn into larger systems and more complex divisions of labor as wage laborers and consumers rather than producers.[4]

If the protagonists of this book were 'ordinary' in falling outside of elite status, they were also ordinary in the patterns of their childhoods, marriages, work, and associations. Their behaviors and values place them well within the mainstream of Hispanic society. The webs of their connections to their society, dense and complicated even from incomplete references in the surviving documents, were unremarkable. Thus, to cite the example of the occupations of bigamists and witnesses, in case after case a broad range is mentioned, and a listing of them, running into the hundreds, could serve as a credible sample of the working population of New Spain. I am, of course, speaking mainly but not exclusively of the Hispanic rather than the Indian world, for the latter, the majority of the population, did not fall under the jurisdiction of the Holy Office. Indians therefore appear in Inquisition records in supporting roles—as wives or husbands, fellow workers, *compadres*, or informants—rather than as the main actors in the story lines of the cases. Nevertheless their presence shows us that they were both integrated and marginal to Hispanic society. They and other humble types give us our view of those at the top—wealthy merchants, mine owners, and top bureaucrats—who figure mainly as bosses, patrons, or judges.

The bigamists and their cohorts in this book worked in 'unskilled' or semiskilled jobs.[5] They depended on patronage and moved from job to job and from place to place, eking out their living and standing up for their honor as best they could. As they did so, they were caught between what E. P. Thompson has called "patrician society" and "plebeian culture"[6] that amounted to the lack of correspondence between the supposed and actual framework for work. The ideal, in New Spain just as in eighteenth-century England, insisted that workers were not free but 'servants,' that men and women without a master were therefore vagabonds. Yet only a portion of workers could be absorbed permanently into the 'cozy' master-servant relationship of mutual reciprocities. The rest moved from place to place taking up one job after another. Some accepted itinerancy as a way of life, some continued to search for the elusive 'good' master to take them in.[7] The 'plebeians' of New Spain, too Hispanized to accept the peasant as an ideal but with too few patrons to go around, took on the picaresque mode: 'free' men moving around and looking to take advantage of situations. But they also wanted to settle down and make a life, and everyday contingencies—accidents, illness, insults, robberies, job offers, meetings—played a major part in determining the directions their lives took.

I saw the chance to follow the dramas of ordinary folk when I began to read the bigamy files compiled by the Mexican Tribunal of the Holy Office of the Inquisition.[8] It intrigued me that there were so many of them, and it appealed to me that they carry little of the emotionally charged atmosphere of cases dealing with major heresy. In fact they have a mundane feel, documenting in great detail commonplace activities of people in everyday settings, often in thick and meaty files.[9] And such a range of people: women as well as men, mulattoes and mestizos as well as Spaniards, idlers as well as workers, newcomers as well as old hands. Nearly all of them managed in a plebeian world, nearly all stand out as individuals. As they speak of their comings and goings, we hear about the places they lived in, the events they saw and heard about, the people they knew, and the conversations they engaged in. This, if not the full picture, was the stuff of their lives.

Bigamy files, of course, center on the marriages of people because this is what the Inquisition wanted to know about. They can therefore be used to learn about marriage and domestic life. But not only in a narrow way, and not only from the normative standpoint of the judges and the court, for the viewpoints of the men and women who married and lived together also appear. Moreover these seldom confine themselves to marriage in a restricted sense, for talk about marriage naturally merges with talk about life more generally. I characterize this more ample view in my subtitle by referring to the *family* and *community* of bigamists. We learn about those worlds not only from the principals of the cases but from the presence and testimony of family members, neighbors, and acquaintances of the accused.

From this testimony we shall see muleteers, shepherds, carpenters, servants, street vendors, and the like—portraying themselves as the protagonists of their stories. I have stressed the agency that they assign to themselves and, along with what they said, have paid attention to how they spoke. In this, as Carlo Ginzburg reminds us, a concern for "philology is . . . related to a kind of respect for the dead" and the best defense against falling into anachronism.[10] Attention to detail and process thus underscores the complexity of life and reminds us that representations of it in words (our own as well as those of our sources) are reductions.[11] But perhaps that tendency can be countered; perhaps we can open up as well as tidy up an exceedingly disparate world and live with a picture of it as a place of complexity and contradiction.

The bigamists of this book, unlike Emmanuel Le Roy Ladurie's Occitan villagers or Carlo Ginzburg's Friulian miller, do not belong to a single community in time and space.[12] Yet they do belong to a coherent Hispanic world of early modern times. That world, which encompassed Spain and the Indies, had its patterns of values, beliefs, and customs imbedded in the culture. Within the complex there was variation and evolution, but at the level of family and private life, beliefs and behavior showed little change during the three centuries of Spanish rule in the Indies. To look at individuals and the ordinary details of their lives, therefore, calls for a periodization stressing continuity—more a composition of themes and variations than a series evolving sequentially.[13]

Although scattered in space and time, bigamists spent a good part of their lives in New Spain. In this they can be seen as men and women of the New World. For those of them who began their lives in the Old World, the Indies loomed large. It beckoned the troubled, restless, and ambitious as a refuge and an opportunity; it was a place to make a new life. For those Hispanics 'native' to the Indies—many of them the mestizos, mulattoes, and *zambos* produced by the coupling of European and African migrants with each other and with the native population—the New World was a vast space in which to move unfettered, a place where one might choose or fall into a new life. Whether one crossed the ocean by sail, or mountain and plain by muleback, one could distance oneself from an old life.

If the scale of life extended, it nevertheless remained confined in networks of human associations. Cities and towns where Hispanic populations clustered can be viewed as small, compact societies, aloof from the larger Indian populations of the suburbs and surrounding villages even as more and more of them were making individual arrangements to hire Indian commoners directly.[14] As well as the many humble types that appear in the files—servants, farm laborers, ranch hands, muleteers, carpenters, shoemakers, tailors, and weavers—were "subsumed," to use Peter Laslett's term, into even smaller units, as dependents of fathers, masters, or patrons in families, shops, or estates.[15] They labored with their hands, owned little real or personal property, and exercised scant power. A few with grander pretenses claimed the honorific *don* or *doña* (often *after* getting to the Indies).

The use of Inquisition documents to flesh out individual lives and to view aspects of everyday life needs no brief. As early as 1956, Pierre

Chaunu urged that they be used, stressing that our own age was unlikely to leave records of comparable intimacy and nuance for the study of manners and social psychology.[16] Moreover the records of the Mexican tribunal are among the most complete of any inquisitorial court. In the past scholars have mined these mainly to place the institution of the Inquisition as a religious and political force in colonial society. Yet Richard E. Greenleaf, a leading modern authority on the Mexican Inquisition, has always stressed the personal and intimate details to be found in Inquisition records: "Kinship and family life show through the procedural apparatus and patterns of speech and behavior reveal the folk culture. The colloquial language of humble people paints vibrant pictures of lower-echelon Spanish and *mestizo* society. Glimpses of daily life, devotion and recreation emerge from the documents."[17]

In the field of social history, James Lockhart notes, historians have "concentrated on fleshed-out portrayals of individual cases and skeletal, aggregate statistics of numerous cases, while rarely adopting the procedure of looking at a moderate number of cases in as much detail as possible."[18] This project attempts the latter, with a sample of 216 bigamy files that concern people who lived from the sixteenth to the eighteenth century. Known birth dates (n = 182) range from 1498 to 1765, first marriages (n = 186) from 1521 to 1777, and second marriages (n = 179) from 1525 to 1787. Birth dates are mostly approximations; I have calculated them from declarations of age by accused persons, from attribution of age by other witnesses, or from the notary's estimate. Of the three, I give precedence to the first, unless internal evidence provides reason not to. Marriage dates are more accurate, frequently confirmed by entries copied from parish registers. See the Appendix for a listing of all known dates.

For a general look at bigamy investigations by the Inquisition, one can consult a typescript index in Mexico's national archive. From that, as worked out by Dolores Enciso Rojas, the entries total 2,305, combining *procesos* that went to trial and simple denunciations that did not.[19] The index, therefore, dates first denunciations and the beginning of institutional intervention.[20] Dates of second marriages can be compared with these to show the chronological distribution of my sample in terms of all known cases (table 1).[21] The sample weighs the sixteenth century more heavily in number of cases (16 percent more), although the seventeenth and eighteenth, with more complete files from the institutionally mature period, include more information about each case.

Men committed the crime of bigamy far more than women, who were more closely supervised and controlled within Hispanic society. My sam-

Table 1. Second Marriages (sample) v. All Bigamy Investigations
Grouped by Century

Century	Sample Number (percent)	Archival Index Number (percent)
XVI (1535–1600)	56 (31%)	345 (15%)
XVII (1601–1700)	39 (22%)	684 (30%)
XVIII (1701–1789)	84 (47%)	1,276 (55%)
Totals	179 (100%)	2,305 (100%)

Source: Appendix and Enciso Rojas, "El delito de bigamia," pp. 80–83.
Note that the growth in the number of entries in the index is proportional
to the growth in the population. In 1789 the Inquisition lost jurisdiction
over bigamy.

ple has a total of 35 women (16 percent), 11 (12.8 percent) of whom fall
within the eighteenth century. This latter figure may be compared with a
total of 86 women out of the total of 554 bigamy entries (15.5 percent) for
the entire eighteenth century.[22]

As for race, a fluid category that also points to *calidad*, or overall reputation, the breakdown is given in table 2.[23] A subset of those racial groupings from the eighteenth century can be set beside all of their cohorts,
comparably clustered, for the same period (table 3).

In chronology, sex, and race-calidad, my sample approximates the overall activity of the Inquisition with regard to bigamy and makes reference
to a broad range of types within the non-Indian population (totaling perhaps half a million people in the middle of the seventeenth century) who
fell under the jurisdiction of the Inquisition.[24] Nevertheless even though
"Indians" could not be brought to the Inquisition's dock, many of them,
as we have noted, appear in the depositions in supporting roles, as godparents, witnesses, coworkers, and so on. As for the sample being racially
'representative,' even though designations found in the index can be re-
fined from material in the files themselves, Enciso has concluded that
bigamy occurred within the racial-ethnic groups in proportion to their
numbers in the population at large.[25] So, in those terms, the archive as a
whole reflects the non-Indian population.

This book, largely a report drawn from archival materials, is something
of a hybrid, for it ranges widely in time, place, and theme. Yet it remains
centered on daily life and the circumstances and details that together make
up a kind of pointillist picture of it.[26] In the text I have tried to let the way

Table 2. Bigamists by Race: Entire Sample (n = 210/216)

Race	Number (percent)
Spaniard	120 (57%)
Indian	4 (2%)
Mulatto	52 (25%)
Mestizo	34 (16%)
Total	210 (100%)

Source: Appendix. The category "Spaniard" includes 89 peninsular Spaniards, 22 creoles, and 9 "other" Europeans; "Mulatto" includes 2 blacks, 8 slaves (black or mulatto), and 5 zambos, an Afro-Indian mixture.

Table 3. Bigamists in the Eighteenth Century, by Race

Race	Boyer (n = 85/86)	Enciso (n = 396/554)
Spaniard	31 (36.5%)	172 (43.4%)
Indian	3 (3.5%)	2 (0.5%)
Black	5 (6%)	8 (2%)
Casta	46 (54%)	214 (54%)
Totals	85 (100%)	396 (99.9%)

Source: Appendix and Enciso, "El delito de bigamia," pp. 101–4. I have combined my own breakdown of ethnic-racial types, in order to match up better with Enciso. The category "Spaniard" includes peninsular Spaniards (n = 14) and creoles (n = 17); Indians, when proven to be Indians, escaped the jurisdiction of the Inquisition; "Black" includes 4 slaves; "Casta" includes 22 mestizos, 20 mulattoes, and 4 Afro-Indian mestizos. Enciso's category "Spaniards" combines peninsulars and creoles (n = 163), which I have broadened to include 9 "other" Europeans; "Mestizo" includes all people of mixed race.

people speak in their depositions (especially their habit to 'quote' past conversations as dialogue rather than as third-person summaries) come through. In this way readers may attend to the mentality and world of individuals more than to the court as an institution in its work of collecting and evaluating testimony. Judges presumed guilt, sought confessions, and effected reconciliations even though, as we shall see, they also tried to understand motives and states of mind.[27]

In general, then, I take the testimony in the files seriously, as reflecting what people thought and did. Even though the notaries' recording of it shifts the words of witnesses from the first to the third person, this is formulaic and predictably delimited. So much so that it might invite 'decoding' words back to direct speech, by returning pronouns, possessives, and verb tenses to forms compatible with the speaker as self-referent.[28] Let a brief excerpt from a transcript serve as an example. On June 22, 1684, Alonso de Guizábal, mestizo, appeared before the tribunal in Mexico City for his first hearing (*audiencia de oficio*). As recorded by the notary, Alonso's response to the request that he give his life history is as follows:

> Dixo q toda su vida la ha gastado y ocupado desde el dho Pueblo de S Xptoval yendo y biniendo a las ciu[des] de Goathemala y San Salvador y S. Miguel con la requa de Antt[o] Botello, español, vezino de dho pueblo y esso responde.[29]

A literal translation of the above would read:

> He said that he has spent and worked all his life out of the said pueblo of San Christóbal, going and coming to the cities of Guatemala, San Salvador, and San Miguel with the mule team of Antonio Botello, a Spaniard and vecino of the said pueblo and that is his answer.

A plausible reconstruction, in English, of what Alonso might have said reads as follows:

> I've spent my whole life in pueblo San Christóbal and from there worked with Antonio Botello's mule team—he's a Spaniard and vecino of San Christóbal—coming and going to the cities of Guatemala, San Salvador, and San Miguel.

But we cannot know this. For one thing any translation only approximates the original. That said, it seems safe enough to drop the "d[id]ho" that twice modifies pueblo and doubtless represents the court's language, not Alonso's. More uncertain is the combination "gastado y ocupado," which suggests the notary's elision of two fully realized clauses that I have opened up a bit. On the other hand, the more common "yendo y viniendo" rings as more probably words that Alonso might have joined. The point is that even in such a simple example, much is left to guesswork. I have not, therefore, transposed the records back to direct speech, but nevertheless remain confident that just below the surface of notarial convention (possibly with some elisions at times) lie the individual voices of bigamists and their cohorts.

Readers should be aware that I have made most citations to the archival file as a whole rather than to a subfile or folio number. The reason for this is to simplify what would otherwise become a very cluttered text, for often a single sentence establishing 'simple' aspects of a narrative, such as the timing and place of an event, will draw from several parts of the file. For quotations, however, I indicate in the text the part of the subdocument that it comes from (for example, the autobiographical statement of the accused or a deposition from a particular witness) and the date. This can be justified because, as we shall see in chapter 1, Inquisition files are predictably structured even though sometimes bulky documents, and students can quickly locate in them the main supports of this study: the testimony of witnesses, the interviews with the accused, and the responses of the accused to the formal accusation and to the summary of the testimony collected from witnesses.[30]

I have organized my discussion of bigamists as a kind of collective ethnography in order to follow them through as much of the life cycle as possible; their stories, as far as the files go, stop when they are caught and punished in middle age or before. To divide a life into 'stages' means not absolute compartments but a narrative convenience.[31] Yet it also reflects the way people talked about themselves, moving forward and backward in time with the help of hindsight and remembered anticipations. This comes through most clearly in chapter 2, a discussion of early socialization and 'training,' as reconstructed from the autobiographical sketches bigamists gave in the dock. Bigamists, as everyone else, became oriented to life and work as children and dependents in households. This stage ended as they took their leave and exerted more independence in the wider world. The patterns set in the formative years often anticipate a long trajectory stretching well beyond them. Chapters 3 and 4 deal with the domestic worlds created by bigamists as they married and set up their own households, not once but at least twice. Because the Inquisition wanted to know why, we can learn something of how marriages began as well as how they failed. Chapter 5 shows how bigamists were discovered and in doing so suggests more generally how information moved from place to place and from person to person.

Before we take up the life cycle of bigamists, a preliminary chapter on bigamy and the Inquisition first places that crime broadly in the context of the tribunal's work and then narrowly exemplifies it by following a single case through the eyes of the tribunal to show how a bigamy file was created.

CHAPTER ONE

MEXICO'S FIRST AUTO DE FE CELEBRATED BY THE NEWLY INSTALLED
TRIBUNAL OF THE HOLY OFFICE OF THE INQUISITION ON SUNDAY,
FEBRUARY 28, 1574

Cover sheet of the file of Andrés González, discussed in Chapter 1. Although the original jurisdiction, "Goathemala," is indicated at the top left of the sheet, this page would have been prepared by and for the tribunal in Mexico City. Note the administrative detail toward the bottom: the placement of Andrés in cell number 9 and the assignment of licenciado don Ygnacio Dávila de la Madrid to defend him. The name and racial designation of each of Andrés's wives, together with dates and places of his marriages, are noted at the left.

Bigamy and the Inquisition

✠ On a July day in 1762, Paula Salazar married Andrés González.[1] She was in her early twenties, he was thirty-four; both were mulattoes. The marriage took place in Escuintla, Paula's hometown, an isolated pueblo in the Pacific coast province of Soconusco at the southeast edge of New Spain. Andrés, an outsider, had come into the district only a year or two before to work as a farm laborer. Before that he lived and worked on a sugar hacienda in the district of Verapaz (northern Guatemala) named San Gerónimo[2] where he had a wife, Manuela, and five children.[3] No one from Escuintla knew any of this, of course, and the marriage took place routinely. As such, no one except those in the family and the locality would have found it remarkable or memorable. Yet it became notorious when locals discovered that Andrés was a bigamist. The Holy Office of the Inquisition arrested and tried him, and the file their officials compiled on Andrés (and on others like him) forms a record that survives to our own time. These materials, a sample of mostly plebeian types in colonial Mexico, stand as the primary documentation for this book.

The story of Andrés's second marriage begins in 1760 or 1761, when he left San Gerónimo to look for work on "the south coast."[4] In Soconusco he worked for "more than a year" in agricultural jobs (possibly on cacao plantations), met Paula, and married her. But like all practicing Catholics, Andrés knew marriage to be a sacrament that forms a permanent bond between a man and a woman.[5] So Andrés risked imprisonment, punishment, and infamy, and we cannot help but wonder why. Our best clue comes from Andrés's brief reply to the prosecutor's indictment (read to him on December 19, 1768) which, in a formulaic way, associates bigamists with "the heretics and Mohammedans who consider having a plurality of wives licit." Andrés rejects this association. Instead he presents himself as having been "carried away by sensual love" and so had "solicited" Paula.[6] In conventional terms, then, the story is this: a man leaves home to find work; he falls in love with a young woman; and, probably to have sexual relations with her, marries her. In doing this, let us note, Andrés rejects only a part of the Christian model of marriage—its permanence for as long as one's spouse lives—and for the rest dutifully conforms to local custom and follows procedures set out by the Council of Trent.[7] In this he behaves in an ordinary way. And against a more complex backdrop, (barely hinted at in the documentation) than we can detail: economic and work conditions in two adjacent regions, rules about sex and marriage as interpreted and enforced by family and patronage networks, and private aspirations and emotions.

Wisely or unwisely Andrés threw himself into a new life. He later recalled with the utmost precision how long it lasted: "from the day before San Pedro [June 29] until the ninth of September."[8] Then he briefly stepped back into his old life by going to San Gerónimo to check on "a house, some cattle, and some mules." He wanted to sell the livestock and other property, it seems, and to help him he "employed" a "black" from Escuintla, Ignacio Figarroa.[9] As a man of few resources, Andrés's plan is understandable. But why bring Ignacio who had a family connection to Paula?[10] We have no way of knowing, but the answer, I think, lies in the conventions of patronage. Andrés would have been expected to pick a partner from 'family,' and this overrode whatever unease he may have had that Ignacio, more than someone outside the family, might note and denounce his marital irregularity. In fact Ignacio did overhear Andrés and some acquaintances talking about Manuela and as soon as they reached the next settlement, San Mateo Zalamá, a pueblo near San Gerónimo, he denounced Andrés to the deputy Alcalde Mayor (of Verapaz province), "captain of infantry" don Jacinto de León.[11] On November 10, 1762, don Jacinto wrote out the denunciation (no notary was available), arrested Andrés, and ordered his sergeant to take him (together with Ignacio, "in case he is needed") to doctor don Juan Falla, commissioner of the Holy Office in Guatemala City.

Thus another bigamist fell into the hands of the Holy Office of the Inquisition. And although Andrés's crime was a minor one compared, for example, with major heresy, and the culprit a man of the lowest ranks of society, the tribunal took great care with his case. Before we follow it further, however, I should like to set the context for it (and for the other bigamy cases used in this study), by showing how the policing of bigamy fit more generally into the work of the Inquisition.

THE INQUISITION AND BIGAMY

The Spanish or 'modern' Inquisition differed from its medieval predecessor in being an agent of the crown rather than of the papacy. Pope Sixtus IV granted royal jurisdiction over it to Ferdinand and Isabella in 1478 (for Castile) and in 1481 (for Aragon). By 1482 the earliest tribunals (in Seville, Córdoba, Valencia, and Zaragoza) had begun to uncover crypto-Jews, new Christian converts who secretly practiced Jewish rites.[12] The creation and early work of these tribunals should be seen, as Edward Peters points out, as part of a mid-fifteenth-century shift in Spanish attitude: from "religious anti-Semitism" to "ethnic anti-Semitism."[13] The former had been concerned only with religious Jews and had welcomed *conversos* as converts; the latter suspected conversos as well as Jews. In fact even sincere conversos who were prominent in their communities became targets of inquisitorial prosecution, envied and suspected because of their success, by the logic of local politics.[14] By 1560 this attitude dominated the Spanish outlook, serving as the base of popular support for no fewer than twenty-three tribunals set up to deal with suspect conversos.[15]

These tribunals had considerable success. By the early sixteenth century, crypto-Jews had been controlled as, by midcentury, had *moriscos* (crypto-Muslims), *luteranos* (Protestants), and *alumbrados* (mystics), the other groups deemed major heretics. Later, at the end of the sixteenth and early in the seventeenth century, the Inquisition launched a major effort against moriscos in Valencia, Zaragoza, and Granada. At the beginning, therefore, the Inquisition worked mainly to uproot major heresies, a task it continued to carry out later in special campaigns in the regions. For the rest it went after old Christians accused of lesser offenses such as blasphemy, heretical opinions, superstition, bigamy, and the like. This more mundane work involved not the presumption of heresy, but the conviction that the faithful needed instruction, correction, and discipline. In the century and a half from 1540 to 1700, lesser offenses made up 58 percent of the Inquisition's case load.[16]

An Inquisition came to New Spain immediately after the conquest. For the first ten years friars manned it, and from 1532 to 1571 Mexican bishops (sometimes also friars) directed it. In 1571 El Tribunal del Santo Oficio was formally established.[17] The timing matters. It means that the

Inquisition in its fully institutionalized form came to the Indies only after completing its project to extirpate major heresies in Spain. By then it had been embarked for a generation on its post-Tridentine project, "the consolidation of the dogmas and moral teachings of the Counter-Reformation."[18] Yet from the 1530s the Inquisition in New Spain had gone through a cycle similar to that of the Spanish tribunals, beginning with the policing of 'major heresy' in the Indian population and shifting to the enforcement of the Counter-Reformation in the Hispanic population. But if comparable, the shift in New Spain came about for different reasons for, from the first, many judged the Inquisition too harsh and too demanding and therefore an inappropriate way to deal with idolatry and paganism. So began the campaign to remove Indians from Inquisitorial jurisdiction, as reports of excessive severity by friars acting as inquisitors in Oaxaca and the Yucatan circulated.[19] It reached a kind of crescendo in 1539, when Bishop Zumárraga 'relaxed' don Carlos Ometoczin of Texcoco to secular authorities to be burned at the stake as a "heretical dogmatizer," a punishment considered too harsh by the Inquisitor General in Spain.[20]

But no one doubted that the Inquisition should deal with the Hispanic population. In fact the reason for setting up tribunals in the New World had been the same as that for founding them in Spain: the fear of crypto-Jews. In particular the crown came to believe that Portuguese Jews had come to the Indies in large numbers. Yet from the first the tribunal took up minor offenses more than major heresies. In 1572, for example, the first full year of work for the tribunal under Inquisitor General Pedro Moya de Contreras, ninety-three cases of "heretical propositions" and forty-four of bigamy came to light.[21] So from the mid-sixteenth century, the Inquisition in both the Old and New Worlds dealt mainly with correcting practices and opinions rooted in tradition and in popular culture. In doing so it delved into matters of sex, morals, and popular beliefs about magic and superstition.[22] These concerns touched not just particular groups but the Hispanic population at large.[23]

INQUISITORIAL PROCEDURES

The Supreme Council of the Holy Office (Consejo de la Suprema y General Inquisición) in Madrid set Inquisition trial procedures and gave direction to all tribunals. Moya de Contreras, having been inquisitor of Murcia, came to New Spain fully experienced in inquisitorial procedures but also carried with him detailed instructions for the founding of a new tribunal.[24] So the unifying force of central direction lay on all tribunals, but even so they varied to some degree depending on place, time, kind of case, and the quality (and qualities) of the officials in charge of the tribunals.[25]

At a deeper level, the assumptions and procedures used by all Inquisitorial tribunals came out of Roman and common law as church canonists applied it.[26] In this the Inquisition shared a common legal tradition with secular jurisdictions, especially that of criminal law. Both, for example, took confession to be "the perfect proof" because accused persons confirmed their guilt directly. More importantly confession 'unburdened' the conscience. Just as crime was sin, so the court-imposed remedy was "voluntary submission to penitence."[27] Inquisitorial courts made this link more firmly than secular courts because heresy, lodged as it was in the inner world of thoughts and intent, could best be corrected through confession and penitence.

Inquisitorial trials moved through three stages: the indictment, a collecting of evidence leading to a formal accusation (*sumario*); the trial proper (*prueba*); and the sentence (*sentencia*). Indictments started with denunciations. The Inquisition wanted these to be 'voluntary' and 'spontaneous,' but edicts of faith, read in churches and posted on church doors, reminded people of what they should denounce in themselves and in others. The edicts were primers that listed errors, gave examples of suspicious behavior, and urged the faithful to examine their consciences.[28] They threatened curses, damnation, and infamy for those who pushed aside this call for personal and collective self-examination.

The threats were so fearful, says Jaime Contreras, that they "could have transformed anyone into the Inquisitor of his neighbor."[29] Mexico's first inquisitor, don Pedro Moya de Contreras, would have agreed. In a letter dated May 24, 1572, six months after he read the first Edict in the cathedral of Mexico City, he wrote that perhaps now blasphemy and immodest speech would stop, for "if they censor and denounce each other with very Christian zeal, they will live and speak decently without the need for punishments."[30] So Moya anticipated a self-sustaining inquisitorial system taking hold in New Spain. If the punishments helped, habits of Christian watchfulness mattered more, for these carried the threat of punishment. The edict of grace combined the two nicely by giving the faithful a period of "grace," usually thirty days, in which to denounce themselves, thereby to avoid a public penance.[31] Moya's first edict, however, only allowed six days; thus, he used it more as a stick than a carrot.[32] For New Spain in general, however, the edicts had a spotty impact because they were read irregularly, were incomprehensible to many, and often were not accompanied by inquisitorial visits.[33] By the eighteenth century the populace had learned to use the tribunal, largely for their own ends, as they denounced their enemies for petty crimes such as witchcraft and superstition, which seemed an ever more tedious waste of time to the inquisitors: "the despicable prattle of some silly women of the lowliest rank," as one of them complained in 1786.[34]

Once judges received a denunciation, along with supporting testimony, they voted (*voto de sumaria*) on whether to complete the *proceso* by bringing the case to trial. A "yes" vote meant issuing the order to imprison the suspect in the secret prison. At this point prisoners were presumed guilty and quite likely already detained to prevent flight. Formal indictment and the trial itself were meant to extract a confession and, through penitence, effect reconciliation. This last came in an auto de fe, the public ritual that culminated and dramatized the process. From the first, autos de fe were enormously popular. On February 28, 1574, for example, in Moya's first auto de fe, a huge crowd of both Spaniards and Indians gathered in the main plaza. From seven in the morning until six in the afternoon they listened to the cases being read out. In particular the important cases, wrote Inquisitors Moya and Bonilla on April 5, 1574, excited "much attention and applause of the people and surprise that there should be such crimes in this land where they had expected not even the shadow of heresy to rest."[35]

The pattern of denunciations, investigations, trials, and autos de fe dates from 1484 when, one year after fray Tomás de Torquemada was appointed inquisitor general of Castile and Aragon, he defined tribunal procedures.[36] By the 1560s (in time to be well imbedded in procedures carried to Mexico in 1571) the Inquisition's Supreme Council in Madrid had standardized them further, so that with minor variations, they were used in all subsequent trials for the next 250 years.[37]

The Mexican tribunal had a structure and mandate identical to those of its peninsular counterparts but had to deal with a vastly larger territory and, according to Solange Alberro, depended on less-principled men to carry out its work. Irregularities therefore resulted, routinely in frontier areas far from Mexico City, but also endemically in regular procedures and processes, especially in the life of prisoners below ground.[38] Yet the Inquisition also policed itself and, on the whole, followed its standardized procedures well enough to produce orderly files.[39] These can be divided into 'legal' and 'personal' materials. The former include dispatches to commission investigations and to collect testimony; orders to arrest, transport, and jail an accused person; queries and reprimands because of delays or improperly collected evidence; prosecutors' arraignments and *consultas-de-fe*, in which the judges, theological advisors, and a representative of the local bishop decided guilt or innocence; and verdicts indicating penalties to be imposed. Personal materials show up in 'life histories' of accused persons; depositions from a sometimes very large number of witnesses; responses to the prosecutor's arraignment and to excerpts from witnesses' depositions; and inventories of a prisoner's possessions.

The present study relies mainly on the personal material. Legal and bureaucratic interleavings of a file can sometimes provide supplementary information and suggest a broader, perhaps more sceptical view of testimony, but they nevertheless represent the voice of the court, not those of individuals. From the latter one glimpses the circumstances, connections, and projects of ordinary people. This occurs for three reasons: the inquisitors encouraged it; the procedures of trials allowed for it; and the witnesses spoke with less inhibition than one might expect.

First consider the inquisitors who elicited testimony. They acted primarily as churchmen and secondarily as judges. Within the ethos of the confessional they worked to reconcile sinners, not merely to punish them. So they drew out a broad range of testimony to probe states of mind, sense of motive, degree of intent, and surrounding circumstances. "With the bare enumeration of our mortal sins," summarized the Council of Trent, "we should not be satisfied; that enumeration we should accompany with the relation of such circumstances as considerably aggravate or extenuate their malice."[40] Here therefore lay the ground for drawing out the accused person's point of view, a process that went far beyond comparable probings of contemporary judges in the secular courts.[41]

Second consider the trial. Witnesses replied to open-ended questions and said whatever they wanted, with no apparent interruptions.[42] More importantly for our purposes, notaries took great care in writing down testimony. They did so because they were instructed to and because the work of the court depended on accurate, complete transcripts. To edit testimony, therefore, would have been audacious, irresponsible, and irreverent. However banal the settings and details described by witnesses, theologians and judges needed to sift through all of it. Moreover testimony had to be read back and ratified as accurate by the witness and by two attesters, and this put the work of notaries constantly under review. Professional, moral, and procedural conventions held notaries to high standards.[43]

Last consider the witnesses who spoke of their lives. As mentioned notaries almost always transposed the testimony into the third person.

The documents that make up an Inquisition file, therefore, are mostly not verbatim transcripts. Yet except for the transposition of tense done in a formulaic way, I have taken them to be essentially that. Recorded testimony comes in a meandering, unstructured shape; remembered dialogues crop up here and there. The "garrulous, faithful memory of the illiterate," in Pierre Goubert's phrase, catches past events and conversations with detail and verve.[44] People casually repeat bits of rough language, showing it to be commonplace in verbal exchanges. Thus Juan de Lizarzaburo recalled his wife shouting "be gone Jewish dog."[45] As if to underscore that peculiar phrases came from the witnesses, notaries occasionally put in a notation such as "this is the way he said it."[46]

The Ordeal of Andrés González

Having looked briefly at the Inquisition and its procedures, let us now return to Andrés González. His case gives a picture of the Mexican tribunal at work and thus shows us how it created its files.[47] Andrés, to summarize, has been denounced, arrested, and sent to the commissioner of the Inquisition in Guatemala City. A constable locks him in a jail on November 10, 1762, and he does not reappear until December 17, when the commissioner, doctor don Juan Falla, interrogates him.[48] Don Juan's questions follow a standard pattern to establish Andrés's identity and offense. For the first they elicit his age, parents' names, civil status, and place of birth; for the second they extract his admission that he has been arrested "for the crime of marrying two times" and record the information he gives about his wives, children, and marriages (places, dates, names of witnesses, *padrinos*, and officiating priests). The commissioner also asks Andrés why he married a second time. The interview ends with the notary entering into the record a description of Andrés: "very tall, with white skin and curly hair, and he lacks most of his upper teeth." Following the interview don Juan returned Andrés to the custody of the constable, Joseph de Amaía.

Now don Juan needed a copy of the entry in the parish register to document Andrés's first marriage. He asked the prior of the Dominican monastery, no doubt because the monastery owned the sugar hacienda, to see to it. The prior subcommissioned the task and it took seven months. After a delay of another ten months, don Juan managed the next step in the investigation, the examination of Manuela, Andrés's first wife. Manuela corroborated what Andrés had already said and ratified her statement three days after giving it. At that time don Juan advised her that the prosecutor of the Inquisition might use it against Andrés. Moving more swiftly now, within two weeks don Juan commissioned the friar Juan Infante, vicar of San Gerónimo, to collect testimony about both of Andrés's marriages. Fray Juan left Guatemala City with these instructions:

> Ask each witness if he knows or presumes why he has been called. If he does not know, you will ask if he knows Andrés González, if he knows that he is married to Manuela López, if he saw them marry, [and if so] which vicar joined their hands, when it [the marriage] was contracted, how long they lived together, how many children they had, what are their names, [and] why the said Andrés González was imprisoned in Zalama. To each question *you will write whatever reply the witness gives* [emphasis added]; you will also ask for a personal description of Andrés González and will close the examination saying: 'Is this the truth by the oath you have made?'

Fray Juan asked these questions of four surviving witnesses, and his appointed notary, fray Juan del Valle, recorded the answers. Then with two friars acting as attesters, they ratified the transcripts. A fifth witness to the marriage had died in 1755, so fray Juan sent a copy of the death certificate, "in case it is necessary." These documents he forwarded to don Juan in Guatemala City in June, 1764, apologizing for the delay, which he said, "was not my fault but owing to the scarcity of witnesses."

Don Juan sent this material to Mexico City, but in a letter dated July 27, 1764, Inquisitor Vizente scolded him and fray Juan for an investigation that was incomplete and lacking proper form. "We find fault with these dispatches, for no authentic copy in judicial form was taken of the entry in the marriage register [and] also missing are the dispatches relative to the second marriage."[49] Apparently to speed things up, now Mexico City decided to get the testimony about the second marriage through their commissioner in Chiapas.[50] Therefore in August 1764, the tribunal instructed doctor don Simón Joseph de Matos y Oliva, archdeacon of the cathedral, to:

> Examine the matrimonial register or registers of that parish [Escuintla] and when you find what would be the entry, copy it to the letter, authorizing it as conforming to the original so that it is valid [for legal purposes]; and you will examine the priest who married them, and the padrinos, and the witnesses who attended, having each of them specify separately with all detail the time that they married, who married them, their married life, how many

children they had from the said marriage, who they are, their ages, where they were born, their occupations, and personal descriptions. . . . And three days after the said examinations you will ratify each one in his respective declaration before honest and religious persons, conforming to what is stipulated in numbers 19 and 20 of the instruction. . . . And having regard to the distance these places are from Chiapas, we authorize you to subdelegate a commission to a clergyman of your satisfaction who may name a notary, receiving mutually the one to the other the oath of fidelity and secrecy with a dispatch serving as confirmation of this.

Moving as slowly as his counterpart, Matos y Oliva did not name anybody to collect this information until November 2, 1765. He chose *bachiller* don Manuel Joseph Chacón, priest of Escuintla, and on December 31 don Manuel chose his assistant, *bachiller* don Martín Antonio Baes, as his notary. Within a couple of days don Manuel and don Martín found references to the marriage hearings and to the marriage itself. Then for some reason, Chacón did no more, possibly because he could not locate any witnesses.

In the meantime the San Gerónimo investigation had also bogged down because Matos y Oliva, the commissioner in Chiapas, died.[51] Not until September 25, 1766, does Matos's successor, don Francisco Navarro y Atercado, attend to Andrés's case. "Until now," Navarro wrote to Mexico City, "the priest of the said pueblo [Escuintla] to whom my predecessor gave the commission has not replied." The reply from Mexico City, dated January 1767, once again asked him to speed the investigation, but four months later Navarro still had nothing from Chacón in Escuintla. Finally in late September, the dispatches arrived, and Navarro quickly sent them on to Mexico City; but again, as with the evidence collected at the sugar hacienda, they failed to meet court standards. A letter sent on November 3, 1767, made this clear to Navarro. It also went over the terms of his commission (inherited from Matos y Oliva).

Not only have the dispatches not complied with what the prosecutor asked for in a previous dispatch, neither do they comply with the commission delegated by this tribunal to make an authentic copy of the entry of the marriage register and the depositions of the witnesses who deposed in the hearing as to their eligibility to marry preceding the said second marriage. And they have not examined any witnesses of the celebration, nor the priest, nor the second wife as ought to have been done . . . so that there is not sufficient proof of the celebration of the said second marriage.

Chacón in Escuintla had failed two commissioners, and the tribunal in Mexico City had become visibly irritated. Navarro bore the brunt of the scolding and, more explicitly than before, was told to get Chacón moving.

> We are sending to Your Grace [Navarro] the commission that was addressed to your predecessor [Matos], our commissioner, with a printed primer (*cartilla*) so that you can send it back to the priest of Escuintla and make him see the complete lack of faithfulness and punctuality with which he carried out the subdelegation entrusted to him. And in order that this case be delayed no more, Your Grace will instruct him in the manner of receiving declarations in conformity with the judicial formulas of the Holy Office to which end you will send him the enclosed primer, and he will become aware of Your Grace's instruction, point by point, those that are in the enclosed commission . . . and let Your Grace make known to the said priest how this proceeding has been delayed, and that the prisoner has suffered a long imprisonment upon which this tribunal cannot look with indifference.

The reprimand worked. Chacón, possibly because the primer had finally spelled out exactly what he was supposed to do, now acted quickly and correctly. He got the evidence from Escuintla to Mexico City by the end of July 1768, probably three months before the equivalent documents arrived from San Gerónimo.[52] On October 29 the prosecutor issued his *escrito de clamosa*, a formal request, based on the evidence of the *sumaria*, that Andrés be incarcerated in the secret prison and brought to trial. Two days later, in a *voto de sumaria*, the judges accepted the prosecutor's escrito. After a standard formula, the vote orders that Andrés be "brought to the secret prison of this Holy Office with embargo of his goods." But in a departure from the normal pattern to bring prisoners to Mexico City, they ordered that the trial be conducted in Guatemala City.[53] Once the file was complete, the Guatemalan commissioner was to send the prosecutor's arraignment (*acusación fiscal*) and summary of testimony (*publicación de testigos*) to Mexico City for final judgment (*sentencia*).[54]

Before these instructions could be carried out, Andrés broke out of jail, traveled to Mexico City, and, on December 7 at 6:30 p.m., surrendered himself to the Holy Office. In a hearing two days later, he explained that "seeing that it has been five years since he was put in jail without a determination of his case he took it as more convenient to come and present himself to this Holy Tribunal to be punished for his crime so that afterwards he can help his children who are in great need."

The judges placed Andrés in the secret prison, listed his possessions and

Table 4. Chronology for the Investigation and Trial of
Andrés González

Event	Place	Date
Birth	San Gerónimo	1728
First marriage	San Gerónimo	11/12/1747
Second marriage	Escuintla	7/3/1762
Denunciation	San Mateo Zalamá	11/10/1762
Andrés's hearing before commissioner	Guatemala City	12/17/1762
San Gerónimo register copied	San Gerónimo	7/16/1763
Examination of Andrés's first wife	Guatemala City	5/1/1764
Commission to collect testimony in San Gerónimo	Guatemala City	5/19/1764
Testimony sent to Guatemala City	San Gerónimo	6/16/1764
Inquisitors find fault with San Gerónimo testimony	Mexico City	7/27/1764
Commission to collect testimony in Escuintla	Mexico City	8/1/1764
Escuintla commissioner subdelegated	Chiapas	11/2/1765
Escuintla subdelegate names notary	Chiapas	12/31/1765
New commissioner in Chiapas takes up case	Chiapas	9/25/1766
Escuintla testimony sent to Mexico City	Chiapas	10/1/1767
Inquisitors find fault with Escuintla testimony	Mexico City	10/29/1767
Inquisitors urge haste in Escuintla investigation	Mexico City	11/3/1767
Andrés breaks out of jail	Guatemala City	10/13/1768
Escrito de clamoso	Mexico City	10/29/1768
Voto de sumaria	Mexico City	10/31/1768
Andrés surrenders to Inquisition	Mexico City	12/7/1768
Cala y cata	Mexico City	12/9/1768
Primera audiencia de oficio	Mexico City	12/13/1768
Segunda audiencia de oficio	Mexico City	12/15/1768
Tercera audiencia de oficio	Mexico City	12/17/1768
Indictment	Mexico City	1/19/1769
Lawyer made available to Andrés	Mexico City	1/28/1769
Publication of witnesses	Mexico City	1/30/1769
Defense statement	Mexico City	2/4/1769
Verdict	Mexico City	2/18/1769
Sentence	Mexico City	3/6/1769
Certification that penance completed	Guatemala City	9/1/1769

described his person (*cala y cata*), and set his board at one and one-half *reales* per day. On December 13, 1768, they summoned him for the first of the requisite three formal hearings (*audiencias de oficio*) each of which ended with the stern admonition (*monición*) to search his conscience and reveal the whole truth, not just part of it. These had begun after he took an oath swearing to tell the truth, to answer all questions, and to remain silent about the proceedings.[55] The Inquisitors' questions listed below show how the discourse between Andrés and his judges was structured. Although these hearings cover much of the same ground that had already been dealt with in Andrés's deposition in Guatemala City, they are more detailed and often contain revealing disjunctures, created when the inquisitor picked on a point or formulation for clarification or elaboration. The hearing began with the court asking Andrés to state his name, birthplace, age, civil status, occupation, and how long he had been in the secret prison. Then he was to give his genealogy, instructed, no doubt, to state it in the usual sequence: (1) parents, (2) paternal grandparents, (3) maternal grandparents, (4) paternal uncles, (5) maternal uncles, (6) brothers and sisters, (7) wife and children. Andrés, like all prisoners, said as much as he wanted to about his family, with no apparent restrictions.

Next came questions to determine whether Andrés could be linked with heresy. What "caste and lineage" were the relatives that Andrés had declared? Had any of them been "imprisoned, penanced, reconciled, or condemned by the Holy Office of the Inquisition?" Was he a baptized and confirmed Christian? Had he heard the mass, confessed, and taken communion at the times ordered by the Holy Mother Church, and was he in possession of an indulgence (*bula de la santa cruzada*)? Then with no directive indicated in the transcript, but doubtless as prompted, Andrés made the sign of the cross; said the Lord's Prayer, Hail Mary, the creed, and the commandments; named the sacraments; and "responded well to the rest of Christian doctrine." Following this, did he know how to read [and write], had he studied in any faculty, had he ever left these kingdoms? Then, and most importantly for our purposes, he was to relate his autobiography (*discurso de su vida*). The hearing concluded with the inquisitor asking Andrés if he knew or could presume why he had been put in the secret prison of the tribunal.

At this point the formula called for the admonition of prisoners. So, as if Andrés had withheld incriminating information, the judges warned Andrés to search his memory and unburden his conscience by confessing all, not just part, of the truth of his guilt. Only in this way would he save his soul and receive mercy instead of justice. Andrés's second and third hearings, each ending with an admonition, followed in short order (December 15 and December 17), as inquisitorial procedures required.[56]

On January 19, 1769, the prosecutor (*fiscal*) read the accusation, made up of eight articles.[57] Because Andrés admitted to bigamy and the collected testimony confirmed this, he was an "apostate heretic of our Holy Catholic Faith or at least suspected of being one." This was the first time Andrés had heard the charges against him, and he now had the chance to respond article by article.[58] The notaries gave the prosecutor a copy of his responses, and with this the indictment was complete.

The case now moved to the trial as such. Andrés had the right to counsel, and on January 28 the court appointed licenciado don Ignacio Dávila de la Madrid. Dávila listened to the reading of court transcripts of Andrés's statements, the prosecutor's indictment, Andrés's response to the charges against him, and "everything else necessary." In the presence of the inquisitors, his counsel echoed that of the judges: he told Andrés to confess the entire truth and retract any false testimony in order to speed the trial and receive mercy instead of justice. The trial began on January 30 with a reading of summaries of testimony (*publicación de testigos*), edited to hide the identity of witnesses, to which Andrés replied.[59]

On February 4 licenciado Ignacio, after consulting with Andrés, made a formal statement for the defense. It followed the normal pattern to concede guilt but plead for mercy. Licenciado Ignacio stressed that Andrés had repented, made a full confession, and in effect had denounced himself by coming directly to the tribunal after breaking out of jail. He also asked the judges to bear in mind the "hunger and privation" Andrés had already suffered during "more than five years" in a Guatemalan jail, hardships he put into perspective with the comment that "even here in this court some prisoners have been known to die of hunger."

A copy of the defense went to the prosecutor, who had nothing to add, and the judge declared the trial complete. The next step was to consult an ordinary and other legal experts and to decide on a verdict (*voto en definitiva*).[60] On February 18 doctor don Julian Vicente González de Andía, "without an Ordinary present because the most Illustrious Archbishop of Guatemala did not name one," but with the benefit of advice from two audiencia judges, reached a verdict.[61] He ordered that Andrés's sentence be read in tribunal chambers, with doors open.[62] It commuted a term of penal servitude at a *presidio* to the time Andrés had already spent in prison and in travel; ordered that he publicly abjure the light suspicion (*de levi*) that he was a heretic; banished him for ten years from the courts of Madrid and Mexico City and also from the town of Escuintla, where he committed his crime; required that he make a general confession (and give proof that he had done so by presenting a note from his confessor) and also that he confess sacramentally from Christmas to Twelfth Night of the first year; and ordered that on each Saturday for a year he recite "the rosary of our Lady the Virgin Mary." As for which of Andrés' wives was to be his legitimate one, the tribunal referred the decision to episcopal jurisdiction, where he was ordered back to his first wife. On September 25, 1769, the inquisitors received certification, in a letter dated September 1, from Guatemala City, that Andrés had complied with the terms of his penance.

THE BIGAMY FILE AS DRAMA AND DOCUMENT

Andrés's file shows two important aspects of inquisitorial proceedings. First, even in a routine case dealing with a minor crime, the inquisitors held to their rules of evidence.[63] In particular they made commissioners and their subdelegates meet judicial standards. Of course this did not help Andrés.[64] It led to such long delays that he himself changed the trial venue by going directly to the tribunal in Mexico City. Second, bigamy documents follow what can be called a "comic fictional mode," to use Northrop Frye's term, because their central theme is "integration."[65] The court, acting on behalf of God, removed sinner-protagonists from religion, family, and community, and through the drama of trial, the humiliation of punishment, and the efficacy of penance, returned them as purged and reconciled. As heroes of their own stories, bigamists were expected to affirm themselves to a degree by confessing their sinful deeds; thus they set the stage to receive mercy and reintegration. The public reading of sentences, the public floggings accompanied by the announcement of a public crier, the solemn processions in the streets, and the abjurations and reconciliations acted as a warning and an example to appreciative and enthusiastic audiences. In Andrés's case, this drama unfolds in eighty subdocuments on seventy-six folio pages.[66]

So in the privacy of the court individuals had their say even though an overall structure of what they talked about was set. Tribunals that wanted to understand motive and circumstance needed to draw out the full details of everyday situations. Bigamy trials especially reflected the banal. First, they dealt with one of the most common of all crimes tried by the Inquisition, and a wide range of plebeian types turned up in them.[67] Second, because they concern marriage, testimony always takes domestic life as its setting. The accused speak of friends, family, *compadres*, bosses, work associates, and neighbors, the dramatis personae of their lives. Many of these people also give depositions to offer other details and perspectives. As a result it is hard to disagree with the judgment of Edward Peters that the Inquisition's "meticulous investigatory methods produced the largest and most important body of personal data for any society in early modern Europe, particularly for levels of society that have left very few traces elsewhere."[68] From the drama of the courtroom come ordinary stories clothed in the trappings of ordinary life, as people placed themselves at home, at work, and in the streets. The worlds of bigamists therefore fuse with those of the lower orders in general.[69]

The shape of the testimony stands as another confirmation of this. It rambles, lingers over odd details, and goes off on tangents. Even though those with little power are speaking to those with a great deal of it, the narratives told to the court have much of the spontaneity and artlessness of conversations anywhere. They point to the circumstances and states of mind that came with chance meetings; they recreate scraps of dialogue; they repeat reactions to a surprising piece of news; they draw backdrops of people and situations that frame the shifting vignettes of daily life. Bigamists, in speaking to judges and facing a prosecutor's arraignment, had every reason to present themselves so as to obtain a merciful verdict. Yet they also placed themselves at the center of their narratives as actors exercising some power in the world. In the dock witnesses asserted themselves more than might be expected.[70]

'Sensitive' matters touching on religious issues might have brought a politics of discourse more directly into play. It would consist of witnesses speaking more guardedly, trying to give the correct answer rather than a spontaneous one, when asked about narrowly religious matters. They would therefore expose themselves less by giving formulaic responses learned in catechism or by disclaiming competence to comment on the mysteries of the faith. The point matters because it can mark in the transcripts a distinction between 'everyday' things that plebeian types knew a lot about and 'theological' concerns that were supposed to be beyond them. Jean-Pierre Dedieu has proposed a test of reliability in testimony that correlates inversely with degree of religious sensitivity.[71] The inquisitors well knew that 'distortion', self-justification, and casuistical adjustment of norms to situations included implied or applied religious principles, but witnesses almost never showed an awareness of them as they related their experiences.[72] The work of the court in fact lay largely in pulling out implied religious heterodoxies from the banalities in which they were embedded. But here the banalities matter more than the construction put on them by the inquisitors. Yet both sides, judge and witness, must be kept in view. Witnesses recounted their experiences, how they situated themselves in their world, and how they made sense of their lives; the court, with its normative thrust, gave a sense of how ideologies and institutions presumed to order behavior and belief.[73]

The dialogues of bigamists with inquisitors, therefore, give us the glimpses of their views and actions that place them as 'ordinary' within their society. Yet one might wonder if they were not a kind of extreme case, a restless minority that were more rebellious than their cohorts. I think not, for as I have already noted (and as we shall see below), they wanted to settle down and got into trouble by following the rules. As for mobility there is of course no precise way to measure it, although Ida Altman, in her study of local societies in sixteenth-century Extremadura, concludes that "leaving home to seek opportunities elsewhere was quite normal" and "marriages often involved relocation."[74] As to the last, the study of bigamists shows that the point may be inverted; relocation often led to marriage.

Bigamy, after all, was not a behavioral but a legal category. It existed to define deviants who violated the central rules of Christian marriage—that it was monogamous and indissoluble. In particular the post-Tridentine church narrowed the definition of marriage to a sacramental event presided over by clerics and tried to restrict sexuality to marriage. But men and women were coupling all the time, in ways that did not necessarily involve marriage but sometimes led to it: engaging in premarital sexual relations, living for long terms in consensual unions, forming casual liaisons, or engaging in adultery while 'living' with a spouse. Officials officially deplored illicit coupling (seduction, fornication, adultery, and informal unions of shorter or longer duration) and separated couples or forced them to marry; the population in general, however, tolerated a good deal of it.

Control was an enormous task and a concern to both church and state.[75] Moreover it took the legalistic high ground with, I think, minimal impact on behavior as such. The Inquisition, for instance, confined itself narrowly to the legal definition of bigamy (rather than the substantive issue of illicit coupling), to judge by the fact that only about one-half of one percent of cases from 1522 to 1700 deal with the suspicious saying "to fornicate is not a sin" or with simple cases of concubinage.[76] So the bigamy category singles out only one particular kind of coupling, because the illicit union had been verbally and sacramentally constituted. Those who contracted such liaisons as private events (the behavior without the ceremony) were legion in Hispanic society, to judge by the fact that Spanish women in the Old and New World recorded "twice and even four times" the number of extramarital births as their cohorts in other Western European countries.[77] Thomas Calvo's study of Guadalajara in the seventeenth century also points to this pattern. At midcentury 58 percent of all children were registered as illegitimate; perhaps "half the households" were irregularly formed, a veritable "rising tide of concubinage and illegitimacy."[78]

But concubinage, often a short-term arrangement, should be distinguished from a long-term and stable arrangement, sometimes known as *barraganía*, an informal union deeply rooted in Hispanic popular culture and accepted to a degree in the Siete Partidas.[79] Illegitimacy rates cannot do that. However, a link has been made by Michael C. Scardaville, based on eighteenth-century police records of Mexico City, between marriage desertion and illegal marriages: "Nearly one-half of all the illegally constituted marriages in Mexico City were formed by at least one person who had deserted his or her family."[80] Deserters would have been more prudent not to marry, for even though the Inquisition taught people to police consensual unions, the penalties for fornication and adultery were simply to separate the offending couple. Sometimes, however, offending couples were forced to marry, and this created the bigamist, just as forcing Jews to convert created the converso. The point needs to be underscored because it emphasizes the coexistence of toleration and prohibition.

Bigamists were men and women who are of interest not mainly because they abandoned spouses, an essentially negative act common enough in early modern times, but because of the risks they took in making a new life. They chose to marry, or when pressured agreed to marry, thus acting according to the basic rules of their society.[81] We should see them, then, not as people bent on disorder but as wanting to fit in and settle in. And from new surroundings, new partners, new associations, came new lives. We turn next to the families and youthful beginnings of bigamists to see in more detail who they were and where they came from.

CHAPTER TWO

A MESÓN, OR INN. DEPICTED HERE IS THE KIND OF
SUBSTANTIAL ESTABLISHMENT FOUND IN LARGE TOWNS,
WHERE TRAVELERS AND TRANSIENTS WERE ACCOMMODATED

Family and Upbringing

✠ As REQUIRED BY trial procedures, bigamists gave information about their families and childhood. This comes in the form of 'genealogies,' brief identifications of parents, siblings, and relatives, and as 'autobiographies,' touching on the early years. However spare this material, it nevertheless contains traces of the private worlds of families and households, where children gained the knowledge, skills, values, and attitudes they would take as adults into the larger world. Childhood, the time of this socialization, will for our purposes here be considered a stage of life that ends on leaving home.

Parents raised children as a matter of course, within daily routines. In the beginning children remained close to the household, but as time passed they ventured afield and felt the influence of neighbors, relatives, priests, teachers, and masters. Some parents placed their children in service (to perform unskilled work as shepherds, farmhands, mule drivers, or house servants), thereby delegating their upbringings to employer-guardians. This drastic course, often forced by destitution, meant little or no further contact with their families.[1] Perhaps the limiting case was the "fragmented families" of plebeians in late colonial Mexico City, with no male adult present, living with "continuous changes and constantly reconstituting [themselves]," in *vecindades* four or five to a room.[2] The compactness of their social space and the requirement that they "share and coordinate" sanitary, washing, and cooking spaces with as many as sixty to ninety other renters meant a more collective existence and resulted in more intense and more complex communal ties (and frictions) than obtained within rural or 'traditional' stem families.[3] Yet humble households with few resources also kept children in residence long after they might have gone. For them children became an economic asset, and the longer period of coresidence meant a correspondingly strong parental imprint on their lives.

In this way children became moored to place and way of life; they learned from everyday contact at table, hearth, and bench, and in the adjacent streets, shops, and churches of their neighborhoods. The customary knowledge they acquired, too full of "subtleties" to reduce to print, Carlo Ginzburg stresses, came from "the living voice . . . gestures and glances."[4] Whether in person or by proxy, raising children came down to a common objective: to join them to society. This took place in a sequence that paralleled the rites of passage as baptism, first communion, confirmation, and marriage marked moments of incorporation, participation, accountability, and autonomy.[5]

We approach childhood not directly but obliquely, because this is all the files allow. Witnesses speak of settings and leave-takings, rather than of processes and influences. Yet something of processes can be inferred by linking settings to the 'formed' adults visible in the inquisitorial dock. This amounts to deducing causes from effects.[6] Leave-takings recount transitions, what came next with reference to what went before. The look backward to childhood, then, shows leaving home either as taking a new direction or keeping to an old one. Narrators often place this moment against a backdrop of circumstances and portray themselves as acting and reacting. They also speak of the ties and memory of family that remained ten or twenty years after the departure from childhood. These distant and all-too-brief references sometimes convey the nature of past family dynamics after time, distance, and new surroundings and influences had made their impact. We shall look, then, at settings to deduce formative processes; at leave-takings to test for continuities; and at family ties still remaining at midlife to see how important they were long after childhood had passed.

SETTINGS

The Household as School

From the time boys began to observe their fathers at work, they imitated and helped them by running errands and performing simple tasks. So they learned. In this way Martín Sánchez of Cebreros, a district capital of Roman foundation in the province and diocese of Avila, must have become increasingly competent as a blacksmith as he frequented his father's shop.[7] By age fourteen or fifteen, he was working with him as a junior partner and so continued for fifteen years until 1559, when the father died. Martín was then about thirty and, assuming his inheritance of the shop, the expected course would have been for him to carry on as before.[8] Instead, however, he moved to Seville and later crossed to the Indies. Twenty years later (in 1581), Martín's lifelong friend Andrés Sánchez spoke of their boyhood in Cebreros and their half-dozen years, both as workers at the mint, in Seville.[9] Unlike so many others for whom Seville was only an interlude, a place to secure passage to the Indies, Martín had settled there and married, fathered six children, was widowed, and married again.[10] Ultimately, as we know, he went to the Indies, but as an impulse more than with advance planning. Serving as a "soldier" on the fleet, he saw Mexico and "the land seemed good," he testified in 1581, so he returned for his wife and immigrated.

By the time Martín was arrested by the Inquisition, he had been in New Spain for about ten years and was then, according to Andrés, a man of "more than fifty years, thin, light-bearded, olive skinned, and one-eyed."[11] Other blacksmiths on Tacuba street, he added, had also known Martín in Seville.[12] But not before Seville, which suggests a common trajectory for many tradesmen in the Indies: emigration from scattered Spanish towns; association based on work for shorter or longer periods in Seville; passage to the Indies at different times; and renewed contact as work and proximity brought them together again. At every stage of Martín's long journey from Cebreros to Seville to Mexico City, he earned his living thanks to the skills learned from his father. Although we have only a bare outline of Martín's movements, they nevertheless show that his work and social ties remained closely linked to the trade he learned as a child.[13]

Just as his father's blacksmith shop became Martín's school, so the buying, transporting, and butchering of cattle for towns became Antonio de Acevedo's (born ca. 1550).[14] Meat contracting was his father's business, based in Tordesillas, a town of some importance situated on the banks of the Duero River (in the province and diocese of Valladolid), and from age fifteen (before that Antonio had attended school), he acted as apprentice and associate, "traveling to and from various fairs in León, Valladolid, Medina del Rioseco, and Extremadura to market cattle."[15] By his mid-twenties Antonio, as a full partner, handled meat contracts for villages on the outskirts of Medina del Campo. His life, so far, projected a pattern for the rest of it: a base of literacy from schooling, apprenticeship, partnership, and eventually ownership of the business. With good prospects at home, Antonio stayed close, married a local woman, and fathered three children.

But then he fell into debt, and ran off to the Indies about 1575, 'pushed' there by his setback. As did many of his contemporaries, he doubtlessly thought he could find in the Indies the wealth that would allow him to return, pay his debts, and resume, maybe on a grander scale, his life in Tordesillas. To help him he had an obvious contact, his uncle Christóbal de Acevedo, a merchant of Mexico City who made Antonio his factor in Oaxaca. That position, Antonio said in his autobiography, meant "travel through Oaxaca and the Mixteca" with goods provided both by his uncle and by other merchants. In the city of Oaxaca, Antonio also had a modest store with "stock and cash worth over 3000 pesos" that served as a retail outlet.[16]

The imprint of Antonio's childhood setting amid his father's mercantile transactions remains visible in the man of thirty-four in the inquisitorial dock, speaking of his life as a provincial merchant. With the mulatto Diego de Hojeda (born 1558; a legitimate son in spite of his mixed racial background), the parental imprint imposed itself even more firmly.[17] As members of the silk workers' guild, his father in Puebla and grandfather in Mexico City (both Spaniards from Medellín) taught Diego their trade: "in Puebla to age five" (with his father, Francisco) and "in Mexico City with his grandfather [Juan] he finished learning it." Diego's statement, more than we might expect, gives weight to the years before five as a time of training, when surely most of it came after joining his grandfather's household. In any case he did finish the training; but instead of working as a silkmaker he took jobs as a muleteer and carter. This, however, must have been to avoid silkmaker cohorts who would have noticed and reported the illicit second marriage he contracted. When sidestepping no longer mattered, at the stage when he was sentenced to five years rowing in the galleys, Diego affirmed the worth of silkmaking and his skill at it. No doubt a ploy to escape the rigors of galley servitude, his plea "to pay his debt in a monastery serving in his trade of silkmaker which he knows very well" nevertheless presumes the logic and values of his society.[18] Otherwise it would have made no sense as a plausible trade-off.

To the kinds of settings we have seen so far, we may add the variable of illegitimacy.[19] Cosme de Robles Quiñones (born 1586), the son of Felipe, a merchant specializing in trade with China, lived with his unmarried parents to age twelve.[20] That is all he says about his early childhood, but it implies a stable household and upbringing suitable for the son, legitimate or illegitimate, of a long-distance merchant. When he was twelve, Cosme's parents (he uses the plural in his autobiography) placed him with a master in Mexico City to begin an apprenticeship in silkmaking. Cosme must have had problems with this man, for after two years he ran away to Zacatecas and found work on *estancias*. But after six months, his father found him, returned him to Mexico City, and made him resume training. Cosme put in three more years to become a silkmaker but instead of working at the trade, signed up for a tour of duty as a soldier at San Juan de Ulúa. This proved to be an interlude of only eight months, for a bad heart led to a discharge, and he then took up his trade.

What did such a setting produce? By 1604 Cosme was well imbedded in a network of men of his and associated trades in Puebla, but they were marginal types of racially mixed castes; he married, and the low quality of his marriage fits with his low standing. His bride was the mulatto Juana Baptista of Guajoçingo, almost certainly illegitimate, the daughter of a free black woman and an "absent" Spaniard.[21] As for Cosme's network, the mulatto Alonso González de Peralta, a taffeta weaver of Guajoçingo acted as his padrino at the wedding, and guests included a silkmaker, a tailor (*jubetero*), "other vecinos," and the *estanciero* Gabriel de Alvarado.[22] After the wedding Cosme and Juana took up residence on the estancia of Alvarado, himself a marginal figure, living on land deep in the Indian countryside (a half league from Guajoçingo).[23] The move underscores, once again, Cosme's lowly status in Hispanic society. Working as a silkweaver would at least have allowed for a life in the city, where the Hispanic world concentrated. And in fact after two and a half years in the countryside, Cosme did return to the city, when he and Juana moved to Puebla and stayed for a year and a half in houses belonging to Juana's mother.

So a disjuncture appears between Cosme's childhood and early adulthood. Although he was illegitimate, Cosme's parents were Spaniards, and they nurtured him in a family setting and placed him in training with a master. The father's intervention to make Cosme complete the training underscores his commitment to his son's formation. Yet from this comes an adult Cosme of lowlier than expected standing; he marries a caste woman, he associates with marginal types in his work, he lives in the houses of his black mother-in-law, he banishes himself to the countryside for long periods, and he works at his trade only sporadically.[24] A year before he went to trial (in 1608), Cosme returned to silkmaking by setting up a "silk store" in Toluca, this after another two-year stint in the countryside, and at this point we lose sight of him.[25] It seems possible, however, that he would continue to use his childhood training, possibly now more consistently than before.

The parental direction that can be inferred from childhood settings oriented, more than it fixed in detail, how children would turn out. Too many unexpected and unforeseen circumstances called for the adjustments, decisions, and associations that led to variation. Again, however, the childhood setting of Joseph Miguel Reyes (born ca. 1730) in a family of storekeepers made a lasting imprint.[26] Joseph, more clearly than Cosme, was marked from early childhood as a marginal figure in Hispanic society. He grew up in the Indian countryside (in Calpulalpa, a subject town of Tezcuco), far from Spanish towns; at twenty he married Tomasa María de la Cruz, a "principal" Indian woman native to the town who spoke at least some Spanish (*ladina*). Before and after his marriage, Joseph lived and worked with his parents and three brothers.[27] He mentions no special training, only that the family ran a general-purpose store and did country work (*labores del campo*), the latter probably a reference to raising crops and stock for their own use. All four brothers (and one sister), then, lived among Indians in an isolated town and, from every indication, would continue to do so after their father died. Joseph, however, broke out of the pattern in 1752 when he got into trouble for gambling.[28] Authorities (most likely Indian authorities) put him in jail, from which he escaped and fled to the mining camp of Real del Monte. After two months, he claimed, he returned to Calpulalpa, but Tomasa refused to live with him, a decision that must have been supported by local authorities. So he left and signed up for a term in a presidio. In his new world at the presidio, Joseph reconstituted his old world, marrying a second time and setting up a store, which also served as a gambling center.

In hindsight, storekeeping at the presidio seems an inevitable continuity with childhood. But choice, not fate, determined Joseph's course, as he could have chosen to remain among the marginal Spaniards in direct contact with the Indian countryside. From his childhood, after all, he would have acquired a general knowledge of country folk.[29] In this he stands with 80 percent or more of the population who, in settings of farm and ranch learned to assess and deal with the endlessly varied circumstances associated with stock and crop raising. The stable and seemingly uneventful upbringing of the mulatto Felipe Rodríguez (born 1725) therefore exemplifies that of many others.[30] Felipe spent his first twenty years with his parents, resident workers on haciendas near Mexico City. What did he learn? We have no listing, but on leaving home at twenty, he found work as a farmhand and a mule driver, presumably the work he had always done. Along the way he also picked up the rudiments of Christian indoctrination, although without the "understanding that he should have had."[31] This much, brief as it is, suggests a firm continuity fixed on the lives of poor men (and women), more in the eighteenth century than before, as generation after generation they worked land owned by others and raised children without means or motive to set out on their own.

They may be contrasted with another type of the eighteenth-century countryside with the means and connections to get ahead. The Spaniard Juan Gómez Franco acquired land near Córdoba and cultivated tobacco.[32] How he came to do this goes back to 1711 when, as an eleven-year-old boy, he set out for New Spain (from Yguera de Vargas, Extremadura) with his father, Pedro. Pedro settled in Córdoba, grew tobacco for ten years, and in 1721 returned to Spain with Juan. During his sojourn Juan had grown to manhood and, doubtless with increasing responsibilities, helped Pedro. At twenty-one Juan had spent half his life in the Indies, had learned to grow, cure, and market tobacco, to read and write, and had become part of a local network.

Now in Spain, however, he apparently meant to stay. He married Inés María de Escobar of San Lúcar, and whatever work he did in the following seven years surely had little to do with his boyhood formation in New Spain. Then the marriage failed; Inés took a lover who, with her blessing, plotted against Juan. He came to fear for his life and around 1730 returned to the Indies and to the growing and processing of tobacco in Córdoba. And with considerable success, to judge by his will that put his net worth at 60,000 pesos in 1756. Shortly before making his will, after a twenty-year 'bachelorhood,' he married a second time (in January 1751). By then he stood out as a provincial notable, a status confirmed in 1752 (shortly before he was arrested by the Inquisition), with a viceregal commission naming him lieutenant in the local militia.[33]

So Juan made a life in the Indies, and its shape had much to do with the formative years with his father. That it ended badly—he died in the inquisitorial prison on January 17, 1756, after a four-year confinement—should not obscure his successful career.[34] In his will he named his son in Spain, don Sebastián Gomes de Escobar, his only and universal heir, "if he is still alive." Otherwise the estate was to go to pious works. To his second wife, the Spaniard doña Francisca Basilia Rodríguez, a native of Córdoba, he left only a townhouse in Córdoba. Doña Francisca, in fact, had been running the tobacco farm in Juan's absence and in a letter of 1752 claimed compensation for her "industry, credit, attendance, and work from cultivating to harvesting, curing and bundling."[35] For all his success, however,

Juan's final resolution of his life lay not with what he had created in the New World but with a part of it he left behind in the Old.

School

School supplemented the schooling taking place within households. From the late fifteenth century in Spain, well before the rest of Europe, church synods required that parishes provide schools and masters to teach children reading, writing, singing, and Christian doctrine.[36] So it became a common adjunct of childhood settings, and its impact can be tracked to some degree in the inquisitorial files.

In New Spain going to school meant different venues and content for boys and girls. Boys went to a parish *escuela*, where a *maestro* taught them reading, writing, arithmetic, and doctrine; girls went to an *escuela de amigas*, where a poorly trained mistress, in her own home, offered rudimentary instruction in reading, in the memorization of the catechism, and in sewing, weaving, and embroidery.[37] So with this gendered distinction, children received some skills and quite a lot of religious indoctrination. For girls the objective was a life of subordinate domesticity; for boys it could be a first stage in preparing to enter one of the professions, commerce, or a trade. Memorizing lists, formulas, and prayers led to little understanding of doctrine, as Jean-Pierre Dedieu has established, yet the link between religious instruction and reading no doubt accounts for a large number of people who learned to read with no apparent 'need' for it.[38]

The mestizo Joseph Muñoz de Sanabria, who grew up in the city and the outlying villages of Querétaro, was such a person.[39] Until 1705, when he was around twenty, Joseph lived with his parents, worked as a shepherd, and learned to read and to write. He apparently retained his skills, for when the Inquisition detained him in 1726, he was carrying a book, *Ramillete de Divinaciones*, and stashed among his possessions were two letters (one from a sister and one from his wife), a promissory note from "one Diego Phelipe vecino of Guanajuato and the tenant of a rancho," plus "other papers." The book, apparently a collection of divinatory formulas, must have been something he referred to frequently, possibly as a roving oracle to isolated country folk. At this level then, Joseph, the son of a small farmer, a simple shepherd and, later, a mule driver, operated as a functioning literate. The essential point, of course, is that people had to use such knowledge or they would lose it.[40]

What should we make of a muleteer's brief autobiographical sketch that stresses details of schooling to the exclusion of almost everything else in his young life? At the very least, it underscores importance by emphasis. The case in point comes from the muleteer Pedro Pablo Rodríguez (born 1721) who, in the dock in 1767, said that his father (a muleteer and farmworker but dead since Pedro was two) and mother (also by then dead) had been "taken for and reputed [to be] Spaniards."[41] He himself had been born in Tomatlán (jurisdiction of Purificación, Jalisco) and

> when very little they took him to Guadalajara where he began to learn to read. Afterward he returned to the said pueblo where he finished learning to read and to write with his master Thomás Rodríguez Calderón. And then being of an age so that he could work in the job of muleteer, he went to Mexico City and to various places in the north, always with mules.

Pedro's statement hinges on the transition from boyhood to manhood. The first he characterizes solely by his schooling, the second he signals by the onset of his working life driving mules. The divide lies at the point of finishing schooling and becoming old enough to work.

The Domestic Settings of Daughters

Our discussion has concentrated on boys rather than girls for two reasons: first, males form the bulk of our sample, and second, the files, even those with a woman as principal, say more about men than women. Women, of course, had fewer options. The usual step that launched them into 'adult' life was marriage, and even that meant merely their transfer from the wardship of father or guardian to that of a husband. Here, for example, are some typically elliptic accounts by women of their childhood. In a deposition given in 1691, the mulatto Lorenza de la Cruz said that she "was born [in 1661] at the Amanalco sugar mill [Cuernavaca] where she grew up and there [at age sixteen or seventeen] she married the said Gerónimo."[42] Bárbara Martina, a *loba* of Indian and mestizo parentage, gave a comparable statement.[43] Born about 1745, she spent her early years with her parents on *ranchos* (her family moved frequently) in the Pachuca mining district and at sixteen married a shepherd of the district.

The upbringing of a creole Spaniard named Mariana Monroy (born 1649) points to a similar sheltered pattern, but from Mariana's sketchy account of it, given in the dock in 1678, a few elaborations applicable to Spaniards, albeit poor, stand out.[44] Raised by her widowed mother who did piecework as a séamstress, Mariana said that she "grew up in her mother's house [in Guadalajara] because she did not know her father and was occupied serving her mother until she was 14."

From her mother Mariana learned to sew, and from a local woman described as a spinster (Antonia Ortiz, no doubt in an escuela de amigas run out of her home), to read and to write. She had memorized and retained the religious material drilled into girls by these mistresses, for she impressed her examiners with her well-spoken recitation of the prayers, credo, commandments, and of the fundamental points of Christian doctrine. At fourteen Mariana married Manuel Figueroa, a newly arrived peninsular Spaniard chosen by her mother. As we shall see in Chapter 4, she was unhappy in this marriage (at least in part because Manuel treated her more as a servant than a wife) and to free herself stressed that she had entered into it against her will.

The pattern repeats itself monotonously: girls confined mostly to domestic settings, learning wifely skills such as sewing and cooking, rehearsing female virtues of modesty and subordination, and then marrying. The upbringing of María Ignacia Zapata, a natural child of Spaniards ("my mother Mariana Deita Salazar . . . now dead in Sochicoatlan, had me out of wedlock [in 1765]; my father is unknown") parallels that of Mariana.[45] Probably from her mother, María learned to sew and to spin and at twenty-three was calling herself a seamstress and spinner. From her mother as well as a *maestra* she learned to read, she said, but only in the rudimentary way for religious purposes: "to spell out the letters one at a time in order to get through the prayers of the catechism." She did not learn to write. When she was twelve, José Hermenegildo Freyre, a *castizo* from nearby Meztitlan, seduced her, took her to Tlacolula (near Tianguistengo), and married her.

It is hard to escape the impression that the meager accounts of their early years given by women in the bigamy records represent, in fact, a spare and narrow range of choices and opportunities. Not until these women were away from their families and caught up in the drama of their usually troubled marriages did they speak about their lives with the detail and agency that places them as actors, albeit often beleaguered ones, in their worlds. Before that we get the repeated formulaic accounts indicating close parental supervision (with hints of variation by class, caste, and cultural linkage, although these are rarely spelled out), rudimentary training if any at all, and the passing to a new stage of life at marriage. Within these statements a suggestive detail sometimes emerges. That the mulatto María Ignacia Cervantes (born 1753) "went to school [and] only learned the prayers of the doctrine and to sew, but not to read or write"[46] once again points to a different meaning of school for boys and girls.[47]

Family Settings of Gentry, Professionals, and Merchants

So far we have the childhood settings of modest households. Here we make an incursion into those with the resources and lineages to exercise more power and influence in their worlds. None of them ranked in the high nobility, but all aspired to wealth and position, mostly in provincial towns, as professionals, merchants, and gentry. The Benavides family, for example, were people of new Christian background from the Spanish city of Toro, a district capital in the province and diocese of Zamora, who were physicians (father and son), money changers (grandfather and son), and notaries (two sons).[48] The youngest son, Gerónimo, born in 1532, concerns us here.

Although his father died when he was an infant, Gerónimo said (in the inquisitorial dock in 1579) that he stayed in school until he was twelve, "growing up" in his mother's house because he did not know his father. At twelve he left home to elude the consequences of a sexual liaison, entered into after a widow extracted his promise to marry her. Gerónimo thereby cut short a formation that surely was meant to resemble that of his older brothers. To get out of the marriage, he got out of town. He went "with a soldier" to Perpignan, then under siege by French forces, but arrived after the siege had been lifted. So Gerónimo went on to Naples where, for five or six years, he shipped "on a lateen fitted out as a privateer whose *patrón* was a Catalan named Jacome Chipriote, son of a Greek."

Some time in 1549 Gerónimo went to Seville, stayed for the usual eight or nine months that it took to secure passage to the Indies, and in 1550 embarked "as a sailor" on the fleet. In Santo Domingo Gerónimo attached himself to the entourage of the audiencia judge, licenciado Alonso de Zorita. When Zorita moved to the Guatemalan audiencia (in the spring of 1553), Gerónimo went with him and no doubt thanks to Zorita received the somewhat lowly position of constable.[49] When Zorita was promoted to the Mexico City audiencia (in 1555), Gerónimo again followed him and again emerged with a constableship, this time in Vera Cruz.[50] He held the post of royal constable (*alcaide de la carcel de corte*) there for seventeen years, and in 1574, by then in possession of the title of "His Majesty's Notary," he purchased the position of notary in Jalapa for 1,500 pesos.[51]

By his early forties, after starting out as if the hero of a picaresque novel, Gerónimo had therefore consolidated his position in the Indies. In 1565 (the year his patron Zorita returned to Spain), he married Marina de Ribera in Mexico City, the sister of the notary Guillermo Román, possibly a man Gerónimo had served as an apprentice. Gerónimo now possessed a position commensurate with his family background and in line with the direction in which he had been headed as a boy.

Although Gerónimo's formation had gone awry, it had been no fault of his family. His childhood in a household of professionals points to a family concern to lose no ground in the struggle to be more like nobility than commoners. In this they would have measured themselves against the likes of the Hoz Espinosas, claimants to gentry status in the village of Poza (in the provincia of Palencia), people of means and reputation, old Christians and hidalgos, who also saw to their son's childhood with evident care.[52] As an only child, Agustín de Hoz Espinosa Calderón (born 1546) stood to inherit the six farms that his father, Pedro de Hoz, possessed. Pedro kept Agustín at home until he was nine or ten (ca. 1556), then sent him to Burgos for schooling. There he learned to read and to write and began a course of studies in the arts; after two years he went to the court (at Madrid) as a page, first in service to the marquesa de Poza, later to don Luis Méndez de Haro.[53]

Schooling in Burgos and three years in Madrid provided sufficient grooming for young Agustín's parents to call him home to marry and take his place among provincial notables. He returned in 1561 "to his parents' house and they married him to a maiden named Cazilda, daughter of Miguel Alonso, a nobleman from Soto de Bureba, three leagues distant from Poza." Agustín lived with Cazilda in his father's house for nine years before she died while giving birth. By then he held the position of alderman (regidor), judge of the rural constabulary (alcalde de la Hermandad), and administrator of poor relief (mayordomo de pobres). The Agustín of twenty-four is enough beyond his childhood formation to underscore how smoothly it meshed with the roles he was destined to inherit rather than to struggle for.[54]

Merchants, like professionals, sought to approximate the status of the nobility. And from the seventeenth century, they were having considerable success, using their wealth to secure titles, offices, and respectable marriages.[55] To conserve and increase wealth, therefore, loomed as all-important. The Malagueñan merchant Diego del Alamo provides an example of a father dealing with a son who failed to grasp this essential point.[56] Manuel's dissolute habits (imitative of the nobility?) acted as a dagger at the heart of family aspirations because they threatened the basis of the Alamos' importance. To reform his wayward son, Diego sent him to the Indies. We pick up the story in 1776. Manuel is 29 and has had primary schooling (reading, writing, and arithmetic) and some grammar.

But as heir to and participant in the family business, he remains completely out of step with the entrepreneurial values behind the family's wealth. As he expressed it later (June 4, 1788) to the inquisitors, his

> nature was to spend on country houses, musicians, on many horses, and other diversions—honest ones but too draining of his parents' estate—because he did not understand that excessive spending is an offence to God . . . The truth is his father scolded him, saying that he had to stop, that he had to realize that in the end he would ruin them.

And so to the Indies he went, but alas no cure awaited him there. If anything its free air incited him to new excesses. On making landfall at Vera Cruz, Diego sold his "good clothing" and other effects that "had cost 1,800 pesos in Spain" and gambled away the proceeds on card games and cock fights. Although he had assumed the honorific *don* (common as it was by then) he became so destitute that he dropped it, together with his surname, out of shame at being reduced to taking the lowly post of night watchman in Zacatecas. Still under an assumed name, Manuel moved up slightly when he began to travel about curing the sick "with the knowledge . . . of medicine he had learned from medical books." Manuel, therefore, used his schooling to educate himself through books rather than through an apprenticeship but, as he appears in the inquisitorial dock in 1787, showed no sign of having set himself on a course to return home. In fact just the opposite; he had given up hope that his father would call him home.

Parental concern for the continuity and advancement of family standing runs through elite childhood as wealth or property acted as a sign or basis of status. To control marriages and inheritance mattered most, but from bigamy files we also find parents tending to values, comportment, bearing, and skills that go with familial traditions and aspirations. In childhood training, younger sons fared as well as older ones, especially among professionals where training, and therefore some level of competence, stood at least in part as the basis for patronage. In comparison, patronage came to well-established hidalgo families as a birthright. Returning to the professional class, with Gerónimo de Benavides (the young *pícaro* who worked his way from runaway, to privateer, to constable, to notary), the intent and pattern of his upbringing was comparable to that of his brothers and fell apart not because of his father's death but because of his liaison with the widow.

LEAVE-TAKINGS

The death of a parent disrupted a child's upbringing because it unbalanced household structures. But as we have already seen with Gerónimo, a household headed by a widow carried on to raise a young child within a pattern already used for grown ones. Children in small and homogeneous communities also grew up much as they would have had the death of a parent not occurred. At age four, for example, Manuel de Campuzanos Palacios (born 1695) lost his father, who drowned when he and his brother capsized in a chalupa while fishing in the Bay of Biscay.[57] So he went through boyhood without his father. Yet tradition and location inclined boys from Laredo, the Basque coastal village that was home, to look to the sea for a livelihood in any case. Two of Manuel's uncles owned chalupas and, like his father and the other men of Laredo, Manuel no doubt took his place in the small vessels that fished the treacherous waters that had claimed his father.

At eighteen Manuel left home, taking up "maritime occupations," as he said in his autobiography, and since then he had "always" been engaged in them. In this he referred to service on crown ships: an armada to the Levant, an escort to the Indies fleet, and, on land for a year in Santander, as quartermaster (*guarda almazén de viveres*). In the 1720s he made several trips between Cádiz and the Indies as a steward and at least one as a helmsman. Marriage to a local woman, also at eighteen, coincided with leaving home and, at the same time gave Manuel another link to the Laredo way of life, with a father-in-law who, like his father and uncles, "used to farm and, in the winter, would fish." Simply growing up in Laredo inclined Manuel to the sea, and for what it was worth, he learned to read and to write and received instruction in Christian doctrine in the "public school."

Manuel's career as a seaman brought him to the Indies on several occasions, but in 1730, crossing as helmsman of *The Cock of the Indies* (*El gallo indiano*) with various notables aboard, he decided to stay.[58] He did not explain why, but his conduct on landing suggests that Manuel intended to solicit patronage. Listen to how he recounted his first days in New Spain, as on leaving Vera Cruz for Puebla he

> joined the señor Inquisitor and six or eight other passengers in whose company he arrived at Puebla. The others continued on to Mexico City but he stayed in the inn waiting for the Inquisitor to depart in order to go with him and with don Dionisio Caro who promised to loan him a mule for the trip to Mexico City.[59]

And so they traveled, but en route Manuel failed to ingratiate himself with the inquisitor, who when he reached Guadalupe (on the outskirts of Mexico City) stopped to wait for colleagues yet to come, while Manuel continued on to the capital. He stayed there for about ten months,[60] made contact with merchants, probably men from his tierra, based in San Felipe el Real (Chihuahua), and traveled north with them. One of them made Manuel a partner, provided him with goods, and sent him to the mining camp of Santa Rosa de Cosihuiriáchic, eighteen leagues to the southwest. There, Manuel said, he "engaged in commerce" (from 1731 to 1732),[61] but work as a factor at a small mining camp[62] hardly could have matched Manuel's initial hopes for patronage and now had taken him a world away from his childhood setting of coastal Laredo. Yet his ending up in Cosihuiriáchic has a logic to it: in the same degree that Laredo's homogeneous society of limited choices shaped Manuel's boyhood, its outlook on the sea also presented him with an invitation to venture into the wider world. Yet once he had ventured, he gravitated to a tiny part of it where his countrymen had already established themselves.

Just as a community, more than a household, shaped Manuel's childhood, so too another kind of community (in this case a Jesuit sugar mill, with its rhythms of production, work routines, and religious observances) served as the childhood setting for Mateo de la Cruz (born 1627).[63] When Mateo was still a baby, his father, a foreman, left with an administrator who had been replaced; his mother died soon after.[64] No one from Mateo's immediate family—father, mother, brother, sister, and a paternal uncle, all of whom worked and lived at Xalmolonga (Malinalco)—became his guardian. Instead Mateo went to the household of his padrino, Francisco Mulato; Mateo had no other surname for him. He grew up on the estate weeding cornfields (*milpas*) with other young boys until he began to help with mule trains. In this it is hard to imagine that his childhood was any different than it would have been had his own parents raised him.

In 1644 Mateo married María Ana, also from Xalmolonga, underlining the narrow confines of his existence. At seventeen he had passed the stage of childhood. Three years later he traveled north to take a higher-paying job as a miner.[65] His account contains idiosyncratic details: not the name of the mining camp, for example, but that he came to owe capitán Juan de Morales 150 pesos; barely a mention of the sickness that forced María to return home (to Malinalco, next to Xalmolonga), but stress on the detail that he stayed to work off the debt rather than accompany her.[66] Did debt outweigh husbandly duties? Apparently so, for men routinely worked at remote sites while their wives remained at home. Mateo, recounting his autobiography to the inquisitors, said that he continued as a miner until about 1655 when "he fell and injured his chest and tail bone [while] working as a pickman." The injury prompted his return to the less-dangerous and less-arduous work of farm laborer. He spent the four years "cultivating a small milpa" in the Indian pueblo of Xochipalan, located in a hot and dry area (jurisdiction of Iguala, now in north Guerrero state). At thirty-nine Mateo had come full circle: from weeding milpas on the Jesuit estate as a boy, to tending his own deep in the countryside as a man lamed by injury.[67]

With Manuel and Mateo, the setting of compact communities shaped their childhood much as it would have had they not been orphaned. By contrast children passing to the guardianship of a relative might suffer greater disruption. At seven, for example, Baltasar Márquez Palomino's (born 1587) parents ("humble, country people" from Jerez, he said) died, and he passed to the guardianship of his uncle.[68] But the change must have unsettled the boy, for he ran away to Seville "with some other lads." He gives no details about his life in Seville (perhaps he lived by his wits in the fashion of the young pícaros portrayed fictionally by Cervantes), only that he remained there for three or four years.[69] He then went to Arcos de la Frontera and, for ten years, served as a farmhand (apparently to a single employer). From Arcos Baltasar felt the pull of Seville and from there, in his early twenties, he embarked for the Indies.[70]

Baltasar's boyhood, as a time of nurturing and training in a household setting, amounted to little. His account passes quickly over his early years and the time in Seville, to stress the settled period in Arcos. Yet his running away marks such a clear transition, in fact a rejection of his uncle, that it points by implication to at least an imagined contentment in early boyhood with his parents. Arcos, in a household working as "a servant in things of the country," returned him to that life. At fifty (in 1633), Baltasar called himself (in his autobiographical statement) a farmworker (*labrador*) and a shepherd. His summary of work in New Spain merely lists places (for example, Vera Cruz, Otumba, Querétaro, Texcoco, Chalco) and the names of masters for whom he worked. The inquisitors would have understood Baltasar's shorthand: he was presenting himself as a servant living under the authority of masters rather than as a masterless vagabond. The work itself needed no elaboration, for the specific tasks associated with farm and ranch work were well known. So Baltasar did jobs that required no specialized training, but he moved more frequently than might be expected, possibly because he found no long-term work, possibly because he sought more-generous employers.

If Baltasar chose to leave his uncle's household, Juan Antonio Ramírez (born 1716) had no chance to remain in that of his parents, Spaniards from Puebla, who died when he too was seven.[71] Juan had relatives in the city who might have raised him,[72] but instead his cousin took him to Puerto Alvarado, south of Veracruz on the gulf coast (jurisdiction of Veracruz, now Veracruz state) and placed him in service to a fisherman.[73] So Juan became separated from an uncle and aunt, cousins, and three brothers. Ten years later when he married (in 1733), not they but Juan's master patronized, and possibly orchestrated, the event. In the intervening years, Juan learned to read a little. He could manage print in books, he said, but not the cursive script of handwriting. He could not write.[74] He also lived for a time in Veracruz, where he "learned the trade of tailor," he said in his autobiography, but instead of working in the trade, he returned to Alvarado to fish. In this his boyhood setting (the household of a fisherman in a coastal fishing village) looms as the strongest imprint on the emerging adult.

Baltasar, who ran away, and Juan, who was taken away, both faced change when their parents died. Other boys ran away from home while one or both parents were alive. Some clearly were running *from* home, but often without a clear idea where they were going *to*; others simply took advantage of the chance to go when it came. In either case they had some control over when and with whom they would go. Here is how the mestizo Pedro Mateo (born 1642), as part of his autobiography (given January 24, 1667), spoke of his leavetaking:

> Already pretty big ("siendo ya grandecillo") [when his father died], he ran away from his mother's house to the Briçeños's *estancia* near Pueblo de la Barca (Guadalajara) where his cousins lived. He grew up there until he was a young man ("hasta ya mancebo grande").[75]

Thus Pedro divided his growing up into two stages. An early childhood ended with his assumption of a kind of incipient maturity—he is "pretty big," and he takes a master. But not just any master, for his objective is to join his cousins. As mestizos on an estancia, they represent the Hispanic world, and so going there means taking leave of the Indian world of his mother's household. A second stage ends on reaching 'young manhood,' and from this moment Pedro takes charge of his destiny more directly than before.

Another young runaway, the *lobo* (of mulatto and Indian parentage) Bernabé Christóbal ran away from home at eight; his going is linked more to opportunity than to any evident aversion toward home.[76] The mayor-domo of a great estate was passing through his hometown of Querétaro in 1704, and he had the chance to go north with him and serve as a shepherd. About twenty-five years later, Bernabé refers to his leave-taking in two slightly different ways: that he had "run away from his parents [when] little [and] went to the Kingdom of León where he served Mireles, mayordomo of the Conde de Peñalva"; and that "Eugenio Mireles took him to Nuevo León, raised him, and [in 1715] arranged his marriage with Lorenza María, free mulatto, native and *vecina* of the sheep ranch."[77]

Bernabé, in effect, chose Mireles as his guardian, for young boys (and in theory grown men) could run not to 'freedom' but to service and the guardianship of a master. Later pairing him with another of his servants was easy enough, but the mayordomo apparently interested himself little in Bernabé in other ways, neglecting, for example to have him instructed in Christian doctrine or to have him confirmed. Only at age twenty-seven was he confirmed, long after his term of service with Mireles. Work as a shepherd continued to be Bernabé's occupation as an adult, not only in León (where Peñalva had his herds) but in the Huasteca district, on the gulf coast south of Texas, and in Río Frío (jurisdiction of Coatepec, now in Mexico state).[78] Bernabé's boyhood break with his family was decisive and permanent; his choice of an employer-guardian shaped his adult life.[79]

Unlike Bernabé who, once he had taken leave of his parents, spent the rest of his childhood with a single master, Juan Lorenzo de Castillo (born 1680), a lobo "tending more to mulatto than mestizo," changed masters frequently after leaving home at age eight.[80] He went with a second master after only a year and, although he gives no details of his service until age twelve, by then he worked as a muleteer with a third master. To judge by how frequently he changed masters (he had had four by age fifteen and seven by age twenty-eight, having served terms of service of one, two, or three years, in places ranging from Querétaro to Sempoala, from Parral to Mexico City), Juan exercised considerable control over his life.[81]

Juan's mobility fits lives working as a muleteer, his father's occupation as well. So even though Juan spent only his first eight years in his parents' household, the time mattered nonetheless. Juan must have watched his father's comings and goings, trying to help, as best he could, with chores of feeding, watering, and tethering the animals, and with the packing and unpacking of them. His leaving for Querétaro removed him permanently from parental supervision, but Juan's wide-ranging travels as an adult and, most recently, those from his home base in Mexico City, allowed him to maintain some contact with his family—at the time of his arrest, his widowed aunt, still in Orizaba; his mother, also widowed, in Puebla with his unmarried sister; his brother, "married to a morisca named Manuela," in Mexico City.

Muleteers served as a ready means for boys to run away because they continually passed through towns and villages, always needed helpers, and went places that might seem more interesting than home. Boys in coastal towns who had access to the comings and goings of ships, as did Juan de Lizarzaburo, had at hand a comparable way to leave home.[82] Juan grew up in Rentería (province of Guipuzcoa, diocese of Pamplona) on the Bay of Biscay in the 1640s. At fourteen, though no longer a mere boy, he said that he "ran away" from his parents' house, embarking on a ship going to Andalusía. On coastal vessels Juan went to Cádiz, Seville, Córdoba, Andújar, Badajoz, and eventually to the Indies. If his early years had made him familiar with the work carried out by his family (his father was a shopkeeper and his uncle a blacksmith), the presence of ships in the harbor offset family example.

In the Indies Juan stayed in the maritime track that his leavetaking set him upon. He served as a soldier in coastal fortifications in Puerto Rico (three years) and in Santo Domingo (twelve years). Then sickness changed his course. He had contracted syphilis somewhere along the way and now traveled to Mexico City to receive the mercury ointment treatment. "After a long wait," he said, the hospital admitted and treated him, but from then on he remained ashore, working as a peddler out of Mexico City and San Juan Zitácuaro (district of Maravatio, province and bishopric of Michoacán). Juan made Zitácuaro his home base for ten or twelve years, running six mules to points "throughout the diocese of Michoacán" and to Zacatecas, Querétaro, San Luis Potosí, and Sombrerete. But his illness gradually wore him down. In 1690, when he appeared in the inquisitorial dock, he was no longer working and, as we shall see in chapter 4, was living apart from his wife in Copandaro, an Indian town ten miles or so from Zitácuaro. The trajectory of Juan's life—from the self-assured and almost-grown boy leaving home to the spent fifty-year-old complaining that his "natural forces were failing" (July 10, 1690)—shows us a man overtaken by age and disease after a hard life at sea and in the Indies.

Triana, Seville's barrio of seamen and transients, even more than the smaller coastal towns must have exerted a nearly irresistible pull on boys who grew up amid its bustle. As the focus of ships and shipping to the Indies, it gave boys the chance to leave home at any time. Juan de Barrera (born 1648) had no seafarers in his family, but took the chance to go at about age ten.[83] Before that he says little (in his autobiography of 1689) about his family setting. His father and eponym was a tailor from Burgos who, with his brother, had migrated to Seville, married a local woman, and lived a settled life practicing his trade. The tailor's family had grown rapidly (Juan was one of seven children), and Juan was sent to a neighborhood master to learn to read and to write. To leave, he

> arranged to go as cabin boy with Salvador Sánchez, a pilot who was making a voyage to the island of Santo Domingo and since then his work has been, sometimes as a cabin boy, sometimes as a sailor, to sail on various ships from Spain to these Indies, to Porto Belo, Cartagena, Havana, Vera Cruz, and from them back to Cádiz or San Lúcar.

In 1670 Juan made his last Atlantic crossing. He stayed in New Spain for a while, married the Spaniard Ana María Milanés (in 1672), and for five years (his testimony says nothing about his work during this time) lived with her in Tehuacán. Then about 1677 he returned to the sea: a voyage across the Pacific on the Manila galleon, service in the Caribbean in the armada of Barlovento, and work on ships plying the Pacific coast to California. Approaching age forty, Juan showed no sign of departing from the pattern established by that first voyage to leave home.

From our examples, then, boys ran away from home at seven, at eight (two), at about ten or twelve, and at fourteen.[84] They took leave decisively and permanently, but rarely said why. Silence as to motive suggests that such leave-takings fall within the range of unexceptional behavior for plebeian, if not elite, Spaniards.[85] However 'personal' their individual reasons, cultural assumptions presumed how and when boys entered society: at seven or eight years, for example, to begin an apprenticeship and by eight, ten, or twelve as cabin boys, helpers with mule trains, shepherds, and servants. The contribution that young boys could make to family enterprises when they existed (stores, farms, ranches, freight haulage, shops) had to be balanced against the costs of keeping them and also against their personal inclinations. After all ambition, boredom, anger, fear, or resentment directed against family or local authorities also pushed boys from home. Such personal components of life were of course also embedded in the culture but with limitless variation possible. A third variable, opportunity, depended on place and circumstance, providing boys with occasions frequent or scarce for approaching potential masters, mostly muleteers and ship captains, but also sometimes clerics and estate administrators.

FAMILY TIES

The Scattering of Families

The mobility of Spaniards scattered families, sometimes sending fragments in several directions, sometimes simply bifurcating them, as when a relative in the Indies became the destination of family in Spain. But whether leaving first or following a relative, the network of relations and compatriots left behind was unlikely to be a part of one's life again.

Boys who detached themselves from their families and tierras at an early age inevitably lost track of their collateral relatives. Let us look at one more of those boy argonauts in the enterprise of the Indies, the Portuguese Manuel Romano, son of a pilot, with six or seven uncles involved with ships and shipping on both sides of his family.[86] In the inquisitorial dock in 1579, Manuel summarized his early years: "Born in Tavila [in 1559], he grew up in his parent's house until age nine and then went to sea. He made five voyages to New Spain and Santo Domingo as a page and cabin boy."

Still only twenty, Manuel had already been in the Indies for four or five years and had worked herding cattle on estancias near Veracruz and in the north. By then he could only identify his family in the vaguest way—"six or seven . . . men of the sea that he didn't know." In this he can be compared with Juan de Barrera (born 1648) of Triana who, as we saw, ran away from home at about age ten.[87] Juan left behind four brothers and two sisters, all young and unmarried, and twenty-five years later knew nothing more about them.[88]

We have already seen that some of those who went to the Indies reestablished themselves with relatives who had gone before. Antonio de Acevedo (born ca. 1550), who crossed to New Spain about 1575, met up with two of his uncles, one of whom, as we noted, was a merchant of Mexico City who positioned his nephew as his factor in Oaxaca and the Mixteca.[89] The rest of Antonio's family remained behind in Tordesillas, in Tordehermos (a neighboring village where his mother's family was based), and in the regional center, Valladolid. They were mostly merchants (but also counted in their number a priest, a farmer, and a physician) and wives or widows of merchants. But to judge by his wife's letter of 1583, they had become increasingly unimportant to Antonio in the eight years he had been in New Spain. The letter, one of many that she wrote, is full of news and poignantly describes her loneliness and hardships, but Antonio rarely answered. Nevertheless his letters, hit-and-miss as they were, at least provided "some relief from my suffering," she said, "for without them I would have taken you for dead."

Families within the Indies

If moving to a new world across the Atlantic weakened family ties, so did moving within the Indies. The second was played out at a 'regional' scale, albeit a vast one in comparison to Spain. But the point does not depend solely on distances. Inquisition files show that the frequent movement of people frustrated efforts to gather evidence, as when Juan Ignacio Bustamante had no way to confirm Bárbara Martina's parentage because he could not locate her baptismal record.[90] He knew that she was born at Rancho de Santa María, deep in the Indian countryside and, it seems, very close to the small village of San Mateo Yxtlahuaca, outside the pueblo of Tolcayuca (jurisdiction of Pachuca, now in southern Hidalgo state), which was visited irregularly by clerics from Tezontepec, and also that her parents moved frequently.[91] When the rancho changed owners, Bárbara's parents and the other renters departed (she was then a small child), perhaps because the new owner canceled their leases. What had been a community, was permanently dispersed. Investigating twenty years after the event (in 1768), Bustamante could not find a single person still on the rancho who had witnessed Bárbara's baptism. "They have all vanished together with the priest and any registers they might have kept. Bárbara Martina's earliest upbringing was a wandering about with her parents." And to add to his difficulties, Bárbara's mother had in the meantime run away from her husband.

Mestizos gravitated more often to the Hispanic than the Indian side of their families, although these could not always be so neatly differentiated. Perhaps in areas where acculturation was well advanced, it was mainly a matter of degree. Bárbara, for example, remained in contact only with her mother's family, whom she termed "mestizos"; she had no contact with her father's, whom she termed "Indians." Pedro Mateo (born 1642) also lost contact with his Indian relatives.[92] Although he called his mother an Indian (from Xalostotitlán, jurisdiction of Lagos, now Altos de Jalisco), she failed to make a permanent imprint on him, even though in his early years he had no contact with Hispanic relatives. Later Pedro could say a little about his grandfather, "reputedly" an Indian, and his 'step-grandfather,' his mother's uncle, who had raised her as an orphan. On the Hispanic side, he had only Magdalena, an aunt married to a mulatto, whose sons worked as muleteers, an occupation that often connected Hispanic and Indian worlds, but more within terms set by the former. As we saw above, Pedro ran away from his mother's household when still young and joined mestizo cousins from his father's family on an estancia. Pedro Miguel, *alcalde de los naturales* of Xalostotitlán confirmed Pedro's failure to integrate himself in the life of the Indian town: "he has not been present in this pueblo," he testified through an interpreter, "but is always away from here."[93]

Networks of relatives stayed in touch selectively as work, mutual assistance, and proximity, not blood ties in themselves, promoted close ties. Thus a family asset (a store, some land, or a team of mules) could become the focus of a family network.[94] The mules of Nicolás del Valle of Tehuixtla (jurisdiction of Cuernavaca, now Morelos) supported his family during his lifetime; after it they served as a reason to stay together.[95] Our glimpse of the family comes after Nicolás died. Juan was the eldest son; he lived with his wife, younger brother and sister, and widowed mother (probably in her house) and had taken charge of his father's freighting business. Two sisters were married to men in a nearby pueblo; one owns mules of his own, the other works as his helper. Two of Juan's uncles (one from each side) feed into the network. The first lives at rancho Tepetlapa, a subject village of Teputztlan on the road to Acapulco, the other in the town of Tistla (capital of an alcaldía mayor, now in Guerrero), about two-thirds of the way to Acapulco from Cuernavaca. All in all, the several units of the family complemented each other, placed as they were to carry freight between the capital and the port, possibly specializing in given legs of the journey.

The high mortality rates of earlier times culled children from families. Those who lived past childhood would have seen an equal number who had not.[96] Christóbal de Ovando (born 1735) had ten brothers and sisters, but in his early forties only three remained.[97] María Ignacia Cervantes (born 1735), the youngest of seven children, was the only one to survive childhood.[98] Antonio de los Santos Chavarría (born in the 1670s) survived his wife and all seven of his children.[99] Of the latter only Joseph Francisco (born 1706) lived beyond childhood, and he died at age thirty in the Hospital de Amor de Dios of Mexico City. Christóbal de Castroverde (born 1576) could name six brothers and sisters who had died as children but not "the rest."[100] María Jesús de la Encarnación (born 1750) lost two sisters: one was named María, the other she could not remember.[101] We need not pile up more examples. These underline that those who survived still 'lived' with those who had not. The tallies of dead siblings, some with names forgotten, means not indifference but resignation. Fate, with no evident criteria, had taken many to an early grave while leaving a few to await a later one.

As the years passed, survivors must have known that family long ago left behind no longer existed except as a faded image of a distant time and place. Juan Rodríguez, after forty years in the Indies, dusted off his memories of family in a village in the mountains of Oviedo.[102] He mentions two brothers and two sisters, one of whom married before he left home. He would have known that they, together with nephews he had never known, might very well be in their graves. Few from his village would have recognized him had he returned.

Conclusion

As enclosed and partly autonomous places, households nurtured children; as social and productive units, they connected them to lineage, community, and culture. The families that made up households mattered, but not all in the same way. Children who remained at home for a longer time, for example, received a correspondingly stronger parental imprint. They came from poor households (but not the very poorest), where they could be an asset, and from comfortable ones, where the cost of supporting them was easily borne. Whether contact ended at five, ten, or twenty, and whether by running away, moving on, or taking a mate, children left home as socialized and in possession of some knowledge. Boys without specialized training foraged widely for work (or patronage), those with it gravitated to shops and construction sites to practice their trades.

As they entered a wider world, young people kept track of their kin, at least to a degree. If relatives showed no particular benevolence or generosity, family connections still probably stood as the most resilient and enduring bonds. When active and current, they served as a network of reciprocal give and take; when absent, as time, distance, and the original qualities that made them supportive or confining eroded them, they nevertheless lived on as a part of personal identity. In either case they oriented and shaped adults. By the time bigamists appeared in the dock (mostly at midlife, after many of their relatives had died, and in Mexico City, usually far from the towns and villages where they began their lives), links to family had loosened.

The death of parents occasioned transitions: to guardians, to a master, and sometimes to a picaresque life of temporary jobs and constant movement. But even without death, boys made such transitions by running away. They went with a master, patron, or employer, as we have seen, and learned a trade, served as cabin boys, helped with mule teams, herded livestock, or worked on farms. If these moves provided a vehicle for running away, they also reestablished boys in familylike settings, headed by patriarchal figures who assumed their guardianship and set them to simple, routine tasks. Still, boys who left home exercised more independence than we might have expected, as they chose masters, work, and destinations. Many of them, especially those from Spain who went to the Indies, lost touch with home.

Even the most doting of parents, in whatever form they existed, could not have controlled all the elements involved in raising children. Locale, economy, family, and character carried too many variables and surprises to allow for any easy predictability. If the autobiographical statements rarely linger over them, they nevertheless give an indication of the ways that children deviated from directions presumed by parents, guardians, masters, and teachers. If raising children was meant to control how they would turn out as adults, it proved only partly able to withstand the unexpected and unforeseen.

Girls, like professionals and gentry, had a more protected and more closely supervised childhood. It centered on hearth and home and so offered far fewer chances for enrichment (wealth and *calidad* made for some variation) than that, based on contact with a wider world, enjoyed by their brothers. Marriage ended their childhood but not their legal minority or, as we shall see in chapter 4, their determination to escape marriages that had become intolerable. They moved to the custody of a husband, but their lives, as Silvia Arrom has shown for the women of Mexico City, were not confined only to "the domestic sphere"; and neither were they "defined exclusively as wives and mothers."[103] In the next chapter we focus on marriage, to see how and sometimes why women and men married and thus became fully incorporated into society as adults.

CHAPTER THREE

THE GILDED CROSS AND PORTABLE CHAPEL OF THE
MEXICO CITY HARNESS MAKERS, SET IN THE CENTRAL SQUARE WITH
THE CATHEDRAL AND CHURCH OF SANTO DOMINGO IN THE BACKGROUND

Marriage

✢ IF MARRIAGE MARKED the transition to adult standing, it did so for a man more fully than for a woman. A woman shifted from the custody of her parents to that of her husband, thus in law and custom her condition hardly changed. Both, in Nancy F. Cott's words, approximated "an indenture between master and servant" little different from other "dependency relations . . . [of] traditional society."[1] If Spanish women retained ownership of their dowries (when they had them), their husbands nevertheless controlled this property and also retained legal guardianship over children.[2] Canon law held a more egalitarian view of marriage (at least in prescribing reciprocal duties between husband and wife) but, as Silvia Arrom has noted, its norms remained theoretical: rarely observed by laymen, seldom enforced by clerics.[3] So wives, as part of a new social unit, lived as subordinates to husbands, bearing and raising children in a domestic setting. Husbands, on the other hand, inherited the patriarchal mantle which gave them uncontested 'jurisdiction' over wives. And even if newly married men continued to live for a time in their fathers' households, the conjugal relationship, sooner or later became the basis for authority over a separate household composed of wife and children and also, sometimes, of servants, relatives, younger siblings, boarders, orphans, and possibly a widowed mother.

Theologians from the time of Gratian to the Council of Trent had worked to join the contractual and sacramental elements of marriage under church jurisdiction.[4] Primarily this meant setting up the supervisory processes to ensure that marriages took place publicly, fully in view of the church and the community.[5] The aftermath—feasting, celebration, and then consummation—could take place much as they always had. Mutual consent, the pledge of a man and woman to marry in the future (betrothal) or in the present (marriage), remained the essential core of marriage. The rest could be dispensed with or, as with the blessing, be pronounced later. Courtship, whether conducted by the father in an arranged marriage or by the couple directly, always included consultation with, and usually the approval of, the family.

So the church, the couple, and the family concerned themselves with marriage. The church defined it as a sacrament, but one to be enacted by the couple itself, for it claimed not to "perform" marriages but to set rules on when, how, and who might marry.[6] Tridentine canons nevertheless restated in more detail than before that the church must "administer" marriages. They grouped barriers or impediments, for example, into those of greater and lesser seriousness. The first, dispensed with only by the pope or a bishop, set minimum ages (twelve for girls, fourteen for boys), forbade force, and disqualified candidates who were closely related by blood or affinal ties (to prevent incestuous unions), who had a spouse still living (because marriage was a permanent union), or who suffered physical problems (of a type that would prevent them from procreating children).

The less serious impediments, dispensed with by parish priests and vicars, involved procedural irregularities—for example, failure to publicize the marriage in the proper way.[7] In parishes candidates underwent a screening process, the *diligencia matrimonial*, to discover possible barriers, a process opened to the community by announcing the forthcoming marriage from the pulpit on three successive Sundays or feast days. If no impediment arose, the priest issued a license, presided over the public exchange of marriage vows, either during or after the celebration of the mass (the nuptial mass as it appears frequently in the documents), preceded by words of instruction and followed by the priestly benediction, the exchange of a ring, and after the Pater Noster, embraces and the kiss of peace.[8] Afterwards the priest recorded the union in a parish register, for the permanent record of the community.[9]

By insisting that persons marrying must do so of their own volition, the Council of Trent would prevent forced marriages. But more importantly the measure established the church as arbiter in cases of parent-child conflict. Clerics may have sided with parents in oppositions (most probably never went to a formal hearing) at least as often as with children.[10] But that mattered less than asserting the primacy of clerics over the process of marriage once and for all. The idea was not new (the requirement that marriages be publicly announced and solemnized dated to the Fourth

Lateran Council, 1215) and did not happen overnight. But after Trent new penalties for noncompliance were stated. Clandestinity, for example, marriages contracted without a priest present, became an invalidating impediment,[11] whereas before it had been considered valid if troublesome.[12]

Assertion of exclusive jurisdiction over marriage rubbed against the regal pretensions of secular states. France, for example, never promulgated the Tridentine decrees. Instead it passed a law requiring parental consent for marriage, thereby undermining Trent's central concern: to assert the centrality of the doctrine of consent and the church's jurisdiction over it.[13] Spain, in theory equally jealous of regal prerogatives, reserved the right to review and prevent publication of papal bulls and briefs when they ran counter to social convention and law.[14] So Tridentine decrees entered the Spanish empire only, as J. H. Elliott has noted, on Philip II's "own terms and at the pace that he himself chose to dictate."[15] But he saw nothing subversive in them and so, unlike France, Spain acted as partner rather than adversary of the church by incorporating them into civil law.[16]

Tridentine marriage regulations form the backdrop for the marriages in the bigamy files, but as we shall see, they do not override individual invention and customary practices. In their autobiographies, bigamists relate how they came to marry in two general ways. In the first they portray themselves as submitting (occasionally after considerable resistance) to the agency of brokers, most often parents, masters, or clerics, who promoted the marriage. In the second they 'marry' sacramentally or consensually on their own. This, in cases of elopement or 'abduction', sometimes meant defying the woman's parents or, when property and status were not at issue, proceeding without reference to parents who remained unconcerned one way or the other.[17] We shall also see how bigamists, involved in sexual liaisons (brief or extended, begun with no intent to marry) turned these relationships into marriages. They began with men and women seducing one another, running away, and cohabiting. But clerics, officials, and sometimes even ordinary people kept an eye on suspicious 'friendships' to see if they needed to be 'solemnized' with a priestly blessing, and policing of this kind pressured some bigamists into marrying.[18]

BROKERS

The mating of two people, before and after the church increased its supervision of marriage, was ordinary, instinctive, and expected. It followed

conventions deeply imbedded in law and custom having to do with procreating children, transferring property, socializing children, gaining advantage through family alliances, and following customs informed by a
patriarchal ethos. Although insisting on the centrality of the doctrine of
consent in marriage, Trent did not alter the ways that parents, masters,
and clerics arranged the marriages of the young.[19] Bigamy records might
make it seem that such people often arranged inappropriate marriages
because, by definition, bigamists abandoned their first spouses and remarried. As we shall see in chapter 4, however, the 'failure' of first marriages
came about for a great many other reasons than how the matches were
contracted. For now we shall be concerned not to evaluate the interventions of brokers but simply to see how they, the couple, and other interested parties played their parts to effect marriages.

Parents

In 1559 Francisco Díaz was the groom in a marriage arranged for him by
his father, a chairmaker of Cartaya (Huelva).[20] He was about ten years old
at the time, well below the canonical age of fourteen for boys, and, as we
might expect, faced an older and larger bride with fear and bewilderment.
As a man of thirty-five relating his life story in the inquisitorial dock,
Francisco said that he remembered "very well" that morning twenty-five
years before in the town of Lepe, near the coast on the Gulf of Cádiz about
midway between Huelva and Ayamonte (in the diocese of Seville). "They
brought him . . . to the main church to marry a young woman . . . and the
priest gave the nuptial blessing. And once blessed he fled out of fear of the
woman who was as big as a Philistine and this one, a boy, was afraid of
her." The bride, Juana García, the daughter of a gravedigger, "had been
brought up" by Juan de Córdoba and Juana García. Juana, as the eponym
of her mistress-guardian, most likely had gone to Córdoba's house as a
serving girl at an early age.

After the wedding Francisco and Juana returned to her master's house
for a wedding meal and "for two weeks lived a married life."[21] Yet Francisco "truly" did not remember, he testified, "whether he knew her carnally because he was so dazed." In any case his older brother Pedro came
to the rescue by arranging his passage to the Indies.[22] Thus Francisco
escaped the marriage decided for him. Years later, however, he remained
perplexed that his own father had been "the one who arranged" it and thus
had occasioned his flight "to this land."

Francisco's marriage had little in the way of property, honor, or status at stake. One plebeian married another in a socially if not personally suitable match. Given the latter it seems that Francisco's taste and sensibility counted for little and that the goal of securing a family alliance, a purpose of plebeian as well as of elite marriages, dominated the decision.

Parental objectives appear more straightforward in families of some, if relatively little, status. Although María de la Cruz, a widowed seamstress, could not endow her daughter Mariana Monroy (born 1649), she nevertheless could represent her as of a respectable creole lineage, long rooted in Guadalajara.[23] This plus Mariana's personal qualities (she was a beauty of medium height, full figure, white skin, rosy cheeks, small nose, dark eyes, and black hair) gave María some reason to hope for an advantageous match. When Mariana reached age fourteen, María pressed her to marry a newcomer, Manuel Figueroa, about twenty, who "sometimes said he was from Seville [Mariana testified fifteen years later], and sometimes from Ayamonte."[24] And so she did, "to please her mother . . . but not willingly because she did not want to get married." In the context of a bigamy trial, Mariana's argument stressing her lack of consent implies that a valid marriage had not taken place.[25] At the time, however, it seems more likely that she readily had deferred to her mother.

Could she have prevented the marriage by resisting? Probably not, for parents and guardians presumed the right to arrange marriages and when faced with filial resistance countered with threats and abuse. The Spaniard Rita Lobato (born 1726) possessed little honor as an illegitimate child fathered by "a certain priest" and also, apparently, no endowment.[26] Yet because she lived in an Indian town (Santa Ana el Grande, *alcaldía mayor* of San Salvador, now Honduras, at the fringe of the "cacao monoculture") she, through her Spanish mother, doña Isabel Lobato, laid claim to superior status and, for what it was worth, also used the honorific *doña*.[27] She got away with inflating her worth because honor was relative in frontier zones where Hispanics were often surrounded by large Indian or slave populations.[28] In such places eligible marriage partners must have been rare, and so Ignacio Buscarones's arrival in 1737 would have been closely noted. He was about twenty, a Spaniard native to Orizaba, roving the countryside in search of a patron or employment; and he found work with don Felipe Ruiz de Contreras, doña Isabel's son-in-law. It was his master don Felipe, Ignacio testified in 1744, who "persuaded him and arranged his marriage to [Rita]," but Rita said no, and as a result, "doña Isabel punished and abused her so much that twice she ran away and took refuge in the house of the three Medina sisters in the pueblo."

In fact doña Isabel failed to break Rita's opposition and so instead of risking a public marriage at the church, she persuaded a priest to come to her house where, with only her and one other witness present, he pronounced the nuptial blessing.[29] Her caution proved wise, for following the ceremony, young Rita redoubled her opposition by insisting that she was not married and, had never wanted to marry. Temporarily, at least, a truce could be declared, as doña Isabel, on the grounds that Rita was too young to consummate the marriage (she was eleven and canon law stipulated twelve as the minimum age for girls), said that Ignacio should wait until the following Easter. By then, however, she was saying that she "hated" (*aborrecía*) Ignacio and "in public said that he would not be joined with her daughter." Ignacio tried to resolve the dispute by asking the priest to intervene, but by now doña Isabel was using Rita's opposition as grounds for saying that a valid marriage had not taken place. As a result Ignacio left town, thinking that he had not really married Rita.

The case, then, illustrates how doña Isabel, to marry her daughter and then to 'annul' the marriage, honored church procedures in the breach more than the observance. First she used a priest as a cover of legality to override Rita's resistance; then she argued that consent had been violated, to deny that a marriage had taken place. The file gives no reason for her about-face, only a picture of it, as she at first intimidated Rita and manipulated the priest, and then as she sided with her and disregarded him.

More commonly parental use of church authority came in suits on behalf of a daughter, claiming that a suitor had given her a *palabra de casamiento* (thereby betrothing himself to her), had taken her virginity, and then had abandoned her.[30] Pedro Muñoz Palomir, a Spaniard from Villa Conil (province and diocese of Cádiz), was not guilty of this entire sequence, but he did delay a marriage arranged by his uncle with Juana López de Heredia long enough that Juana sued for breach of contract.[31] An ecclesiastical judge placed Pedro in jail while he heard the complaint, and in 1707 ordered the marriage to take place without delay. The judgment found that the oral agreement made by Pedro's uncle was binding even though, as don Pedro, márquez de Herrera, a witness, observed, Pedro had objected with "violence and repugnance" to the match. And as a result, Herrera recalled, Pedro "left Juana's house on the very night of the ceremony on the pretense that he was going to change clothes and never came back."

The young man ran away to the Indies, perhaps his only option, given that family and local authority stood firmly against him. It may seem surprising that in 1707, with the principle that marriage be a consensual contract so well established in canon law, the judge forced it in this way.[32]

But a woman's honor (or more precisely her family's honor) was at stake, and the judgment looked to repair that by the overriding consideration that a promise to marry constituted a binding contract. Requiring that it be fulfilled solved everything and nothing: Juana's honor had been vindicated, but she experienced not even one day of married life. Until her death some thirty years later, people of the village would know her as "Juana the badly married."

Pedro went through the motions and then freed himself with the traditional 'self-divorce'.[33] Resistance at an earlier stage conflicted with the deference that young people owed to their elders. But probably in most cases, attitudes of parents and children coincided more than they clashed, because children freely 'chose' prospective spouses according to values instilled from childhood. This in fact constituted one of the central rules of the marriage market, that in racial and class terms, like married like.[34] Yet there were disagreements, and children sometimes had to decide whether to defy parental authority by resisting a marriage or submit to it by acquiescing to an undesirable one.

One way to finesse the issue was to marry without parental consent. Such a course, of little concern to laborers and peasants without land, mattered a great deal to people with property and with a concern to maintain family status.[35] Catalina de Vega, a young Spanish woman who married clandestinely, thus provoked parental outrage. In Mexico City one night in 1563, Catalina de Vega agreed to marry her young suitor, Pedro de Ribero, as he courted her through the iron grill of a window in the house of don Bernardino Pacheco de Bocanegra, one of the richest and most powerful men of Mexico City.[36] Catalina was thirteen, a native of Seville and in Mexico City only since 1561, having come to the Indies with her father, the widower Tomé de la Vega. Tomé had purchased the position of notary in Cuyoacán (part of the marquesado but also in the corregimiento of Mexicalzingo, now part of the Federal District and the state of Mexico)[37] and placed Catalina in don Bernardino's household where she served his wife, doña Isabel de Luján, a woman of considerable substance in her own right.[38]

Even in the household of such important personages, Catalina did not repress unruly habits. At least Marina Díaz, who had known her all her life, implied this in testimony she gave in 1573: "She was a fickle young woman; would take advice from no one because she had too much pride; and she boasted that she took advantage of the said Bocanegra's absence to get married." Marina's characterization fits what would have been said about a girl who had so boldly disregarded her masters' authority. The betrothal, words of "future consent," not only made a binding contract, but began "the process of marriage" that became complete with sexual relations.[39] This Pedro found out, by consulting Father Jorge de Mendoza, chaplain of the *colegio de niñas*, and as a result, he tried to begin a married life with Catalina. She, in the meantime, had faced a furious doña Isabel who scolded her, put her in protective custody in the colegio de niñas, and started a legal inquiry. Tomé de Vega threatened to attack Pedro.

Catalina acted independently of her master and therefore fits Marina's description of her as insubordinate. This I think explains doña Isabel's anger: a thrall in her husband's household had acted with no regard to her and her husband's authority over her; she had thereby insulted and dishonored them.[40] Tomé de Vega's outrage has a different explanation. His project to match Catalina with a man of honor and substance, perhaps in a marriage arranged by her masters, had been thwarted. If doña Isabel set upon Catalina as the target of her wrath, Tomé set upon Pedro as the target of his, on the standard convention that honorable women seduced or abducted were not party to what had befallen them but were innocents.[41] With Catalina inaccessible in the colegio and the imminent threat to his safety, Pedro decided to flee. Later Father Jorge testified (July 27, 1573) that Pedro told him "he had to leave this city because . . . the said Tomé de Vega was after him to punish and do him harm."

It took about a year for ecclesiastical authorities to confirm the marriage and release Catalina from custody. But to no avail, for Pedro had disappeared. In fact he had gone to Peru, but no one knew that until later. As Father Jorge remembered it:

> About two years after the said Pedro de Ribero left Mexico City [1565], he received a letter from him sent from the city of Lima . . . together with others for the said young lady, for Tomé de Vega, for Bocanegra, and for the mother of the colegio where Catalina de Vega had been put in custody. [Pedro] said that he was well and had returned to Lima from an expedition of conquest (*entrada*) that he had gone on with a general and other soldiers. From the entrada he got two or three pueblos [in encomienda] and was waiting to find out how much they would be worth. [Pedro] begged him [i.e. Father Jorge] to deliver the said letters and to make the said Tomé de Vega hand over his daughter because she was his wife. He said he would come for her and would bring a lot of gold and silver and would take her and that he [Father Jorge] should advise him of the resolution of this.

If mediation should fail, Pedro added, would Father Jorge begin a lawsuit in Pedro's name? So if Pedro had not followed standard procedures, he nevertheless had taken his vow seriously. And now that he had raised himself to the status of encomendero, he seemed confident that Tomé and others directly involved (and failing that, the intervention of the ecclesiastical court) would see him in a different light.

But Father Jorge barely bestirred himself. He could not find Catalina or her father (so he claimed), and the mother superior in the meantime had died. As for don Bernardino, by then he may have been disgraced and banished following his implication in the conspiracy that formed around Martín Cortés from about 1563, which was cut short by his arrest and that of others on July 16, 1566, and the subsequent beheading of the Avila brothers three months later (October 3).[42] In truth Father Jorge seemed indifferent. He lost Pedro's letters and sent no reply. His lethargy illustrates a principle: those in need of a broker in colonial society should choose *compadres* and relatives rather than strangers.[43] As much as anything, father Jorge's lassitude left this marriage, and consequently the lives of Pedro and Catalina, unsettled for more than thirty years. Only in 1596, when Catalina petitioned to take up the long-lost marriage, did a resolution appear. Addressing her petition to the Holy Office, she said that

> the said Pedro Ribero has just come to this city in order to live with me as his legitimate wife and I need to receive the nuptial blessings. I therefore petition your Lordship to . . . give me a report of what happened so that I can receive the said blessings and live a married life with the said Pedro Ribero my husband.

At forty-six, then, Catalina is properly subdued and cautiously awaiting the completion of her marriage, the nuptial blessing, before beginning the long delayed married life with Pedro. But for her guardians and her father, she would never have been separated from him; but for the Inquisition, she would have forgotten him and lived out her years married to Alonso Sosa. As it was she lived with Alonso for ten years before the Inquisition prosecuted her for bigamy, thus disallowing the relationship.[44] The judgment consigned her to a 'marriage' that was only an abstraction, one never consummated or experienced, and with a man with whom she would not meet again for another sixteen years.

Catalina's marriage to Pedro in 1563 came just before the Council of Trent tightened its prohibitions against clandestinity.[45] In any case Tridentine reforms would not have disallowed this marriage, only required that it be formalized publicly in a nuptial mass or at least a nuptial blessing.

After about a year, as we have seen, the church sided with Catalina against 'parental' objections, but this came too late for Pedro who had already fled. Catalina, apparently in good faith, married again, but this was technically an adulterous relationship, and any children she might have had in her prime child-bearing years would have been "adulterinos," a particularly odious category of illegitimacy. So Catalina paid the price for taking the initiative because others presumed that it had not been hers to take. Her marriage disrupted her father's aspirations for her, and also, quite possibly, his chances for staying on good terms with don Bernardino. Instead of a wealthy and powerful compadre, Tomé de Vega had only disaffected former employers, irritated at his daughter's affront to their honor. Although Father Jorge insisted at the outset that Catalina and Pedro had indeed married, his inability to counter the anger and opposition of a father and an employer, especially one so powerful, reflects the personalized politics of life in the largest of Spanish colonial cities.

We should see Father Jorge, then, as adjusting church teachings to fit the realities of power and influence. As did everyone else in Hispanic society, priests tied themselves to patronage and family networks, cultivating some and not bothering with others. And in certain circumstances, families courted priests as well. The Mesquita family of Oaxaca failed to appreciate this when in 1558 they tried to marry a daughter, Francisca de Alvarez, to a local encomendero, Francisco de Aguila.[46] But Martín de Mesquita, the head of the family and local notable (he held a city magistracy, alcaldía ordinario), arranged the marriage with no reference to the church. At the time Francisca, a creole Spaniard, was twenty, and Francisco, a peninsular Spaniard claiming to be an hidalgo, 60. Mesquita proposed the marriage in September, 1557, his motive, surely, to secure for his family Francisco's encomienda. Although it yielded only 400 pesos a year in tribute, the prestige of joining the encomendero class and the gaining of access to workers from the Indian towns seemed a prize to covet.

All went according to plan and in June 1558, the couple "joined hands as husband and wife," Francisca testified, and "married with the words of present consent at the door of her father's house."[47] Catalina, a black slave of the household, and Martín de la Mesquita, Francisca's brother, witnessed the exchange. Three months later, toward the end of September, Francisco and Francisca repeated their exchange but in a more festive occasion: "last Saturday night," according to Francisca, "clandestinely, with the words of present consent." Both occasions, then, were clandestine, because no priest presided and no nuptial blessing was given. And the couple, as well as the entire Mesquita household (father, mother, brothers, sisters, two brothers-in-law, and servants), were implicated. Francisca testified later that "Francisco had her virginity," probably in the period following the original exchange in June.

Anticipating Tridentine rulings, a vicar annulled this marriage on the grounds that it was "not a true marriage because it was not preceded by the reading of the banns and not [conducted] in the sight of the Church (*in facie ecclesiae*) as is the rule and custom of the holy mother Church." So much for the assumption of the Mesquita family that they could contract a marriage strictly as a private, family event. Even pre-Tridentine teaching stressed the sacramental nature of matrimony, insisting that it be public, that it take place in a church, and that possible impediments be checked for. Yet in spite of these objections, clandestine marriages, once they slipped through, were supposed to be binding (especially when a woman of honor had lost her virginity), when checked for impediments and confirmed with a nuptial mass or blessing.

So why, in this case, did church authorities insist on the narrowest definition of valid marriage? The answer has to do with politics. The church, at least as represented by the prior of the Dominican friary, had already foisted a marriage, by proxy, on an unwilling Francisco, to one María Valdés Sotomayor. Thus he was already 'married,' but curiously the church annulled the marriage to Francisca not on these grounds but, as noted above, because a priest failed to preside over it.[48] Although the fault easily could be repaired, as it often was, with a priestly blessing at a nuptial mass, the vicar insisted that the affront be expiated with a fine: 30 pesos for both Francisca and Francisco, 15 for each of the Mesquita children, and an unspecified sum, possibly 30 pesos, for Mesquita himself. Two years later (March 2, 1560), Mesquita, appealing for a reduction of the penalty, said that the fine "would destroy me and my children because I have many of them and am very poor."[49] His distress and his inability to pay (the fine was commuted to labor on a church) underscore how useful the encomienda tribute would have been. The judgment, then, gave occasion for the church to assert its control over marriage but in general and procedural terms rather than as an instance of bigamy.

Bigamy records have allowed for some glimpses of parents arranging their children's marriages from the midsixteenth to the early eighteenth century, but from the standpoint of children. This yields a sometime exercise of parental authority as arbitrary, ill-considered, and resented. Some of this comes after the fact, but much of it does not. It shows us children in conflict but not in the dock, as they perceived marriage arrangements as having little to do with their own contentment. Overall, however, parents exerted their authority, a matter of honor even in plebeian households, sought tactical advantage (on however humble a scale) through family alliances, and made matches that approximated their own social and economic standing. The last, in modest households, came mainly through the negative test of trying to avoid a drop in status or prestige.

Masters

Masters considered all members of their households to be under their authority, and their presumption to arrange and patronize marriages differed little from that of parents. At best attachments to masters, as with all forms of clientage, involved affection and trust, and this formed the broader context of whatever economic benefits the relationship yielded. Ana Díaz, a Spaniard, had been born in Fez (Muslims had taken her parents captive) around 1519.[50] By 1570 she was well established in Zacatecas where she counted among her possessions "some houses" and a black slave named Juan Sape; in her community she was known as a healer to both "poor and rich." Although she did not indicate how and when she arrived in New Spain, she must have come at least twenty years before and then established herself in the household of Alonso Carreño of the mines of Zultepec (an alcaldía mayor in itself or jointly with Temazcaltepec during the colonial period, now in the southwest part of the state of Mexico), most likely as servant, but also as mistress and mother of children fathered by him. But this led to no undue presumption on her part; she continued to call him "lord and master," and in 1554, at his order, in his house, and under his supervision, she married Pedro Rodríguez. After the marriage she looked to Carreño as patron just as she had before it, serving in his household but now with Pedro. Then, after about a year and a half, Pedro requested leave to move with Ana to Zacatecas, and Alonso granted it. There rumors that Pedro had a wife in Portugal bedeviled the marriage, until Pedro departed, ostensibly to go to Portugal to get the affidavits to disprove them.[51]

In Zacatecas Ana waited more than a year with no word from Pedro and then, by letter, explained her trouble to Carreño. In reply he once again made a major decision for Ana. "Alonso wrote back not to wait for Pedro," she testified in 1572, "that he too had heard that Pedro was married in Portugal, and that if [Ana] should find a suitable young man she should marry him and that he would patronize and help him."[52] Again, then,

Carreño endowed Ana and her marriage prospects with the promise of continuing patronage.

As servant, as mistress, and then as 'daughter' to pass on to another man in matrimony, Carreño treated Ana as more than a mere employee. Their tie can stand for the familylike protocols that became part of all employer-employee relations.[53] A typical expression of these came in the arranging of marriages. Normally masters would match servants within their own households, and what better way to do this than view a newly arrived worker as a suitable candidate for a daughter or relative. In his mid-thirties Francisco de Riberos (born 1576 in Conde, Portugal) was employed by Antonio de Carmona of Seville to act as master (*arráez*) of a *barco de embarcación*, probably a lighter that ran between Seville and San Lúcar, along the Guadalquivir river.[54] Before this he had knocked about for years in the Atlantic shipping lanes, engaged mainly in the slave trade between West Africa and the West Indies. Riberos testified that he stayed with Carmona for at least a year and a half, probably a longer-than-normal stint for him, "because he always gave good pay" and that after a time Carmona "became fond of him and tried to marry him to Mariana de los Reyes, saying that she was his relative."

The negotiation began correctly enough, with Carmona asking Riberos if he were married. Riberos said yes, to María Francisca in Conde, although he had gone eight or nine years without any news of her, and some from his tierra had said she was dead. Carmona took this as a qualified "yes" and wanted to proceed. Francisco, however, wanted to check to see if María Francisca was alive. Carmona apparently agreed but three months later still had not found anyone to travel to Conde. Evidently in a hurry, and without consulting Riberos, he then arranged for three witnesses (one his own wife) to attest in a marriage investigation that Riberos was single. The statements, of course, were perjured to speed things up, for had the witnesses declared Riberos a widower, the marriage could not have proceeded without confirmation of María Francisca's death. These shortcuts, Carmona knew, placed Riberos at risk. After giving his own deposition, he returned to his unsuspecting shipmaster and consigned him to his fate. Francisco, in his autobiographical statement (seventeen years later, in January 1620) recalled the moment Carmona told him that the matrimonial investigation was complete and "there was nothing to do now but entrust [the matter] to God . . . [for] he could now marry the person arranged for him. [Carmona] also offered to help him however he could and so this [witness] determined to marry Mariana de los Reyes, vecina and native of Triana." Francisco's account conveys that the process began tentatively, picked up momentum, and then reached a point of no return. Although it amounted to a betrothal rather than a marriage as such, Francisco viewed it as tantamount to marriage now that Carmona made it visible as publicly in progress rather than a private negotiation. The offer "to help" and Francisco's "determination" to marry merely embellished a fait accompli.

We need not doubt that Carmona's fondness for Riberos was genuine to wonder why he could not find a more suitable candidate in Triana or Seville. The circumstances, in fact, suggest a family emergency, the need to find a husband quickly for Mariana, possibly because she had been seduced by an unacceptable or now absent suitor or even raped. In the three months intervening between Carmona's initial approach to Riberos and his extraordinary performance before the ecclesiastical judge, the family was searching for a man to marry Mariana. Ideally he would be of the plebeian ranks (all Mariana's family were carpenters and mariners) but respectable, known in the community, and already connected to the household. Riberos, except for his possibly still-living wife in Conde, fit the profile perfectly. And if the worst happened and Riberos were arrested for bigamy, not Mariana and her family, but he alone would bear the infamy, loss of honor, and punishment. Family came before friendship; paternalism was a means not an end.

In the same way that plebeian masters married their relatives to employees, they also married their daughters. Bartolomé de Renaga, a muleteer based in San Juan del Río (jurisdiction of Querétaro, now in Querétaro state), for example, found Domingo Rodríguez, a mestizo from Puebla in his early twenties to be "industrious and accommodating," and so proposed that he marry Luisa Ramírez, Renaga's mulatto step-daughter.[55]

How masters 'courted' these young plebeian men can be seen in more detail in the case of Pedro Mateo (born 1642), a mestizo native to Xalostotitlan (jurisdiction of Lagos, now in the Altos de Jalisco), but who grew up on cattle ranches to the south near La Barca, Pénjamo, and Piedragorda.[56] At eighteen he gravitated back to Xalostotitlan and found work with an Indian named Pedro Hernández who asked him to marry his daughter, Francisca. At first Pedro declined, saying that he was poor, just a boy (*muchacho*), and without money for the marriage investigation and other expenses. Hernández countered that he would arrange everything, pay the costs, and establish Pedro in his household. So Pedro agreed. And Hernández did his part, but in a way to let Pedro bear the costs after all. After choosing padrinos he supplied Pedro with a new name (Mateo González), and with aliases for his parents so that Pedro could be presented as Indian. This meant a reduced fee but more importantly set up a deal to commute the fee: the priest agreed to enter 'Mateo González' in the marriage register as an Indian in exchange for Herńandez's pledge "to some day harvest his maize crop," an obligation, of course, to be passed along to Pedro.

Thus Hernández worked within marriage procedures as set by the church, but adjusted them with the help of a cooperative priest to further family ends. An incident that occurred a year or so later makes this even clearer. Pedro decided to leave the Hernández household and go back to an estancia (La Mesa) where he had formerly worked. As he prepared to take Francisca with him, he recalled in his autobiographical statement that Hernández had said "no, that he would beat him before allowing him to take her ... He said 'go,' that he would support Francisca just as he always had while he was raising her and after she married." The impasse had to do with power: would Pedro submit or would Hernández give in? The latter would have been too much to expect from this plebeian pater familias. Hernández refused to surrender his authority over Francisca, despite her marital status.

Masters on a household scale such as Hernández and Renaga used their daughters as a resource for adding young men to the family economy. Each chose a son-in-law after assessing the young man's strength, industry, and potential loyalty. The last consideration was perhaps linked to youthfulness that presumably could be molded into commitment to the new household and family. This was crucial, for in addition to recovering the costs of marriages, masters wanted to keep their daughters as part of a productive unit. The process should not be seen to be cynically motivated, as if acting out a petty tyranny to mistreat underlings (although in-law ties could be abusive), but as stemming from the ethos of clientage that embedded labor within personalistic bonds. Hernández's impatience with Pedro came because the young mestizo failed to make the transition from outsider to family.

If masters arranged marriages directly, they also facilitated them indirectly. They might, for example, advance the money to cover costs. This was not necessarily routine, because it included an element of risk. When a priest of Santa Clara ordered José de Mora (born 1718), a Spaniard native to La Piedad (Valladolid) to quit his "illicit friendship" with María de Josepha de los Reyes (they had lived together for eight years), José agreed to marry her.[57] He asked Joseph León and his wife, Indians of Santa Clara, to act as sponsors, but as he testified later, they "declined because they were poor Indians and not able to confer the honors and the candles but [José] answered that they should do it anyway because his master had offered to charge everything to his account."

In fact advancing money in this way could also be a way to hire a worker. So it became in 1735 for Nicolás Antonio de Arauz, a mestizo from Calpulalpa (jurisdiction of Tezcuco, now in the state of Mexico), in the impromptu offer of one Pedro Aguador (Pedro Waterman) to cover the costs of his marriage.[58] Nicolás had been pasturing some hogs for a gate-keeper (of Mexico City?) who lived just beyond the village of Guadalupe, north of Mexico City. After delivering the hogs, he was heading north when, as he testified, he "met an Indian named Dominga" who lived with her mother and three brothers, selling food to travelers next to the pueblo of Santa Clara, beyond Guadalupe, on the *camino real.*

Nicolás took up with Dominga and instead of continuing northward went with her to Mexico City. On meeting an acquaintance, Joseph Alvarez, he asked for a loan to pay the costs of getting married; but Joseph, saying that he was poor and did not have the money, could not help.[59] Pedro overheard the exchange, offered to pay the costs, and, with his wife, stood as marriage sponsors. Once married Nicolás and Dominga moved into the Aguador home, and Nicolás became Pedro's helper in carrying water to houses.

Pedro bound Nicolás to him through debt, ritual kinship, and by settling him in his household. Was the loan a device to indenture Nicolás at less than market wages? Probably not, for a large floating population in Mexico City could always be found to perform unskilled labor. Moreover Pedro's cash advance on wages was money at risk (minimized in his mind, perhaps, by the newly established *compadrazgo* bond) that might not be repaid if Nicolás chose to skip town. And in fact Nicolás did skip, after four months, although it is not clear if by then he had cleared the debt. Probably he had not, and Dominga, working as a house servant, would have completed the obligation.

From the examples of Nicolás and José, one might infer that masters readily provided credit to employees in the form of advances on wages. Here the relationship was mainly employer-employee, but that slid naturally into patron-client and compadre-compadre, even though neither master played the directing role in bringing about a marriage. It is important to notice the process, for it points to ways that masters bonded with workers at many interlocking levels: as patrons, creditors, benefactors, compadres, landlords, advisers, and friends. More importantly it transformed mere employees into clients and compadres, thereby cementing deeper loyalty. If this was a linkage that from the employer's standpoint might have been merely instrumental, it was not consciously so. Paternalism inhered in mastership, the exercise of authority over others. Even humble figures aspired to the role. Witness Pedro, a man with only his occupation for a surname, acting as patron in the same way, if not to the same degree, as personages with far greater resources.[60]

Clerics

As representatives of the church, priests viewed marriage as the sole licit setting for sexual relations, the "remedy" for lust, and the only legitimate context for procreating children.[61] As we have noted, they screened applicants, announced upcoming marriages, presided over the exchange of vows, and pronounced the nuptial blessing.[62] Their correct role was to guarantee proper usage and procedures rather than to arrange marriages directly. This might result in apparently contradictory behavior, sometimes standing behind a couple to face parental opposition, sometimes behind parents to overcome filial resistance. In either case church regulations could be adjusted to suit circumstances; for clerics, like everybody else, lived in a world of personalistic networks, maintaining themselves by siding with friends and allies.

It therefore catches our attention to see a priest playing the part of arranger of a marriage to a man and woman who were unconnected to his own family, as did fray Juan González de Mendoza, an Augustinian.[63] A few days before Christmas in 1581, he went to extraordinary efforts to convince a wealthy widow to marry a newcomer to New Spain, the Spaniard Agustín de Hoz Espinosa Calderón (born 1546).[64] Why he did so does not appear in the file although it seems to have been at the behest of Agustín himself, who arrived in the Indies down-and-out after fleeing his creditors.

Having been a local notable in Poza, a small village in the province of Palencia (he had held a seat on the municipal council), Agustín also pretended to noble status in New Spain. He secured a good mount, sported sword and dagger, and on occasion carried a harquebus. He may have made a favorable impression, therefore, but as he himself knew, his costume only temporarily covered his destitution. He persuaded fray Juan to approach Mari Gómez de Barajas, "a rich widow, señora of estancias and livestock," with a proposal of matrimony.[65] Fray Juan ingratiated Agustín with Mari's mother and other relatives, and as a result, they wrote to encourage the match. Mari, recalling the process, testified (in 1584) that "she was at Ocaquaro, one of her estancias in this bishopric of Michoacán, and her mother and others of her relatives sent some letters saying that Agustín de Hoz Calderón was a respectable man and it would be a good thing to marry him."[66]

Afterward fray Juan and Father Juan González, beneficiary of Tlazazal-ca, brought Agustín to the ranch, and Mari recalled that "for three days they importuned her to marry the said Calderón." When she remained undecided, they tried a final ploy as they pretended to take leave. "Gentlemen, let us go [Mari remembered Agustín saying], for this is not a matter to be forced like a battle. Let the señora look into this further and we can come back in two months." Father Juan then drew Mari aside to give this advice: "Señora, if you lose this chance it will be a long time before another as good comes along." With this Mari put aside her reservations. Father Juan immediately sent for witnesses and without reading the banns and without a marital investigation (omissions that would have required special dispensation), he solemnized the marriage in the ranch chapel.

An even more heavy-handed effort of clerical go-betweens to effect a marriage occurred in Oaxaca midway through the sixteenth century. Once again the objective was a person of property, the Spanish hidalgo and encomendero Francisco de Aguila (born 1498).[67] The prior of the Dominican monastery, fray Bernardo, time and again approached Francisco (in person and through third parties), urging him to marry doña María Valdez Sotomayor. But Francisco refused and to end his harassment once and for all, addressed the following message to doña María and sent it to fray Bernardo:

> I stress that I am a man sixty years old, most likely more rather than less, and I have a town [in *encomienda*] that yields no more than 400 pesos of *tepusque* [copper coins] each year. I do not even own my own house but live in a rented one that costs me 100 pesos a year. I haven't the licenses (*derechos*) to marry nor do I have at present the possibility of buying them.

With this Francisco concluded, "the señora would cease to want me for a husband." Four days later, when Francisco saw fray Bernardo, he orally added a postscript: "Should the said doña María reply to my message I don't want to see it or receive it." The prior, angered by Francisco's determination, began to threaten him. First unless Francisco proceeded with the marriage, he warned, doña María's brother would return from Peru and, presumably to vindicate her honor, kill him; second he would arrange to have Francisco's encomienda taken away; third he declared that

Francisco's written message, contrary to Francisco's obvious meaning and intent, had in fact legally bound him to marry doña María. He then obtained a power of attorney from doña María and claimed it sufficient to have the marriage enforced by justice officials.

With this fray Bernardo had broken Francisco who was reduced to falling to his knees to plead for mercy. With tears streaming down his face he said that "for the love of God . . . he cannot be made to marry the said doña María by force because his will was not to do so . . . and if she wants half of his yearly tributes which comes to 200 pesos of *tipuzque*, so that she could eat, he would give it as a charity."

But fray Bernardo was unmoved and responded as if the matter had already compromised doña María's honor: "the said . . . cares nothing for the 200 pesos but for her honor and will demand it to the death." So Francisco was defeated and, protesting to the end, submitted to the authority and force of fray Bernardo López, who, acting as doña María's proxy, took Francisco's hands and, in the presence of witnesses, exchanged marriage vows with Francisco.

Later Francisco testified that he had never seen doña María in his entire life and did not even know who she was. After the ceremony he neither saw her nor wrote to her. Nor did she contact him. It is hard to imagine any other motive in this affair than a scheme to secure inheritance rights to the encomienda. This end, in the guise of defending a woman's honor, justified extracting 'consent' through intimidation.

LOVE MATCHES

A marriage arranged by parents or clerics for social and economic ends, as we have seen, could seem arbitrary and inappropriate to the contracting parties. Another model of marriage, what Beatrice Gottlieb calls the "love match," obtained when the contracting parties found each other, became "sweethearts," and eventually made it known to parents and community that they intended to marry.[68] If parents objected, usually because they perceived their son or daughter to be marrying a partner of lower status, lovers might seek clerical intervention, sometimes by eloping first, or they might find themselves thwarted.[69] The kind of clerical intervention that we saw above as direct, energetic, and even ruthless in arranging marriages, in these cases consisted of routine supervision of the initiatives by young people or of the contracts settled on by their parents, in the case of arranged marriages.

First an instance of a thwarted marriage. About 1556 sixteen-year-old Gómez de León, a native of Seville, fell in love with the daughter of a merchant who resided in the neighborhood of the duke of Medina Sidonia.[70] Pedro de Trujillo, Gómez's confidant at the time (by 1570 Trujillo was a notary in Mexico City) testified (in 1571) that "seventeen or eighteen years ago,"

> Gómez de León was having a love affair with a girl of about fifteen . . . [Pedro] does not remember the girl's name except that because she was small and talkative they called her *La Merlina*. And to meet her, the said Gómez told [Pedro], sometimes they would open the door and he would spend the night. And the merchant moved from Seville . . . and took with him his whole household including his two daughters.

As if playing the role of the tricky servant, a stock character of contemporary comedy, a trusted black servant, probably a slave, facilitated Gómez's entries.[71] Probably at the outset, to legitimize the sexual relations, Gómez and Merlina became betrothed. In the house but with Merlina's father's unaware, the servant and a sister witnessed Gómez and Merlina exchanging the vow to marry with hands clasped. Thus they had married and consummated their marriage, but out of view of the church. Thus it was "clandestine." These circumstances regularly constituted the elements for breach-of-promise suits, when the groom, most typically, failed to transform an engagement into a marriage or to solemnize a clandestine marriage with the nuptial blessing of a priest.

In this case, however, Merlina's father moved his household to Badajoz before any of this became public. Pedro recalled Gómez coming to him

> one morning when the said merchant was departing . . . and when they were alone told him with bitter tears that the merchant was taking his whole household, his daughters, and his sweetheart. And he knew that La Merlina was his wife and that they had married . . . in the presence of Merlina's sister and a black who used to open the door.

Pedro told his friend to speak to the ecclesiastical judge, for he too believed that Gómez had married. This explains why five years later (1558), Pedro denounced Gómez to the Inquisition after he married Francisca de Torres.

The reasons for the merchant's departure do not appear in Gómez's file, but some of them can be inferred. The timing, haste, and completeness of it suggests that it links to the discovery of the betrothal and deflowering of his daughter. If he investigated Gómez, he would have found the young suitor wanting in several ways. Though the son of a woman of distinguished family, he was fathered by a priest and therefore an illegitimate child of the most despised kind. In addition around Seville Gómez was notorious as a gambler. I suspect that the merchant judged Gómez's calidad as well below his daughter's. Rather than assenting to this 'marriage' by letting it become public knowledge, he spirited the girl away, presumably to a place where a more appropriate suitor could be found.

If young people married clandestinely to bypass the authority of parents, that very circumstance, in this case, made the marriage vulnerable to parental annulment. In taking his daughter away, Merlina's father skipped over church authority to secure his own house. To avoid such an outcome, couples needed to publicize their union as a fait accompli and have it sanctioned by the church. Pedro, as we saw, understood the mechanism well in advising his friend to appeal to an ecclesiastical court. For some reason (possibly he feared retribution, possibly he felt restrained because of his lack of honor as an espurio) Gómez failed to do this.

Not all young men acted so tentatively, and not all young women so docilely. In 1613 the Spaniard Agustín Vázquez found his youngest daughter, Catalina (born 1591), a mulatto like Agustín's wife, stubbornly committed to her beau, no matter what he said to oppose the match.[72] He was Juan Vázquez (no relation), a muleteer who had worked with or for Agustín; but that connection in this case worked against Juan. Catalina's attempt to gain her father's permission for the match, neighbors testified, came to heated arguments, periodic shouting, beatings, and a final blowup, when Agustín pushed Catalina out of his house and threw rocks at her. In the face of such resolute opposition, Juan sued to remove Catalina from parental jurisdiction, thereby blocking Agustín from further interference. But that may have been unnecessary, for Agustín in the meantime disowned Catalina. In the end Juan and Catalina went through all the approved procedures and, in spite of rumors that Juan was already married, exchanged vows in Tepozotlán, in the presence of a priest and friends.

Agustín tried to subdue Catalina with the usual parental instruments of control: intimidation, threats, violence, and finally disinheritance, whatever that would have amounted to in his plebian circumstances. When his daughter dishonored him by refusing to submit to his authority, he withdrew. Here the will of two young people determined to marry defeated a father's opposition. This must have occurred frequently, with greater or lesser histrionics. Lesser, for example, in the case of Sebastiana, an Indian of Malinalco.[73] In 1644 her daughter, the mestiza María Ana, wanted to marry Mateo de la Cruz, a *mulato-lobo* from the nearby Jesuit estate, Xalmolongas, but she opposed the match and so did María Ana's brother and sister (her father, not married to Sebastiana and absent, played no part in the incident). The opposition, then, consisted of voicing disapproval but nothing more. When María Ana persisted, they refused to participate in or witness the marriage, so she asked an acquaintance in the village, the mestiza Ursula de Lara, to attend her in the ceremony. Ursula testified (in August 1666) that the wedding day began when

> María, a mestiza whose surname she doesn't remember, came to her house one morning about eight o'clock and told her that her mother would not let her marry Mateo de la Cruz . . . and begged her to go to the convent with her so she would not have to go alone and so [Ursula] did and witnessed the marriage as godmother.

Only at the last minute, therefore, did María Ana speak to Ursula who, to judge by her ignorance of María's surname, had only a casual friendship with her. This is corroborated by the fact that she apparently learned for the first time of María's problem on the wedding day. María Ana's isolation came as a surprise to the priest, who wondered why the bridal party consisted of only two people.

In the cases of María Ana and Catalina, we find no clear reasons stated for parental opposition. It seems, however, that common concerns focused on social and procedural matters. The first involved seeing that the calidad of a suitor matched that of his intended; the second that impediments defined by the church would not mar the match. Petrona de la Candelaria, a mestiza of Mexico City, valued the assurance that her suitor, the lobo Juan Lorenzo del Castillo, was unmarried more than her own virginity, which she had already surrendered to him.[74] In 1706, having had an "illicit friendship" with Juan ("more mulatto than mestizo," she said) for about a year, he asked Petrona to marry him. Petrona was then about seventeen and living with her mother; Juan was about twenty-six. "She resisted," she testified three years later, "saying to him that as long as he does not bring a paper, or a person who knows him, she doesn't want to marry him." She referred, of course, to acceptable proof that he was free to marry. As it turned out, Juan, in spite of being already married, produced affidavits that satisfied Petrona as well as her mother. The story shows us, then, how Petrona followed social norms selectively, adopting a relaxed view of illicit sexual activity but holding firmly to marriage procedures defined by the church.

If Petrona accepted sexual relations outside of marriage, the Spaniard Juana Montaño held, more conventionally, that sex came only after marriage or betrothal, not before it.[75] In this she exemplifies the assumed link between an unmarried woman's honor and her virginity.[76] The Spaniard Marcos de la Cruz (born ca. 1625 in Pátzquaro) accepted the rule, as we can see by the account of his infatuation with Juana, which began in 1657. At the time he was already married and so had good reason to think twice before getting involved. But he did not or could not. In the dock in 1671, the inquisitors asked him to explain why, given his correct understanding of the permanence of matrimony, he would commit bigamy.[77] He answered that he had been "dragged down by human weakness because he wanted her so much and, since she was a virgin, there was no other way to gain access to her because Juana said he could have her only if they married. Thus carried away and defeated by passion he committed the error." Marcos had lost all judgment in the throes of his "uncontrollable sexual passion," a basis for marriage that parents increasingly attacked as irrational, unstable, and, in the words of one father, "the effect of a lascivious juvenile appetite."[78] In fact he was twenty-seven, hardly a juvenile, and already married. Yet he was out of control, and Juana used his condition as a basis for talking about marriage.[79]

Eloping was a simple and effective way to counter parental opposition. It consisted of running away, exchanging vows, engaging in sexual intercourse, and returning to report a fait accompli to a priest or ecclesiastical judge. If parents persisted in their opposition, they would usually be isolated by ecclesiastical and legal procedures (mainly the removal of the young woman from parental jurisdiction, as we saw in one case above), which would legitimize what had been effected by stealth. Legitimation through a nuptial mass was, of course, the decisive step.

All of this was common knowledge possessed by plebeians such as Pedro Mateo, a mestizo who had always worked on cattle ranches.[80] At age twenty-five (in 1666), he said that he could not recite the confession because "he forgot it." Nor did he know anything else about Christian doctrine for, as "a *pobre miserable* he has not had anybody to teach him." Yet lacking as he was in doctrinal knowledge, Pedro nevertheless knew how to spirit the mestiza Nicolasa de Chávez from her parents' household when they rejected his suit.

After the elopement Nicolasa's parents found them and brought their daughter home. But it was too late. Pedro could now enlist the church on his side and did so by going to Father Tomás de Alcocer, a parish priest who, a year later, testified that "the said Pedro appeared before him saying he and Nicolasa had exchanged marriage vows (*palabras de casamiento*)." Father Tomás therefore took Nicolasa from her parents, deposited her in the house of a respectable citizen, and prepared to bless the marriage. By then the rumor was circulating that Pedro was married elsewhere, but Father Tomás ignored it, probably because he heard it from Nicolasa's mother and discounted it.

In fact it was true, and later the inquisitors asked him why he had contracted a bigamous marriage. He answered that he had been "blind and compelled by the arrogance of Nicolasa de Chaves's mother who said that he was a poor Indian." Thus the reason for opposing Pedro fits with a standard interpretation of parental opposition suggested by J. A. Pitt-Rivers, C. Lisón-Tolosana, and Verena Martínez-Alier: the perception that the suitor fell below his intended in social standing.[81]

The case of Pedro takes us further into the process, however, because it documents the suitor's reaction. Taking the judgment as an insult, he resolved to have Nicolasa whatever the cost. So here parental opposition had an outcome contrary to its intent. It shifted Pedro from the position of suitor of Nicolasa to that of defender of his honor. But why was the comment so insulting, when it may very well have been true? Pedro himself admitted to some confusion when he testified that he did not "know if he is Indian, mulatto, or mestizo, because he did not know his father or even who he was and he only knew that his mother was Indian." Thus he may have been illegitimate as well, or at least perceived as such. But the insult had less to do with biological specifics than with Pedro's calidad. Labeling him an Indian presumed him a servile type unworthy of Nicolasa. Here again Nicolasa's mother spoke the truth, but it was a question of degree. All indications projected Pedro to a low place in society but not, in Pedro's view, so low as a "poor Indian." Plebeians constantly haggled over calidad, it seems, in the social marketplace. At the lower end of the hierarchy one could claim a higher or lower place within a range (admittedly a fairly limited one), and so heated disagreements arose over the disparities between self-designations and the attributions of others.

Rustics as well as men of higher status used elopement to repair the dishonor implied by the opposition of a girl's parents. The response fit an expectation for males in Hispanic society that they dominate and conquer women.[82] It included 'taking' women from the household of their fathers for the purpose of marriage or seduction, an extraction that could be carried out by trickery as well as by stealth. In 1727 the mestizo muleteer

Manuel de Lizona combined the two, when Sebastián Ruiz Medrano of the mining camp of Guadalcázar (an alcaldía mayor, 1618–1743, or te-niente-subdelegato, 1743–, now San Luis Potosí state) refused to allow Josepha Medrano, an Indian foundling he had raised, permission to marry him.[83] Why? Not for social reasons, but almost certainly because he wanted to keep Josepha as a servant in his household. Manuel countered with an elaborate scheme. After a season driving mules, he had earned enough to buy pieces of silk, wool, Brittany cloth, and some ribbon from his boss's store, which he brought to Ruiz's house. He presented the goods and asked Sebastián to "give them to the señoras."[84] "Now let's be on good terms," he added, for "I've found a cave that seems to be used by robbers where there's a lot of goods and we must go there, for it's not far away, on the side of the peaks that lie between San Luis Potosí and Guadalcázar."

With an embellishment or two (say, for example, the untimely return of the robbers) the account approaches something from the *Thousand and One Nights*. Even so it must have been a local classic, to judge by don Manuel's well-rehearsed retelling with the actors' words given as direct speech and with the scene carefully drawn. The rest of his testimony dwells on how well the scheme worked, that indeed Manuel the trickster used Sebastián's greed to achieve his ends. The older man suddenly warmed to his daughter's suitor and agreed to ransack the cave with him. He hitched a team to a cart and, with Manuel giving directions, the two men headed into the rough country. Once there, Manuel pretended to be confused, told Sebastián to wait with the cart while he scouted ahead, and moved quickly out of sight. He then circled back to Guadalcázar, where Josepha awaited him, and then 'abducted' (*hurtó*) her. They traveled east-ward to Valle del Maíz, married, and afterward returned to Guadalcázar. Later Josepha's biological father, who gave Josepha to Ruiz to be raised, referred to Manuel's "capture" of his daughter as undertaken with her consent.[85] Ruiz, as was usual in elopement cases, accepted the accom-plished fact; besides he had some consolation in the gifts that Manuel had brought in the first place.[86]

ILLICIT FRIENDSHIPS

Seduction

Because the church confined sexual relations to marriage, it goes without saying that a hasty promise to marry, whether sincere or not, would accompany some liaisons. We noted in chapter 2, for example, that Antonia Sánchez, widow and hatmaker of Toro, exacted a palabra de casamiento from twelve-year-old Gerónimo de Benavides (born 1532) before she accepted the boy's proposition to engage in sexual relations.[87] Gerónimo spent three nights with the woman, "knowing her carnally," but this and the fact that he had betrothed himself to do so, horrified his older brother Pedro. Still in Toro thirty-five years later (1577), Pedro testified that "he did not want his brother Gerónimo de Benavides to marry the hatter, saying to him 'look at what you've done, that it would lead you straight to the devil' . . . and he persuaded his brother to go to New Spain because that woman would be lost and that was [his] conscience."

Antonia's attempt to use sexual relations with an inexperienced boy to marry him can be compared to the raping of a young girl that included no plan for marriage. Ana Pérez (born ca. 1514) was raised in Zamora, in the household of an aunt and uncle.[88] She testified (in 1539) that

> in Zamora she knew a Christóbal García carnally. He had her virginity [when] she was in her aunt's house and after he had it, the husband of the said her aunt, brother of the said Christóbal García who had it first, also had sexual intercourse with her [on two occasions]. She was a young girl (*muy muchacha*) and one day she was alone in the house and in bed and he [Christóbal] entered her room and had carnal access with her.[89]

Even as transmitted into the third person by the notary, the account seems to reflect a child's trauma, for the statement simply goes over the same ground, with slight variations, three times. Ana, it seems, had never been able to go beyond the event itself, which had stripped her of her honor as a woman, perhaps before she had been aware of possessing any honor. Her account focuses on Christóbal, the agent of the deed (who he was and when and how he took her virginity); the scene, weighted with normality (a day at home and she alone in bed); and the act itself, the familiar figure of her uncle entering her room and, somewhat euphemistically, 'having her virginity.' The account is emotionally distant, but the details point to strong feelings nevertheless. And is it not remarkable that after this initiation, sexual relations continued with both of the adult men of the household? For the rest of the story, Ana stresses the agency of her aunt, who effects a conventional justice: "Afterwards when her aunt found out how [Christóbal] had corrupted her, she made him marry her."

Rape and marriage are followed by six or seven years of married life with Christóbal and the birth of six children. At this point, perhaps in 1530 or

1531, Ana revealed, apparently for the first time, the details of her sexual initiation to a priest in the confessional. But why then? Perhaps through contact with catechal teachings, she became aware that marriage to an uncle was an invalidating impediment. The priest in any case told Ana that her marriage to Christóbal was invalid, and so she left him and the children and went to the Indies to begin a new life. In New Spain she cohabited with Beltrán de Peralta until "believing that she would serve God by removing herself from sin she married him." After a year, however, Peralta took up with an Indian woman of Vera Cruz, saying, Ana remembered, that "he was married in Spain with a Francisca Morena who lives in the city of Baeza [diocese of Córdoba] and with her had a daughter." But that did not stop him from contracting a third marriage, to the Indian woman. Ana in the meantime also married a third time, after stating her situation to local priests and receiving a dispensation.

Some of Ana's marital complications (those stemming from her involvement with Beltrán de Peralta for example) may be traced to the state of flux existing in the Indies during the first half of the sixteenth century. However, we must not let that obscure Ana's initial predicament and its resolution: the loss of her honor was repaired by marrying her to the man who had taken it. Ana's aunt enforced the 'solution' with her considerable authority in her household. Ana in fact places the aunt at the very center of her narrative: it was her house, her husband, her finding out, her making Christóbal marry.[90]

Relatives had a duty to protect their women's honor when it looked as if a suitor wanted to enjoy her sexual favors without following through with marriage. In so doing they protected their own honor, for the behavior of daughters, sisters, or cousins reflected on the honor of fathers, brothers, cousins, and uncles. In Portugal in the 1550s, before he came to the Indies, the mulatto Francisco Rodríguez, a native of Tabila in the Algarve, established a liaison with Isabel Hernandes, daughter of a muleteer of Tabila.[91] To the inquisitors he testified (in 1578) that

> about twenty-two years ago, he made love with the said Isabel and promised to marry her. But before giving her his word, he had access and participation with her. He did not actually marry her but visited her as a person that he had promised to marry. They had a son but he doesn't remember anything about him. Once her relatives found out that they were not really married, they attacked him with knives.

As Francisco tells it, the relatives discovered, all of a sudden, that a marriage had not taken place. More likely they had been monitoring things right along and had acquiesced in a natural progression, with betrothal initiating sexual relations (in fact Francisco was at pains to state that the latter had begun *before* the betrothal) but with the expected marriage delayed for too long. Was Francisco stalling? Was he trying to avoid marriage altogether? Isabel's relatives must have thought so and therefore forced him to go through with it.

The betrothal implied by the initiation of sexual relations between doña Clara Ochoa and Francisco del Valle, a Spaniard of Mexico City, mobilized her relatives to restore her honor by forcing Francisco to marry her.[92] Because both parties claimed high social status, more was at stake, and the drama generated more emotion. Francisco, born in 1606 of a family with a tradition of serving the crown in war and in peace, had filled a number of positions in New Spain (governor, deputy governor, constable, militia captain, and judge), at the behest of one or another viceroy and also in the domain of the marqués del Valle. His trouble began in August 1654, when on finishing a term as governor of Tuxtla (an alcaldía mayor, now in Vera Cruz state), he was traveling to Cuyoacan to rejoin his wife, an invalid, who had remained behind during his term of service. We learn of it from his autobiographical statement, given in the dock of the Inquisition in June 1656.

At Puebla he found 'lodging' at the home of doña Clara Ochoa, located on the road to Cholula (a separate jurisdiction near Puebla, now in Puebla state). But instead of a brief stopover, don Francisco settled in for a more leisurely stay as he and doña Clara dallied in an "illicit friendship." After a couple of months, doña Clara's relatives decided that this open liaison must be legitimated by marriage. To this end they circulated a report that don Francisco's wife had died, sent messengers to tell him, arranged for city officials to offer condolences, and then urged him to marry doña Clara. The new widower understandably tried to delay the process. He wanted the alleged death confirmed, but the family portrayed this as simply stalling. To increase the pressure they applied economic leverage: he would agree to the marriage or else pay immediately an outstanding debt of 2,300 pesos. This would have meant the seizure of Francisco's property and person until he could pay.

Trapped, don Francisco agreed to the marriage, but secretly tried to evade it. He continued to request correct procedures, for example that the banns be published in Mexico City, which would have been in order because he was a vecino there. Doña Clara's relatives said this was "unnecessary" and, as they orchestrated a rapid run up to the marriage, made don Francisco a virtual prisoner in doña Clara's house. In this predicament don Francisco decided on a desperate plan to escape. After nightfall at the entry of the house he arranged a meeting with his sister's blind servant, the mestizo Christóbal, and directed him "to bring him a horse from [her] estancia" so he could escape to Mexico City in a predawn gallop.[93]

But doña Clara herself overheard the conversation (perhaps she was keeping a close watch on her 'fiancee') and told her brother and cousins. In the meantime an unsuspecting don Francisco returned to his room and retired early. But alas there would be little rest, for at 10:00 P.M. an angry crowd, led by doña Clara's brother Juan Ramos, burst into his chamber. With drawn dagger and a pistol in his belt, Ramos angrily confronted the startled Francisco: "So you wanted to abandon doña Clara and make her a laughingstock." Then as if the protagonist of a melodrama, he turned to the others in the room and recounted Francisco's plan to run away. Facing his adversary once again, with threats and oaths he shouted that Francisco would marry that very night, or "he would have to kill him." In fact he had already sent for a magistrate (alcalde ordinario), who arrived at 11:00 P.M., together with even more family partisans. The magistrate, according to don Francisco, was

> more irritated than all the others. He said to him 'you don't have an out, you are going to have to marry now,' and he ordered that he be seized and taken to the jail for the debt he owed to the king, to the said Matheo de Ledesma, and to other persons, that he would have to die in jail if the relatives of the said doña Clara did not kill him first.

Don Francisco was defeated, and his final antagonist was a peer and colleague exercising in Puebla the powers he himself had just relinquished in Tuxtla. His dalliance had turned into a nightmare. His attempt to delay the denouement, even to adhere to normal processes, had been thwarted. His plan to flee had backfired. After the dramatic scene was over and Francisco was alone with the magistrate, he appealed one more time to him as a colleague:

> On the way to the public jail he pleaded with the said alcalde to take pity on him, that he was a nobleman who had held offices and administered justice and that he should [therefore] take him to his house and enclose him in a room until the truth as to whether his wife, doña María de Acarçe, is dead can be investigated. And even in case she was dead it was not his convenience to marry the said doña Clara for many reasons. [For one] she was so poor that there was no advantage whatsoever in marrying her. [For another] he could

not permit the large blot and affront to his lineage [that marriage to her would bring, for] afterward how would he be able to face the Viceroy or his friends.

Francisco supposed that a collegial understanding within the magistracy overshadowed the ties between magistrates and locals. But not in this case, as he might have known from the already ample proof of this official's partisanship for doña Clara's family at the house. Yet Francisco challenged this directly with his candid and unflattering assessment of doña Clara's worth relative to his own.

With no escape the marriage took place, and afterward don Francisco immediately left Puebla never to have further contact with doña Clara again. From the standpoint of her family, his departure was no longer a problem, for they had vindicated her honor. The entrapment of Francisco was of his own making, at least in part, for he seemed to have used the promise of marriage (whenever his first wife should die?) as the backdrop to forming the liaison with doña Clara. Even more striking is the political point that a man so well connected in the viceregal court could be so powerless in a provincial city. An important family of Puebla had enough local influence to isolate an outsider completely and, most importantly for our purposes, church officials were completely integrated into this local network.

Another instance of this puzzling pattern (allowing an apparently single male to enter a household, thus tacitly granting him sexual access to a single woman) took place in a plebeian family headed by the mestizo María Josepha del Próspero.[94] Bartolomé Ortiz, a Spaniard of Mérida in his midtwenties, had been on the road for several years and had adopted several aliases to avoid being arrested as a vagabond. He drifted into Chiapa de Indios in May 1721, a few days before the feast day of San Antonio; within a week he had been invited to a fiesta and had begun a liaison, the last apparently with the encouragement of the girl's mother. From Bartolomé's testimony eight months later (February 28, 1722) we have an outline of how this happened.

> They invited him to a fiesta in honor of San Antonio that was taking place in the house of a mestizo woman named María Josepha del Próspero. And having gone and attended the fiesta in which they provided him with a harp because he said he was a musician, on the following day the said María sent for him so that he could write a letter which he did and on this occasion he got involved in an illicit friendship with Rosa María de Avriola, a daughter of the said María Josepha, who was eighteen.

In the confessional Rosa told Francisco del Pozo, the parish priest, that Bartolomé had given her a palabra de casamiento. Bartolomé denied this, but the promise to marry so commonly accompanied seduction that her version rings as more plausible. Rosa also had the advantage that she was the resident and Bartolomé the stranger. And as Bartolomé noted, Pozo customarily protected women who claimed breach of promise after surrendering their virginity. He summoned Bartolomé, scolded him, and demanded to know if it were true that he was engaged in such a friendship. Bartolomé admitted it, and Pozo took steps to marry him to Rosa.

Bartolomé, pretending to cooperate, raised a procedural issue. Because he was a stranger, no one in Chiapa de Indios could testify that he was free to marry. He proposed, therefore, to go to Guatemala to secure the normal affidavits and then to return. In fact had he been allowed to leave, he said later, he would not have returned. Pozo, perhaps suspecting as much, countered with his own plan. Bartolomé was to write "a paper," addressed to Pozo but dictated by Pozo himself, certifying that if he did not qualify for matrimony in Chiapa de Indios, he would take Rosa to Guatemala. Pozo took the note to the vicar general (provisor) for a judgment and he, accepting it as evidence of Bartolomé's good faith, lowered the usual standards for proof of eligibility to marry to what could be done locally "in the best form possible." Pozo could now proceed. He used witnesses who had known Bartolomé for only twenty days for the marriage investigation and read the banns in the parish church. The vicar declared this "sufficient," issued the licenses, and Pozo married Bartolomé and Rosa on July 29, 1720.

In this way Pozo and his vicar general protected local women. Their policy had a precedent in canon law: the bypassing of two readings of the banns to speed cases in which outside pressure might override the will of the contracting parties.[95] In fact Bartolomé's proposal to obtain testimony in Guatemala, where he was known, conformed more closely to proper usages. But Pozo judged this less important than blocking Bartolomé's escape so as to protect Rosa's honor.

Families and communities, therefore, protected their daughters, perhaps in some cases by entrapping eligible men into marriages. The crux of concern focused on the alleged loss of a maiden's virginity, more than sexual activity as such. Yet any woman who engaged in sexual relations, whether for the first time or habitually, could claim that the promise to marry had accompanied a liaison. This implied connection obtained strongly enough that it even affected the mulatto innkeeper Leonor Vázquez, a "woman of the world," who in truth had no such concerns.[96]

She dispensed her sexual favors freely and apparently enjoyed herself with many men.[97] Testifying in 1565, when she was in her late twenties, she remembered an occasion when a twenty-year-old mulatto, had "stopped to sleep two or three nights" in her house in Mexico City. The man, Christóbal de Ayala, testified that he had had "carnal access with her as if she were his mistress but the said Christóbal never promised to marry her nor did she him, for she had already promised to marry the mestizo Francisco Mendezín before knowing Christóbal."

For Leonor, then, it amounted to a straightforward liaison without complications. Others at the inn, lodgers or customers in for a drink of pulque, must have thought the same, as it became 'public' and the occasion for ribald comments.[98] One lodger (Francisco Velázquez), apparently a permanent one, since he also declared himself a vecino of Mexico City, remembered the end of a jocular exchange in which Leonor said to Christóbal: "Yes, I would like to marry you." He noticed how the remark had silenced Christóbal and how Leonor, a bawdy type apparently enjoying Christóbal's uneasiness, repeated the comment. At this point, he testified, "an Indian woman urged Christóbal to marry Leonor," that is, to respond to the comment in kind. And so he did. A liaison, a flirtation, a facetious remark had suddenly become serious, as Christóbal took Leonor to the vicar to apply for a marriage license. But here Leonor had the sense to stop, to get away from Christóbal, and to run to "a mestizo [Francisco]" to whom she was already betrothed.[99] Later, running into Leonor in the plaza, Christóbal gave her several hard slaps and dragged her to the archbishopric's jail. Doctor Anguis, vicar of the archbishopric, questioned each of them and upheld Leonor's prior betrothal to Francisco. He also ordered Leonor whipped, "because she had not told the truth to Christóbal in representing herself as free to contract marriage."

The little drama of Leonor and Christóbal illustrates the complex interplay of sexual mores and matrimony. Neither of them presumed a necessary connection between sexual intercourse and marriage. But once that connection was made, albeit at least for Leonor, in a joking way, the banter was easily misinterpreted. Discussion of marriage, especially when a man and woman 'agreed' to marry, was more serious than sexual liaisons as such, for it constituted a betrothal. The crucial moment that transformed this exchange came with the innocent intervention by the Indian woman who did not get the 'joke' (Christóbal's silence suggests that he got it but realized that it was suddenly serious business) but instead pressed Christóbal to take Leonor's comment in its literal, not just its ironic sense.

So the picture is one of people socializing, joking, and intervening in each other's lives (possibly in Nahuatl or a mixture of Spanish and Nahuatl, to judge by the presence of the Indian woman and the fact that Leonor herself testified in Nahuatl),[100] with advice and urgings of various sorts. Moreover the group of mostly mulattos took the Indian woman's suggestion as seriously as anyone else's. Through the entire episode Leonor must have known that she could not follow through with her charade but, after a certain point, how was she to extricate herself? That she eventually did shows that she too respected matrimony, or at least feared the penalties that came from violating the norms that defined it. However irreverent and brazen her joking, she knew that betrothal firmly set her on the way to marriage. Christóbal knew this too. Witness his initial hesitation, his decision to go directly to the vicar, his angry confrontation with Leonor in the plaza, and his suit for breach of promise.

In the above six examples falling under the category of "seduction," sexual relations were linked to marriage. In four of them betrothal was presumed. Of the other two, in the first marriage restores a girl's honor after she loses her virginity; in the second 'betrothal' comes from joking about marriage in the aftermath of a liaison. Given this association the promise to marry clearly played a part in persuading women concerned with protecting their reputation to engage in sexual relations. Admitting as much in 1722, the Spaniard Miguel de Herrera testified that "he solicited some women, promising to marry them but as a pretext to satisfy his lust, not with the intention to keep the promise . . . Sometimes this became public and people thought he married [these women] but he did not."[101]

Miguel's words, "pretext to satisfy his lust," have the tone of the formulaic speech prompted by confessionals as a kind of ritual contrition. Many, in fact, must have repeated such phrases to authorities, to distinguish between "feigned" and "serious" promises.[102] But it might be difficult for those who heard such promises to make the distinction. This may have been the reason, Miguel speculated ingenuously, why "some" of these women claimed that he had married them.[103] In fact breach-of-promise suits over a palabra de casamiento, according to Lavrin, make up the most frequently heard kind of complaint in ecclesiastical courts, thus indicating the widespread use of this model of seduction.[104] The results of the complaints against Miguel have been lost, probably because he ran away quickly and avoided apprehension and prosecution. He must have been a common type, however, in using to his advantage the conventional tie between marriage and sexuality.[105]

Abduction and Concubinage

Seduction, abduction, concubinage, and marriage can be seen as a continuum. Couples passed through some or all of these stages, which in one way or another went from courtship to stable pairings. Marriage always stood at one pole, however, as the proper resolution for any of the others. Earlier we saw one kind of abduction that in fact was nothing more than elopement in the face of parental opposition. Even more commonly, I think, abduction occurred as a part of illicit friendships, the coming together of men and women with no particular intent to marry, at least not right away.[106] Yet these can be seen as informal marriages, for they become cohabitations rather than one-night stands.

As with elopements, they begin with a man 'abducting' or 'stealing' a woman. The language accurately mirrors a structural rather than phenomenological reality, in that women (except for widows) lived as minors under male jurisdiction. In theory they acted largely through the agency of men, but this was a male view of things. "As far as men were concerned," in Edward Shorter's words, "she did not make things happen; they happened to her.[107] To take a woman from that jurisdiction irregularly (without permission, consultation, or leave of the church) indeed amounted to robbery. In truth, however, this language and these assumptions do not pick up the agency of women, who did 'make things happen' by consenting to, encouraging, and sometimes engineering their leave-takings.

Parents heading plebeian households with minimal property and status placed no great importance, in Ramón Gutiérrez's words, on "whether or whom their children married."[108] These types accepted the abduction of a daughter as a routine event of no particular concern. In 1582 or so, the Spaniard Miguel Muñoz, a native of Triana living in Celaya, found one day that his daughter Isabel had been abducted.[109] She was then about fourteen and, as he described her, "a mestiza . . . his bastard daughter." In Celaya (Miguel had lived in Mexico City when Isabel was born), Isabel had little claim to status in Hispanic society. In fact it may have pleased Miguel that Isabel and her beau spared him the bother of a formal wedding, which would have entailed some expenses. In a nonchalant way, he testified (in 1588) that she had been abducted six years before, when

> a vaquero [serving] Gaspar Salvago—he doesn't know his name except that he
> is a mestizo and he lived on the estancia Los Llanos, three leagues from
> here—took her from [Miguel's] house in this town . . . He heard that [the
> mestizo] took her to Guadalajara and then to Zacatecas . . . where three years

ago she married Francisco Ortiz, native of Cádiz, who serves as a soldier in the presidios of that kingdom and his daughter lives with her mother-in-law in the new inn next to the Tlalpuxagua mining camp [an alcaldía mayor now in northeastern Michoacán] and he doesn't know if she married before with someone else.

Yet Miguel had a pretty good idea of Isabel's movements. He knew, for example, that she was not living with her husband but, probably servant-like, with his mother, running the inn. As for the abduction itself, two aspects of the statement give the impression that he considered it a commonplace. For one he never bothered to pin down the individual identity of the abductor. Instead he defines him socially through his master, his work, and his 'quality,' which place the young man, in our terms, as a propertyless wage earner of mixed race—roughly speaking, Isabel's social equal.[110] In addition to Miguel's casual view of the abductor, let us also note his apparent indifference (surely he could have found out through the grapevine) as to whether it had resulted in marriage or not.

Isabel's abduction led to marriage but in a roundabout way.[111] Officials arrested her abductor, not for taking her but for another unspecified crime, and sentenced him to the galleys; they sent her to serve in the household of an audiencia judge in Guadalajara. After three years another man, the one whom Miguel had heard she married, ran off with her, and in Zacatecas they tried to pass as married. But Officials spotted them as living together illicitly, arrested them, and arranged their marriage.

The two abductions of Isabel both initiated marriagelike cohabitations. Officials 'annulled' the first because of crime and ratified the second by formalizing it. The initiative, planning, and commitment implied by running away, then, amounted to a kind of folk marriage, and when officials moved to transform these informal unions into proper marriages, there was little reason to resist, except possibly to avoid the costs or, in the cases of the already married, to avoid bigamy. After formal marriage, life went on as it had before, except that couples were now bound by a formal and sacramental tie instead of an informal one. The latter had the advantage that it could be ended at any time without further complications. Many, in fact, must have ended neatly and quickly for one or another reason.

Such an ending proved fortunate for Bernabé Cristóbal, termed a lobo to signify his racial mix of mulatto and Indian, because he was already married when he began a period of cohabitation with a woman.[112] He worked as a shepherd and therefore spent long periods away from his wife, Lorenza María, a mulatto whom he had married in 1708. During one such absence, in the shearing hut on the heights of Ibarra (jurisdiction of, and now in the state of, Aguas Calientes), he met María, an orphan and like him a loba. She had been raised by an Indian named Antonio who tended the hut and, with María's help, cultivated a plot of land. Contact in this isolated place led to Bernabé and María running off together. They settled in the Huaxteca, the area of the gulf coastal plain under the jurisdiction of Pánuco where, as before, Bernabé worked as a shepherd. After a time, however, María's brother, acting as a kind of guardian of his sister, tracked her down and took her away. So it ended with no damages and no recriminations, as if nothing much had been at stake.

A shift from the casual pairings of mestizos and mulattoes to the concern for respectability of Spaniards brought more emphasis on formal marriage. In 1586 the Spaniard Ana de Hierro, a vecina of Huexocingo, threatened Miguel Alonso with a criminal suit when he began to cohabit with her daughter, Luisa de Los Angeles.[113] The charge most likely would have been fornication, together with a suit for damages for loss of virginity, on the grounds that Miguel seduced Luisa by promising to marry her. In fact Luisa herself may have taken the initiative, to judge by Miguel's testimony three years later in his bigamy trial.[114] "The said Luisa de los Angeles, his second wife, left her mother's house and moved into his for which her mother summoned him and threatened that she would have to take the matter to adjudication. And he calmed her down by saying that he would marry her."

Miguel stayed with this version, in which he stresses his fear of a law suit. He testified, for example, that the second marriage "was not in contempt of the sacrament but to avoid the accusation and criminal suit over [her] saying that she found him with the said Luisa de Los Angeles." And again, later in his testimony, Manuel covered the same point, saying that he married to deliver himself from "prison and the punishment of the justice." This of course served poorly as a defense, but conveys admirably his fear, apprehension, and anxiety. If Luisa "left her mother's house and moved into his," Miguel nevertheless knew that the judges would read this as 'he abducted her,' for in the nature of things men, not women, 'made things happen.'

Luisa's mother, scandalized that her daughter was cohabiting with Miguel, cut it short and intimidated Miguel into marrying the girl. Formal marriage solved the problem, because it fit the church prescription as the honorable context for sexual relations. A liaison with a Spanish woman could be dangerous precisely for this reason: families and communities rallied to defend the honor of their daughters. It all became a plausible ritual, even if a woman was not a virgin, when they caught a suitable marriage partner dallying with one of their own while away from his home territory.[115] In this way an entire province arrayed itself against Pedro de Valenzuela in 1604, after he 'abducted' a local woman.[116] The story begins when Pedro, married to Juana del Castillo in Lima, received word from Jerez that his father had died and set out for Spain to collect his inheritance. For his journey he took Juana's gold chain, worth 400 pesos, which had been part of her dowry. He reached Cartagena but for some reason proceeded no farther and, after acquiring goods in Cartagena to resell in the interior, began the return trip to Lima across Nueva Granada.[117]

In Tocayma he met Francisca de Sosa, a Spaniard, daughter of a deceased merchant, whom he later termed a "woman of the world." The implication of the designation, as we have already seen, was clear enough. Although of respectable family and still living with her mother, Francisca apparently was no virgin and freely approached men. Pedro slept with her one or more times and then, he claimed later, "she pleaded with him to take her to Lima as she had others before him." This at least is how Pedro described Francisca's behavior in his autobiographical statement, thus portraying her as taking the initiative and himself as merely acquiescing in it. They traveled as far as Timana, about sixty leagues away, and then the local constabulary (*hermandad*) arrested Pedro with warrants sent from Tocayma. A local judge (*alcalde de hermandad*) ordered Pedro secured with "two pairs of shackles and a chain" and, for good measure, ordered him placed in the stocks and watched by two guards. He sequestered Pedro's possessions, which included his porter, a black slave, and his most valuable possession, the gold chain. Evidently no one entertained one typical solution to situations of this kind, that Pedro pay a sum to endow Francisca, on the pretext that he was compensating her for the 'loss' of her virginity.[118] Pedro offered a standard defense that Francisca, a loose woman, had come on her own initiative. But this fell on deaf ears. Faced with the prospect of the long trip back to Tocayma in chains and confrontation with Francisca's partisans, he agreed to marry her "in order to regain his freedom," he said later, "and to get back his possessions."

Marrying Francisca solved Pedro's immediate predicament. A priest of Timana officiated, with local residents acting as witnesses, among them two "soldiers," apparently Pedro's former guards. Now free but shackled with a second marriage, Pedro resumed his journey. Ten leagues down the road he ran into a muleteer and with him sent Francisca home to her mother, together with a letter explaining that he already had a wife in Lima and could therefore not be married again. Then, by way of

Campeche, he went straight to Mexico City and denounced himself to the Holy Office. He chose Mexico City rather than Cartagena, he said, because the latter city was under the jurisdiction of the Holy Office in Lima, and he hoped to avoid the notoriety of imprisonment and punishment in his home city. Except for this hope to minimize his dishonor, he seemed resigned to the punishment for bigamy.[119]

So men and women through their own agency came together in various forms of spontaneous coupling, and sometimes their unions set into motion a policing reaction. If they began as "abductions" and carried on as "friendships," they nevertheless amounted to a quasi-marital arrangement. These informal unions, for example, avoided the veto that was sure to be given them when impediments would have prevented sacramental marriage. The castizo Joseph Muñoz de Sanabria, for example, had been living with María Rosa for about eleven years in 1719 but, like many engaged in such cohabitations, he had begun it as an already married man.[120] He could not licitly marry María, yet in a life they built together that began after he abducted her, they moved from place to place in the north.[121] Joseph testified (in 1719) that "he changed his name and they acted as if they were married but when it came out that they were not, they put him in jail [in Saltillo]. He was afraid and decided to marry the said María Rosa."

In effect this was a 'marriage' that began as an abduction. Its illicit nature remained undetected for such a long time because Joseph and María worked at avoiding detection; they moved frequently, he changed his name, they pretended that they had married legally. At the same time that they were living a married life, therefore, they also had to hide the fact that it was not really a marriage. But in the living, it in effect became that, and Joseph chose to regularize it and risk bigamy rather than walk away from it.

Officials policed even long-standing, apparently legal couples, such as Joseph and María, but the problem was so prevalent, at least in some places, that it seemed overwhelming to individual clerics. Consider, for example, fray Joseph de Arcocha, writing to the Holy Office in Mexico City from Sombrerete in 1686: "Advise me on what I should do about the scandalous free unions of 10, 12, and 20 years [of couples] living together as if they were married. Some of them have been denounced, but I haven't followed up on the matter, preferring first to notify and receive directions from your lordships." So many long-term unions suggests many years of clerical negligence. But they were marriages in everything but the formality of a priestly blessing, and this somehow confounded fray Joseph. He, in any case, would have had no jurisdiction over the parishes of the camp administered by secular clerics. That he wrote the Inquisition instead of his bishop indicates that he expected no leadership at the diocesan level.[122]

But newcomers more than long-term residents received the closest scrutiny by officials, masters, and priests. So much so that marriage irregularities came to be associated with vagabondage and with some justification, in the case of a type such as the mestizo Isidro del Castillo (born 1688) who, like Joseph, left his wife and stayed on the move.[123] Unlike Joseph, however, he cohabited with one woman after another. "Isidro Castillo is a lazy vagabond," the prosecutor of the Inquisition wrote, "who for nearly twenty years has had no known occupation except that of concubinage." Unfortunately testimony establishing the basis for the sarcastic barb does not appear in the file.

The file does, however, include material on his most recent liaison, with the mestiza Dominga Petrona, because she became his second wife. A native of the pueblo of San Lucas Amalinalpa (a pueblo in the jurisdiction of Tlalmanalco, now in the federal district), she was the widow of an Indian. Isidro joined up with her in 1726 in Chalco and took her to Tacuba. They worked on an hacienda owned by doña Isabel Anselmo for two years, but "the wages were short," Isidro recalled. So they moved back to Chalco, where friar Marcos, a Franciscan, arrested Isidro and told him that he had to marry Dominga, whom, in the meantime, he placed in custody. Twenty days later (barely enough time to publish the banns and secure affidavits in Amalinalpa, let alone elsewhere) fray Marcos married Isidro and Dominga. The greater good of transforming a consensual union into a marriage justified speeding up proper usages.[124]

The routine and mechanism of policing consensual couples can be seen from a vignette that must have recurred countless times in New Spain. It consisted of a priest visiting isolated settlements and haciendas and marrying couples living in concubinage. Our example concerns Manuel Romano of Tavira (Portugal), who in 1577, at age eighteen, was working as a vaquero on the estancia of Pedro Núñez, six leagues from Veracruz.[125] There he lived in concubinage with "Juana India" and in his autobiographical statement testified that

> about a year and a half ago a priest . . . who used to visit estancias in the district came to visit and told him to clasp hands with the said Indian and the said priest then took their hands in the presence of Pedro Núñez and other vaqueros who were two black slaves and a free mulatto. He doesn't know what the priest said or how the rest of it went except that he took their hands and afterward he slept with her just as he had before.

The marriage made no sense, for as Hispanic society calculated it, they were badly mismatched. He was an immigrant, albeit a humble one, from the peninsula; she was a native, possessing only the generic "India" for a surname, speaking only Nahuatl. Their union had been a sleeping arrangement and nothing more. Why then did the priest marry them? First of course to regularize an illicit friendship. But more fundamentally, I think, to help a master keep and control his servants. This compromised no Christian principles, for within the natural order, as a seventeenth-century confessional manual makes clear, masters held authority over servants no less than fathers did over children: "not only the body, but more importantly the soul, is under his guardianship."[126] There is little doubt that Núñez, who paid the priest and was on friendly terms with him, easily arranged the marriages of his cohabiting servants. An overworked priest on circuit, trying to keep up with the demands of a far-flung rural parish, no doubt welcomed and counted on such cooperation.

As might have been expected, Manuel left Juana after a couple of months. He traveled north and near San Miguel married the free mulatto Juana de Herrera. In doing this he corrected to a degree the social and cultural mismatch of the marriage with Juana India, for Juana the mulatto had a surname, a family, and a place in the Hispanic world. In his bigamy trial, Manuel said that he "did not take that which happened with the said Indian to be a marriage." He had three reasons: it had not been preceded by a matrimonial investigation and the reading of the banns; it had not taken place in a church; and it had been "arranged (this last from Juana herself) to keep him on the estancia."

Manuel, at least for his trial, distinguished between mere concubinage (even one covered with a priestly intervention because of the ulterior motive of tying him to the estancia) and proper marriages.[127] So did others, and with good reason. The mulatto Francisca de Paula, testifying nine years after she married Manuel de la Trinidad Rodríguez, explained that "as a weak woman she had a friendship with her husband before and didn't want to marry him because she well knew his bad character but her mother and sister forced her."[128]

The state of mind she refers to takes her back to 1739, when she was nineteen. In accepting the "friendship" and, at the same time, rejecting the suit for marriage, she made a crucial distinction, for marriage tied a woman permanently to a man of questionable character; cohabitation did not. But Francisca's mother, Damiana, also played a role in the drama. She called the friendship a *mala vida*, or "bad life," thereby connoting her moral disapproval but also her concern that Manuel was subjecting Francisca to an unsettled existence.[129] "He has never wanted to subject himself to live a settled life," Damiana said in 1748, "but kept moving, today here, tomorrow elsewhere, jumping from one pueblo to another." By then the eighty-year-old woman must have realized that her original moral concern had been misplaced. As a result of the marriage, Francisca suffered "many hardships," she said, and Manuel "gave her bad treatment." All of this Francisca had anticipated in her original preference for concubinage rather than marriage.

CONCLUSION

Marriage is complex. It takes place as a private transaction and as a public one; it springs from passion and from planning; it is based on consent yet subject to pressure, cajolery, and intimidation; it enabled licit sexual relations and occasioned, through the promise to marry, illicit ones. Bigamy records give some indications of how and why pairings took place because they include the testimony of the young people who were setting up new households. Naturally they received advice and the attention of parents and relatives, of masters who considered themselves guardians or patrons, and of the post-Tridentine church, which claimed exclusive jurisdiction over the sacrament. They resisted or cooperated with interventions in one way or another, depending on their temperaments, personal inclinations, and ideas about how life should be lived.

Inés Hernández, alias Florentina del Río, a Spaniard born at the very end of the fifteenth century, certainly had her own ideas.[130] She faced the prospect of living alone (her husband had long ago disappeared) or remarrying. In 1525 she chose to marry, thereby risking bigamy. The justification she gave to the inquisitors consisted of an axiom of popular culture: "Better to live [as a bigamist] in one sin than as a single woman in many." In fact the saying paraphrases a passage from the *Siete Partidas* that excused informal unions (called *barraganía*) among men:

> Holy Church forbids that any Christian man have *barraganas*, for to live with them is mortal sin. But the wise men of old who made the laws permitted that some men might have them without civil penalty, for they held that it was *a lesser evil to live with one woman than many*, and that the paternity of the children would be more certain."[131]

Inés's version conflates bigamy with barraganía, inverts gender, and disregards the underlying intent to control for paternity by restricting women to a single sexual partner. She shows, therefore, how legal principles, at the level of popular culture, could be stretched to suit individual purposes.

By keeping an eye on the views and behaviors, on the actions and reactions, of the contracting parties, we can view processes of marriage formation in a real-life contexts. So we have named individuals and told their stories. If their approaches to marriage and life fell within a "system of predispositions" arising from upbringing and place in society, they nevertheless were personal, varied, and subject to contingency.[132] So much so that they defy easy formulation as a system. What does come through is their humanity, as they complained about and resisted the brokerage of others or submitted to it; as they ran away to marry or to cohabit; as they fell under the purview of policing mechanisms and submitted to marriages to correct their illicit cohabitations.

However casually marriages were contracted, the parties understood the importance of marriage as a context for their lives and for forming a family, the essential unit within which they would exercise some leverage on the larger society. Symbolically the contracting of marriages mattered as well for, as Beatrice Gottlieb has stressed, bigamists went "through the complete series of proper procedures" to effect "normal" marriages.[133] By this they defined themselves as respectable citizens, conforming to social expectations. Nevertheless we have seen how young people viewed outside interventions as distasteful, disappointing, and threatening. Outsiders, for example, all too often brokered marriages for reasons of their own and, as a result, sponsored inappropriate matches. Marriage, a supremely organizing moment at the threshold of adult life, could become a fundamentally disorganizing one, as cupidity, passivity, and legalistic interventions based on church doctrine rode roughshod over the sensibilities of the contracting parties.[134]

Yet people learned. Passivity before marriage brokers correlates roughly with youthfulness and inexperience; self-assertion (as can be seen in the way people approached second marriages or, sometimes, preferred to cohabit rather than marry) with experience. The exertion of more control, sometimes only in its negative form, by exercising greater caution, may have come from the higher risks attending illicit second marriages. Nevertheless men and women contracted second marriages in much the same way as they did first ones. Even informal unions, the coupling of men and women without the step of a formal marriage ceremony, replicated the courting process normally issuing in marriages.

So men and women coupled, before, during, and after they married, and sometimes they married twice. When this happened the inquisitors wanted to know why. Bigamists and their spouses tried to explain, and to do so spoke of their marriages, separations, and reasons for marrying a second time. These explanations will be our window on domestic life, the subject of the next chapter.

CHAPTER FOUR

THE PLAZA AND CHURCH OF SANTO DOMINGO,
WITH THE INQUISITION DIRECTLY TO THE RIGHT OF THE CHURCH

Married Life

✝ MARRIAGE AFTER TRENT increasingly came under church control in its design to channel all religious life to the parish.[1] As Tridentine reformers reaffirmed traditional doctrinal positions, they also set out to improve religious practice. And by the end of the seventeenth century (probably earlier in Spain and the Indies), they had succeeded.[2] Married life, however, falling as it did beyond the requirements of attendance at mass and the partaking of the sacraments, barely felt the intrusive winds of Trent. Once marriages had been contracted, domestic patriarchies presided over families, as they always had. Pastoral exhortations urging husbands to respect wives and moderate harsh treatment merely reinforced that authority, for the 'good government' of the family, that most basic of society's cells, depended on the male heads of them as the essential agents of social control.[3]

Parish priests and ecclesiastical judges concerned themselves with family matters, perhaps most particularly with drunkenness and adultery, but had no thought of interfering with the structure of the family. Interventions, when they occurred, acted to "avoid disorder," as François Giraud has noted with regard to cases of sexual violence, and thereby to restore an "equilibrium."[4] But if the church intruded little into the domestic arena, what mechanisms did regulate married life? Probably the traditional ones of popular culture: charivaris, pasquinades, mock trials, ritual humiliations. But once again to traditional ends: to defend patriarchal authority, to protect the local pool of marriageable women, and to insist on the inviolability of sex roles.[5] So the deeply rooted norms of popular culture possessed considerable inertia, thus contrasting, in John Bossy's phrase, with the "silent revolution" of Trent, which moved from the top down.[6] For our purposes the point matters, because it underscores the church's limited engagement with domestic life. Once couples were properly married, clerics had little to say about the quality of life within marriage (the occasional exhortation to act less harshly perhaps accompanied by reference to the iconography of the peaceful domesticity of Mary and Joseph) that would place it in opposition to traditional norms. These, for example, viewed a husband's adulteries as acceptable but a wife's as worthy of death; looked at a husband's beating of his wife (and children) as the exercise of discipline but a wife's beating of her husband as infamous. Although the church had theoretical positions to encourage moderation, these, as we have noted, reinforced the traditional patriarchal order.[7] Deviation from this key norm led to censure by the church and to charivaries and other humiliations through processions and mock trials by the populace. Otherwise clerics, parents, masters and neighbors showed little inclination to intervene in quasi-autonomous household units headed by men.

One might think that the marriages of bigamists, at least first ones, were by definition less successful than those of nonbigamists. But the issue is not so clear-cut. As we shall see, bigamists lived in harmony with partners they eventually separated from as well as in discord. They were adulterous and sometimes ran off with another partner, but who can say whether in greater numbers than the population in general? Separations came often enough because work, debt, and flight from the law occasioned absences and the loss of contact; second marriages followed after a new life had been established. Bigamists contracted them because they thought their first spouse had died, because officials forced them, because they became carried away by passion, or because they thought they could get away with it. In any of these circumstances, bigamists lived out their domestic dramas with the same concerns that anybody else had: getting along, making a living, running a household, raising children, and maintaining links to bosses, patrons, neighbors, and authorities.

SHAKY FOUNDATIONS

As we anticipated in the previous chapter, forcing an inappropriate partner on a reluctant or passive young person may have been a 'marriage' in law but hardly in fact.[8] We saw, for example, the already married Pedro de Valenzuela arrested, put in chains and, with property impounded, held until he married Francisca, a young "woman of the world" he had picked up in a small town of Nueva Granada;[9] the boy Pedro Muñoz Palomir, forced against his will by an ecclesiastical judge in Spain to fulfill a marriage contract arranged by his uncle;[10] and Francisco Rodríguez, procrastinating after promising to marry Isabel Hernández, in order to engage in sexual relations with her, reluctantly fulfilling his promise as he is threatened with death by her relatives.[11] Francisca del Solar's parents surprised Juan Antonio Chacón Gayón alone with her in her house and, threatening to kill him, demanded an explanation.[12] "This one responded," the transcript reads, "'I am with my wife.'" The answer saved his life but committed him to an unwanted marriage. In these cases and others, the objective was to force marriages in order to satisfy family honor. Once that had been done, the men were allowed to escape. Pedro de Valenzuela resumed his journey and sent Francisca back to her mother; Pedro Muñoz fled, eventually to the Indies, without consummating his marriage; both Juan Antonio and Francisco stayed with their wives about two years, without enthusiasm it seems, and then abandoned them.

The cases above point to a society taking marriage as a formal nuptial too seriously. It became an end rather than a means, a legalism to satisfy family honor or protect against scandal. It sacrificed content to form because it lost sight of the long term: family life and a stable environment for raising children. It infringed on the doctrine of consent and it created bigamy as a by-product of forcing couples living in illicit friendships to marry. In time this 'solution' was likely to be discovered and then punished, as a crime against the sacrament of matrimony, a more serious offence than various forms of fornication.

At a first level, weak foundations for married life resulted from the parties simply disliking one another. In Zacatecas in 1572, Petronila Ruiz (born 1555 in Havana) objected so strongly to the marriage her master arranged that he overcame her resistance to it only by locking her up, chaining her, and threatening her.[13] Eventually she 'consented' to marry Francisco de Aguilar, but this was mostly a legalism. She hated Francisco no less as his wife than as his prospective wife, and within two weeks this almost cost her her life. Francisco tried to kill her, and "he would have," Petronila testified six years later (August 22, 1578), "but for the resistance I had in my legs and the other people who stopped him."[14] But these bystanders could not protect her, when Francisco had her alone at home. Here recorded as direct speech by the notary, Petronila gives some details.

> He abused me in many other ways, branding me on my face and on other parts of my body, beating me, selling my clothes, and not providing me with

food because he is an incorrigible man and a criminal so that the said marriage is null because it was forced . . . because in conformity with the law of
God, marriages must be in accord with the will of both persons without the
intervention of third parties.

Francisco's violence, sadism even, was not entirely arbitrary. That he
branded her, for example, symbolizes a degree of control akin to that of
master to slave more than of husband to wife. It suggests that he determined to 'own' Petronila, yet he could not break down her resistance. In
fact just the opposite, for his abuse strengthened her resolve to escape. But
however badly mistreated, Petronila, when dealing with officials, spoke in
legal terms, stressing that lack of consent, not bad treatment as such,
invalidated the marriage. In this she adjusted her language for officials who
she knew would count violated procedures for more than a violated wife.

From Petronila's experience we may infer something of the dynamic
between masters and the servants whose marriages they had arranged.
What in theory constituted the primary relationship, marriage, depended
almost entirely on the secondary one, the master-servant tie. Perhaps
marriages of slaves constituted the extreme. Pascual de los Reyes broke
his primary tie to his master when, about 1737, he ran away, changed his
name, and passed as an Indian.[15] As a matter of course he sacrificed his
'secondary' tie to his wife and fellow slave, María Olaya.

But free servants also, at times, acted in a similar way, as we have seen.
The shepherd Bernabé Cristóbal changed masters in his peripatetic occupation; he also left behind Lorenza María, the woman his former master
had married him to.[16] Pedro Mateo, recruited by his father-in-law in order
to attach him to his household as a worker, ended his marriage when he
went to work elsewhere.[17] Pedro's marriage was created by and depended
on the will of the paterfamilias; its end came as a byproduct of changing
masters. Did this represent a casual attitude toward marriage? Not necessarily, but it does indicate that marriages instigated by and for masters
lived or died because of their continued utility to the master. In a third
case Manuel Romano saw his marriage to the Indian Juana, with whom he
had been living in concubinage, as his master's way to keep him on his
estancia; two months afterward he discarded Juana, when he moved on to
find another job.[18] Even though he contracted it in the presence of a
priest, the marriage hardly made an impression.

These cases represent an instrumental, if not casual, view of marriage
and depended on the agency of the master. As the tie to him loosened, so
too did the marriage tie, a casualty of the *real* marriage between servant

and master. In at least two of the three, the marriage procedures themselves were seen as flawed, at least in hindsight. This became the focus of the mulatto Beatriz Ramírez, who insisted that she had gone through an incomplete ceremonial sequence.[19] In 1560 she and Diego, and Indian vaguero living on an estancia near Apaseo, publicly declared their intention to marry. The banns were read and the priest told them to go to San Miguel el Grande for the marriage, but they never did. Instead they lived together as if they were properly married, until Beatriz tired of Diego's abusive treatment. "Because the said Indian gave her a bad life (mala vida)," she testified to the inquisitors in 1574, "and beat her whenever he saw her, she left." Yet she also admitted that she knew that the exchange of promises had bound her to marry. Her argument that an 'incomplete' marriage was not a marriage merely justified her 'self-divorce' and marriage to another man.

This argument, similar in a way to Petronila's above, shows how people dissatisfied with married life spoke knowingly of lawful and unlawful procedures as a way to justify 'divorce.' The process amounted to a kind of folk casuistry, which made the Tridentine requirement that marriages receive a priest's blessing (velaciones) an escape clause. The trick was to avoid that solemn occasion in order to deny, or pretend to deny, that a marriage had been constituted as final. This could become contentious between married couples. Teresa Núñez, for example, testified (in 1670) that "many times she urged [her husband] Marcos to arrange the nuptial mass because he was delaying it."[20] Another reluctant groom, Manuel Angel Domínguez, calmly acquiesced to a bigamous second marriage but fled at the prospect of going through the upcoming nuptial mass planned by his wife's brother.[21]

Marriages coming out of abductions, more than those that lacked a nuptial blessing, could have an uncertain status. The issue hinged on whether the woman cooperated or resisted. In any case, as we have seen, women were legally minors and therefore not responsible for their acts. Thus running off with a man was termed a "theft" or an abduction. Compliance implied elopement, resistance rape, although the distinction became blurred, and rape was rarely prosecuted.[22]

In fact communities seemed to spend more energy finding illicit but consenting couples than running down rapists. To avoid such policing, some couples stayed on the move. Antonio de la Cruz, serving as a vaguero near Tlaquiltenango (jurisdiction of Cuernavaca, now Morelos state) in 1706, married the mayordomo's daughter, María de la Encarnación.[23] But after six months, Joseph del Vario, a sometime worker on local haciendas and a muleteer, ran off with María (she went willingly, it seems), took her to Amecameca (jurisdiction of Tlalmanalco, Chalco, now part of the Federal District) and lived with her for two years. In the meantime Antonio was "feeling lonely," he said, and took up with the mestiza Rosa Munice. Before the inquisitors twenty years later, he recalled that he and Rosa "moved through all of these towns and provinces covering the territory between the Pacific coast and the Mixteca with the story that she was his wife." As a couple, therefore, they presented themselves as married to cover their informal tie. After two years Rosa became tired of life on the move, terming it a mala vida, and Antonio returned her to her home village, Tistla (capital of an alcaldía mayor, now in Guerrero). And so ended this cohabitation, without rancor and with no further complications.

As for his wife, María, Antonio said that she had "run away" ("se huyó") with Joseph. Joseph, for his part, said that "he abducted María de la Encarnación [while] peddling clothing." Antonio's version makes María the agent of her leave-taking; Joseph's makes himself the agent. What actually happened points, in fact, to a parallel trajectory for María and Antonio, after María dissolved the marriage by running away. Each reformed into a consensual union that lasted two years. Although Antonio eventually married again (hence the reason we know about him), María stayed unmarried. When she testified to the Inquisition in 1732, twenty-six years after running off with Joseph, she was still living in free union, now with one Joseph Garfías, an overseer of orchards in Atrisco (an alcaldía mayor, now in the far west of Puebla state).[24]

Husbands of course did not take it lightly when their wives ran off with other men. Probably without exception, they found such leave-takings humiliating, an affront to their honor, and an excuse for vengeance. Sometimes they pursued with intent to kill both their wives and their abductors. The issue was sensitive enough that even abandoned women who returned to their families and lived 'honorably' might fear the vengeance of husbands. Eleven years after Teresa Núñez and her three daughters returned to her family's house in Guadalajara, she testified (in 1670), her husband Marcos appeared at odd hours of the night to spy on her.[25] Perhaps he hoped to catch her consorting with another man, thereby giving him an excuse to kill her. Such a motive is easily imagined, for Marcos had married a second time, and killing Teresa might have seemed a way to avoid prosecution for bigamy.

Joseph Muñoz de Sanabria announced just such a plan to his second wife, María Rosa, explaining that killing his first wife, Josepha, would 'save' their illicit marriage.[26] This was in 1726, after five or six years of married life, and shortly after María discovered that Joseph was already married. From the Silao jail, Joseph asked María to help him break out. In her denunciation of him (July 6, 1725) she testified that

> in jail he repeated that he would kill his first wife and within six months would go and live with [María] in the North where she was to await him. She said that more likely he would receive his first wife and serve God by living with her. The said Sanabria made so many entreaties that she agreed [to meet him] but only to quiet him so she could go to the Commissioner [of the Inquisition] to report the matter.

On first reading it might seem that María Rosa rejected the plan only because she doubted that Joseph would go through with it. She must have wondered, however, why she should believe that he would compound one crime (bigamy) by committing an even more serious one (murder). Even more telling the comment shows María Rosa imagining a more logical alternative: why not simply resume married life with his legitimate wife?

María Rosa must have been afraid, for she moved quickly to escape Joseph. Yet men may have spoken about killing a wife more commonly than we might have thought. Imagine, for example, Thomasa de Orduña's feelings on hearing her husband, Sebastián, recount his killing of his first wife.[27] She had just told him that a neighbor said he had had another wife and, as she testified later (December 1671), "he said it was true, he had been married, but because he found his wife with a man he had killed her and with that she did not deal with the matter further." If this seems a placid acceptance of Sebastián's self-possessed account, what else could she have done? Society would have agreed that those circumstances justified vengeance. More directly, of course, the exchange reminded her that sexual misbehavior as a married woman brought the harshest possible sanction.

So far we have seen little of day-to-day married life, only some instances of it beginning badly. The unhappy runaways from such marriages often enough denied that a marriage had taken place. They said that they had not given their consent or that procedures had been incorrect or incomplete. Lack of consent, experienced as a personal violation, is most often linked to separating; incompleteness of procedures, a technicality constructed later, to justifying second marriages. Both form part of the discourse on Christian marriage, as did even the tactic to seduce women after promising to marry them. Miguel de Herrera, as we saw, carefully differentiated between betrothal, which was the promise to marry (words of future consent), and marriage (words of present consent).[28] The distinction, a fine one not so visible to his victims, shows him carefully skirting church regulations. It was also seized upon by the older brother of twelve-year-old Gerónimo de Benavides, who promised to marry the widowed hatmaker in order to sleep with her. Before this engagement could become a marriage, he arranged Gerónimo's flight.[29] The innkeeper Leonor Vázquez got into trouble not because she engaged in sexual relations with Christóbal de Ayala, but because she joked with him about marriage.[30] She answered for her irreverence with a whipping, but that was better than the penalty for bigamy; typically for a woman of her station, lashes, abjuration of her error, and three to five years confinement.

Abandoned in the Old World

If men and women found ways to escape impossible marriages and to flee unwanted engagements, they also walked away from marriages considered, at least by others, appropriate and workable. Women left behind by men at least felt abandoned; they wanted their husbands back, their marriages restored, their children supported. Why then did men leave? Not in the main because they were 'pushed' by an unhappy domestic life, but because they were 'pulled' by the larger world. Departure should be seen therefore, as a process rather than an event. It began as men went to war, took a job, began service to a master, or tried out a liaison (all absences presumed temporary) and culminated as husbands moved farther and farther away from their old lives, until finally they shifted to new ones.

The way that three men (Nicolás, Francisco, and Luis) spoke of their leave-takings from married life illustrates the pattern. In 1524 Nicolás Chamorro married Juana de Moñón in Medina de Rioseco (province of Valladolid).[31] Married life lasted "some days," Nicolás said, and [later] Juana gave birth to a daughter. "Afterward," Nicolás testified in 1537, "he went to Valencia and Andalusia to look for a living and was in those parts for three years without returning to his house. Then he passed to these parts [the Indies]. Just as he was about to embark he received word that Juana had died and then he left without inquiring further or knowing [more]."

The second, Francisco García (born 1523), spent his youth in Broças and Campomayor (El Campo[32]) as a swineherd, shepherd, and muleteer, married (in 1551) Violante Ruiz Pizarro, of the numerous Pizarro clan of

Trujillo.[33] After three or four years of married life, he took his four mules and headed for Seville. After he had been gone for some time, Violante went to look for him. Later she testified that she had resented traveling "from place to place, like the gypsies, looking for him."[34] In fact her searching had not been random. Accompanied by her uncle, the weaver Pedro Alonso, she had gone straight to Seville, on hearing that Francisco was there. And as Pedro testified (June 1572), we learn that they found Francisco "living with a mulatto woman and he [Alonso] returned. But Violante stayed three or four months and then came back—three months pregnant—saying that she could not suffer being there any longer because of the bad life that she had with him because of his love for the said mulatto with whom he was in concubinage." Francisco's testimony (July 1579) differs from Pedro's, in that he has Violante returning to El Campo after a few years, not a few months, and himself going to the Indies nine years after that. This makes her the deserter more than the deserted. In Puebla, where he worked for a year as an innkeeper, his paisano Sayago from El Campo (dead by 1579) told him, he said, that Violante had died.

The third, Luis Rodríguez (born 1556) of Moguer (province of Huelva), had been married to María de Cabrera for only three months (in 1575) when he went to Seville to practice his trade of pastry chef.[35] Finding work and settling on Sierpes Street, Luis moved in with Juana de los Reyes, the daughter of another *pastelero*. A couple of years later he heard that María had died, and he married Juana. Six or eight years after that, in 1585, he sailed as a cook on a ship going to the Indies. Although he had been paid only 10 ducats of the 80 he was to receive for the trip (the remainder to be paid on arrival back in Seville), he jumped ship in Vera Cruz and remained permanently in Mexico.

All three of these abandonments, then, began in an apparently innocent way. The search for work took each of the men to Seville, where two of the three established consensual unions. As time passed each became settled in a new life and received 'news' that his wife was dead. Killing the old life (signified metonymically by the wife) validates the new one. As well it correlates with going to the Indies (coming just before departure in two cases and just after arrival in the third), a further step in the creation of a new life.

As men worked their way toward a new life in a new world, women remained behind in their old worlds. So much so, in fact, that in 1525 Seville seemed to the Venetian ambassador to be "in the hands of women."[36] Women expected their husbands to return and became desperate and angry as temporary sojourns turned into permanent disappearances. Witness, for example, the plaintive letter that Isabel Pérez wrote in 1583 to her husband, Antonio de Acevedo, after an eight-year absence.[37] "Every day I miss you, for it seems such a long time and I am so melancholy and wounded by your absence." She related news of the children ("Luis is with my brother Juan Pérez who is teaching him doctrine, virtue, and to read"; "Antonio . . . goes to school and applies himself well"; "Ana is well, and God be served, a good girl and a very gracious young woman"), the cousins, an aunt and uncle ("They kiss your hand many times"), her mother ("better but very tired"), and his father ("He is well and is the butcher of this town"). Although Isabel asks Antonio to send money, she adds: "I would rather see you, for without you I feel so used up and lost . . . that sometimes I feel dead." So Isabel reminds Antonio that his old world is still intact, that it still consists of everything that should matter to him—wife, children, family—and awaits his return to resume his place in it.

In fact Isabel *constructed* Antonio's world as intact, by stressing that nothing essential had changed. She could do this, perhaps, because she had some contact with him through letters. There came a point, however, when women stopped hoping for the return of husbands and turned their energies instead to making a new start. Beatriz González, of Málaga, saw her husband Juan embark for the Levant in 1521. She testified that for ten years "she raised her daughters with much labor and fatigue, without compromising the honor of her person or her life."[38] During this time neighbors and relatives (including in-laws) would "say to me every day that the said Juan González was dead or that he had died in Italy." Eventually she agreed, gave up on her old life, and embarked for the Indies. She justified this course to the inquisitors in the strongest terms: "By right all those who are absent in distant and remote places should be presumed dead so that their wives can remarry without penalty."

Women took longer to give up their old lives because they remained in them, whereas their husbands periodically absented themselves anyway. Beatriz, most immediately, had two daughters to raise. Yet temporary absences after a time seemed permanent, and so women agonized in the eighteenth century no less than the sixteenth. First efforts lay in reestablishing married life to its full integrity, as we can see, for example, in the letter of Mariana de Itá (of Cádiz) to her husband in 1746.[39]

> Agustín, I would like to know what motive you have to not remember a daughter and a wife whom God has given you. I would like to know if it is ill health that causes you not to bother yourself at all. I charge you with enjoying

yourself and forgetting us. Remember you have but one soul and you will lose it for not tending to your obligations . . . and I pray to God that you will return as every day I do *novenas* asking God to bring you back. I think I shall become blind so many tears have I shed.

But years went by, life continued, and abandoned wives had to carry on.[40] They might be absorbed in the household of a father, brother, or brother-in-law, look to live off the charity of a relative of their husband when they had none of their own, or support themselves and their families through their own labor, most commonly perhaps by becoming domestic servants.[41] A common concern, to return to Isabel Pérez's letter to her husband, Antonio, was "to shape these children in discipline and virtue."[42] Another was the social limbo they found themselves in, a "suspension in the air," as one woman termed it, as neither wife nor widow.[42] The urge to transform oneself from deserted wife to widow must have tempted many, for it solved a lot of problems. But a missing husband had to be certified as dead, for no statute of limitations existed. How could a woman find this out conclusively or at least infer it with relative safety?

For one thing they made inquiries. Antón González, pilot of an escort ship in the Indies fleet, remembered how Isabel Gerónimo approached him in 1579.[43]

Five years ago he was passing through Ayamonte on the way to Cádiz. He spoke with a woman there and she, knowing that he had just returned from the Indies, asked him if he knew any men named Cañada in New Spain. He answered yes, that he knew a So-and-so Cañada. 'Know this, then,' she said. 'He is my husband. And this girl that you see'—showing him a young girl by her side—'is his daughter and mine. He has been gone now for twenty-two years.'

With that Isabel entrusted González with letters for her husband.

Catalina Rodríguez made similar inquiries when she approached Father Juan de Pinilla and other travelers from the Indies in search of news of her husband, Christóbal Quintero.[44] Father Juan testified (in 1542) that

two years ago he was at his *posada* in Seville and a woman whose name he does not know came up and asked after Christóbal Quintero, a black staying in Vera Cruz. He told her that he left him married in Vera Cruz to a woman of Castile, that he had shown him a *probanza* [proof] showing that his first wife died. And the woman said 'how could he marry, the evil man as he is my husband and I am alive'.

A year later Catalina spoke to Martín Hernández (a vecino of Seville who probably sailed regularly on the Indies fleet) and sent him back with a strong message for her husband. Here, from his deposition given in Vera Cruz, is how Martín remembered the incident:

It was [Saint Mary] Magdalena's day in July [22] 1539 and he spoke with the said woman and saw her alive. She asked if her husband was alive and he said yes. She then said to tell him that he'd better come to these parts, that he'd better send her money to support her, that if he did not she would go there and take him away from the wife that he now has.

On returning Hernández duly relayed the message and received the response, "she can go to the devil." Hernández, as far as we know, did not upbraid Christóbal for lax morality. But González, the pilot from Ayamonte, eventually ran down Isabel's husband, Pedro Cañada, who was then about to remarry. When Pedro claimed that Isabel was dead, González testified that he had then shouted "you dog, enemy of God, you're lying. I just spoke with her and I left her alive."

So strangers sometimes took the part of the women who enlisted their help to locate husbands and pressure them to send money, to return home, or to abandon illicit marriages or the plans to contract them. However impassioned the anger of González, though, it did not prevent Pedro from going ahead with his marriage. It is equally clear that Christóbal wanted nothing more to do with Catalina.

Was the next step for a woman to go to the Indies? Possibly, if she was in good health, could afford passage, and had family to go with.[45] The last mattered in two ways: it gave women protection for the journey and allies for confronting their errant husbands. After all an absence of eight or ten years amounted to 'divorce.' By the time a missing husband had been found, he no doubt had formed strong ties to a new place, new associates, a new spouse, and new progeny. Now newly rooted, the reappearance of his old life in the form of a wife's message, or worse her arrival, sparked dismay, hostility, and disbelief. We already saw Christóbal's reaction to his wife's threat to take him from his new wife; "she can go to the devil" might very well epitomize most Old World intrusions into the new world of bigamists.

Yet wives persisted by refusing their husbands 'divorces.' Juana de Herrera, in the fourth of five unanswered letters to her husband Francisco Rangel, asked him to return to Mexico City from the north, insisting that she had an absolute claim on him.[46] "Many people here know that you want to [re]marry. Watch what you do, for you are a Christian and my husband and you know very well that before God, when you left you didn't even say farewell and I didn't know a thing about it."

Note that she concerns herself less with the marriage Francisco might contract (perhaps because she knew it would not have legal standing) than the one he has failed to maintain. This ordering repeats itself in her coupling of a warning not to marry with the apparently trivial complaint of his hasty departure. Yet this mattered a great deal, for it symbolized her destitution as an abandoned woman. Her condition rankled all the more because, as she wrote, she had "found out that it goes well with you and that you have money. For the love of God you ought to give some to your daughters who have nothing." In all of this Juana speaks as a woman presuming her marriage to be intact (as indeed it was in the eyes of church and state) and so concludes in the same way: with the formulaic but nevertheless affectionate sign off, "God keep you happy until he lets me see you which is my desire, your wife who esteems and loves you."

Abandoned wives presented a traditional view of married life as companionship, economic partnership, and a project to care for and nurture children. Women wanted this not in the abstract but concretely with the man they married; men wanted it too but in a general way, by reconstituting the model in other places with other women. The pattern can be seen in the case of Francisco del Puerto, who found himself "temporarily" in the Philippines.[47] But time went by, and he became ever more permanently cut off from the happy marriage, two daughters, and network of family and friends that earlier had blessed his life in Málaga. When Francisco told his story to the inquisitors in 1721, he was fifty-four, and by then had been apart from his wife and family for more than twenty years. In Málaga he testified that "many people envied" his happy domestic life, but then a cargo ship in which he had an interest was lost and he therefore fell into debt. "Seeing that he had become a slave, he said to his mother and wife that he would like to go to the Indies to see if he could get on his feet again."

And so he went, with his mother's blessing and his wife's permission. What happened next is not clear, except that Francisco, so far away, got the idea that his wife and mother had died. They did not hear from him for nine years and did not know where he was. His mother, doña Juana de Arriola, in a letter dated October 3, 1705, one of many she wrote to try to reestablish contact gave an idea of the family's distress with Francisco's interminable absence.

> I am completely broken in health because of your absence, or, to say it better, because you have forgotten your obligations. I can see a daughter [in-law] living with many burdens who is carrying them with great virtue. My heart is even sadder when I see the two daughters that you left who are naked, not able to hear the mass for lack of clothing, and with their mother in the same plight. Would that our Lord open your eyes and give you to understand your hardness of heart, for when honorable men, because of the accidents of life absent themselves, they are not thereby freed from meeting their obligations to their wives and children.

Doña Juana's rebuke of her son can stand for the voices of other women (wives, mothers, sisters) left by their husbands in Spain. These range in tone from shrill and angry to fatalistic and resigned. They repeatedly express distress that the head of the household has removed himself from his economic and paternalistic roles as provider and leader. They show us that from the sixteenth century, a divide had opened up in the valuation of domestic life. On one side men, pulled by the wider world, valued marriage and family life relatively; on the other women, focused mainly on their households, valued it absolutely. When a man such as Francisco del Puerto finally got around to thinking about it, he spoke movingly of his former life and happiness in Málaga. But he, like other men who established new lives in the Indies, had reconstituted it in a new place with a new woman. We turn now to follow men whose work and the call of wider worlds pulled them from their marriages.

WORK AND THE LARGER WORLD

So far we have seen that bigamists went to the Indies as a matter of course, to escape debt or a spouse as well as to seek their fortune. The excitement of the early Spanish expansion into new lands exerted a strong pull on men, and Diego de Villareal can stand for the type.[48] He had arrived in Mexico about 1522, in time to play a secondary role in the conquest, and sustained a wound that required the amputation of one leg below the knee.[49] After marrying María de Aguirre in 1529, Diego settled in the town of Santa María de la Victoria [Tabasco] and fathered four children. But in 1544 he went to Peru, lived for a time in Potosí, and as a reward for his role in "pacifying and populating" Tucumán, received an encomienda in the district of Santiago del Estero (probably in 1552).[50] After his departure María knew nothing of Diego's adventures and subsequent life in Santiago where, according to the testimony of an acquaintance in Peru, he moved about on horseback or on a chair carried by his Indians.[51] In fact he had begun a new 'married life,' informally of course, with Francisca de Vega, the "servant" who lived with him for nine years and to whom he left a "quantity of gold pesos" in his will. Back in Victoria, María, after six years, gave up on Diego and remarried.[52]

Francisco, modestly successful in New Spain, abandoned his wife when given the chance to go to Peru. So did Jacobe Luxeri, who left his wife, Inés, in Guatemala City in the early 1540s.[53] Jacobe, however, occasionally saw his wife; after twenty years he saw her for three or four days while en route to Mexico City where he stayed for three or four years; and on returning to Peru, once again for a few days. He then dropped from Inés's sight again for fifteen years. A brief file has nothing in it to indicate what Inés thought about this 'married life.' Jacobe's son Christóbal, however, testified in 1580 that he had gone to Peru around 1556. At the time he was eighteen and intended to collect his inheritance (reports had arrived that Jacobe had died) but found his father alive. Father and son reunited at the mining camp of Almaguer ("eight leagues from Popayán"). Christóbal testified that "reacquainting themselves as father and son," he stayed for two years. Inés waited and finally, in 1579, remarried on hearing (unfortunately falsely once again) that Jacobe had died.

The early period of conquest and settlement pulled forcefully at Jacobe and Diego. But the larger world had pulled men from their homes before the Indies opened up and would do so afterward. For the women left behind, expecting news or the return of their husbands, disappearances amounted to the same thing, whether in the heroic mode to go to Peru or simply to another region in search of work. Pedro Ortiz, for example, gave no reason for leaving his wife, Juana Rodríguez, but in 1570, after about a year of married life, he took her to the town of Sonsonate in Guatemala, left her and their daughter in the household of Gómez Díaz de la Requera, and headed for the province of Mexico.[54] She never heard from him again. From testimony given in 1581 by Francisco Hernández, lieutenant governor and *justicia mayor* of Gracias a Dios, we learn of Juana's life afterward. "Seeing that her husband did not return, send support, or news of himself, the said Juana Rodríguez returned to her father's house in this city and, until she died five or six years ago, Pedro Ortiz never returned and there was no word of him except they heard that they had hanged him in Mexico City.

There is some reason to think that Pedro intended to reestablish a married life with Juana, for had he planned to abandon her permanently, why arrange so carefully her placement in a household? But as we have seen, temporary absences had a way of becoming permanent ones, sometimes in spite of the intention and attempts to reestablish contact.[55] Hernando de Rosas, for example, after living for six years with his wife, Ana de Salazar, in Mexico City, signed on (in 1605) for a tour of duty in the Philippines. "I am the most wretched of men," he wrote Ana in 1615, "for in ten years I have seen only one letter from you even though I have written every year." If he has failed to meet his obligations as a husband, he adds, it has not been "for lack of love, desire, or resources, which, thanks be to God," were considerable. These he cheerfully listed as 1,000 pesos cash, a house worth 600 pesos, two slaves, and successful business enterprises. But they and he remained in Manila, hostage to dangerous sea lanes across the Pacific.

> If I have failed to come to see you it is not my fault but yours. I have written letters, one with auditor Diego de Chandía . . . and twice embarked with my goods (*provecho*) [for New Spain] but they unloaded them, for year after year there is nothing but war and more war. So you can well believe that the fault lies in trying to govern the many enemies of these islands. And so *señora*, my very own, once again I beg you to come to my rescue by letting me see your letter . . .

Work and Mobile Types

If the circumstances of living in an expanding and far-flung empire pulled men away from home, so too did their search for work. Most emphatically here we are concerned with mobile types such as seamen, muleteers, or shepherds, whose work took them from home as a matter of course. We have, for example, a precise chronology of Diego González Carmona's career and can infer how it affected his marriage with Elvira Sánchez.[56] Both came from the mountain town of Araçena (jurisdiction of Huelva) and married in 1578. They lived together for two years and then, in 1580, Diego joined Spanish forces invading Portugal. On returning Diego testified (in his autobiographical statement of 1614) that he was based in Seville for eight years.

> The first four [years] the said Elvira Sánchez, his wife, came to see him from Araçena and she was with him two months until the galleons of don Francisco

Colonna that came to Cartagena were ready and he embarked on them and spent on that armada one year and a half. He returned to Spain and was there another three years and four months in the port of Santa María and in all this time did not see the said Elvira his wife nor hear whether she was dead or alive.

At this point Diego had drifted well away from his married life with Elvira and finished it off by embarking for the Indies "on the fleet of Pedro de Escobar Melgarejo about fourteen or sixteen years ago [1600]"[57] and "it will be about seven years ago [1607] that he married a second time in Mexico City understanding that his first wife was dead."[58]

Other mobile types imposed similar pressures on their marriages. Although muleteers moved shorter distances than seamen, they could nevertheless be lost from view as far as their wives and communities were concerned. Here is how a routine leave-taking could turn into a permanent one. One day in 1731, the muleteer Juan Antonio Mascareñas of Sinaloa, married for thirteen years to Francisca de Armenta, father of four children, left on a job headed for Mexico City.[59] In southern Sinaloa he became sick at the mining camp of Nuestra Señora del Rosario and his boss left him behind. On recovering he was hired by don Juan de Mosquera, based in Acaponeta (an alcaldía mayor, now in the northwest part of Nayarit state), fifty miles or so to the southeast of Rosario to run some mules to Guadalajara; after that he went to Mexico City, to Vera Cruz, and, hired by "a *gachupín*," to Parral. Then he signed on as a soldier in the presidio of Cerro Gordo.

Juan's movements from job to job have a random quality, as if he were a leaf blown by the wind. And indeed the contingent nature of work pulled men from place to place and, little by little sometimes, farther from their old lives. The circumstantial ordinariness of this kind of drift can be epitomized by a 1752 leave-taking of another muleteer, the mestizo Pedro Pablo Rodríguez.[60] He and María Marcelina de Baes had been married for four years when, in the words of the prosecutor's summary of testimony against Pedro,

he told her to make him some tortillas, that he was going to the pueblo of Mascota [jurisdiction of Guachinango, now in Jalisco state] with letters sent by the alcalde major don Christóbal de Mendoza y Alvarado. So he left with this pretext the Friday after . . . the feast . . . of the Immaculate Conception of our Lady the Virgin Mary [December 8] and with word that he would return the following Tuesday but he did not until August 1767.

Pedro therefore disappeared for fifteen years. His failure to return must have baffled María, for she described (in 1768) her married life with him as a happy one, "living together with all peace, love, union, and serenity and her husband made their living . . . and together they urged on some mules that he had with which they maintained themselves comfortably."

What had Pedro been doing in all these years? He as well as the prosecutor seemed hard pressed to give a coherent picture, but here is the prosecutor's summary: "He went to various pueblos and places and *even* practiced the office of shoemaker in . . . the mining camp of Cosalá (Culiacán, Nueva Galicia) where he tried to marry."[61] Pedro confirmed this, adding details about stays in the area of Tepic (an alcaldía mayor by the midseventeenth century, before that in the jurisdiction of Compostela, now in Nayarit state), Zacatecas, and Santa Barbara (an alcaldía mayor in Valle de San Bartolomé, Nueva Vizcaya, twenty miles or so south of Parral, now in Chihuahua state), working sometimes as a groom or shoemaker but always returning to muleteering. The end came on an ordinary trip with the mules (as Pedro testified), when

> Domingo Morán sent him with his [Moran's] mules to San Sebastián [jurisdiction of Copala, now in southern Sinaloa state] to pick up a load of maize. But he did not find any and Morán had him return to Pánuco (jurisdiction of Zacatecas, now in Zacatecas state] and then go to Acaponeta to try to get some. He ran into his brother there and, because he told him that his wife María Marcelina was still alive in Tomatlán [jurisdiction of La Purificación, now in west Jalisco state], he went to Hacienda San Lorenzo. From there he made two trips to the mining camp of San Francisco,[62] one with fruit and the other with meat. Then he went directly to Ameca [jurisdiction of Tala just west of Guadalajara, now Jalisco state] and was put in jail.

Eventually Pedro married a third time (he had married María Marcelina as a widower), after living in an illicit friendship for a year with Juana María Bobadilla. Juana testified that he was "prompted by violence because of the denunciation the judge of the district made that he would banish him unless he married." In spite of the "violence," the marriage can be seen as a kind of ratification of Pedro's life at that moment, drifted into little by little, until it had reached a point far removed from the old life with María.

The answer to a still troublesome question, why Pedro left a 'happy' marriage with María in the first place, remains unanswered. Fortunately the inquisitors also wanted to know, and in response to their query Pedro said that "he did not find [María] sufficiently faithful and rather than suffer the loss of his honor by his wife, he left and thereby did not have to strike her as a jealous husband." Missing are the specifics. Had María become too bold or a little insubordinate at the festival of Concepción? We cannot know. Perhaps Pedro had forgotten or simply spoke formulaically of honor in a way that would make sense to other men. Assuming some basis to the statement, however, we have Pedro recalling what he remembered as a real dilemma, either to "strike" María or to abandon her. In this way a plebeian defended his honor and quit an otherwise happy marriage. If he had too much pride to return to María on his own, the net closing in on him as a bigamist provided the extra push. And the reunion was a happy one. María said that "he greeted and embraced her . . . with expressions of love and of happiness."

Shepherds and Vaqueros

Shepherds and vaqueros, also mobile types, had to be away from their wives regularly and sometimes for long periods. When the Inquisition investigated the marriage of José Francisco Ortiz (born 1743),[63] a shepherd at Hacienda del Pozo, in the district of San Luis Potosí (the hacienda ran sheep and goats in an arid country that required much land to sustain the animals),[64] they received a deposition by Miguel de los Santos López, mayordomo of the hacienda, who testified in 1780 that he had known José "on the rancho called Charco de la Piedra, accessory of the said hacienda of Pozo, since he was about twelve." He had seen "the gathering of people for the wedding and celebration" when José and María married in 1773 and knew that "the hacienda paid the marriage fees." But he did not enter the house at the time of the festivities.

Salvador Carrizal, about seventy and "without a trade before arriving at an advanced age," but then an "ager of stock to be slaughtered," remembered the event only at second hand because he had to be with the animals. Others, busy with their work, Juan Salvador Pérez for example, said much the same thing. As "assistant to the foreman of the goat hacienda, property of the Hacienda del Pozo, he was with the livestock as required by his occupation." Nevertheless Juan knew José and his wife María Josefa for about two years, and his testimony gives a clear picture of the married life of shepherds.

The said María Josepha did not actually live on the goat hacienda but at Pozo [where] the rancheros normally keep their wives. They [the goatherds] always run around—they're like couriers [*correos*] doing different jobs in distant places—and it is more comfortable for the wives to stay on the said hacienda although that does not mean that they do not have a married life as much as they can.

This pattern of marriage, sketched so clearly by Juan, allowed for liaisons, concubinage, and bigamy or polygamy. The mulatto shepherd Alonso de Alvarado, for example, had three wives.[65] Moreover, the prosecutor of the Inquisition charged, "he usually had an Indian woman as his companion" while herding sheep near San Miguel el Grande. Not until 1691, twenty-five years after his first marriage, did his loose way of life catch up with him, for it easily went unnoticed as men moved long distances with flocks, lived away from towns and even small settlements, and left their wives behind. One of Alonso's wives, Agustina, remembered her "needless" jealousy of Alonso's Indian consort, whom she had begun to beat: "She stopped when a man told her 'señora, don't beat her, because Alonso de Alvarado told me that you are not his wife'." Only a licit wife need bother to beat her husband's mistress.

MALA VIDA AND DISCORD

If work pulled men from their marriages, the mala vida (abuse, overwork, lack of support, beatings) pushed women from theirs. Women engaged the problem in a discourse informed by norms of Christian marriage, for common as the mala vida was, it was so designated as the inversion of some sort of ideal *buena vida*. We saw above, for example, that friends and neighbors recognized Francisco del Puerto's marriage in Málaga as an enviable one.[66] The tanner Joseph de Luque, who saw Francisco and his wife María daily in the 1690s, testified in 1707 that "they were a husband and wife with more affection than other married couples; they did not quarrel or inflict the mala vida on one another but always were very lovingly married." Debt rather than discord pushed this couple apart, but with most marriages, 'external' forces such as debt cannot be disentangled from 'internal' ones such as discord. The first often provided the pretext and the second the motivation for separating. Here, nevertheless, we shall highlight directly expressed dissatisfaction with marriages, often termed the mala vida, as an indication that men and women chose to begin new lives because their old ones had become unsatisfactory.

Joseph makes clear that the mala vida could be inflicted by either partner on the other. In fact, however, men imposed it on women far more often than women on men, as they directed or neglected the affairs of their households. Law and custom supported male dominance and assumed male superiority. "In wisdom, skill, virtue and humanity," Juan Ginés de Sepúlveda wrote, men surpassed women just as Spaniards exceeded Indians and adults children.[67] The role of husband and father, however, included reciprocal duties and the benevolence associated with ideals of paternalism. Mariana Monroy of Guadalajara recognized the discrepancy between ideals and reality when she bridled at her servant-like condition as wife (she married in 1663) of the peninsular Manuel de Figueroa.[68] She testified (in her autobiographical statement of 1678) that he made her rise at one o'clock in the morning to do household chores, and "if she did not do things to his liking he abused and beat her many times." Three years of this culminated when Manuel beat Mariana for failing to serve him "as quickly as he wanted," and she fled to the house of Manuel de Escalante, prosecutor of the audiencia of Mexico City.

The move came after considerable thought, it seems, for by then she said that she "hated him and always lived in discord with [Manuel] because he made her work so much." More tellingly she had a way to turn this into an argument for divorce, by prefacing her feelings with the point that "she married against her will." The last counted as an argument to invalidate the marriage. Mariana intended, it seems, to have it put before a court, to argue for annulment on the grounds that the doctrine of consent had been violated. But after waiting all day for Escalante to appear, Mariana gave up (perhaps in the knowledge that the justice system, just as individuals, hesitated to intervene in another man's domestic affairs) and instead took refuge in the convent of Santa Catalina, where she remained from Shrovetide until Holy Week, a period of about six weeks. Only then, because she believed (wrongly as it turned out) that the viceroy was going to punish Manuel by sending him to the Philippines, did she take leave of her sanctuary.[69]

That Mariana believed this shows how she thought her society worked. She thought it natural that the highest official of the kingdom, proxy of the king himself, would concern himself with her mala vida and, solely on the basis of her friend's complaint, exile her husband. The weak, the abused, and the victimized looked to benevolent protectors to act on their behalf.

In her autobiographical statement as well as in later ones (the response to the indictment and a specially requested supplementary hearing after all evidence had been presented), Mariana returns to the themes of consent and mistreatment. The first, without detail, acts merely to frame the bitter list that itemizes Manuel's tyranny, beatings, and merciless slave driving. To Manuel, Mariana's loathing was also a protest and evidence of her lack of subservience, a challenge to his male authority that must have intensified his harshness. Summing up their relationship at the end of the trial, Mariana characterized it as one of "continuous war, disagreement, and disunion."

Manuel's defective character, Mariana concluded, accounted for the trouble, and in an inspired leap she associates this with heresy. "He has a perverted nature, so bad and so disturbed that she decided that the said marriage was null and void and invalid. In her view it was as if he were a heretic and she considered [the marriage] no longer binding." The progression outlined by Mariana therefore is framed by lack of consent but moves from bad treatment to defective character to "as if a heretic," the first and last both grounds for annulment.

Not many instances of the mala vida can be documented in so much detail. If all wives coming into their husband's households entered as outsiders and subordinates, they nevertheless expected some limitation to their subservience. This came at the hands of husbands who imposed a servant like condition, a kind of 'indenture,'[70] as we just saw, and at the hands of mothers-in-law.[71] The mulatto Lucía Guadalupe testified in 1744 that she had put up with five years of married life beginning in 1726, "until she had to run away to this village [Córdoba] because of the bad treatment (mal trato) from her mother-in-law, Juana de Pisa, and her husband, the mulatto Antonio de Pisa."[72]

Lucía ran away "accompanied by the Indio ladino Antonio Ramos," according to her neighbor Leocadia Gertrudis. She made her way from Izúcar (an alcaldía mayor, now in Puebla state) to Córdoba and became a servant in the house of don Rafael de Olivera. But thirteen years later, she declared that she "desired to rejoin her husband whenever possible." But what an odd turnabout (was it tailored just for the inquisitors?) after so much effort to remain out of Antonio's hands. He, at least for a time, had searched high and low for her. A glimpse of him looking comes from the deposition (in 1744) of the Spaniard Juan de Pastrana, who ran into Antonio in the village of Xalostoc (jurisdiction of Cuernavaca, now Morelos state). "He was crying while telling the story of Lucía's flight and asking help to search for her." On the one hand, then, Antonio mistreated his wife; on the other, he grieved her running away. Most likely the grief had more to do with loss of face than change of heart. More importantly Lucía 'solved' her own problem, a point that can be underscored from Leocadia's account of Lucía running away "accompanied," not abducted, by Antonio.

The Spaniard María Guadalupe Delgadillo Hernández, some fifty years later, also traced her mala vida to her mother-in-law.[73] She ran away twice, the first time in 1773, after a year of married life, the second after being returned to and living with her mestizo husband for another nine months.[74] What went wrong? María testified (in her autobiographical statement of 1780) that she ran away to escape the "punishments and bad treatment" of José and his mother. But before that she had also "explained to José that she would leave him if he did not treat her better." She had also asked the parish priest to intervene. And later, from Mexico City, she wrote letters. None of this did any good. If anything her complaints made things worse and strengthened the resolve of mother and son to tame her. In this José's mother took the initiative: she restricted María to the house, barred José from giving María even a half real, and forbade him to sleep with her. This, then, was the content of the mala vida for María. Young as she was (fourteen at marriage), she resisted such treatment and, in a letter, told José that he had violated "the obligations of matrimony." In effect, therefore, he had abandoned her, not vice versa, as was true literally.

Women, from the examples we have seen, experienced the mala vida as soon as they married, but endured it for a time (three years in two cases, one year plus another stint of nine months in the other). A male version of the mala vida also appears in bigamy testimony, but it seems to refer mostly to problems of 'insubordination.' María's husband José no doubt would have viewed in this way her refusal to acquiesce in her servile condition. With an unruly wife, he would be subject to taunts and possibly the organized demonstration of a charivari, calling into question his manhood.[75] Men could euphemize this as "various discords," as did don Joseph Serrano y Mora in characterizing his marriage (in 1760) of only four months to doña Francisca Ricarda Molina of Málaga.[76] A dispute led Francisca to return to her mother's house,[77] and when don Joseph went to get her, his mother-in-law's servants ejected him from her house. The incident wounded his pride. Referring to it fourteen years later, he testified that he had been "shamed by this insult to his honor" and so went to Carcabuey, to Cádiz, and then to the Indies. Doña Francisca said that she did not know where, but she must have known why, don Joseph had gone.[78]

Whatever the "various discords" had been, don Joseph abandoned doña Francisca because he had failed to maintain authority over his wife and therefore lost face. In this he underscores a difference from the mala vida as experienced by women. Unhappily married men did not suffer 'discordance' for so long. The mestizo Nicolás Antonio de Arauz managed just four months with the Indian Dominga María whom, as we saw in chapter 3, he took to Mexico City and married (in 1735) with the patronage of Pedro the waterman.[79] In the dock six years later, he recounted a brief and troubled marriage "with her in the house of his padrino, whom he helped carry water to the houses, . . . and because he could not stand his wife with whom he had no peace, he left her and went to the rancho of Nicolás Díaz with his uncle, Pedro de Arauz, an Indian tributary."

Díaz had raised Nicolás, and so this represented a homecoming, even though the older man by then had died. His widow, the mulatto Rosa, and two sons took Nicolás in tow and "at different times" asked if in the time he had been away from their house he had married. Nicolás always answered no. So they counselled him to marry the Indian María Rosa, a girl of sixteen or eighteen of "unknown parents" from Guachinango (an alcaldía mayor, now in Jalisco state), who worked as a house servant. Nicolás said that he agreed, "thinking that in the epidemic [1736] his first wife would have died." Nicolás's denial that he was married and his silent wager that his first wife had succumbed (a common and plausible supposition in an age of cyclical epidemics and high mortality rates) shows us a man who had put a brief but unsuccessful old life behind him.

While the mala vida for women meant mistreatment, abuse, and overwork, for men it meant 'discord,' a less-specific term that included insubordination, disaffection, and conflict. Husbands viewed this unruliness as the cause of the "discord," as did the muleteer Juan de Santana Izquierdo, who in 1783 used the term to characterize his unhappy married life with the mulatto Josepha Castellanos in Piguamo, a village in the mountainous zone of Michoacán (jurisdiction of Zapotlán, now in Jalisco state).[80] "After six years, having had various disagreements (discordias), he went to the pueblo of Tamazula [still in the region of Zapotlán, about forty miles to the north] where he has been married now for four years with the Indian Juliana Valerio, vecina of the said pueblo, daughter of Margarita la Ortega and an unknown father." Juan's statement highlights a simple sequence: discord, leaving, remarriage. If bigamists created new lives for themselves, this one began with the 'push' of an unhappy old life rather than the 'pull' of the larger world.

BEATINGS

Probably more than is usually thought, violence was part of the day-to-day content of married life. Thus it would be a mistake to think of it as abnormal or aberrant. It only becomes visible, however, at the extreme, when women complained that beatings had become excessive, even life-threatening, and cited them as the reason for running away. When women talked about beatings as an element of the mala vida, they were therefore making a distinction between the slaps, cuffs, and rough language that constituted everyday 'correction' and the sustained, full-fledged attacks with weapons as well as fists and feet that threatened life and limb. Women tolerated the former to a degree but also tried to combat it by using the spells and potions of witches, by seeking protectors, and most frequently, by running away.[81] Men dissatisfied with married life less rarely used witchcraft but mainly resorted to violence or, as we have seen, abandoned their wives.[82]

The married life of the mestiza María de Villagrán with the mulatto Domingo gives an indication of the place of beatings in a marriage.[83] It began in 1566 as a kind of elopement. Domingo "took her" (*la sacó*) from the home of the storekeeper in Mexico City who had raised her, probably as an orphan, and who used her as a servant. Domingo began to live with María without marrying her, and officials arrested him, placed him in the viceregal jail, and called in a priest to hear their vows and to bless them. Afterward the couple went to Cuernavaca. The marriage ran a stormy course during its fifteen years, it seems, for María ran away at least twice (almost surely on occasions when Domingo had beaten her), only to be returned home.[84] She testified (in her autobiographical statement of 1586) that in one beating "ten or twelve years ago, her husband abused her with lashes and wounds and left her for dead and she never saw him again." Here the beater, not the beaten, ran away, perhaps fearing that he had gone too far and wishing to avoid complications with authorities.[85] Meanwhile María recovered and returned to Mexico City. We cannot document the degree to which Domingo's most violent outbursts poisoned his relations with María, but we must assume that they were extreme moments in a pattern of scores of lesser beatings in their years together. That such a marriage could survive for so long (when she did run away it must have been only to temporary refuge, until Domingo sobered up or cooled down) suggests that women tolerated considerable violence from husbands.[86]

But how much? When had a beating gone too far? Domingo's occasion to flee, after leaving a woman for dead, marks one extreme but no guide for moderation in the long term.[87] These, such as they were, appeared in church confessional manuals. They are useful because they focus not on theological abstractions but day-to-day pastoral concerns.[88] Fray Jaime de

Corella's instruction, in a manual for confessors, allows for undisputed male authority but calls for it to be exercised with moderation: "The father is the true head of his family . . . [yet] any person in a superior station [must] be an example of good to his subjects; otherwise he sins against justice."[89] But how to apply this? Corella demonstrates in a dialogue between penitent and confessor.

> P: Father sometimes I lose control when I punish her; otherwise I cannot control her and she does not carry out her domestic duties. Other times I just treat her badly for no particular reason.
> C: When there is a legitimate reason it is licit (*lícito*) that a husband punish and even strike (*poner manos*) his wife, but with moderation and to the end that she mend her ways.

"Yet all authorities agree," Corella adds, "that a husband may not punish his wife without reasonable cause, for arbitrary punishments severely administered are a mortal sin."[90] The problem becomes one of who monitors arbitrariness and severity. Consider Corella's three didactic possibilities from the penitent's opening statement: that husbands often lose self-control as part of the process of wife control; that husbands must discipline wives to prevent their neglect of "domestic duties"; that husbands sometimes treat wives badly "for no particular reason." Corella has thus isolated real problems inherent in family patriarchies (because unchecked power over others corrodes the self) but has no solutions. How could he, for he accepts the premises of patriarchy and thus leaves husbands to decide for themselves what constitutes 'moderate' and efficacious punishments.[91] Punishments were not only licit but necessary, and no extrafamilial mechanism controlled when and how they would be administered.

This left women to cope as best they could with their individual patriarchies, and they must have done so in a variety of ways. For every woman who ended such treatment by running away, many others must have endured it. The cases of running away themselves suggest the pattern. María Jesús de Encarnación of mulatto-Indian extraction testified (in her autobiographical statement of 1781) that she "lived quite a few years of married life at Hacienda de los Hornos [jurisdiction of Lagos, now in the northeastern part of Jalisco state]" before she ran away (to Acámbaro, to Pátzquaro, and then to Valladolid), "because [her husband] José punished her."[92] The statement, a mere summary without the circumstantial detail we would have preferred, nevertheless makes clear that a beating occasioned running away and that she fled only after a considerable time.

The marriages of María de Villagrán and María Jesús indicate that women tolerated violence from husbands for years, until such treatment no longer seemed 'normal' to them but instead excessive and gratuitous. The moment of truth, when it could no longer be tolerated often came during a fiesta, when a man's honor was on public display, and accompanied by alcohol, when his judgment was clouded.[93] It could be precipitated by real or imagined unfaithfulness, insubordination, neglect of household duties, or no reason whatsoever, except a compulsion to demonstrate control and authority.

María Jesús used the word *punish* (*castigar*) to characterize the beating, and this can serve as a clue for bridging the normative and practical assumptions about wife beating. As we have already observed in the confessional manual, pastoral theology authorized the "laying on of hands," that is beatings, stipulating that they be corrective and therefore edifying. To the degree that a woman accepted this idea (and most surely did), she would tolerate, or at least resign herself to 'disciplinary' treatment. To the degree that she observed it to be 'irrational' and arbitrary, brought on perhaps by too many fits of jealousy or bouts of drinking, she might declare the treatment intolerable. The open-ended and vague notion of corrective punishment always put women on the defensive. The burden of proof lay with women, but to what end: not to deny a husband's right to punish, only to gain the ruling that he had abused it. This could be secured with difficulty, for judges presumed 'provocation'.[94] In fact the testimony of women in general was discounted by the court system (as was that of Indians), especially in complaints of rape and violence.[95] Husbands, therefore, largely acted on their own counsel, held the preponderant power, and received the support of legal institutions. Because they controlled the occasion and administered the blows, anger, jealousy, alcohol, and even sadism could cloud judgment and lead to ever greater excesses.

Women had some basis for objecting to beatings, therefore, when they became detached from their corrective function and degenerated into arbitrary abuse. But they had to make this distinction before they could give themselves a legitimate reason to resist. Mariana Monroy, as we have seen, did just that in pronouncing her husband "perverted" because he treated her so cruelly.[96] Neighbors and others within the same or neighboring households closely observed wife abuse but rarely intervened; they tended to describe its results in detached terms.[97] Such a tone characterizes testimony describing the beatings endured by Rosa Maldonado who, as a young widow twenty-five (in 1767), eloped with Juan Nicolás and settled on a rancho near Guadalcázar owned by Juan's mother.[98] Juan's brother Antonio and his wife María, also residing at the rancho, observed at close range Juan's treatment of Rosa. María testified in 1774 that she "saw the injuries—they were reddish bruises—that Juan used to give her, especially when she fought with him." *Especially* when she fought, but apparently not *only* then and "when *she* fought with him," not vice versa. Juan's blows did not amount to 'fighting'; Rosa's resistance did.

Francisco Xavier Albiro, a "miner and farm laborer" doing seasonal work at the rancho, corroborated María's impression in a deposition given a few days before María's. "For periods her face was free of any marks indicating that she had not suffered abuse but mainly when she quarreled with her husband he beat her senseless leaving her unable to talk." Francisco traced the beatings to Juan's "excitable and choleric temperament" and like María related them to Rosa's arguing back. Yet he did not say whether he thought them excessive. Local officials seemed to consider them so, however, and at least once placed Rosa in protective custody by "depositing" her in the household of a third party. But protection arranged by local officials would only have been temporary. Except in extreme cases, wives were always delivered back to their husbands; and so was Rosa.

How can Juan's 'punishments' of Rosa be explained? First, as we have seen, the ethos of patriarchy allowed it, encouraged it, and failed to set limits to it. Second, Rosa was an attractive woman and flirted (so Juan would have thought) with other men. Francisco described her as a small woman with "olive skin, curly hair, full figure, small nose, and good-sized eyes who was known for her lively singing and dancing at the dances." Such lack of modesty, attracting the attention of other men no doubt, would have incited Juan's jealousy, the basis for much family violence in colonial Mexico.[99]

Third, Rosa's tendency to fight back caused her additional grief. Because men expected submission from women, resistance would have intensified Juan's anger. She above all would have known this, yet she defended herself against her strongly built husband. That she did so not just once but habitually thereby challenged his authority as a male. This, to Juan and to most men, marked her as defiant and deserving of harsher blows. We have no way of knowing if Rosa expected Juan to become more moderate. Certainly she had little reason to think that Juan's family and friends or local officials would intervene. Yet she refused to change her personality or appearance. Perhaps most of the time she bought peace by affecting a modest demeanor while becoming more unrestrained at the *fandangos.* In the end, however, the beatings took their toll and reduced Rosa's options to one, that of running away.

To a modern sensibility, it may seem surprising that women endured harsh treatment for long periods. They did so because they expected to be dominated by their husbands. To think otherwise would have gone against some of the deepest assumptions of the society. Only the cruelest domestic tyrannies pushed women into revolt, as we can see from the married life of the mestiza María Ignacia Cervantes, a girl of fourteen when she married the tanner Ramón Anastasio García in 1767.[100] Replying to the official arraignment, she testified in 1788 that

> two weeks after having married, she began to suffer the mala vida with her first husband in whose company she remained for about five years experiencing abuse from her husband, from her mother-in-law, and from two sisters-in-law. . . . Her husband gave her the mala vida and treated her with the greatest cruelty as she can let you see in [the scars from] eight wounds he gave her. Various blows and other abuse caused her to abort six times. . . . Having had her fill of this mala vida and left alone in Marfil while Ramón was away, she joined in concubinage with Raymundo, a young black soldier who was unmarried.[101]

María's summary makes clear, then, that she endured a great deal of abuse over a long time, maintained some sort of intimate life with Ramón (witness her six conceptions), and finally reached a point where she determined to escape. The first leave-taking was temporary. Ramón found her, took her home, and the mala vida continued. It took sixteen years before she made a decisive break, and this time she went alone instead of with a companion. In her first destination, the town of Silao, she had hoped "to change her luck," for with Ramón, she "found herself held back." Although María's departure must be seen against the backdrop of her mala vida, it is remarkable that she focused not merely on escaping what she could no longer tolerate but on creating a new life that would be more satisfying. María manifests this spirit in her critical attitude toward her first job, as a house servant of one señora Franças. "She did not like the arrangements," she said, and therefore quit after a week. Although we have fewer details than we would like, there is enough to see that María emerges from the punishing years of married life not as a 'battered wife,' but as a woman with direction and self-assurance as she sets out on a new life.

In cases of violence, the claims of women against husbands were rarely received sympathetically by judges. A final example is therefore invaluable, because it puts the violent treatment of women in the framework of community norms. We return to 1559, when Luisa de Vargas (she married Alonso Franco in Seville in 1556) went with him to Mexico City.[102] An outline of their life together emerges from the file after they had lived for three years in barrio Santa Catalina. The merchant Juan García Montero, for example, a friend of Alonso's who lived in an adjacent house, testified that one day he entered Alonso's house and saw Luisa with her "entire face scratched (*arañada*), bruised, and covered with blood."[103] He asked her what had happened, and she told him that Alonso had come home drunk the night before and, with sword unsheathed, chased and beat her.

Juan confirmed Luisa's story in a conversation with Catalina Hernández, a neighbor who, in a deposition of 1566, also recounted a separate incident.

Four years ago [1562] Franco left Mexico City and entrusted Luisa de Vargas in her keeping. After four or five days he returned at night after she had locked up. Shortly afterwards the said Luisa yelled from the window facing the street 'open up sister, my husband is killing me.' She opened [the window] and saw Luisa with her hair disheveled, naked, and covered with dirt as if it had been plastered all over her, as if she had been dragged along the floor. She went to Luisa's house and found Franco asleep on the bed, his naked sword near his head, and the sheath on the floor.

Other neighbors observed Alonso's violent treatment of Luisa. Pedro Montalvo, a twenty-four-year-old merchant, testified in 1566 that "without any reason that he could understand Franco wanted to kill Luisa, threatening her with his sword." He also remembered the time when Alonso "shattered a small box by hurling it at her head." His summing up of the neighborhood villain marks him as deviant from norms another man would consider correct: "Franco is a vagabond and not a man to support his wife and when he is away from this city he doesn't leave her a *tomín*. He also heard that he has a mistress in Guanajuato." His comment, however, stays with the issue of lack of support rather than with excessive violence.

By 1567 or so Luisa had had enough of this life and went to a neighbor for advice. From this came her petition to divorce Alonso, and the inquisitors asked Luisa about it. She said that "she does not know anything about what a divorce is except that three years ago [1567] she wanted to separate from Franco. She communicated with a woman who was a vecina in barrio

San Pablo who said that she had to file a petition before the vicar general of the archdiocese." The petition was drawn up while Alonso was in Toluca selling cacao, but Luisa did not follow through with it after he returned. The reason, she testified, was that she lacked the energy because she was "weak and sick." Nevertheless that document summarizes Luisa's complaints as of that moment:

> many and various times numerous and cruel blows without cause or reason . . . with his sword he slashed her face and cut her lips; he has sworn that he would kill her; he called her a whore and a bitch; he does not want to give her support although he has seen her suffer hardship and hunger; he ordered her not to associate with decent folk after their marriage; after they married he committed adultery with other women and left her for them. [All of which illustrates his] bad way of living and she asks for divorce and restitution of all the goods and pesos of gold that he received in dowry when they married and all else that pertains to her.

At some point during this dismal period, Luisa asked her brother, Gaspar de Vargas, an alderman of Oaxaca, for help. This had some effect, for out of fear that Vargas would kill him, Alonso fled to Acapulco. In fact Vargas had had little regard for Franco from the beginning and according to Hernando Sánchez Merino, Luisa's second husband, had said that "Franco did not have the quality to be his sister's husband and rather than see them married he threw them out of his house." This referred to the start of the relationship, when Alonso, apparently, had already seduced Luisa and for the sake of family honor they were passing as married. Hernando entered the picture as an interloper; he said that he had known Luisa "five or six years" before marrying her in 1569, during which time he had had "carnal access" to her. Thus his liaison with Luisa occurred during the period when Luisa's mala vida with Franco was at its worst and therefore it may have triggered Franco's jealousy and violence. Hernando, for his part, justified the liaison on the grounds that "he always intended to marry her, taking her for a woman free of impediments [to marry]" (perhaps to portray himself as unknowingly a party to adultery) "although not going ahead until this was certified."

Without the benefit of a divorce from Alonso, Luisa married Hernando and, as one acquaintance put it, "they remained very contented with each other." Luisa, on her own initiative but with support from a brother and lover, left the mala vida with Alonso and established a more rewarding life with Hernando. At first she considered filing for divorce but, as with so many other cases of separation, gave up on legal procedures and instead relied on the unofficial channels of family and her own initiatives to effect a 'self-divorce.'

ADULTERY, NEW PARTNERS, NEW LIVES

Adultery strained marriages but in itself did not break them. Society, after all, accepted a double standard, and men sought adulterous liaisons at the same time that they insisted on their wives' fidelity and their daughters' chastity. Thus the Spaniard Miguel de Acosta's good-humored admission (in 1777) of his adulteries exemplified a pattern: "one and another peccadillo (*fragilidad*) with some other woman" during a six-year marriage to Ignacia de Castro, he said, without "treating her [Ignacia] badly and without ceasing to have conjugal relations with her."[104] Ignacia saw it differently and testified that "Miguel treated her very badly perhaps because he was illicitly involved with Teresa de Anaya, unmarried, resident of this town [Molango, jurisdiction of Meztitlan, now Hidalgo state]." We have, then, contrasting visions of adultery: the first regards it as a matter of little consequence, harmless to married life; the second, as the source of her "mistreatment." Still Ignacia remained tentative, as if a husband's infidelities did not necessarily ruin marriages.[105]

However discordant the double standard for wives, they probably acquiesced in it, worked to regain their husbands' affections, and tried to keep temporary liaisons from becoming permanent.[106] The latter would mean serious trouble: abandonment, withdrawal of support, and, more likely than not, children to raise alone. Yet how could women prevent such drift, when mobile occupations offering occasions to establish and renew illicit friendships routinely took husbands away from their wives for shorter or longer periods? Here is a typical instance, when in 1714 Josepha de la Nava saw her husband Miguel de Herrera off. "He said he was going with someone who was going to pay him a peso a day," she testified in 1722, "and would be back in four months."[107] In fact he roamed about, seduced a number of women, and eventually married one of them. Josepha, in the meantime, remained in Mexico City and in eight years saw Miguel only three times.[108] It seems doubtful that in the beginning Miguel intended to abandon Josepha, but finally one of his liaisons in Michoacán pushed him into that step. By the time he stopped by to pick up a hat left behind with Josepha (two visits in May may suggest that he was monitoring the condition of the now ill Josepha and hoping for her demise, thus to remove the evidence of his crime), his new life was well established.

Wives feared adultery if it portended abandonment. If the mulatto María Robles seemed to accept that her husband, the mulatto Felipe Rodríguez, would have sexual relations with other women from time to time, she drew the line when a liaison threatened to break up their marriage.[109] As she summarized twenty-five years of married life that had begun in 1738, she noted that Felipe's work as a muleteer frequently took him away from their home in Zumpango (jurisdiction of Guautitlan before the late seventeenth century and alcaldía mayor afterward, now the northern part of Mexico state). After several years of married life and seeing the birth of three children, Felipe left and stayed away for four years. When María tracked him down, he was living with a woman named Gertrudis. To get him to come home, she threatened to report him to don Antonio Correa (a man who acted as a patron to her?), formerly "captain" of the audiencia chamber. Felipe returned, this time for five or six years and the birth of three more children. His next long period of truancy began in an ordinary way, when Felipe departed with a mule team owned by Joseph Morales. After about a year, María again found him, this time in Mexico City, and brought him home. And once again, María recounted in testimony she gave in 1775, she conceived a child but miscarried. The absences punctuated by the homecomings in María's account, therefore, correlate with the birth of her children, as if she sought to emphasize that Felipe, not somebody else, had fathered them.

She also noted a third long absence, "seven or eight years ago [ca. 1767], and for no reason at all, for there was no quarrel, anger, or anything else." Indeed not, for from Felipe's testimony we learn that he had then realized that he was tired of María and simply left. It might be inferred that married life for Felipe and María had been a tenuous matter for some time. Without María's initiatives to bring him home, Felipe two or three times seemed well on the way to drifting out of the marriage. However frequent his trips, together with occasional longer periods away, the marriage still confined Felipe too closely, it seems, and there came a point when he determined to separate permanently. But note how María and Felipe disagreed on why this happened with María unable to imagine a 'motive,' even though she had lived with Felipe's erratic pattern of absences for nearly twenty years.

María and Josepha expected their husbands to be away for varying intervals. Josepha, for example, spoke of Miguel's projected four-month absence to work for a peso a day as if it were routine. Nor did María worry when Felipe was away for similar periods. María also tolerated the adulteries that seemed to go with Felipe's absences, as long as they did not imply a cessation of their marriage. The liaison with Gertrudis, for example, had had such overtones, and she found a way to stop it. A distinction can be made, therefore, between liaisons of short and long duration. Both of course were sins and officially prohibited; both consumed time and resources to which wife and family had prior claim. Yet a short-lived, passing adultery did not threaten a marriage, until it became a regular liaison and the basis for another life.

At that point, with her husband 'permanently' living with another woman, a wife might give up hope. At least the mulatto Juana Martínez did, after a five-year marriage to Andrés Ramírez, also mulatto.[110] It began at an hacienda near Querétaro "on Tuesday, the day before Ash Wednesday in the year after the *matlazáhuatl* [epidemic] of 1738," Juana testified in 1750, when she and Andrés "married and received the nuptial blessing." In fact it was a group wedding, probably to regularize a number of informal unions, as Juana's aunt and "many others" from the hacienda also married. Afterward they feasted in the quarters of Juana and Andrés with "all the servants of the hacienda present." The newlyweds stayed at the hacienda for ten months, then went to Guadalajara (six weeks), Mexico City (four months), back to the hacienda (ten months), and then to Ocoyoacac (jurisdiction of Tenango del Valle, now in Mexico state), where for three years they both served a priest. Then Juana left Andrés, she said, "because living in concubinage with Agustina Quesada, he subjected her to the mala vida."

Juana's charting of her married life with Andrés seems a fairly routine prologue to the central point: she left him. The wording here matters. She might have reversed it, to convey that Andrés left her. That she did not underscores the assumption that taking a mistress did not in itself mean abandonment of a wife. Notwithstanding Agustina, Andrés had not left Juana, but Agustina's presence in the marriage meant the mala vida for the rightful wife.

Eventually Juana attacked Agustina with a club and tried to kill her two children. The judges, in fact, ordered her not to speak to or attack her rival. Yet the children were an inviting target, for Andrés had fathered them (the eldest was then six, thus indicating that the liaison had been going on at least since he married Juana). But why strike at this moment, and why target the other woman instead of Andrés himself? The timing links to Juana's realization that she indeed had been supplanted. That she attacked Agustina instead of Andrés points, once again, to the disparity in power between husbands and wives. Instead of lashing out at Andrés directly, Juana chose the safer course of attacking the rival who had displaced her.

If losing a husband to a mistress was a process, at the early stage wives might see the danger signals in the loss of affection and support. Francisca de Torres, for example, a woman of sixteenth-century Seville, had to cope with her wayward husband, Gómez de León (she married him in 1558), who openly associated with prostitutes, had mistresses for shorter or longer periods, and gambled away his substance.[111] His friend and compadre, Christóbal Ruiz,[112] bluntly said (testifying in 1572) that in the early 1560s Gómez had been "a whoremonger who gave the mala vida to his daughter." He recalled that Francisca, addressing him as "señor compadre," asked, "why had he consented to the said Gómez her husband associating with other women?" Francisca therefore links her distress, at least in part, to her husband's adulteries, which, in Christóbal's emphasis that Gómez was giving the mala vida to his daughter, not his wife, suggests nonsupport. By this time, in fact, Gómez had confided to Christóbal that he regretted marrying Francisca, saying that he had been too young and had gone through with it to get the funds (from her dowry?) to qualify as a notary.[113]

Men who drifted into consensual unions away from their tierras could pass as unmarried, but because they were unknown ("vagabonds," "travelers," and "strangers" in the language of the Third Provincial Council of Mexico, 1585), they were expected, more than locals, to demonstrate their freedom to marry.[114] But in practice the extra vigilance did not seem to screen out already–married strangers so readily. In fact just the opposite, in many cases, for newcomers whose personal histories were unknown and who were living in concubinage were assumed to be unmarried to the degree that officials and families threatened and urged them to marry. In this way the distancing of space and time set the stage for a 'trial' life to become a 'permanent' one, as it did in the case of Nicolás Cervantes, alias Nicolás Hermenegildo Hidalgo.[115] After marrying María Martínez in 1754, he lived with her for three years. But in the next three years or so, he spent, in the wording of the inquisitorial sentence (handed down in 1782), only "two or three days [with her] . . . every four or five months," before he "absented himself completely." That Nicolás married two more times reveals less for our purposes than the fact that his third wife, Antonia Josepha, had previously been one of his mistresses while he lived a married life with María. Nicolás testified (in his autobiographical statement of 1782) that "he moved to the city of Salvatierra [jurisdiction of Celaya, now in southeast Guanajuato] and . . . married a third time with the said Antonia Josepha who, years ago . . . he used to know in that city when he made his trips to the North." For Nicolás an occasional but periodic liaison prepared the ground for his third marriage and a new life.

Differing versions of Joseph Manuel de Molina's sudden abandonment of his wife, María Rosalia, illustrate perceptions of adultery that are poles apart.[116] The first comes from the mulatto Pedro de Zúñiga, who at sixty could say that he was native to and a vecino of the hacienda of San Agustín in Nueva Galicia (jurisdiction of Fresnillo, now in Zacatecas state) and had watched Joseph grow up, marry (in 1743), and live on the hacienda with his wife, the mulatto María. He testified in 1770 that

> they lived a married life for a number of years until the administrator, don Miguel de Olea, expelled some *peones* and he went to the mining camp of Bolaños [an alcaldía mayor, formerly Tepeque, now in northern Jalisco]. But perverted by a woman, he ran away with her but after three or four months the witness knew that he was very contentedly living again with his wife and a young lad named Simón Lobatero, known as Patales, told him this.

Pedro's story combines two explanations. First, a 'structural' one refers to a kind of reorganization of hacienda labor brought about by a new boss. *Peones* are expelled and one of them moves on to a mining camp. Second, a 'personal' one makes a conjuncture with the first but is subordinate to it: temporary insanity 'caused' by a woman. So Joseph is blameless because he was powerless. Somehow, though, he managed to come to his senses (Pedro seems to approve) and return to his wife. In this telling the episode is a minor one, a small aberration in an otherwise stable marriage.

In a second version, María Rosalia's, the episode looms larger, because she states the relevant chronology more precisely. "He made a married life with her—she had seven children, five are alive—until the beginning of the 1760s. Then he separated from her, having abducted María Casimira, and for eight years the witness had no news of him and then he returned and resumed married life until they arrested him."

In María's telling Pedro's "number of years" of married life becomes more than seventeen, his "three or four month" absence becomes eight years. María Rosalia had no idea what had happened, but she, Pedro, and Joseph agree on the centrality of Joseph's infatuation with the other woman. In a familiar plot Joseph himself testified in 1770 that the story consisted of abduction, illicit friendship, the birth of children, work at the mining camp, and finally the word from "a man from Zacatecas" that

María Rosalia had died. The progression mirrors Joseph's new life unfolding and, with the timely 'news' of a wife's death, marriage (ca. 1765) puts the old life permanently to rest.

Women Adulterers

If male adultery had its place, female adultery was, to say the least, less acceptable.[117] Husbands portrayed runaway wives as loose and immoral, adulteresses bent on going with other men. Such a construction put women on the defensive but, as can be seen from the way Lorenza de la Cruz defended her virtue (in her autobiographical statement of 1691), running away, even with another man, could still be seen as compatible with a conventional female identity.[118] "The said Gerónimo [her husband] gave the witness a very bad life and abused her [and in 1683] after six years of marriage with him she could not stand it any more and ran away from him and went to the city of Guadalajara." As it happened, she ran away with a mulatto who happened to be at Temisco, the sugar estate where Lorenza and Gerónimo worked. Hence Gerónimo's charge. Lorenza's rebuttal, however, clarifies that he was the vehicle, not the cause, of the flight.

Lorenza and the women who used other men to flee their husbands should be differentiated from those who were abducted by force and raped. The former were women who abandoned their marriages by choosing other men as companions in flight, whether they were family, friends, lovers, or strangers. The only requirement was that they be near at hand; for once a woman determined to run away, she focused first on running from an old life, not to a new one.

Married men who abducted the wives and daughters of other men were engaging in a common behavior but one nevertheless irritating to inquisitors. In chapter 3, for example, we saw the prosecutor's sarcastic question put to the mulatto Francisco Gómez ("Is it your trade and custom to abduct married or single women?"), who in 1622 had allegedly abducted María de Figueroa.[119] In truth the sarcasm was misdirected, for Francisco's flight with the Spaniard María de Figueroa came entirely at her initiative.

Here is how it happened. María had married the Spaniard Alonso Martín Cabello in 1621, but after six months of married life, he abandoned her, 'abducted' another woman, and remained out of contact for two and a half years. At that point, in January 1624, he appeared before don Juan de Saldivar Maldonado, judge of the rural constabulary of León. He petitioned that María, "his legitimate wife," be arrested, noting that "a mulatto named Francisco at hacienda La Sieneguilla has her . . . and the said Francisco went to the estancia of his father-in-law, the Spaniard Pedro de Ortega . . . violently took her from him, and abducted her."

The complaint represents not what happened in a literal sense (he was not even living with María), but the event euphemized to recount her leaving in legal and patriarchal terms. Another version comes from the testimony of María and Francisco. In her life apart from Alonso, María testified that she suffered a mala vida at the hands of her father and grandfather while living on her father's estancia. She reached a point of desperation one night [in December 1723?] when they threw her out of the house. From her testimony it seems that she then spoke directly to Francisco, but we do not know exactly how. Most likely, I think, she went straight to a lean-to or rough shelter of some sort where passing travelers were allowed to bed down for the night. In any case she found Francisco and spoke to him.[120] He testified (a week or two after the event) that "one night about midnight María de Figueroa came to this witness and begged him to take her, for 'the love of God', to Zacatecas or wherever he wanted, because her father Pedro de Ortega and grandfather Santiago give her the mala vida." Gómez hesitated, saying that "she should excuse him so that her husband would not come out and kill him, for she was a Spaniard and a married woman. She answered that she was not married nor had she relatives who would be able to harm him and then she climbed up behind him on his mule."

We should not forget that María had not seen Gómez before that night. She was entrusting her person to a stranger, and a casta at that. In approaching a man in this way while denying that she was married, she was opening herself to his sexual advances (a calculated quid pro quo?). María's unconventional indifference about this and her heedlessness as to where she would be going (almost anything now seemed better than mistreatment at the hacienda) show how singlemindedly she sought to escape. As a woman caught in and victimized by the conventions of her society (a husband's adulteries and abandonment, a patriarchal tyranny, and perhaps a mulatto stranger's lascivious expectations), she opportunistically chose the third to escape from the first two.

What about Alonso's place in all this? Although he was living with another woman, he expected María to live modestly and chastely in his absence. Yet he himself had done exactly what he accused Francisco of doing. He judged the mulatto a violent abductor because males assumed the right to 'steal' women but not to have their women stolen. And here, as Francisco had recognized at the time, a man of mixed race was adding insult to injury by running off with a Spanish woman. María eventually chose to ignore well-entrenched assumptions about male-female relations, for Alonso had forsaken married life and also abandoned her to mistreatment at the hands of her own family.

Married women ran away less frequently than men, just as they took lovers less frequently. The reason: they ran far higher risks in doing so. If caught in the act of adultery, for example, they could be killed, an action sanctioned in law as justifiable homicide. The Spaniard Juan Antonio Ramírez of Alvarado (Vera Cruz), for example, had been married for only seven months when he surprised his wife, the morisca María Valdivia, with another man.[121] This was in January, 1734, and Juan, expected to be away for six weeks, arrived home about midnight. On seeing the entwined figures covered with a blanket, he seized a knife, drove it home, and then left town. Miraculously, he missed them both, although he apparently thought he had had his revenge. The important point, however, is that no one questioned his right to strike. Afterward in Mexico City, he maintained contact with Alvarado, in a letter from María's sister, for example, and news from other Alvaradans. María's adultery justified Juan's response, which in satisfying his honor also ended his marriage.

The assumptions behind Juan's action prevailed among men of all classes and stations. In 1700 when their crisis came, Felipe de Santiago and Rita de las Nieves, both slaves, had been married for six years.[122] We know about it from the deposition of 1706 of Father Juan López, assistant (*teniente*) to the priest of Llerena (jurisdiction of Sombrerete, now in northwest Zacatecas state), who had spoken to Felipe in the local jail. He said that Felipe, "arriving at his house one night, found a man sleeping with his wife on his bed whom, along with his wife, he beat, wounded, and left for dead." Later Felipe asked after his wife, and a friend told him that his "enemy" was alive (apparently a man in a position to harm him), and "he had better not stay in the area, because he had killed his wife, Rita. So Felipe fled, 'abducting' Mariana, a single woman who went with him willingly, for company, and headed north.

Did this really happen, or did Felipe make it up as a pretext to escape slavery? Rita's deposition (she had not been killed) raises some doubts. She said that she and Felipe "loved each other, that she did not give occasion or motive whatsoever for him to leave." She also mentions another factor, perhaps the real cause of Felipe's flight: he had gotten into trouble with the mayordomo who threatened to whip him; and he, in turn, had complained to his master. Yet Rita may have omitted details of a liaison she had had, whether forced or consensual, that might very well have been with a mayordomo or another administrator, perhaps the very one who was out to get Felipe. Otherwise Felipe would have had no reason to flee. The defense of one's honor, allowed for reprisals against a wife but not against rivals of superior station. A later glimpse of Felipe reinforces the impression that we have gained of his character so far. Although a slave, he was volatile and quick to avenge encroachments on his honor, whether supposed or real. A brief reference, in fact, records that later Felipe killed Mariana whom, in the meantime, he had married. She died in 1705, three years or so after running away with Felipe, from what must have been an exceedingly brutal beating, referred to with understatement as "some blows."

Juan had the unimpeachable evidence of his own eyes and ears with which to judge his wife. Felipe too left behind a vivid statement that he had caught Rita in the act of adultery, and it is possible that he killed Mariana for the same reason. The reaction of the mestizo Domingo Rodríguez to his wife's adultery provides another variation on the theme of men defending their honor.[123] Domingo married the Indian Juana Agustina in 1619 and they lived and worked on a wheat-growing hacienda.[124] In his autobiographical statement of 1621, Domingo recalled that one day "a man named Lorenzo, supervisor of the crops, carried Juana off on horseback mounted double." We do not know where they went or whether this was rape or a consensual escapade, but as soon as Antonio could get his hands on Lorenzo, he attacked him with his knife and wounded him. The swift retaliation with a real 'weapon' (as opposed to a hoe or a stick) indicates that he prepared himself as he awaited the return of horse and riders. But here he attacked a man above his own station and this meant fleeing afterward.

Juan, Felipe, and Lorenzo struck back with whatever force they could command, avenging their dishonor by striking at their wives or their rivals. They acted with passion and apparently with little premeditation. In other circumstances, however, they might be so badly overmatched that the only possible action would be to slink away, as did Juan Gómez Franco, whose wife, Inés, added insult to injury by openly siding with the interloper.[125] This occurred after seven years of marriage (in 1728) in San Lúcar de Barrameda, in which Juan (testifying twenty-seven years later in his autobiographical statement of March 13, 1755) recalled that "he came to see that he was in danger of losing his life over her because of a man who was soliciting her for lustful reasons." Juan asked local authorities to intervene but that solved nothing; and he dared not attack directly (perhaps because his rival was too powerful, perhaps because Inés too had joined against him). "On two occasions, for the sake of his said wife, they were going to kill him." So Juan embarked for Córdoba in New Spain, where (as we saw in chapter 2) he had spent ten years as a boy growing tobacco with his father, and where he put together a new life.

The blatancy of Juan's rival can be compared with the shadowy, possibly only imaginary, suspicions harbored by the mestizo Antonio de Barahona.[126] In his five or six years of married life with the mestiza Gertrudis de Artiaga in Cuernavaca (1695–1700), Antonio became ever more worried that she was being unfaithful. In 1700 he suddenly abandoned her and she had no further contact with him. Yet Gertrudis had lived, it seems, with no awareness of Antonio's suspicions, for following his arrest for bigamy in 1706, she, in a deposition, could offer no motive whatsoever for his leaving. Antonio's statement, however, recovers something of his state of mind. "Some people told him and he himself saw that his wife was illicitly involved with a young lad named Miguel, mestizo, with whom she had this said relationship before he married her. And with her he had a daughter and she is alive today and he has verified this himself."

What Antonio "saw" was Gertrudis's former lover still in the community, and he therefore imagined that they had continued or resumed their liaison. So Gertrudis' past haunted Antonio's present. His suspicions could have been true, but they came from hearsay and rumor rather than eyewitnesses. One can well imagine onlookers watching Gertrudis and Miguel at every opportunity, alert for signs that they had exchanged words or even managed brief eye contact across the plaza of a small town.[127]

For our purposes it matters more that men such as Antonio held their suspicions so strongly than that they may have been poorly founded. The incident points to the anxiety of men to control the sexuality of women connected to them: daughters, servants, and especially wives. Yet men who monitored the behavior of women had no control over the past. What if later, for example, a man 'found out' that the virginal status of his bride had been 'misrepresented.' For one thing we should be suspicious, for deflowered women could overcome their disadvantage with attractive dowries. Yet such compensation, promised but undelivered, could serve as a ready excuse to abandon a wife. Witness how Juan Rodríguez in 1603 looked back to 1575, the year he married Catalina Morena, whom he abandoned after four months.[126] He testified that even though her father "promised him a dowry of 3,000 ducats" he received "not even a maravedí [1/34 of a real]," and "although she was a beautiful girl and [the father] said she was a virgin that was to protect her honor because in truth she was not." The deal came down to the agreement to present Catalina as a virgin in exchange for the dowry. Had it been delivered, the marriage might have succeeded, or at least would not have failed so prematurely.

More than a hundred years later, Juan Lorenzo del Castillo used the same tactic, the 'sudden' discovery of the nonvirginal status of his bride, to abandon a marriage.[129] Here, however, he acted after six years of married life and with no dowry at stake. Listen to his explanation, as he revealed to the inquisitors (in a supplementary hearing in 1709) that ten years before, he had abandoned the mestiza Teresa de la Cruz "because he came to detest her because her father . . . said that she was a virgin and the three kids that she looked after . . . belonged to her brother. But after he married her he found that it was not that way but instead they are her children which is the reason he left her."

The account is puzzling in two ways. First, Juan's *coming* to detest her indicates a gradual process rather than a sudden realization. But is it possible that he did not realize right away that a woman who had given birth to three children had not been a virgin? Otherwise why remain with her, feeling so strongly about the matter, for six years? Second, the powerful emotion detestation springs into the account with no warning or run up, thus suggesting a justification more than a description. Are we in the presence here of Edward Shorter's archetypal traditional marriage, a joyless, affectionless couple living in "quiet hostility and withdrawal"?[130] Possibly yes, and Juan's means to escape it was to seize on this issue of virginity.

Men therefore lived in fear that their honor would be impugned by the behavior, chosen or forced, past or present, of their wives. In this they shared a common anxiety but not one that resulted in a fraternal bond. In fact just the opposite, as we have seen. They preyed on each other by coveting and abducting one another's wives and daughters. A man whose wife had been abducted likely abducted a woman in turn. And whether the woman he joined with was married or not mattered less than his chances of eluding or intimidating her "protector," if she had one. So men treated women as if they were property, possessing and protecting them but also preying on them and abducting them. But as we have already seen, it is more complicated than this. Women were not just passive and victims, they also took matters into their own hands. They used intimidation, manipulation, and guile to fend off despotic treatment or to control their own affairs.

Adulterous women stand out, therefore, because they acquiesced in or invited liaisons, behavior most likely to harm their husbands' reputation and to put themselves at risk. Husbands confronted with such behavior placed the agency on male abductors but, as we have seen, also punished their wives. José Francisco Ortiz, a worker on Hacienda Pozo de los Carmeles (jurisdiction of San Luis Potosí, now the San Luis Potosí state) is one of the few who did not euphemize his wife Inés's adultery.[131] After five years of married life (1773–78), and three children (one of whom survived), Inés ran away with Ignacio, a hatmaker, while José was away for six months herding cattle. After two weeks officials returned her to José. Later, when José was discharged from Pozo (he apparently was a seasonal worker), he traveled about alone until he found long-term work as a bricklayer in Matehuala (jurisdiction of Charcas, now the northwest part of San Luis Potosí state). At this point, he testified later, "he sent for his wife and was with her for half a year but then she ran off with a man named Antonio Arévalo." What did José think of his wife's behavior? Obviously it troubled him, although he did not try to pursue and punish either his rival or Inés. Later, answering the prosecutor's accusation that he had abandoned her, José insisted that "she abandoned him, not the other way around, offending him further by joining herself to another man."

José's absences (they would have left Inés unsupervised and perhaps unprotected) seem to have opened the way for her running away. But they occasioned this only indirectly, for at the time she left, José was living with her and supporting her in a normal way. She chose to leave, therefore, for reasons similar to the mostly unverbalized ones that motivated male adulterers: a simple preference for another partner. Bárbara Martina, a mestiza who married Andrés Joseph Márquez in 1765, can only have left for similar reasons.[132] Although she accompanied Andrés when he took cattle to summer pasture at Ocuila (Malinalco), his work nevertheless required that he be away from her at least some of the time.[133] This may have given Bárbara the chance to form a liaison with one or more men, and after five years of marriage she testified (in her autobiographical statement of January 1771) that "she left [Andrés] to run away with Bernardino de Sena, in calidad an Indian, married with Felipa, mestiza, vecinos of San Mateo."[134]

The file does not reveal how Andrés reacted to Bárbara running away, but he must have alerted the officials who found her after two weeks. Normally husbands themselves also searched for runaway wives and their 'abductors.' Witness the mestizo Manuel de la Trinidad Rodríguez, whose wife Isabel María, an Indian, ran off with a "young lad" (in 1740) after five years of married life.[135] Manuel gave chase, fought with the youth, and threw him into a *barranca*. But the chase and the struggle had so exhausted him that he collapsed and lost consciousness, thus enabling Isabel to get away. From this point Isabel drops from view for six years, and then (in 1746) she resurfaces to denounce Manuel to the Inquisition for marrying a second time. She must have done this to harm him, possibly hoping that his conviction might break her tie to him. Otherwise how can we explain her remaining completely out of his sight and away from him as if intending the separation to be permanent?

So men who saw their wives succumb to the advances of other men, whether consenting or coerced, found their dishonor painful and often lashed out in anger. The reaction, however, was personal, for liaisons and consensual unions caused little stir in general. Bárbara Martina and her lover Bernardino, for example, lived in a thatched hut, hiding that each was married to somebody else, but not that they were living in concubinage. Even that mattered little, at least for some, to judge by the matter-of-fact way the Spaniard Eugenio Martín spoke of his son's abduction of a married woman.[136] "About a year and a half ago [1783?] his son Manuel . . . abducted Francisca Lisarda Rosas, wife of Juan Francisco López . . . from the pueblo of San Francisco Xalapexco (jurisdiction of Izúcar, now in Puebla state). Afterward he ran into them in the town of Amozoc (jurisdiction and immediate district of Puebla de Los Angeles) where Manuel served Felipe Zepeda as a muleteer." López, the victim of this abduction, admitting that Francisca had "absented herself with another man," said that he looked for her "in various places," heard in Tehuacán (an alcaldía mayor, now in southeast Puebla state) that she had died, and so remarried. Thus the well-rehearsed sequence to explain himself for purposes of a bigamy trial.

DEBT, CRIME, AND PUNISHMENT

Vignettes of married life by bigamists and their spouses give us some idea of the causes and occasions for separations; their accounts of leave-takings, show us something of the mood and makeup of married life. Pressures that sometimes worked against married life came from the 'inside' (clashes of personality, taste, and expectations) and also from the 'outside' ('structural' tendencies embedded in economy and society). In this section we shall be concerned with the latter, largely in the form of pressures exerted by the state to punish crime and enforce debt collection.

The mestizo Matías Cortés (born 1665), for example, stole a mule and other property worth 1,000 pesos, while serving the alcalde mayor of Colima.[137] A judge sentenced Matías to four years labor in a sweat shop (*obraje*) in Mexico City and his wife, the mestiza Hypólita de Alcántara (they were married in 1701), stayed with him for perhaps a year.[138] Hypólita testified in 1706, however, that she left "because of the mala vida that he gave her in the obraje." No doubt the conditions were dreadful, but the change was one of degree, not of kind, to judge by her summary of life with Matías before the imprisonment: "six or seven years, never settled in one place (*sin pie fixo*), always coming and going, and much abused in word and deed." All three children from the marriage died young.

The imprisonment therefore made an unhappy marriage more unhappy while, at the same time, giving Hypólita the chance to escape it. Hypólita left Matías and the obraje but, remaining in Mexico City, took refuge in the convent of San Bernardo, working as a servant (for a month), served in the house of the condesa de Peñalba (eight years), and, shortly before testifying, moved to her mother's house. She spurned the chance to rejoin Matías when he completed his sentence by keeping her distance, claiming, she said, that she could "always see his face [at a distance?] because it is so ugly."[139] This refusal to rejoin Matías emphasizes the central point, that Hypólita wanted out of this marriage, obraje or no obraje. If Matías's penal servitude made her mala vida worse, it had not created it.

The Indian Mariana de Espinosa also found the justice system an ally in freeing herself of an unwanted husband.[140] She had married the mestizo Joseph de Molina in 1586, and their married life lasted two months, living in Joseph's mother's house "in San Pablo behind the tanners." Then a magistrate put Joseph in the viceregal jail "because of a certain murder." This we learn from Joseph's autobiographical statement of March 1600. Mariana testified seven months later (November 5, 1600)[141] that

> she married Joseph de Molina thirteen or fourteen years ago. They did not have a nuptial mass because Joseph was always away from this city. Their married life was no more than two years. He would come to see her at her mother's house because she was still just a girl and he would bring his mistress. The two of them would beat her up and so she went to the house of a doña Leonor de Chávez . . . and, for a long time after [doña Leonor] died, was at the convent of Santa Mónica, and at present . . . is with Lucía de Monroy.

So Mariana documents her mistreatment. However, here we are concerned less with the abuse itself than the fact that Joseph's trouble with the authorities gave Mariana the chance to get away from him. After his arrest she refused to see Joseph or to send any message to him until she knew the outcome of his trial. No doubt hoping to be permanently free of him, she counted on a harsh sentence that would send him away for a term of penal servitude.

We can infer this by returning to Joseph's story recounting that authorities freed him after six months and he returned home to find Mariana missing. "Her mother said she had run away while he was in jail," he recalled, and then he gave a rambling account of his searches for Mariana in Chichimecan estancias and in towns such as Zacatecas, Pátzquaro, and Guadalajara. He also tried Mexico City again and spent considerable time in western Nueva Galicia (Compostela, Tepic, Valle de Banderas). All told Joseph waited ten years before deciding that Mariana was dead and married a second time in Tepic (in 1593), to the mestiza María López, a house servant of the Spaniard Alonso Sánchez Rubio, who also brokered the marriage. This last comes from the testimony of Diego de Piña (in 1600), regidor of Compostela and estanciero; and from that of another regidor, who acted as padrino and (with obvious exaggeration) said that he had known Joseph "for twenty years *in these parts.*" So by the time the Inquisition arrested Joseph early in 1600, he had settled into a new life, had lived with María for seven years by then, had fathered two children, and had firmly established himself in the clienteles of local notables. Mariana was well rid of Joseph, then, but the Inquisition found him out, tried him, and sentenced him to five years in the galleys, after which he was to resume married life with her. Yet her chances of permanently staying away from him remained good, given the high mortality rates of galley servitude or, failing that, given her proven success in keeping from his view.

A more dramatic and far-flung instance of the pressures exerted by policing forces takes us back to Sahagún (León) in Spain where, in 1595, don Francisco del Quiñones married doña Ana de Escobar.[142] Don Francisco testified (in his autobiographical statement of 1615) that after five years and the birth of a son (dead at 18 months) and a daughter ("alive today, now sixteen, and he does not know if she has married"), he "had the misfortune to kill a man and therefore fled to the city of Orán in Africa where he served his majesty in that presidio as a soldier for three years. Then he killed another man, and so he came to these parts [the Indies]."

During his 'exile,' don Francisco and doña Ana stayed in contact through letters. "He wrote that he was in these parts looking for a sum to come home with to settle that death [in Sahagún] and in his last letter, that he was coming in next year's fleet [1616] to live with her." Even if this had been true, it was by then too late. Since 1607 don Francisco had been married to doña María de la Guerra of Cholula and, at the time he allegedly wrote his letter, the Holy Office was about to arrest him. Time, distance, and the satisfactions of his new life postponed and then prevented the return to Spain. Don Francisco put it that "many times our Lord inspired him [to repent] by showing him the embarrassment and ugliness of his infamy yet he continued because of the love of his wife [doña María] and children [a son and daughter] and in vain confidence that his crime could not be proved in this faraway place.

The account highlights don Francisco's internal conflict: his infamy, as defined by the church norms with which he was indoctrinated; versus his happy life, as experienced with a loving wife and family. And it could not be resolved. As the new life in the Indies became ever more strongly his 'real' life, don Francisco's 'action' was to hope, passively and yet passionately, that the old one would not overtake him.

Don Francisco's crime, requiring that he pay damages, made him a debtor and, without funds to settle, a fugitive. The crime of debt itself, contracted in more ordinary ways, also played havoc with families. We have already seen how the Malagueñan merchant Francisco del Puerto, although happily married, separated from his wife and went to the Indies to clear his debt.[143] Did he fear confiscation, imprisonment, or the ruin (and vengeance?) of bondsmen and partners? We lack details, although it is enough to recall that he termed his situation an "enslavement." In going to the Indies, he pursued the double objective of restoring his fortune and avoiding his creditors.

Agustín de Hoz Espinosa Calderón, under greater immediate pressure than Francisco, suffered a more complete debacle because of debt. Yet it was one that could be managed with less urgency than settling a homicide.[144] Thanks to his marriage to María de Barahona (in 1573), his fortunes improved dramatically.[145] The parish priest, for example, testified that he had taken Agustín "for a poor man because he arrived in a very needy state . . . in fact he does not think he had anything, for whatever he acquired came from the estate of his wife, María de Barahona." Probably suffering losses while speculating in wheat (he was keeper of the municipal grain warehouse), Agustín fell into debt and, to escape his creditors, hid at a farm owned by a convent. Miguel Gutiérrez who visited him there testified in 1583 that his friend told him that he intended to go to the Indies. That was the last time he saw him. Had it not been for the debt, Agustín's marriage to María might have continued indefinitely, its permanence or transience a product of the hazards of reproduction and disease and of the ups and downs of the relationship itself. Agustín enjoyed some prestige from María's noble birth (she was called a *donzella noble y hijadalgo*) and wealth but she retained title to her estate so he could not tap into it to clear his debt.

Debt also disrupted the marriage of a much humbler man, the mulatto Nicolás de la Cruz of Mexico City (born 1609).[146] Nicolás had married Clara, a black slave, when he was nineteen (in 1628), but married life lasted just a few days because Nicolás's master, don Francisco Sicher, accused him of stealing (possibly a trumped-up charge to indenture him) and demanded restitution. To work off his debt, the justice sold Nicolás to Pedro de la Sierra, owner of an obraje in Coyoacán. In the file he resurfaces seven years later in the testimony of his mother-in-law, who said (in August 1635) that "last Easter a black man sent by Nicolás contacted her in the plaza where she was selling beans. Thus for the first time she learned what had happened to Nicolás and that he was now in the obraje of Diego Caro on Pedro de Sierra's orders until he pay money that he owes."[147]

Moreover Nicolás was in debt to others in Mexico City and explained (in his autobiographical statement of December 1635) that "they called him Nicolás de Pisa in the obraje to differentiate him from another mulatto named Nicolás de los Reyes. Then he called himself Nicolás de la Cruz, the name he uses today . . . to hide his identity so that some people, to whom he also owes money would not attach him." Nicolás's unanticipated confinement in the obraje, together with his long sentence and change of name, kept him from Clara's view. As if that were not enough, Clara's owner in the meantime took her to Querétaro, in the general exodus of refugees abandoning Mexico City in the wake of the flood of 1629.[148]

Marriages at Work: Roles and Expectations

We have seen that personality clashes, petty tyrannies, and loss of interest pushed men and women apart; that structures of law enforcement and economic organization pulled them apart. These help to explain how married couples separated. Virtually every separation, however, was followed by a recoupling, which, as formalized by marriage, of course became the crux of the bigamists' problem. What matters most here is the cycle and its tendency to return to the same resting point. Couples, however unsuccessfully married, maintained an ideal of married life.

Occasionally husbands and wives managed to approximate an ideal of harmony, thriving together in a domestic division of labor in a life together as partners. In the 1570s, for example, Antonio Sánchez Navarro (born ca. 1533), a muleteer-storekeeper, complemented the work of his wife (they married in 1563), the innkeeper Isabel Maldonado.[149] Antonio, a native of Seville (he had been known there as Pedro Navarro) crossed to the Indies in 1574 and settled in Santo Domingo, where he sold "spices, wines, and other things" from his store.[150] He spent another two years in Jamaica (again dealing in wine), passed to Havana, where he served as a mayordomo to a man named Vellaneda, and then moved on to New Spain, where in Orizaba (an alcaldía mayor, now in central Veracruz), he worked as a "muleteer and Isabel Maldonado [his wife] stocked and sold wine." The tailor Francisco Ortiz, native of Seville but then a vecino of Veracruz testified (1581) that "he knew Pedro [Antonio] Navarro more than nineteen years ago in Seville in their barrio where the tailors are on the [Guadalquivir] river front and Pedro dealt in fish and smoked sardines which he would buy and then sell."

Our view of Antonio and Isabel comes in 1581, when they were operating an inn at San Juan de Ulúa. Before that they had lived in Puebla and Orizaba and, according to one acquaintance, they were thinking of moving again: "he is trying to go to Mexico City soon and thinks he can live there and earn a living by running a few mules on this highway."[151] What exactly was their work? Antón Rodríguez, a muleteer who "runs on this road from Mexico City via the San Antonio highway," had been a neighbor when they were in Orizaba. He testified that "all of their possessions were in common. She used to sell wine and other goods and he used to go with his mules to look for wheat and other things to sell and to stock in their house."

The testimony of the Basque Juan Butrón (in 1581), a vecino in Vera Cruz, indicates that Antonio and Isabel's life at San Juan followed a pattern similar to the one at Orizaba. "Antonio lives on the island of San Juan de Ulúa . . . with his wife and they rent an inn there . . . and his wife runs the inn and Antonio goes with his . . . mules and brings flour, biscuits, and supplies [including quinces and pomegranates from Vera Cruz] for the inn and other times he remains at home."

The record of Antonio and Isabel's partnership runs for eighteen years. As they move around and aspire to move again to Mexico City, their association in petty commerce complements their union as husband and wife.[152]

The partnership of work did not insure the permanence of a marriage, but it surely helped, because the failure of partners to carry their share of the day-to-day burdens of earning a living acted as a major source of discord. Consider a situation, for example, in which the husband no longer fulfilled his role as provider and protector. The Spaniard Juan de Lizar-zaburo, by the time he faced the inquisitors in 1690, had for some time been so weak that he no longer worked as an itinerant peddler.[153] When asked if he knew or could presume why he had been imprisoned, Juan could only think of the sometimes raucous quarrels that he had had with Angela Muñoz, his wife of thirteen years who, he said "has a harsh tem-perament and on one occasion, during an argument last Easter, said to him 'be gone Jewish dog.' And he does not know why she would have said such a foolish slur because he is a Christian and the son of Christians.[154]

Three days later (June 9, 1690), Juan returned to the same theme when he asked the court to secure his property (five pigs, a horse, and a saddle) in the Indian pueblo of Copandaro (jurisdiction of Zitáquaro, now in eastern Michoacán state), where he had lived for "many days," he said, because "he could not live with his wife [any longer in Zitáquaro, four leagues away] because of her harsh temperament and the little or no attention that she paid to the person of this [witness]."

There can be little doubt that Angela had a strong personality and, well-equipped with an earthy vocabulary, spoke forcefully enough to dis-comfit Juan. But because Juan's file does not include her testimony, we must infer why, perhaps more than usual in the rough and tumble of plebeian marriages, she insulted and neglected Juan. The answer lies in Juan's weakened condition, which in becoming more pronounced, pro-voked an ever more strident reaction from Angela. For years he had been battling syphilis, having picked it up during a twenty-year career as a seaman traveling between Spain and the Indies, with long stays on the isthmus of Panama. Although he had undergone the mercurial ointment treatment in Mexico City, his health continued to deteriorate, and at the time of his arrest, he suffered fevers, weakness, and loose bowels (*cursos*). Angela's dominance in conjunction with Juan's frailty inverted their do-mestic politics as she abused him actively with insults and passively with neglect. This culminated when Juan, suffering the mala vida, retreated to Copandaro.

The harshness of Angela's insults points to her strong dislike of and even contempt for Juan. It might also represent a bit of revenge for rough treatment handed out to her when he was stronger. Now she could rail at Juan spontaneously and gratuitously without inhibition or fear of reprisal. And because this abuse was not connected with any particular grievance, at least not from Juan's point of view, he found it all the more upsetting. But Angela had a general grievance. Juan had ceased to contribute to their living. Angela's refusal to serve him constituted a retaliation in kind. In a society that expected men to dominate, Angela lost respect for Juan as she saw him increasingly unable to carry out his role of provider and household head. There is no reason to think that other women of Hispanic society would have behaved differently.

In the way she drove her husband away, the mulatto María Micaela can be compared with Angela.[155] Her mother brought María from Pachuca (born ca. 1705) as a girl to Mexico City and placed her as a house servant with don Joseph de Abendaño, auditor of the tribunal of accounts. Two developments came from this: María acquired a taste for expensive clothing and she became pregnant. Both probably link to don Joseph himself, for if we may trust Thomas Gage's observation, elite Spaniards of the capital flaunted elegantly dressed mulatto mistresses in the fashion of the day.[156]

After María married the mulatto shoemaker and coachman Joseph Francisco de Chavarría in 1721, the couple joined the household of María's parents.[157] Joseph, summarizing their married life, testified that he

> supported her for about six years without any notable absences, working at his trade of shoemaker and other times serving various people. At the end of this period he left, fed up with his wife's nagging and insults (*impertinenzias y desazones*), for his said wife did not leave him in peace because she insisted on wearing clothing of the highest quality and other things that he was not able to acquire with only his work.

Elsewhere in his confession Joseph called his marriage a "mala vida . . . because his energies were insufficient to give [María] all that she wanted." Thus arose the mismatch between a humble man of limited means and a woman whose tastes had been 'artificially' elevated above those that normally befell those of her station. Rather than lower her expectations, she railed at Joseph.

Joseph may have exaggerated, but in outline his characterization of María seems accurate. Her own testimony, in fact, corroborates it in the way she spoke of a temporary reunion with Joseph.

> When the *sala [de crimen]* burned [at the stake] two men this last time, he appeared here serving as coachman to a priest of the said camp [Guanajuato]. . . . And running into her husband in the crowd gathered for the burnings she quarreled with him for running away and told him that she heard that he had married. He denied it, confessing only that he had had his weaknesses as a man with [various] women.

The answer satisfied rather than angered María, for she seemed more concerned with his failure to support her than with his adultery, complaining once again that "her said husband came and went to her house but without helping her with anything although he had money." Perhaps hoping to keep Joseph at hand and squeeze some support from him, María and her mother searched out señor Miguel Castillo, Joseph's employer, and told him that Joseph should remain in Mexico City so he could live a married life with her, and Castillo should therefore discharge him.

And so he did, but without the intended result. Although discharged by Castillo, Joseph nevertheless headed north again and three years later in 1735 in Guanajuato, married Matiana, a slave. Why, when he had so recently seen María alive in Mexico City? And why a slave? Joseph, showing that his ideal of marriage survived the unhappy one with María, answered that he "married the second time to see if he could experience a better life than in the first one. He did not hear that [María] died, he just thought she must have because when he left [Mexico City] she was sick."

The brief explanation comes as a familiar pairing: the leaving of an old life and the attempt to make a new one, with the projection of a 'probably' dead first wife to make it licit. Note, however, that Joseph did not have to marry Matiana. No one had threatened to whip, jail or banish him for being in an illicit relationship with this slave. He proceeded because he wanted to, because he could not conceive of his projected "better life" as merely an illicit friendship. Rather he wanted it constituted as a fully authorized marriage. We know that Joseph thought his first wife too demanding. Perhaps the main characteristic he hoped for in his second one, symbolized by her slave status, was submissiveness. This would restore the proper lines of authority in marriage and affirm him as a man worthy of respect in his community.

In Joseph Francisco and Juan de Lizarzaburo we have the unusual circumstance of men claiming to be subjected to the mala vida by women. María Micaela demanded that Joseph support her at a level beyond his means because she had acquired expensive tastes. But surely she could not have indulged herself and so hounded Joseph without the support of her parents and don Joseph. Perhaps this was the reason why he failed to oppose her with brute force, but instead adopted the 'female' tactic of enduring for a time and then running away and starting over. María and Angela both expected more than their husbands could provide; Joseph and Juan, passively and defensively, only wanted a 'peaceful' life, but lacked the forcefulness or allies to assert themselves within the traditional role. Flight rather than endurance or confrontation became the way to escape from so much unhappiness.

Another beleaguered male, on the defensive because he had failed to consummate his marriage, shows us the inversion of the usual power relations between men and women. The Spaniard Baltasar Márquez Palomino had crossed to the Indies in 1613, married Agustina de Buitren six years later, and then was beset by impotence.[159] Agustina and her mother, Gerónima de Pálido, understandably upset, made matters worse by insults and threats of a lawsuit to annul the marriage. Shaken, Baltasar ran off to Guastepec and conferred with a friar Natera at the Dominican monastery. Describing this meeting to the inquisitors, he testified in 1634 that

> he asked for a cure so that he could consummate the said marriage and, after examining him, [friar Natera] said that he had no disease or impotence but that [Agustina] must have put a curse on him and therefore the witness must commend himself to God. He left, tired of the whole business and in Las Amilpas [an alcaldía mayor, formerly part of the marquesado, but escheated to the crown in 1583, now in Morelos state] began to serve don Juan de Agüero.

From time to time, Baltasár recounted, he returned to Mexico City and tried again, but "every time he came to see his said mother-in-law and wife they treated him so badly that [eventually] he was forced to agree to a separation and so the three of them went together to the house of a lawyer, Contreras, now dead, and he drew up a petition that they presented to the Vicar General of the city." On the vicar's order, two midwives examined Agustina and declared her a virgin. Baltasar refused to submit to an examination and fled.

He stayed away for three years because he feared his mother-in-law's threat to have him "banished to China." But surely she did not threaten him primarily because he was impotent, although he may have been confused about that at the time. Agustina and her mother no doubt sought to recover the considerable dowry of 3,000 pesos they had delivered to him. After the three years, perhaps largely because his nemesis, the mother-in-law, had died, Baltasar reestablished contact with Agustina and once again tried to consummate the marriage. In her testimony of 1633 Agustina remembered the occasion. Speaking of Baltasar's problem to the inquisitors, she said, with clinical detachment, that he "did not return to Mexico City for three years and then for three nights they were on good terms (*buen amistad*) and Baltasar tried to consummate [the marriage]. And it seems that he does not have a member capable of knowing a woman although he appears to have semen because she has sometimes felt some wetness underneath."

Baltasar, admitting that he had been unable to consummate the marriage, was clearly perplexed that "when trying to have access to her he was not potent within the natural receptacle yet away from it he was." Agustina suspected that Baltasar was purposely withholding his semen to nullify the marriage; Baltasar was ashamed, confused, mystified, and worried about giving back the dowry. Together with friar Natera, he probably felt that he was still under some sort of 'spell,' for he had already explained to Agustina (as she remembered it) that "with other women who were not virgins he was not impotent but with virgins he was." From this Baltasar drew a reasonable inference.

It seems to him that Agustina shares some of the blame, for when he was absent from her he had normal intercourse with many other women, fathered children with several of them, and twice impregnated the one he married in Agua del Venado [jurisdiction of Charcas, now the northwest part of San Luis Potosí state]: the first a miscarriage and the second to be born, he has heard, in four or five months.

Baltasar had a point. And surely his exploits while away from Agustina and his relation of them to the judges vindicated his manhood. Yet there was a price to pay, for he had just confessed to bigamy. Why did it come to this? Might not Baltasar have continued with his itinerant life and the enjoyment of sexual relations with many women? His answer to this question shows that all along, through the unsatisfactory relationship with Agustina and compounded by her mother, he had clung to a more idealized notion of married life.

From Zacatecas he went to the mines of Papagayo where he spent what little money he had. There fray Gerónimo Pangual asked him if he were married and whether he wanted to marry a young virgin who was poor but virtuous. And envious at seeing that other vecinos lived quietly with their wives he said he was not and, after a month, agreed to marry the girl.

Not an entrapment of passion, not the calculation of gain, not the threat of authorities, but the simple return to a quiet domestic conviviality drove Baltasar. The month that he took to decide must have been spent calculating the risk. And in human terms it was a risk he judged worth taking. To the inquisitors Baltasar triumphantly stressed the detail that "the same night he consummated the marriage without any difficulty, even though he found her a virgin." But the precariousness of his newfound domestic contentment weighed heavily on Baltasar's mind when he confided his secret in Jusepe Ramos, his friend and former employer in Zacatecas. Jusepe testified in 1632 that "Baltasar Márquez wrote him a letter telling him that he married a second time and asked that he keep it a secret because his honor was now in [Jusepe's] hands."

Baltasar's merging of his honor and his new life amounted to a personal affirmation, his entrusting it to his friend Jusepe a social one. It underscores that honor grew from the self-respect and personal contentment of an untroubled family base, the all-important platform from which one presented oneself to society. But why entrust a friend with such potentially damaging information? The answer, I think, has to do with Baltasar wanting his life to be not only a private reality but a public presence, legitimately constituted. To live as if only the former mattered was the incomplete outlaw life of the vagabond and outsider, without the substance of connections to locale and family.

Conclusion

In part, as we have seen, domestic life functioned as a self-contained system, where a gendered politics based on male authority and female subordination played itself out. Households became virtually the sole places where plebeian as well as other males in colonial Mexico became unquestionably dominant. They expressed that dominance by insisting on the subordination of women, and often they inflicted the mala vida on them. What we can learn of their words and behavior in this domestic context, therefore, stands as a relatively uninhibited expression of what they thought it meant to be a male, a husband, and a father in this society. Yet their authority was not unquestioned, nor was it absolute, for women sometimes found ways to return insult for insult, to fight back, to run away, and to seize the advantage when husbands could be put on the defensive. Domestic interactions more than any others, I think, defined, shaped, and expressed identity, for in a hierarchical world in which plebeians deferred or pretended to defer to those who dominated them, the household was where that domination ceased and one took charge.[160]

However self-contained married life, it nevertheless connected to society at every turn. Indeed the very mentalities that people had internalized as their role models and expectations came from the larger culture. Married life can therefore serve as both a reference point and a vantage point for viewing the larger system. As a reference point domestic life acted as a kind of home base (a place of shelter, nourishment, companionship, and of work) from which people moved outward to contact other groups, regions, and the formal institutions of their society. Our examples of such exchanges help to epitomize the patterns, workings, and rules concretely rather than abstractly. As a vantage point, and speaking now in interpretive terms, domestic life gives precedence to the informal associations of family, neighborhood, and clienteles more than to formal institutions of church and state to explain the movements and actions of people in society.

In our next chapter we shall continue to use the domestic life of bigamists as a point of reference but now as seen farther from home base, as we follow the movements and actions of bigamists to the periphery, to see in more detail their links to society. To do this we shall look at how people kept track of each other or, in more immediate terms, how bigamists were caught. This will give us a broader look at society through the trivial and ordinary transactions of people passing on gossip and information and thus a better sense of the context of the lives and marriages of bigamists.

CHAPTER FIVE

A PROCESSION ON GOOD FRIDAY IN THE SIXTEENTH CENTURY

The Flow of Information

✛ VERBAL EXCHANGES—CONVERSATIONS, messages, reports, directions, inquiries, chats—are usually seen as means rather than ends and therefore seldom studied directly. Yet they can be crucially important, to reflect the mentalities and processes of everyday life. Throughout we have assumed that the memories people had of their days, as reflected by what they said to inquisitors and as recorded by notaries, recapture at least something of particular incidents and the narrator's state of mind about them.[1] As with all narratives, storyteller-protagonists shaped them for particular audiences.[2] Yet however shaped, the events are remembered. They reflect act *and* attitude, and therefore direct us to how people engaged what they saw, thought, felt, and did in the past.

The individuals who appear in bigamy records had remarkable memories. They recalled the circumstances and content of their verbal exchanges in such detail that we might wonder whether they invented and embellished more than they 'remembered.' As narrators they must have done both to recreate the dramas of their comings and goings as actors in their worlds. The result is a surprising degree of specificity in regard to both everyday affairs and of states of mind about them.[3] Most noticeably in the vignettes and fragmentary stories found in the Inquisition files, the storyteller's art consisted of using layers of detail so that an audience could visualize the setting and actions of the protagonists.[4] It also meant that narrators tended to simulate conversations rather than summarize them.

Thus the testimony in the bigamy files, recreating scene and substance, dramatizes but does not 'make it up.'[5] We shall keep this in mind in this chapter, as we look at what people talked about, how and why they came together to exchange news and gossip, and what patterns can be found in their interactions. The chapter begins by noting some standard patterns of conversational give-and-take. Then it looks at "the carriers of information," the people who were having these exchanges, in order to detail the random, curiosity-driven ways in which news and gossip were collected and broadcast. Third it deals with "inquirers," people looking for specific information and making queries of those likely to have it. And finally it roughs in a scheme of traffic patterns to show that news and gossip moved within a framework, albeit a loose one subject to chance and variation.

THE CONTENT

What did people talk about? And in what ways? The simple answer to the first question is "other people." There can be no doubt, as M. Chevalier has reminded us, that people of early modern times, as now, were interested far more in each other than in "the relations between men and things."[6] The answers to the second question are already scattered throughout this book in the words of people who told their stories, explained their views, and recounted meetings and conversations. Here we shall linger a bit more on how people began and patterned their exchanges.

Who are you?

The process by which strangers joined up on the road, identified one another, and found the common ground of a mutual acquaintance is illustrated in the way the mule driver Alfonso Sánchez fell into step with "a silversmith" newly arrived in New Spain.[7] The meeting led to Alfonso making a denunciation in Antequera on April 6, 1615. It was "about twenty-two days ago," he began, and he asked the stranger where he was from "and he said . . . Oviedo in Asturias and this witness said 'I know a man from that same land, Hieronimo Meléndez, married in the city of Antequera.'" Meléndez, it turned out, was the newcomer's cousin and now the object of his consternation. "But how was he able to marry here if he was already married in his tierra with a woman who, because she is so young—not yet 12—they had not handed over to him?" As they talked, Alfonso learned more about Meléndez's life and marriage. He had been given 500 ducats of the girl's dowry "on account" and had been in the Indies for fifteen years. Until that moment the stranger had thought his cousin "in Havana living in concubinage with a Portuguese woman who worked as a baker." Absconding with the dowry and living in concubinage he took in stride; bigamy shocked him.

The 'who-are-you' opening of so many exchanges began by stating one's tierra, the essential category for getting started. Once this was established, known compatriots (sometimes relatives and compadres) became the topics. Knowledge or ignorance of compatriots, whether at home or in the Indies, tested whether people were who they said they were. Up to this point, Alfonso had known Meléndez strictly within the boundaries of his life in Antequera, together with the mere label of tierra which had been innocuous until this conversation with a compatriot. Suddenly Alfonso had to shift his view of the seemingly ordinary man who was his neighbor in order to think of him as a bigamist living illicitly.[8] Time, distance, and settlement in an obscure place failed to shield Meléndez from the searchlight of a compatriot's knowledge.

We can see how the connection of tierra also came into play as Antonio de Hamaniego, about to depart for Michoacán (from Mexico City?) in 1582, took leave of his countryman Francisco de Salas, at that moment standing with "a Salazar, hidalgo, near the Dominican monastery."[9] Francisco recalled that Salazar, realizing that he "resided in Michoacán" asked if he "knew Agustín Hoz Calderón." Francisco "said 'yes' and that he was rich . . . and he said 'is it true that he married?'" Again Francisco said "'yes, with a rich widow who is señora of estancias and livestock'." Salazar then told Antonio that Hoz Calderón was married in Spain, and so the secret was out. Later Hoz said that his enemy, Diego Cuellar, made up the accusation, but in fact Salazar was Hoz's compatriot from Bribiesca (Burgos) and had known him and his wife there.[10]

The connection of tierra, which called for Antonio's farewell to his countryman Salas led to Antonio's secondary exchange with Salazar, because Antonio and Hoz, their subject, both lived in Michoacán, and Salazar could link Hoz back to his tierra in Spain. That Antonio became rich, repeated twice in a brief exchange, underscores how notorious Hoz's good fortune had become. His transformation stood out, perhaps, because it had changed him into a local notable. He represented, therefore, a subject of envy but also of curiosity, the last because he would be expected to change in some ways the political dynamics of the locale.

Yet the outsider-insider conversations did not have to be so dramatic. Consider for example the low-key exchange remembered by Hernán González in a deposition he made in 1615.[11] About thirteen years before, he had been in the pueblo of Navito (jurisdiction of Culiacán, now in

Sinaloa state), "and saw there a white man with a red beard, of medium height—neither short nor tall—and one of the three Spaniards he was dealing with said to him 'that Fleming over there married Juana de la Bastida in the villa' [Culiacán]." Because Hernán had no other contact with the informer, he did not know his name. Thus an ordinary exchange, a moment when local society stopped to keep track of itself.[12] It came as a brief parenthesis, not an interruption, in the conversation of four men, a passing notice of the newcomer, not with drama or intensity, but as a minor curiosity of only local significance, taken in a leisurely way. Even such seemingly irrelevant tangents, punctuating virtually any conversation, to judge by González's vivid memory of the incident, absorbed the full attention of people.

If the presence of newcomers attracted interest, so too did topics touching on scandal. They came up in a similar way as people passed the time and homed in on subjects close at hand. The testimony (in 1586) of the Spaniard Pedro Yrazábal, a vecino of Puebla, for example, includes his account of a conversation he had had a little over a year before.[13] He said he had been

in Mexico City two days before and two after 'the threes' [Epiphany?]. The witness was having lunch in the house of the stonecutter Martín Casillas who said that he had heard that the wife of a [Juan de] Pantoja had been cloistered and kept in seclusion at the convent of the penitents because they said that another husband of hers was coming from Spain.

Others in Puebla also seized on the subject. Christóbal Baltasar was speaking to a servant of Benito de Lara, cutler, in the latter's store when "a man arrived . . . and said 'this is the limit (*basta*), Pantója's wife is already married.'" Jerónimo Hernández heard his employee, Christóbal Cantero, say the same. Jerónimo had come from Spain with Pantója eleven years before and therefore, along with everyone else who knew him by sight or reputation, followed the unfolding drama closely.

Locale and Region

It is hard to measure the currency of stories that circulated in a region as well as a locale but, as we shall see, these mostly moved irregularly and within 'corridors' between central and outlying places. In 1662 a twenty-five-year-old Spaniard, Matías Martínez de Torres, was traveling the province of Soconusco, selling goods out of his home base in Guatemala

City.[14] Although he had been in the Indies for only three years, he had begun to sort out regional gossip and news. He testified in June 1663 that ten months before, he had been at the Jesuit hacienda of Santa Ana, "now a cattle ranch, but before it used to produce sugar."[15] Over a meal Matías and the hacienda administrator, father Domingo Martín, spoke of local news. Domingo, for example, mentioned that "a mulatto named Sebastián de Loaysa, branded on the cheek, bald, and taller than average, was a fugitive slave of the sugar estate (*ingenio*) of Manuel de Yrasaga in Las Amilpas, and he was married in the said estate."[16] Matías took notice because he had known Sebastián in Guatemala City. For a time, he said, he had lodged him, along with "a mestiza named Tomasa de Orduña by whom he has two children." On returning to Guatemala City, Matías told Sebastián about the conversation, heard his denials, and then pursued the matter further in his travels. In Las Amilpas a week later, he asked about the "escaped slave" and his abandoned wife and then went to see her.

Meanwhile Father Domingo had also continued to interest himself in Sebastián. "The sons of don Antonio de Aguilar," he said, told him that Sebastián lived in the neighborhood of Santo Domingo (in Guatemala City), worked as an ironmonger, and was married to a mestiza. Six months later he also arranged to check on Sebastián's alleged wife in Las Amilpas, a task he delegated to a friend, Father Juan Martínez de Tobar of Puebla, whose travels would take him to the village. Domingo asked him to find out, "with scruple," if the woman was alive.

The two 'investigations' of Sebastián's bigamy therefore ran concurrently after the initial meeting between Matías and Father Domingo. Each verified the existence of Sebastián's first wife, as Father Domingo broadened his interest in Sebastián from runaway slave to bigamist, while Matías focused on bigamy, as he had from the beginning. Bigamy in this case overshadowed running away, for Father Domingo and Matías could have notified authorities that Sebastián was in Guatemala City.[17]

The subject of the 'escaped slave–bigamist' became topical on a regional scale, not because it was inherently different or more compelling than more local news, but because it ranged outward with Matías's movements and Domingo's Jesuit contacts. Sebastián, the central character, also himself helped regionalize the story because he resided in a central place, Guatemala City. Digging out and verifying the truth about Sebastián's past became more and more interesting for Matías. In this he became a kind of agent for the Inquisition, but that is not why he did it. Rather we should think of him as a man indulging his curiosity and in his travels enjoying telling and retelling a story, compelling because its hero, known or known of by many, was now revealed as a criminal. It resonated as true because it played upon stereotypes that blacks and slaves were lawless, faithless, and sacrilegious.

By definition the arrival of travelers from the outside enlarged the scale of the exchanges. Yet this became most interesting when it connected to locals. We can see this from the testimony (on December 11, 1761) of bachelor don Pedro Joseph Calzido, priest of the mining camp Cosalá (jurisdiction of Culiacán, now Sinaloa state), which allows us to stand with him as he eavesdropped on a conversation one day.[18] The circumstances were ordinary enough. Two strangers, don Clemente, a carpenter, and a man named Rivera, probably his helper, had just arrived and were in the anteroom of a private house, recounting the misfortune of a drifter (*vago*) named Juan Esteban Pacheco. It seems that "some robbers had stolen his wife," María Teresa Barrona, after they had been married for only three months. Don Pedro found this especially interesting because he had known Juan when he lived in Cosalá some two years before. He made a mental note of this information and, as we have just seen, later recalled it for the Inquisition.

The strangers, themselves subjects of curiosity, served to update knowledge of a former acquaintance. But don Pedro structured his account to keep Juan, the concern of the inquisitors, the focus, while reducing his own role in the incident to that of bystander. But not only that. He also acted by monitoring the arrival of the strangers, by following them, and by standing around and listening.[19] In this don Pedro becomes the hero of his narrative. Moreover although he does not say so, he must have joined the conversation by recounting something of Juan's life in Cosalá. Thus he would have engaged the strangers further on this and other topics, at once assuring himself that he had learned all he could and prolonging the diversion for its own sake.

In the never-ending quest to satisfy curiosity, conversations incessantly *placed* people. Who are they and who are their companions? What do they do? Why did they come *here*? Where do they come *from*? These kinds of questions constantly needed to be updated to find out what people were doing now. If something has changed (place, work, companions), *why*? From the testimony of the Spaniard Domingo de Gara, administrator of San Joseph Cocoyoc, a sugar estate near Cuernavaca, we can see, for example, how the presence of a young woman in an unexpected place provoked inquiries from a passing observer.[20] Domingo said that he was giving meat rations to the slaves on the afternoon of the seventh [July 1691] when Joseph de Pineda, a mestizo, arrived. And when he saw the young mulatto Lorenza de la Cruz, he asked . . . what she was doing on this hacienda because she was married on the ingenio Temisco to a free mulatto. And [Domingo] responded that 'it was not possible, for that one said she was a native of San Juan Peribán [jurisdiction of Xiquilpa, now Peribán de Ramos in Michoacán state] and very recently she had come to the hacienda married to a slave on the said hacienda and they married in jail in Guadalajara.'

In this exchange Domingo and Joseph define Lorenza and her husbands by race, civil status, and place. The last roused Joseph's curiosity because it represented change. In response to Joseph's identification of Lorenza, Domingo's restatement of the incomplete identity she had made known to him was not meant to challenge the newly arrived information about her but rather to stress (underscored by the exclamation "it is not possible") the importance of the discrepancy. He presumed that Lorenza had lied and denounced her to the Inquisition.

Association with a place put people in the position of being a source of news from that locale. In April 1745 the Spaniard don Manuel Francisco de la Torre, vecino of Querétaro, was passing through the mining camp of San Pedro Guadalcázar when Asencio Sánchez, knowing where he was from, approached him to ask how things were with don Joseph del Acevedo.[21] Don Manuel (his deposition dates from December 1745) recalled saying that "right now . . . [he] is out of work after losing his job as maestro and foreman in the construction of the monastery of San Agustín." Then Sánchez asked about Acevedo's brother, Manuel de Lizones, and don Manuel "said that he only knew him by the name of Reyes, and that he was married in Querétaro. Sánchez said 'that is impossible, since he has been married for many years in San Pedro with a woman named [Josepha] Zúñiga.'" So the conversation reached a focus. That marriage, in fact, had been notorious throughout the region, as we have already seen in the account of how Reyes ran off with Josepha by luring her father into the mountains in search of a robber's cave. This might have been a chance for Sánchez to retell the story and don Manuel to hear it for the first time. And with enjoyment, no doubt, for in his deposition to denounce Reyes, he recounted the details and scene as if he savored it for its own sake.

Routine Inquiries of Friends and Family

So far we have looked at the meetings of strangers and the subjects they found as common ground for conversations. Here we note how acquaintances worked through formulaic and routine exchanges to arrive at subjects of greater interest. The "old mestiza" Barbola Descolín, unmarried, servant of a barber-surgeon of Oaxaca, testified (on April 15, 1660) that she kept track of the mulatto Lorenzo de Otalora Carbajal of Guatemala City "because his mother was her friend."²² She therefore would "ask the muleteers" for news of him. About a week before she testified (on April 9), Barbola and her daughter, "Chita,"²³ were with the slave Pedro de Obando (formerly of Guatemala City but resident in Oaxaca for a year by then) and Pedro's wife, María Nicolasa (who had just been reunited with Pedro after living apart for a year in Guatemala City). As was her wont, she asked about Lorenzo, describing him as "mulatto, blue-eyed (zarco), raspy-voiced (ronquillo), the slave of don Juan de Otalora." María Nicolasa, with fresh news from Guatemala, said that he was well and married. Barbola and Chita were shocked, for they also knew that "he was married in Antequera with an Indian named Micaela who used to live next to the Augustinian monastery." María prodded Pedro: "Don't you remember this mulatto and when he married?"²⁴ Pedro admitted that he did, and shortly afterward he denounced Lorenzo to the commissioner of the Inquisition, saying that "he did not see [Lorenzo and Antonia García] marry but heard the banns read and saw them go to the church on their wedding day, return to their house, and in view of everyone, have a fiesta and later live together in one house."

As we would expect, to ask after one another's spouse, family, and compadres was, and still is, a standard conversational gambit. The mestizo Pedro de los Santos Alexos testified in 1780 that he had known José Francisco Ortiz and his wife María Josepha for at least ten years.²⁵ He knew, for example, that about ten years before, María used to bring food to José when he had been in the public jail of San Luis Potosí, that after getting out of jail José and María had gone to the mining camp of Matehuala, sixty miles or so to the north, and that José had left María there. Whether he thought this a temporary or permanent absence, he nevertheless went through a routine conversation when "about two years ago, in San Luis Potosí, he saw José and asked after María Josefa and José responded that she was to be commended to God, giving the witness to understand that she was dead."

In fact Pedro had just seen María alive, in a place called Puesto de Coyotes, and knew the reply to be blatantly inappropriate.²⁶ Here an unexpected answer to the conventional "how is your wife?" turned the routine exchange into an occasion for active suspicion. This suspicion, in turn, became a topic to broach in other conversations, until Pedro reported it to the Inquisition.[27]

Like Pedro, Joseph Benito de la Palma, a weaver native to Mexico City, passed through the standard courtesies on meeting his friend Manuel Tapia, a man he had known for many years.[28] He rarely saw Manuel's wife, María, yet as he testified in 1778, "on the occasions that he saw Tapia he always asked after his wife and received the impression that they were happy together." All of this became relevant only later, when the Holy Office charged María with bigamy. What matters here, however, is Tapia's recognition that his meetings with Tapia followed this conversational pattern. He directed the conventional "how is your wife?" to Tapia himself, a greeting and a courtesy to the head of a household, and not, to be sure, a question meant to elicit a detailed report. And no doubt the equally conventional string, "she is fine," gave him the impression that all was well.

The 'Other'

The patterns and formulaic courtesies of ordinary exchanges, therefore, sometimes evolved into interesting material about what was current and curious in the lives of others. This did not require a spellbinding story, such as that of Reyes's deceiving Josepha's father with the ruse of the robbers' cave. On the contrary, to be of interest news merely had to touch base with acquaintances and with minor day-to-day incidents, concerns, and musings within communities. Among these must have been mostly ignorant and unsympathetic characterizations of the world of the Indian 'others' that surrounded and touched on the Hispanic world in varying degrees. The shadowy terrain of Indian wisdom, lore, and magic stood as a fascinating universe surrounding Hispanic society yet a virtually inaccessible one.[29] It intrigued Spaniards because magic was power and Indians, according to Calvo, tried to maintain their reputation as possessors of the techniques, especially herbal preparations, that helped one find lost objects, tame a violent husband or master, seduce a young woman or attract a potential husband, heal a mysterious sickness, or retaliate against an enemy.[30]

In the 1780s the Spaniard Christóbal Ovando tried to penetrate this world, even though his methods and the quest itself placed him on the margin of respectable society.[31] His method was "to make and sell *chinguiritería*," a brandy made from sugar cane, and use it "to discover the secret ways and ideas of the Indians." He brought his alcohol to their gatherings and also made it available in his home. At least some of what he discovered he told to the priest, but for no good reason, according to the inquisitorial prosecutor, who said that "he carried their stories and jokes to the priest daily and by this, perhaps, fomented a most harmful disunion in the pueblo." And surely the tricks, knowledge, and occult practices Christóbal could represent as coming from his Indian sources (without doubt garbled and distorted, perhaps purposefully so by the 'informants') became a staple in the content of his conversations.

The Inquisition, mainly concerned with Christóbal's alleged bigamy, saw him only as a mischief-maker, not a dabbler in sorcery. They may have misjudged him, for he had a compulsive and ultimately serious interest in native beliefs and lore that he veiled only thinly by mocking it in his reports to the priest. The fascination may have been mutual, but if not, the reports seemed to buy off priestly censure for trafficking in alcohol, for they could be seen as a necessary means for keeping tabs on the secret world of the Indians. The bonus for Christóbal was its profitability. All of this put Christóbal at the margin of the Hispanic world and increasingly uncomfortable with what his wife referred to as "decent foreigners." Whenever such persons came to Coscomatepec (jurisdiction of Córdoba, a sujeto of Ixhuatlan, now in Veracruz state), his wife said, he became "agitated and preoccupied" and "would disappear, wandering the streets until daybreak . . . and at other times go into the milpas and mountains for days at a time."

Another Spaniard, don Joseph Serrano y Mora, became obsessed with the idea that an Indian shaman could "show him where money was buried."[32] Don Joseph confessed to the inquisitors on September 3, 1774, that "on eighteen or twenty occasions during the period of four months that he was in Tepexi del Río [four leagues south of Tula], . . . he brought [the shaman] Ramoncillo to his house and gave him presents to this end but he only said that he did not know about gold." Don Joseph did not leave it at that. He also showed Ramoncillo some powders and a marble object that he had taken from another Indian named El Sol when the latter was put in jail. Again Ramoncillo frustrated him, saying that "he did not know or recognize those things."

Did such 'conversations' take place frequently? Probably yes, on those many occasions when Spaniards sought shamanistic power to solve everyday problems.[33] The examples of Christóbal and don Joseph give some idea of their awkwardness, for momentarily they inverted the social structure. The transactions followed a kind of model of seduction: affected friendliness, hospitality, alcohol to release inhibitions and loosen the tongue, all in the effort to gain access to the gnostic power of the other. Yet in the background lay the correct social order. Don Joseph consistently refers to the shaman as Ramoncillo, a patronizing diminutive in this case, and Christóbal, at least to the priest, affects a mocking attitude. Neither man entered the Indian world. Their greed was too transparent, their 'seductions' too clumsy. The 'otherness' of the Indian in these encounters, therefore, remained beyond reach. Ramoncillo endured the vulgar courtship with dignity, simply denying that don Joseph's concerns had anything to do with his own.

If Indians surrounded the Hispanic world, Jews were imbedded within it, an insidious other because they appeared as no different from old Christians after persecution and forced conversion led them to blend in. Part of this resulted in intermarriages. If we can believe the testimony of don Joseph Serrano y Mora in 1774, he suffered an attack of anxiety fifteen years before when "recent arrivals in Málaga said that doña Francisca, his wife-to-be, was descended of Jews."[34] Unsure of what to do, he "went to see a gentleman of advanced age, one of the most distinguished of the town." The older man derided the information as false, and don Joseph went ahead with the marriage. But the rumors continued, he claimed, when in "conversations on various subjects, the militia sergeant's brother . . . said that [the name of] her grandfather or great-grandfather was on a board above the church prison." Others said that "a relative of the mother of her mother" had been tried by the Inquisition. Such "conversations took place among plebeians (*gente plebeya*)."

In this way don Joseph depicted conversations current in Málaga around 1760, seeming to imply that the allegation and the 'evidence' for it were topical. He saw it as undermining his reputation. And no doubt it did, as it made for a nice topic with which commoners might bring one of their betters down a notch or two. This in fact explains why commoners found the matter so compelling. Their apparently endless fascination can be contrasted with the old gentleman's scornful dismissal of the rumors as "false and a lie." Elites and plebeians were divided, and the former viewed with some uneasiness the loose tongues of commoners out of control as they decided who of their betters was tainted.

THE CARRIERS

Curiosity

So far we have stressed that people talked about other people by placing strangers and updating each other's movements. Driving the process was an ever-present curiosity about acquaintances, friends, relatives, and paisanos. People eagerly listened to and passed on what they were told about each other, and the ups and downs of marriages provided endless topics.[35] Through conversations they enlarged and modified the stories they started with and also, sometimes, the significance they attached to them. A common pattern found compatriots from Spain meeting in the Indies to talk about compatriots at home and in the Indies as well. Thus in 1615 we have Anna Gerónima of Cádiz, married to a barber-surgeon, arriving in New Spain just one fleet after her countryman Juan Francisco, whom she had known in Cádiz.[36] Anna met up with him in Puebla and gave him a letter from his wife, Francisca. Although we do not know the contents of this letter, Anna's testimony, given on May 7, 1615, includes her account of meeting Juan: "He asked after his wife and gave [Anna] a letter [addressed] to Francisca to send in the first despatch ship (*navio de aviso*) and asked this witness to write the said [Francisca] to apply herself to her responsibilities, look to her honor, and expect money for her passage so that she could come and make [a married] life with him."

Had Juan Francisco already said this in his own letter, or was this part of an attempt to mislead Anna? We do not know, but the exhortation, about what would have been expected from an absent husband, backfired when Anna found out that Juan Francisco had married in New Spain. She was conversing with the silk dealer Antonio Morales just after he returned from Oaxaca and (as he testified on May 6, 1615) he told her that Juan, his "friend" in Puebla, had been married in Oaxaca for four months.[37] Antonio remembered Anna's "indignation" and her determination, "because she was Francisca's friend, to write a letter giving the news of the evil (*maldad*) that the said Juan Francisco had done in this land."[38]

The convergence of information about Juan Francisco became notable and therefore documented, because it became an ever-tighter net closing in on his bigamy. Here, however, let us concentrate on how the process evolved. Initially people found Juan to be topical not because they suspected him but because he was a countryman, friend, or acquaintance. News of his illegal marriage, passed along as part of the 'he-is-doing-well-in-Oaxaca' report, became damaging, the basis for prosecution, because Anna, fresh from Spain, could be sure that he had committed bigamy.

A similar process, innocently focused on a 'what-is-Felipe-up-to-now' exchange, helped to uncover the bigamous second marriage of the mulatto Felipe Rodríguez.[39] Sometime in the 1750s, after a marriage of perhaps fifteen years but with frequent absences from his home base of Zumpango (one, as we saw in chapter 4, lasted four years), Felipe took off with his team of mules, apparently without intending to return. The testimony of his wife María Robles in 1775 tells how the first scrap of information about him got back to Zumpango.

> He left about seven or eight years ago. There was no motive: no dispute, anger, or anything else. Only once was there news from Felipe when Alejandro Leonardo, vecino of Zumpango, ran into Felipe on the road to San Juan del Río [jurisdiction of Querétaro, now Querétaro state] and Felipe told Alejandro to say to everyone that he was well and hadn't suffered any setbacks.

No cause for concern here, for over the years, when he was away for long periods, Felipe must have relayed similar reassurances to compatriots from his tierra. This time, however, Felipe had been gone longer than ever before. Perhaps only María, who twice before had fetched Felipe home from a new life in the making, would have seen this as deviating from a pattern. Alejandro certainly had no suspicions, and he innocently and routinely recounted the meeting and message.

Yet by this time, about 1768, Felipe had moved decidedly out of the orbit of his old life, and six years later he formally constituted a new one with a second marriage. Within a year news of this found its way back to Zumpango. Once again it was a curiosity-driven exchange of bits of information as individuals, haphazardly gathered, formed a temporarily enlarged pool of information. It occurred on a Thursday in May of 1775 at the plaza of Guadalupe, where María's cousin was selling maize. His interest quite naturally alighted on the arrival of his cousin's husband, and he wondered aloud who his companion was. Thus he activated the network around him and from "one and another" learned that both men served Canon Malpica of Valladolid and that Felipe was married there. In this way they discovered Felipe's new life and then denounced him to the Inquisition.

Contrasting Felipe's different fortunes at the hands of his wife's cousin with those at the hands of his compatriot Alejandro shows us that simple curiosity fueled the endless and mostly aimless process. Hearing about the associates, whereabouts, adventures, run-ins, and foibles of others (however banal the settings, however ordinary the protagonists) passed the time, provided amusement, and reinforced in-group solidarity. And sometimes information coming together in this way, especially but not only when the curious realized that one of their own had been victimized, was reported to authorities. Norms therefore penetrated into popular culture but not only and not mainly as abstractions. Yet popular concern over illicit behavior also reflected the legalistic stance of society in placing so much emphasis on an event (the illegal marriage) rather than a process (the long abandonment that led up to the marriage). Alejandro, for example, knew that Felipe had long lived apart from his wife and family but gave that no particular significance. Thus his 'Felipe-is-doing-fine' report to María. Without news of Felipe's second marriage, the conversation of María's cousin might also have lapsed, although as part of María's family, he might have had a more pointed 'you-aren't-supporting-your-wife' line on Felipe which could have been cause to suspect the presence of another woman. As it turned out, however, the routine 'Felipe is married in Valladolid' brought María's cousin immediately to attention, for he knew as a certainty that Felipe was already married.

Once rumors got back to the tierra of their subject, they must have become generally known overnight. In the early 1660s, for example, the entire community of Xalapa (an alcaldía mayor on the gulf slope west of Veracruz, now in Veracruz state) homed in on the report that the mestizo Juan Luis de la Cruz was a bigamist.[40] The rumor began to circulate six years after Juan married a second time, in 1656, to María Núñez of Xalapa, and consisted of talk that "he was married in Puebla to an Indian who sold in the plaza." This at least is how Sebastián de la Cruz expressed it in his deposition of October 2, 1662. Sebastián's boss, Juan Dias de la Cueva, became curious and, in the course of having other business in Puebla, sent Sebastián and Juan Martín, one of his slaves, with instructions to "ask around and find out if what they are saying about the said Juan de la Cruz is true."[41]

Sebastián and Juan found Juana Agustina selling lengths of cord (*mecates*), and she identified Juan Luis as her husband, although at the time she married him, she said, he called himself Juan Ruiz. More dramatically, as Sebastián talked to her, he realized that Juana was his long-lost mother after she tentatively recognized him and then recounted some family details: that she had married Juan Ruiz who had deserted her after a year and a half of marriage; that her son had been born in Cholula and she had sent him to an apprenticeship in Mexico City when he was little. Sebastián declared himself the lost son and embraced her.[42] Although Juana had not seen her husband for twenty years, she was not completely in the dark about him. The muleteer Melchior, a slave of Juan's former employer, had reported to her that Juan was in Xalapa, using the surname Cruz, and married to "a Spanish woman." When Sebastián and Juan brought news of Juana back to Xalapa, the murmurings about Juan became more assured.

They reached into his very household, and Juan's second wife, María Núñez, remembered asking him "for the love of God confess to me if all this is true so that I can get things settled."⁴³

As the net began to close around Juan, those with a financial interest in him scurried to recover anything they had entrusted to him. A Xalapan merchant commissioned the Spanish tailor Antonio de Castro, for example, to find Juan and collect money that Juan was to pick up from a merchant in Veracruz. This action anticipated Juan's arrest and the embargo of any property in his possession. As he made his way to Veracruz, Antonio ran into the muleteer Luis López, headed for Xalapa. Juan, of course, was topical and Antonio, on learning that Luis had subcontracted Juan to freight some cacao, warned him of possible losses. Luis (testifying on August 28, 1662) recalled him saying "look out for the cargo that Juan de la Cruz is bringing because it is on your account and you'd better get hold of it because they've told me and written [to me] that they are bringing to Xalapa an Indian wife of the said Juan de la Cruz and without a doubt he is married twice." But "thinking that there was no basis for [the report]," Luis remained sceptical. He must have had second thoughts farther along the road, however, when "a Spanish youth not of this jurisdiction" inquired after Juan in the name of doctor Christóbal de Salzedo, with the object of collecting "some money and other things that he is bringing to the said doctor." Luis, telling the young man that Juan was behind him and wondering why he was in such a hurry, received this answer: "because of word that Juan has two wives in Xalapa and to avoid litigation" over goods that surely would be impounded.

As for Juan himself, the moment of truth came in Veracruz, as he was about to depart for Xalapa, his mules loaded with Luis López's cacao. Juan's helper, the Indian Juan Luseno, remembered that

> they gave him a paper and it made him very sad and he would not eat or drink
> . . . and he said he was very sad because his wife was sick and although [Juan]
> told him to eat something he did not want to . . . and, having left some
> bundles of cacao in Vera Cruz because his mules could not carry them all,
> they traveled to La Rinconada where he delivered the loads he was bringing
> to Luis López . . . and Juan said he was going to see his wife and he went
> without [Juan] seeing him again.

Our final picture of Juan shows him tidying up his affairs as best he could: getting the cacao to Luis and leaving the mules behind (they had come to him as part of his second wife's dowry), while keeping to the fiction that his wife had fallen sick and he was going to her. La Rinconada, nothing but an inn some twenty miles from Veracruz on the Xalapa road, was, according to Thomas Gage, "the hottest place from San Juan de Ulua to Mexico," which had remarkably "refreshing water," "abundance of provision," and at night, "swarms of gnats [that] no device of man is able to keep . . . off."[44] From here, a necessary stopping place for muleteers, Juan departed to establish himself elsewhere. We do not know where he headed, but his file suggests that he found yet another life to live in a place where the Inquisition never located him.

Muleteers

Everybody had some gossip, rumor, or news to relate as they met one another, passed the time, and filled in details about people, events, weather, crops, and other topics that mattered in everyday life. Thinking of this as delimited to region or locale, the dynamic aspect would have been the news from the outside that allowed for the constant revising, renewing, and enlarging of a pool of information. So those coming into a district (muleteers, seasonal workers, peddlers, and travelers in general) acted as agents of the process. Communities relied on such people to pass on what they knew, to pick up what they could, and to convey elsewhere what they had seen and heard.

As a muleteer Nicolás Sebastián had been "all over New Spain" before marrying in 1671.[45] This was a second marriage, contracted, Nicolás testified, because Mateo, another muleteer just returned from "the gulf," had brought him news that his first wife had died. As it turned out, Mateo had been wrong, but here, let us note, Nicolás accepted the report as probably true because he habitually relied on muleteers for news.

María Teresa de la Cruz, approaching a group of muleteers loading biscuits at Captain Joseph Hidalgo's bakery (biscochería) in Puebla in 1707, held the same assumption as she asked for news of her muleteer husband, Juan Lorenzo del Castillo.[46] And she was not disappointed, for the mulatto Antonio Gamboa stepped forward with plenty to tell her. He had been padrino of Juan's second marriage, eight months before in Mexico City, a last-minute replacement, he said, because "Juan de Amaro, mulatto slave and loader of Miguel Hidalgo's mules, backed out because he had no money." The marriage took place at Santa Catarina Church attended by muleteers and cart drivers most of whom were mulattoes. A celebration followed at Juan's house, and the next morning, Antonio said, he and Juan were back on the job, heading for Acapulco with Hidalgo's mules.[47]

María Teresa made Antonio promise to report Juan to the Inquisition, and she too went immediately to the commissioner in Puebla to denounce him. The important point for us here, however, is her presumption that muleteers (a kind of fraternal network, dispersed but periodically renewing contact with one another on the road, at inns, and in distribution centers) would know about one another. Witness, for example, Juan's wedding, very much an affair of muleteers, from guests to padrino.

Yet muleteers also made mistakes and sometimes brought conflicting reports. At thirty the mulatto laundress Juana Tadea, of Indio Triste Street in Mexico City, spoke in 1746 of the differing reports that had come to her of her husband, Sebastián.[48] He had been gone for seven years,[49] and in that time she said that she had "not had news except for that from some muleteers from the north, some from Guadalajara, and others from Za-catecas and Chihuahua. But a few days ago she heard from some coun-trymen that he was in Chihuahua and had married again but others say he is not and she is not sure." The contradictory information confused rather than clarified Sebastián's status, but at least she had reports to work with that gave her the chance to try to confirm one or another of them.

For his part Sebastián faced the opposite problem: the dearth of news about Juana that reached the isolated presidio of Conchos (a large district with the commander of the presidio acting as justicia mayor, now in southeast Chihuahua state). He ended up trusting too much a single report that proved to be mistaken; at least that is what he told the inquisitors on March 2, 1748. "About four years ago, having been at the presidio for three or four months, a muleteer named Juan Joseph Montes arrived who had passed through this city [Mexico City]. Since he knew this witness he said that his house had been infected by disease and his wife and mother-in-law had died." After the marriage it took nearly three years for correct information to reach Sebastián in Conchos, but long before that (within a year) a fellow soldier who had traveled to Mexico City discovered Juana alive and denounced Sebastián.

Visitors from the Old Life

If rumors persisted and those who supplied them seemed reliable, they sooner or later led to accusations. In a case involving the mulatto Chris-tóbal de Castroverde (born ca. 1576 in Seville), the process took about four months.[50] It began in the spring of 1616, when the Spaniard don Francisco de Nuncibay y Borques (about thirty, probably the nephew of a man Christóbal's mother had served[51]) was running some colts and mules from

Villa de los Valles in the Huasteca to Pachuca (a journey of well over fifty leagues in rough country). Near the end of the journey, don Francisco ran into Christóbal, recognized him, and called out to him: "Señor Castroverde, don't you recognize me?"[52] Christóbal said that he did not, but don Francisco persisted: "Don't you remember don Francisco Nuncibay, son of licenciado Francisco de Nuncibay?" Don Francisco, in fact, was a ghost from Christóbal's past, hardly a person he expected or wanted to see on this stretch of road or anywhere else. Here is how don Francisco remembered his reaction: "Señor, Your Grace would be very much like him but as you appear so dark and now older, I did not recognize you."[53] As they talked don Francisco said that he had a letter, given to him when he left for the Indies four years before, from Christóbal's wife in Seville. In the meantime don Francisco noticed that Christóbal seemed anxious to be off. "He said that he was going to mass and he was late in finishing some work for a Castañeda and therefore begged me to see him on my return from Pachuca."

So they went their separate ways, but shortly afterward don Francisco was back in Atotonilco ([el Chico], jurisdiction of Pachuca, now in southern Hidalgo state) and, speaking to Christóbal de Ojeda, recounted how he had just run into his countryman. As they talked Ojeda discovered that Christóbal was married to "a mulatto in Seville," and don Francisco, that he had a wife in Omitlan, ten or twelve miles southeast of Atotonilco. As Ojeda remembered it, don Francisco said that "within two days he had to go to Mexico City and would notify the inquisitors."

Thus Ojeda had no urgency to report the news about Castroverde to the authorities, and a month or two passed before he happened to be in Omitlan. There, before an interested audience, he relayed the news to Antonio Moroato, a man he barely knew.[54] Moroato took it up as a piece of interesting gossip, spread it around, and worked to have Castroverde arrested. Running into Castroverde himself two days later, he advised him to turn himself in, but Castroverde denied everything. Moroato also spoke to Francisco Lozano, Castroverde's father-in-law, who told him that it was wrong to slander Christóbal. Instead he should report what he had said to fray Juan de Santa Ana (*calificador* for the Holy Office in Omitlan) or, in case he could not find him, to the alcalde mayor, "so that [Christóbal] could be arrested."[55]

Lozano's reaction seems contradictory: on the one hand he calls the rumors slanderous, as if they had no basis in fact; on the other, he urges that they be reported to the authorities, as if they did. No doubt he had found his family's association with the emerging scandal painful, but he also knew that it had to be resolved. So, with no quick intervention by the authorities, he himself seized on the chance to confront Castroverde (out of Omitlan for over a month since the suspicions first surfaced) in a family setting. And indeed it was a family matter, for if it were true, Castroverde's two children with Lozano's daughter, a son now three and a daughter eight, would be adulterinos, bereft of inheritance rights and of honor. From Lozano's deposition of July 1616, we learn how he confronted Castroverde.

> Yesterday, the day before San Pedro's day, it will have been a week since [Castroverde] came to the house of this witness where he has kept his wife after he married her and this witness said, in front of [Castroverde's] wife, their children, and his own [wife] that how was it that he was such a bad Christian that being married in Seville he married a second time.

As time went on, then, the community began to accept the reports as true, as if their mere repetition confirmed them. Even Lozano, to judge by his accusation, had come a long way from his first reaction to the report of four or five weeks earlier. Licenciado Mateo de Otaço, priest and vicar of the mines, at first had given them even less credence than Lozano. Mateo had known the details of the reports for three months but continued to call them "rumors," even in the face of "publicity in the past few days." His skepticism gave way only after Lozano confronted Christóbal with the allegations and in response, as Lozano remembered it, remained silent and "lowered his head as a guilty man." Licenciado Mateo, like Lozano, took this as an admission of guilt, and Lozano went to the alcalde mayor (in Pachuca) to request that his son-in-law be arrested.

The reports about Christóbal persisted not because authorities took them up but because ordinary people did. The former, with no more evidence than hearsay and gossip, remained sceptical. They did not trust plebeian stories as true out of hand but assessed them more dispassionately as not necessarily what they seemed to be. We see this attitude in the face of the testimony of "a sailor" who, when the banns were read in 1554 for Ana Díaz's (born ca. 1519) marriage to Pedro Rodríguez in the mining camp of Sultepeque, told Ana, the vicar, and Ana's master, Alonso Carreño, that Pedro was married in his tierra, Portugal.[56] Carreño spoke to Pedro who offered an explanation. As Ana recalled, he had said that "when sailors collect their salary they do not pay the unmarried men and Pedro said 'pay me—I am also married—so I can send money to my wife,' and he said this with cunning." Carreño thought this probably conventional deception explained why another sailor might mistakenly think Pedro already married and allowed his marriage with Ana to proceed.

He, not the vicar, made the decision. But the reports continued to reach Ana, and they troubled her. Later in Guayangareo [Valladolid and, after 1826, Morelia], for example, she served a Franciscan friar who taught at the college there while Pedro was away looking for work, and "many persons . . . told her that Pedro was already married in Portugal [she testified in June 1572], and with this she went crying to the friars of San Francisco of the pueblo and told them what was being said publicly about Pedro and asked them what to do." They, however, dismissed the rumors and advised her that she should "live with the said Pedro her husband and she was not obligated to give credit to what was being said."

Possibly the matter seemed less urgent than it might have otherwise, for Ana and Pedro had no children who would have been adulterinos. As far as local officials were concerned, they might have continued as before in spite of the rumors. Pedro, as in his initial interview with Carreño, convincingly denied them. The friars were sceptical. The breakthrough in this stalemate between popular rumor and official scepticism came when a bailiff of Zacatecas interested himself in the case (perhaps he was more closely attuned to the rumor mill), questioned Pedro, and threatened to arrest him. With this Pedro fled, ostensibly to clear his name but more likely to escape the closing net. Except for the bailiff, then, those with authority seemed to think of plebeians as repeating gossip indiscriminately. Carreño and the friars refused to take the reports at face value but saw them more as 'stories' unworthy of official action.[57] So here and elsewhere they proceeded as a kind of local entertainment that sometimes, probably to the surprise of many, proved true.

The Denunciation as Personal Attack

Denounced persons, as a first line of defense, might associate allegations against them as maliciously intended. Defendants, in fact, always had the right to name enemies who might have testified against them (they of course would have had no precise knowledge of prosecution witnesses), so that the court could disallow such testimony or at least examine it with special care. Agustín de Hoz, we saw, alleged that an enemy would have been the source of the denunciation against him.[58] He said that "Antonio de Cuéllar . . . whom he knew in Spain, may have testified against him because he refused to give him money and therefore became his enemy."[59] Martín Luis, who in 1588 was in prison for debt, also claimed that he was a victim of malice, when Luis Gómez denounced him as married in Portugal (as well as in New Spain) and, presumably to avoid detection, living under an assumed name "because this is what he has heard."[60] Martín put the denunciation in another light when he said that he "had beaten a young man named Luis González with a stick" and it was therefore nothing but maliciousness, "raised because he is an enemy." The judges agreed that this circumstance discredited the denunciation and released Martín.[61]

No doubt a revenge-minded Luis had acted opportunistically. He seized hearsay that came his way and used it to get back at his antagonist. The crucial aspect, however, was that such denunciations be plausible, that they be not *only* revenge. In 1560, for example, Catalina García's denunciation of Pedro Hernández of Antequera seemed plausible, simply because he was in the Indies without his wife.[62] Catalina testified that he had been "publicly in concubinage with a married woman" and that he had stated that "friars, pretending to confess women, instead 'screw' them right in the churches" and, for good measure, that "the devil is the leader of all priests and friars."[63]

Pedro's witnesses presented material to impugn the character and motives of Catalina. Her original denunciation had been corroborated by her sister María, but another witness said that María had testified under threat of eviction from Catalina's house. Another witness said that "Catalina customarily raises false testimony, that she has a malicious tongue, and is wont to say bad things about some people." All in all, as Pedro summarized it, Catalina was "a bad Christian who drinks wine and pulque in her house, and [is motivated by] the anger and enmity she has for me." By contrast, he, according to his witnesses, had not been seen consorting with the woman in question, nor had he "defamed anybody," and he was well known as a charitable person and a good Christian.

Such testimony might seem sufficient to drop the case except for the overriding circumstance that Pedro was in the Indies without his wife.[64] Whatever the merits of Catalina's charges, the inquisitors held Pedro suspect. They sentenced him to return to Spain and resume life with his wife within a year. And in the meantime they fined him six pesos, ordered that "from now on he have the appropriate respect and reverence in word and deed for the ministers of the Holy Mother Church," and that he stay completely away from the house of the woman in question. The sentence presumes guilt (even of the obviously made-up charges of sacrilegious remarks) not from the solidity of the 'evidence,' but because men such as Pedro, who lived apart from their wives, were automatically suspect.

Community interest in María de Aguirre's possibly bigamous marriage also fell within the logic of local factionalisms.[65] The case, embedded as it is in the conquest era, reflects that unsettled time. It began in 1529 when María married Diego de Villareal. He lived with her for fifteen years in Mexico City, Guazacualco (an alcaldía mayor until the eighteenth century, now at the eastern edge of Veracruz state), and Chiapas, and then went to Peru in 1544. María and her four children had no news of Diego for six years, and in Mérida, where they then lived, reports arrived that he was dead. She therefore married Francisco Manrique. Seven or eight years later, however, word arrived that Diego was alive. María, before the inquisitors in 1563, characterized these rumors as

> murmurings not based on certain information, firm knowledge, or eyewitnesses which came to the attention of the Franciscan friars who at that time administered ecclesiastical justice, and to some people who were motivated by passion and enmity for the said Francisco Manrique, especially licenciado Miranda, dean and vicar general who first dealt with this cause when they tried to separate María from Francisco . . . [but] all the people of noble birth of Mérida took Diego for dead.

In other words, María charged, the unfortunate rumors had been taken up by the rabble and the friars, thus laying bare the social divisions in the community. Miranda ordered that Francisco separate from María, but he "did not accept nor did he obey." Francisco had enough support in the community to dismiss the order with impunity. Here the news that came into a town took the form not of an entertainment but of an issue to be seized upon by an opportunistic faction.

The coincidence of damaging information with local politics came as a happy circumstance to the denouncer and a bitter pill to the denounced. In 1678 Mariana Monroy spoke self-reflectively about having to swallow just such a pill.[66] Francisca de Garibay, who "has been and is her enemy," she said, circulated word that Mariana's husband, whom she hated and had presumed dead, was in fact alive. Mariana refused to believe the report for nearly a year. To the inquisitors she admitted her inner resistance and turmoil before finally acknowledging it and confessed that "she had had irritation, hatred, and ill will toward the person who spread the news of the survival of her husband as certain through this city [Mexico City]."

The issue here became the informants' motives, which when transparently self-interested, might also discredit their accusations. We already saw that Pedro Hernández portrayed his denouncer, Catalina, as compromised because she drank pulque and habitually gossiped. Her charges, therefore, should also be seen as frivolous and perverse, especially because he countered them with the word of disinterested persons of 'quality.' María de Aguirre, whom we just saw embroiled in social and political rivalries in Mérida, used a similar tactic. In her defense she called no less a personage than "don Francisco de Montejo, lieutenant governor who was in these provinces," who testified, in truth quite vaguely, that "in the town of Vitoria de Tabasco he received very certain news from a priest and two Spanish soldiers" that the man in question had died.[67] Yet to good effect, it seems, possibly in recognition of his status and that of María's other allies, for the vicar found that María had been "invincibly ignorant" that her husband Diego was alive (by now he had been confirmed as dead) when she married a second time. He therefore declared her blameless and eligible immediately to remarry Francisco.

Who Said What?

The weight of presumption, therefore, rested on who said what, as don Juan Antonio Ulloa, in 1686 explained to the inquisitors. "Obviously one cannot marry a second time while his wife is alive, but when a husband is away and a person comes and tells him that his wife is dead and this person is trustworthy, then he can marry with a clear conscience."[68] Specifically don Juan claimed that he relied on a letter from his father-in-law and the word of Joseph Bernardo de Quirós, who "having just come from Toro [Zamora] not only told him but affirmed it with an oath." For don Juan, then, the word of two honorable men who were eyewitnesses, not merely the recipients of hearsay, made the news dependable.

Messages brought straight from one's tierra (from Spain to the Indies or from one part of the Indies to another) were therefore presumed true. So reasoned Juan Bautista Alemán, a runaway slave owned by Augustinian friars, who left his wife, son, and daughter at hacienda San Lucas, jurisdiction of Guatemala City.[69] He had lived for ten years as a free man in the town of Tacotalpa (jurisdiction of Guazacualco, now Veracruz state) and, he testified in 1735, "a compatriot, the mulatto (*pardo*) vaquero Juan Salvador, told him that his wife had died and he [Juan Salvador] then served as a witness in the hearings for his second marriage."

Juan Bautista's hasty remarriage suggests that he was already living informally with the woman he was ready to marry. The news that made the marriage possible, therefore, must have been welcome, not least because it seemed solidly grounded by an eyewitness. We can contrast it with Juan de Barrera's reference to a message he supposedly received, as he described in a self-denunciation of August 17, 1686. The report, he said, came not from a compatriot but "a mulatto he ran into whose name he does not remember who told him that his wife in Tehuacán had died and he had seen her buried."[70] We have, then, the vaguely described nameless mulatto, who could not be traced, who nevertheless Juan represented as an eyewitness to the burial. The inquisitors could hardly be expected to take such a report as reliable. And rightly so, for Juan admitted that he had married a second time less because of the alleged report (most likely he made it up) than because he was already engaged in a new life with Elena de la Cruz. If such a report arrived at all, it came at a suspiciously convenient moment, when Juan was being pressured to marry Elena.

We must assume the all-too-human inclination to welcome the 'good' news and deny the 'bad.' Messengers with the first were taken as credible, those with the second, as mistaken or mischievous, the last a kind of symbolic slaying of the proverbial bearer of bad news. In this regard consider the denunciation given by the Spaniard Matías Martínez de Torres (June 21, 1663), who in the 1660s peddled goods in the region of Guatemala City.[71] Seven leagues from the city, at the Jesuit hacienda de Santa Anna, he learned of an escaped slave whose description (bald, taller than average, and branded on the face) fit the mulatto Sebastián de Loaysa, whom he knew in Guatemala City. Here, taken from Matías's deposition, is how Sebastián reacted to the report: "The father or whoever said it was drunk."

While not in a position to impugn Matías directly, Sebastián certainly spoke rudely of him as a source of information. Had Matías been a mulatto or Indian and Sebastián a Spaniard, we might well have expected the messenger to have been discredited then and there, a prejudice that sprang up automatically when Indians or mulattoes brought unwanted news.[72] Witness then the assurance of the Spaniard Marcos de la Cruz who, in a statement before the inquisitors in 1671, explained how he resolved conflicting reports about the alleged death of his first wife, Teresa.[73] Indians brought the disagreeable report (he had by then already married a second time) that she was alive; a Spaniard, the welcome confirmation that she had died. The latter he took as true, he said, because "he heard it from Diego López Pazuelo, a Spaniard married in Sayula, now dead, and he did not make any inquiries at all to see if it was certain or not." Later, Marcos testified, word reached him

in Zapotlan [an alcaldía mayor in the sierra de Michoacán, now ciudad Guzmán in southern Jalisco state], a pueblo beyond Sayula [six or seven leagues southeast of Zapotlan, an alcaldía mayor from 1615, now in Jalisco state] where some Indians told him that they had come from Guadalajara and had seen and talked with Teresa, but he did not believe them because they were Indians.

The assumption that Indians were untrustworthy, in this case, served Marcos well, for Teresa had to remain 'dead' so that he could carry on with his new life.

Even when 'well-disposed' toward Indian witnesses, Spaniards assumed a well-practiced patronizing posture, and, in the dock, Indians an equally well-practiced servile one. In 1621 the Inquisition called in Juana Agustina, an Indian who knew no Spanish, to testify about her marriage to the mestizo Domingo Rodríguez.[74] For an interpreter the court used Francisco Martín, vecino of San Juan del Río (jurisdiction of Querétaro, now in Querétaro state), a mulatto "who has served his majesty as a soldier in the wars with the Chichimecas in the said pueblo and its region, and knows well the Mexican language." Juana prefaced her testimony, possibly formulaically inserted as she was sworn in, with the proviso that "although she is an Indian, she wants to tell the truth of what she knows and what she has heard." Whether volunteered or imposed, however, Juana testified within the shadow of the inferior standing ascribed to her, one that was underscored by judicial protocols.[75]

Mestizos and castas impugned the word of Indians less handily because they were not as decisively above them in rank. Francisco Catalán, for example, was raised by his Indian mother and spoke her language, even though his father was a Spaniard.[76] In 1652 he married Agustina, an Indian of San Juan Amatitán (jurisdiction of Guatemala City), and two years later, thinking his wife was dead, married again in Orizaba (an alcaldía mayor on the gulf side of the Citlaltépetl volcano, now in central Veracruz state), where he worked as a muleteer for a Captain Olmeda. Improbable as it might seem, he lived for thirteen years with his second wife, María Martínez, before hearing that Agustina was alive. Francisco testified in 1667 that the information had reached him

fifteen days ago [when] he was coming from Orizaba to Puebla de Los Angeles with iron[77] loaded on his master's mules for a Juan Cruzado, vecino of Puebla, and having delivered it . . . he went to the Inn of the Angel in the neighborhood of Analco on the other side of the river to see if there were some Guatemalans there with news of his tierra. He ran into an Indian lad named Baltasar . . . and, along with other news of his tierra of Guatemala,

[Baltasar] said that Agustina, [Francisco's] first wife, was living in pueblo San Juan . . . and had been on her last legs from smallpox, so close to death that it only remained to put her in a shroud.

With no sympathy for Agustina, Francisco told Baltasar that the news was a piece of "bad luck" because he had married again in Orizaba on hearing that Agustina had already died of smallpox.

The fact is he was fully engaged in a new life, and the news dragged him back to his old one. If his disquiet came from no particular malice toward Agustina, it nevertheless represented the breakup of his present. It would have been easy enough to deny the news or impugn the carrier as merely an Indian, but (and this for our purposes is the interesting point) he accepted it as true. He returned with the mules to Orizaba, delivered them to his master, whom "he told what had happened so he could direct him as to what he would have to do." For Francisco the information was authoritative because it came directly from his tierra, a criterion that overshadowed the fact that an Indian had transmitted it.[78]

THE INQUIRERS

Our discussion of carriers stressed the randomness of chance meetings and the way that curiosity fueled the exchange of news and gossip. We also looked at how people tried to screen out inconvenient news and, by examining denunciations as personal attacks, how hearsay might be seized upon opportunistically. We saw the movement of news as an integral part of normal routines and movements, as part of the baggage of mobile types, and as 'entertainments' to tell and retell as people passed the time, discovered common ground, and exchanged what they had seen and heard. Inquirers differed from carriers in that they were looking for specific information. In this we see them approaching their sources more systematically, as if they were in fact dealing with a system.

Family

The distinction between carriers and inquirers can be illustrated in the way that the mestizo Lázaro Domínguez of Pénjamo (jurisdiction of León, now in Guanajuato state) acted when he heard that in Xalostotitlan (jurisdiction of Lagos, now the Altos de Jalisco, Jalisco state), some eighty miles to the northeast, his son-in-law Pedro Mateo had another wife.[79]

The report came to Lázaro in 1666, a year or so after Pedro's second marriage, from Indians of Xalostotitlan who were in Pénjamo asking for contributions (*limosna*) for their hospital. Lázaro decided to investigate, and the testimony in 1666 of a local man, the mulatto Simón Hernández, servant of bachelor Martín, probably holder of the benefice of Xalostotitlán, tells of his coming to the pueblo.

> A mestizo [Lázaro] came from Río Grande [possibly the presidio in the jurisdiction of Nieves, now in northwest Zacatecas state] four to six months after Pedro Mateo left Francisca Hernández [his first wife], . . . and asked [Simón] if Pedro was married in Xalostotitlan. This witness said yes, that he had been padrino. And the mestizo said that he had sent Pedro to Zacatecas to sell shingles (*tajamanil*) which gave him the chance to make this investigation . . . and to come more secretly he brought bananas and oranges to sell.

Lázaro thus confirmed that Pedro had married twice and spread the word. Two local men joined in the effort to arrest Pedro; one of them, the mestizo Miguel Gómez, testified that "he had scolded [Pedro] and said 'don't you have any shame to have married while married [already] in Xalostotitlan, for we all know that your wife is alive.'"

Lázaro had to find out if his son-in-law was already married, for that would have invalidated his daughter's marriage. It also made the children of such unions illegitimate and put dowered property at risk. If second wives faced these problems, abandoned first wives had the opposite problem: to locate legitimate, rightful husbands, sometimes years after they had gone. So it happened that Bartolomé Pérez de Reyna, twenty-four years after his father-in-law Melchior Ortega left his wife Catalina and made his way to the Indies, followed him, accompanied by other members of the family.[80] On arrival they made the search for Melchior their first concern and made inquiries that led to finding him in Mérida, where he was living away from main traffic routes, remarried, and with a thirteen-year-old son. Melchior, rooted as he was in his new life, resisted his son-in-law's news that Catalina had come to New Spain. Only the evidence of letters written by Catalina's two brothers convinced him. Thus he returned to his legitimate family, an association of less than three years that he abandoned some twenty-five years ago, and took leave of his illicit one, the daily context of his life for some fourteen years.

Melchior, in an out-of-the-way location, tried to reduce the risk of getting caught. No one expressed that consideration more bluntly than don Francisco de Quiñones, married for a second time in 1607, who testified in 1615 that he thought "it would be impossible to discover his crime in such a distant outpost."[81] To improve his chances more, he changed his identity (in the Indies he called himself Alvaro de Quiñones) and named an uncle and aunt in Naples as his parents. At the same time, however, he could not quite cut himself off from his legitimate wife in Sahagún (they married in 1595), with whom he continued to correspond. Becoming ever more deeply enmeshed in his life in the Indies, he none-theless never quite set aside his plans to return to Spain. The decision could no longer be postponed when, in a letter of "about three years ago," he said, his nephew Rodrigo de Prado of Sahagún "demanded that he separate from the second wife and get out of this bad state quickly or else he would make it known." Don Francisco took the threat seriously and, in an answering letter, remembered that he had "pleaded insistently [with Rodrigo] to keep silent, giving his word that he would be returning very shortly, that this would be the last time he would postpone leaving and would prove it by coming on the next fleet." Yet three years later don Francisco had not returned, and Rodrigo had not carried out his threat to denounce him. At that point, on August 29, 1615, Francisco denounced himself, evidently to calm a troubled conscience; having "many times thought he was about to lose his life," he came "to this Holy Office to make known his crime with much repentance."

So Rodrigo's attempt to solve a family problem quietly failed. Interest-ingly two confidants in the Indies shared don Francisco's secret. One was the alderman and municipal standard bearer (*alférez*) Juan Ortiz, a co-chineal merchant, whom don Francisco called "his comrade and intimate friend." Ortiz returned to Spain on the fleet that don Francisco promised his nephew he would be on. The other friend, Gonzalo Fernández, notary of the city of Puebla and native of Sahagún, had brought Rodrigo's letters when he came to the Indies two or three years before. If out of friendship and loyalty these men remained quiet about don Francisco's crime, it was probably because he had also promised them that he would soon comply with his nephew's demand.

Because don Francisco's crime was a sin, neither he nor his nephew and friends would likely conceal it indefinitely. Yet they avoided going to the authorities. Instead they threatened to do so while working behind the scenes to reunite don Francisco with his wife in Spain. They complied with church teachings but 'enforced' them flexibly. Such leniency amounted to an informal way to comply with legal norms (or at least not to resist them frontally), while shielding blood and fictive kin from the full force of church and state authority.[82] No such flexibility obtained, however, in dealings with errant in-laws. We have already seen, for example, that when Pedro Yáñez came to New Spain in 1557 or so, he had left his sister Isabel behind in Tavila (Portugal), married to Francisco Rodríguez.[83] Twenty years later Pedro ran into Francisco and found that he had remarried, supposedly after proving, with letters, that Isabel had died. Pedro, illiterate and distrusting the proof, set out to verify the information for himself by questioning new arrivals disembarking in Veracruz. Eventually he confirmed that she was alive, and he denounced Francisco to the Holy Office. Testifying on March 5, 1579, Francisco repeated the account he had given to Pedro: "sixteen years ago [1562] he came to this tierra and about ten years ago he found out that Isabel Hernández was dead from people of her tierra whose names he forgets and he got the same news in letters which he now has lost."

Francisco's vagueness looked all the weaker when the Holy Office had no problem locating a sailor from Tavila in Veracruz who, with first-hand information about Isabel, declared in 1579 that "she is a big woman with a fair complexion and a cyst of the same color on her face . . . and because her tierra is poor, she moved to Seville in order to earn her living and now lives in Triana [next to the sailor's aunts]." With the inquisitors we may doubt that Francisco received credible information that Isabel was dead. Vague accounts of 'reports' from unremembered informants (naturally alleged to be from one's tierra) and of lost letters appear all too frequently as excuses in the testimony of bigamists.

Employers and Godparents

If families inquired after their own, so did employers and godparents. In 1737 Bernardo Díaz of Tulancingo (an alcaldía mayor, now in southeast Hidalgo state) arranged the marriage of his house servant, María Rosa, an Indian foundling raised by Bernardo's parents, to the mestizo Nicolás Antonio, but not before checking to see that Nicolás was unmarried.[84] "Because he had been away from the district for a time," Nicolás testified in 1741, "Bernardo Díaz questioned him at different times to see if [in the interim] the witness had married." In fact Bernardo's inquiry proved insufficient, as he explained in 1741, for after the marriage "he became aware through rumors . . . that Nicolás was already married to another [woman] . . . whose name is Dominga." To expose Nicolás, Bernardo took him to San Cristóbal Ecatepec (an alcaldía mayor, now on the northern outskirts of Mexico City) without telling him why and delivered him to the alcalde mayor to whom he confessed. We cannot recover exactly what

Bernardo thought he was doing when he sprang his trap. As master of both Nicolás and María Rosa and the instigator of the marriage, however, it behooved him to bring Nicolás to justice.

In 1580 Christóbal de Pastrana acted with equal diligence when he investigated the mulatto Diego de Hojeda, the husband of his slave Ana.[85] Hearing that Diego had a wife in Puebla, he sent two men (one was his relative Diego de Pastrana) to check. In Puebla they found Diego's father who said that indeed his son had married. He had disapproved of the match (she was an Indian) and in anger he beat the young man with a rod. They also spoke to the padrino of the marriage whose account confirmed that of Diego's father.[86] With this information Christóbal wrote to the inquisitors: "It has come to my attention that this mulatto [Diego] was married in Puebla before he married my Negress."

If masters made these checks with evident care, they also sustained interest in them for surprisingly long periods. Antonio de Saavedra, for example, remained vigilant for fourteen years.[87] His involvement began in 1558, when he went to Gaspar Salvago's estancias near Apaseo (jurisdiction of Celaya, now Guanajuato state), probably to serve as a mayordomo. He took a servant with him, Beatriz Ramírez, a fat mulatto short of stature, according to the brief characterization of her on the cover sheet of her file. After a time she wanted to marry Diego, an Indian ladino of the estancias. And so she did, but after two years she ran away: first to Guanajuato, then to Puebla (she married the black Diego López there in 1569), and then to Oaxaca. Somehow Salvago kept track of this, for in 1574 he approached Diego who, testifying later, on April 20, 1574, described the meeting:[88] "a month ago Gaspar Salvago . . . told him that Beatriz was publicly married to an Indian on one of his estancias." Salvago then closed the net more tightly on Beatriz by bringing this Indian to Mexico City. So Salvago assembled the case against Beatriz and the inquisitors found her guilty of bigamy, sentenced her to appear in an auto de fe, to abjure a light suspicion of heresy, to receive two hundred lashes in the streets of Mexico City, and to be banished from the archbishopric for five years.[89]

Doña Antonia Guerrero of Puebla was not above arranging a covert surveillance to confirm the misdeeds of her servants and their consorts.[90] She began to wonder when she saw Juan Antonio Pavón, the husband of her house servant María de la Cruz, suddenly rejoin her, "to do what God commands," he said, after an absence of eighteen years.[91] At the time, it seems, María accepted the return as within the order of things. Doña Antonia, however, suspected foul play and to investigate hid in a room adjoining the kitchen of her house (on plaza San Antonio) to observe Juan when he entered the kitchen to speak with María.[92] A month later she repeated the observation for the benefit of doña Josepha de Iguera, who identified Juan as married to Magdalena, a servant at her sugar mill. Doña Josepha testified on October 25, 1726, that she had hired Juan fourteen years before and then had dismissed him, "because he ran off with the wife of a black of the ingenio and afterwards came to the house of this witness and spent quite some time begging her to let him back but she refused." To support her charge that Juan was a bigamist, she cited the word of María and of "a Negro slave of the estate, now a servant in her city house in Puebla" (the latter a witness of the first marriage), whom she had questioned.

Why did masters go to so much trouble? And why did the marital standing of servants or former servants matter to them after years had passed. The answer, I think, is that they enjoyed it. It was part of the patriarchal model to exercise power over others. Moreover to do so under the banner and at the service of church dogma underscored and legitimized themselves as worthy of their place at the top of a sociomoral order. Servants and underlings validated this identity by acquiescing in it. And acquiesce they did. Witness Nicolás de la Cruz, serving a criminal sentence in the obraje of Pedro de la Sierra in Cuyoacan (now Coyoacán), who when found out as a bigamist (he married a second time in the obraje) went to his master and confessed.[93] Pedro told him that he had to go to the Holy Office, and the black slave Mariana de San Miguel, Nicolás's wife in the *obraje*, remembered that he "walked around very sad and broken until . . . their master took him to Mexico City."

Even though Pedro was a kind of surrogate prison warden, Nicolás looked to him for guidance in this crisis. For his part Pedro had no choice but to deliver his charge to the Holy Office, even though this might mean losing a worker.

Paisanos

Inquirers often came from the same tierra, thus acting as the starting point, motive, and occasion for checking on a countryman. They knew enough to be curious when something seemed amiss. Thus "a man from Campeche" was in Valladolid on the feast day of San Francisco in 1574 and recognized Francisco Gutiérrez, a man from his tierra, walking hand in hand with a woman in the procession.[94] He asked who the woman was and found that she was Ana de Melgarejo, Francisco's wife of fifteen years. "How can this be," Ana's half-sister, Francisca Velázquez (on July 14,

1574) remembered the stranger asking, "for this Gutiérrez is also married in Campeche." Francisca's husband reported the remark to the alcalde mayor, who arrested Francisco. In spite of Francisco's fifteen years of marriage and deep roots in Michoacán, his former paisano brought this life down in a moment.

The point is that a paisano, even one long resettled elsewhere, had to be noticed, remarked on, and brought up to date. The last sometimes came as a delayed response, as paisanos who saw their countrymen remarried had occasion to confirm that their first spouses were indeed alive. Here for example is how the Spaniard José de Castro, thirty-six, a native of Orizaba, came to denounce Fabián Orvel in 1766.[95] He testified that he was

passing through San Juan Huetamo [jurisdiction of Cuisea for most of the colonial period, now in Michoacán state] and recognized his paisano Fabián Orvel . . . where he was married to a woman whose name seems to be Fabiana. And the witness asked [Antonio] how he could have married again since he was already married, and he answered that his [first] wife was dead. But the witness [later] ran into the legitimate wife, whose name is Micaela Izquierdo.

Paisanos kept track of each other; they also asked each other to help with their inquiries. So Catalina de la Cruz in 1584 asked her friend from Toledo, Catalina Gómez, a widow about to go to the Indies, to look for her husband.[96] She directed her to try to find her husband's "great friend So-and-So Díaz, son of the Toledan mint worker Bartolomé Díaz, now dead who would know what happened." The man in question, Juan Díaz, held a foremanship (capataz) at the Mexico City Mint, receiving the marked and weighed silver before consigning it to workers to be coined. Juan proved easy to find and in 1584 testified that

about twenty years ago he knew a bricklayer, So-and-So González living with his wife—he does not remember her name—living behind the Magdalena [in Toledo]. In that city he was a personal friend of the witness.[97] And eleven years ago [in 1573] this witness left González and his wife in Toledo . . . and never saw him again until 1583 when he saw the said González next to the mint. They recognized one another and embraced, and this witness asked him to tell the story of his life. He said that shortly after this witness left for this tierra he took his wife to the country, a mule kicked her in the stomach leaving her unable to speak for ten days, and she died. Then he had come to this tierra and, in Tehuantepec, had married and has a wife and children.

González's story must have seemed plausible to Juan, who had few contacts from Toledo. But Catalina Gómez, just arriving from there, gave Juan news of the supposedly dead wife as still alive, and he reported González to the Holy Office.

If it took eleven years for paisanos to track González down, it took more than thirty to locate Pedro Muñoz Palomir.[98] The unlikely protagonist who did this, Juan Márquez Moreno, had to reconstruct events that had taken place in his tierra (Conil, province of Cádiz) before he was born, in order to denounce Pedro Muñoz Palomir in 1741. The story went back to about 1707 when an ecclesiastical judge forced Pedro to marry a woman named Juana of the same town.[99] Pedro did as ordered but then fled to the Indies. Later Juan, who called himself a merchant, followed and in 1732 met his countryman in Havana. "Treating one another as paisanos," Juan testified in 1741 that he

> asked Pedro if the woman he was living with was his legitimate wife, for this witness knew that he was married in Spain. He said yes, but this witness always doubted it, instead taking her for a concubine, because although he had heard that he was married in Conil, he did not know for sure even though this was commonly said throughout the town.

It took another nine years for Juan to figure out that Pedro probably was a bigamist. By then he was in Mérida and Pedro came up in a conversation with another paisano, Joseph Román.[100] Because Joseph was older (he was then fifty-five), he may have had a more exact memory of the infamous marriage, but he said little, probably because he had gone to the Indies before it took place. He did, however, provide Juan with more information about Pedro's life in the Indies because Pedro, presuming the familiarity and hospitality of a paisano, had sought him out. From Joseph's deposition of 1741, we see that they found each other when Pedro

> came to his house saying he was his paisano, a native of Villa de Conil. He gave him news of his relatives which persuaded the witness that he was from his country where he had heard of the Palominos . . . and he talked of how he made his living as a merchant, what places he had been, and how, in Valladolid, he had married a girl from Havana and, after a married life of some days in the said villa [Valladolid], he went to Havana where his wife died.

So Juan, together with Joseph, found out about their countryman Pedro as the bond of tierra implied hospitable relations and the comparing of notes about home, each other, and other paisanos. Juan brought to the Indies the key information that Juana was alive, but he did not believe that Pedro had remarried. He also may have been too unclear about the events that took place before he was born to accuse Pedro of bigamy. Thanks to Joseph, however, he pieced enough together to denounce Pedro to the Inquisition, nine years after meeting him in Havana. Pedro acted as if he had nothing to hide from the two other men from his tierra, but the information about his marriage in the Indies became a problem because Joseph was able to corroborate the original marriage in Conil.[101]

The 'comradeship' of common tierra presumed friendliness, but that shaded to a stern paternalism as paisanos acted as their brothers' keepers. Consider Diego de Lemos's meeting with Antonio Pinero.[102] While aboard a ship going from the island of Margarita to Veracruz, Diego discovered that Antonio was from Aveiros (Portugal) and told him that he was looking for Antonio Pinero. Antonio identified himself and Diego "embraced and greeted him and said that he knew he was married in his tierra and in Campeche. And Antonio became angry and [then] sad and . . . begged him not to tell anyone or say that he was married in Aveiros, promising in the coming year to go with this witness back to Aveiros and rejoin his wife."

Diego ignored Antonio's proposal and instead denounced him straight-away to the Inquisition. The investigation that followed included a statement from Antonio Pérez of Barcelona, master of a frigate who said that, he had "navigated with Antonio Pinero, who has an uncle in Española, on several occasions and the uncle sometimes quarrels with him, telling him that he should go home to his wife." Antonio's uncle, not a threat to denounce him, pressured him informally, but his countryman Diego denounced him.[103]

One might expect that priests, officially the guardians of Christian teachings, would initiate many of the inquiries to uncover bigamists. There is much to suggest, however, especially in frontier regions, that they were apathetic and overwhelmed by the scale of their far-flung parishes and the stubbornness of their parishioners. I am tempted, therefore, to regard a vignette remembered by Manuel Angel Domínguez (in testimony he gave in 1763) as atypical. Manuel, a peddler, had left Querétaro on circuit peddling goods about seven months before and arrived one night in 1760 at the mining camp of Mesquital (jurisdiction of Nieves, now in northwestern Zacatecas state).[104] "The night he arrived," he testified, "a notary came looking for him saying that the priest had called for him. And passing to his house he asked if the witness was married and where his wife was." In this out-of-the-way place, then, small enough to mark all new arrivals, Manuel had to immediately give an account of himself. The priest, either observing Manuel's arrival himself or acting on a report, took the stance that vagabond types were probably marital outlaws.

That priests depended on ordinary people to point out suspected bigamists can be seen in more detail by following the evolution of neighborhood suspicions about the Spaniard Bartolomé de Zúñiga in a barrio of Puebla.[105] The mulatto Manuel Nicolás Marañón, "master of the military arts," started the process by denouncing Bartolomé in 1700. He described the suspicious behavior of Bartolomé who "about a year ago he ran into on San Pedro Street [in Puebla] and because of their friendship said 'how's it going, señor Bartolomé, how many years has it been since we've seen each other?'" Bartolomé, now using the alias Joseph de Zúñiga, pretended not to recognize Manuel. "No, sir, I am not Bartolomé; I am not that person."[106] The unexpected brush-off troubled Manuel and he investigated further. From the mulatto Magdalena, who resided in the same house as Bartolomé, he verified that the man was a sculptor and carpenter, as was Bartolomé, and had married about eight years before in Puebla. This pointed to bigamy (about a year before Manuel had seen Bartolomé's first wife in Mexico City), hence the denunciation.

In the course of his testimony, Manuel, as requested by the judges, provided the names of others who would be able to speak of Bartolomé. A priest named licenciado Guicham was one: "He is Bartolomé's compadre and Bartolomé made all the figures that the said licenciado needed for his Nativity scene." Diego de Amaya was another: "He wears the habit of the third order of San Francisco and has a bakery next to the convent of Nuestra Señora del Carmen." In fact neither of these men testified, but the inquisitors did call Magdalena, who had already collaborated with Manuel in his checking of Bartolomé. Manuel kept her informed of his growing suspicions and told her when his confessor ordered him to denounce Bartolomé to the commissioner of the Holy Office.

The priest of Santa Cruz parish, doctor don Rodrigo Múñoz de Herrera, became involved on receiving reports from Bartolomé's neighbors. The most persistent of them, the tailor Joseph de Veas, "in appearance between a mestizo and a Spaniard," said that Bartolomé and his alleged wife Josepha had lived in the neighborhood for eight years. He suspected them of "living incontinently but hiding that fact by spreading the word that they are married."

In fact Bartolomé and Josepha, to reassure Joseph and the others, once let it be known after returning from a stay in Mexico City that they were no longer living in an "illicit friendship."[107] The ever-suspicious Joseph, however, continued to watch them and to voice his misgivings to the priest don Rodrigo who again spoke to the couple. Meanwhile the commissioner of the Inquisition approached Manuel, the original denouncer, and directed him (Manuel said in a second deposition of September 1701) to go "to Mexico City to find out if Bartolomé's wife is alive." And so he did, acting as a kind of deputy and coming back with the report that she "is alive and lives on the street called Cordobanes and because he knows her he went to her house and told her that Bartolomé was alive in Puebla." She told Manuel that twenty years before, Bartolomé had deserted her, leaving her pregnant with her now-grown son, fray Manuel de Zúñiga, and had never returned. María and fray Manuel composed letters addressed to Bartolomé, and Manuel carried them to Puebla to hand to the commissioner as evidence.

The net seemed to be closing around Bartolomé, but the commissioner, perhaps because a second marriage had not been proved, did not arrest him. Nearly two years later, in April 1703, the parish priest, don Rodrigo, apparently not privy to the information being collected by the Inquisition, was still asking Bartolomé to supply him with a certificate of his marriage. Shortly afterward, in fact, Bartolomé finally did produce a document saying that he and Josepha had married on May 2, 1696. This satisfied don Rodrigo, who considered the matter settled. A few weeks later, however, he and licenciado Carlos Lozano Lechuga, prosecutor for the bishopric, were at the parish church for a meeting of the confraternity of Santa Cruz, with licenciado Carlos presiding. Licenciado Carlos used the occasion to speak to don Rodrigo alone about the troublesome couple in his parish. He surprised don Rodrigo with the news that he had harangued Bartolomé and extracted his confession that Josepha was his mistress, that he was "in an illicit friendship with the said woman, and that the certification of marriage which had satisfied don Rodrigo was false." In the future, he warned the priest, he was "not [to] put into the books under his care similar certifications, for they are not truthful." As it turned out, licenciado Carlos had much earlier (in 1701) scolded Bartolomé directly for causing a scandal in the parish and had ordered him to supply the proof of his marriage within one month. But "with so many things to attend to for the whole bishopric," he testified to the inquisitors in 1703, "he did not remember this matter until last Resurrection Week when another denouncer told him that Bartolomé was persevering in his illicit friendship." In the end the key to breaking

Bartolomé's story was licenciado Carlos's threat of intervention by the municipal judges of the city.

Several levels of authority interested themselves in Bartolomé and Josepha: the parish, the diocese, the Inquisition, and, at least as a threat, the municipal judges. Parish, diocese, and municipality worried about the scandal of concubinage, the Inquisition about the sacrilege of bigamy. As long as the former suspicion was the dominant one, the Inquisition remained in the background. Ironically Bartolomé's 'solution' of counterfeiting a marriage certificate might have caused Inquisitorial interest, suspecting bigamy, to quicken. If Bartolomé seemed capable of putting off the religious authorities indefinitely, he declined to skirmish with city alcaldes. The relentless curiosity, suspicion and pressure exerted by neighbors, however, provided the energy behind all the bureaucratic action. This kept the case alive even when officials forgot about it in the press of other business.

TRAFFIC PATTERNS

Information in early modern times circulated in a random, hit-or-miss way that reflected the spontaneity and the movement of life itself. Yet it was also a system. We have seen, for example, patterns of interaction based on links to family, masters, paisanos, neighbors, coworkers, friends, and acquaintances. It remains for us to sketch traffic patterns in a larger sense. In simplest terms information borne and shaped by its human carriers traveled along roads and sea lanes and collected in larger pools in the cities, towns, villages, haciendas, or ranchos connected by these routes. Traffic ebbed and flowed with the seasons, the rhythm of commerce, the feast days of the church calendar, and the size and activity of the places linked. Regular and periodic movement between places, therefore, implies some patterns; but in terms of information available at a given time or place, the amount varied with the individuals passing through. We may view this as a series of perimeter-hub networks, with central places surrounded by outlying ones.[108] Centers ranged from small to large, from bustling to sluggish, and this correlated with how much information would have circulated in them—from very little in isolated estancias to a great deal in the viceregal capital.

Mexico City as a Central Place

From the time of its founding on the ruins of Tenochtitlán, Spaniards made Mexico City the central place of Mexico. It was home to royal and religious bureaucrats, large merchants, and elites with ties to mining and ranching. The wealth of such people pulled in streams of humbler types (builders, craftsmen, tradesmen, servants, and hangers-on) and, more temporarily, provincials seeking credit, partnerships, markets, or goods. The centralized bureaucracy drew virtually anybody who had to deal with more important lawsuits, administrative problems, and questions relating to taxes. From outlying points traffic converged on Mexico City. We can see Mexico City, therefore, as the center of a network so pronounced that virtually everybody went there—to conduct business, to find work, to file petitions, to attend festivals, to purchase specialized wares, to drink and hang around in an environment free from "village rules of comportment," or to be tried by the Inquisition.[109]

This reputation of the viceregal capital can be seen in the muleteer Alonso Sánchez's account of a conversation he had with a stranger in Veracruz in 1615.[110] The man, whom he only remembered as "a silversmith," just arrived from Spain, fell into step with Alonso, and they traveled together as far as the pueblo of Santa Cruz, five or six miles outside of Teguacán. There (as Sánchez remembered it in his statement to the commissioner of the Inquisition on April 6, 1615), the man spoke "a great deal criticizing the dullness of this town [Teguacan], whence he turned toward Puebla saying that if he did not find proper comforts there he would seek them in Mexico City." The brief vignette shows that the newcomer understood the setup. Mexico City was a sure thing; Puebla, worthy as it was as the second city of the viceroyalty, was on probation, worth a try mainly because it was en route.

Even humble types went to Mexico City more commonly than to secondary towns closer to their immediate districts. In his entire life, Joseph Manuel de Molina said, he had "never left the mining district of the north except to go to Mexico City."[111] His contact with the capital was a normal and expected exception to what would otherwise be regional insularity. In a similar way, Juan de Santana Izquierdo and his family focused their lives closely on the town of Colima and its region.[112] Juan lived there in his father's home when he was not hauling freight with mules. His three brothers and five (of six) uncles or aunts were vecinos of Colima; his maternal grandparents were buried there; and he even lacked knowledge of his paternal grandparents because they were "from some place other than Colima." Although Juan lived in Colima until he was thirty (in 1773), he ventured out regularly, but only along two corridors: one between Colima and Guanajuato, the other between Colima and Mexico City.

Joseph Francisco de Chavarría also had a sometime connection with

Mexico City where, in 1721, he married María Micaela, lived with her for six years, and then went to Guanajuato without her, as the coachman of a priest.[113] So employed Joseph had occasion to return to Mexico City where he made no move to see María but instead lodged with his sisters "who live on the corner of San Pedro and San Pablo." Yet María saw him as they attended a public execution. Although she tried to get him to stay and support her (as we noted in chapter 4), he headed north again. From Mexico City she nevertheless kept track of Joseph to some degree, by questioning travelers from the mining district. She testified in 1736, for example, that "a few weeks ago she ran into the lobo Antonio, a mule driver from Guanajuato who said that 'that man' [Joseph] was no longer in Guanajuato but had gone to Salamanca [jurisdiction of Celaya, now in Guanajuato state] and married a slave." In fact Antonio was on his way to denounce Joseph to the Inquisition when María spoke to him. Although his reason for coming to Mexico City had nothing to do with informing on Joseph (or for that matter, with speaking to María about him, for his meeting with her had been a chance one), once in the city he set out on this errand as if it were routine.

There is no doubt that in its capacity as an administrative center Mexico City drew in every kind of person, humble or distinguished. So came Nicolás Mayorga and his wife María Gertrudis from Pachuca (in 1727) to petition for a writ to change María's status from slave to free.[114] They claimed that María's master, Joseph Orchate, had promised to manumit her on his death.[115] On this understanding Nicolás married her, fully aware that she had been Orchate's concubine of many years and had had children by him. The expected manumission must have seemed 'normal' given these circumstances. In Mexico City Nicolás and María presented their case to don Juan de Osilia y Rayo, a judge of the criminal court. But first they arranged to have a notary prepare their papers, one who lived on the plaza of San Gregorio, Nicolás recalled in his hearing of March, 1743, a place that at first he had trouble finding "because he was a foreigner and had not lived [in Mexico City] continuously."[116]

In the area set aside for petitioners María and Nicolás waited but failed to gain access to a magistrate, and so they went to the viceregal palace to consult their notary. At that point don Antonio Terrino de Orchate, "merchant and baker who lives in Pachuca," arrived and asked what they were doing.[117] They explained, and he called the whole business "foolishness and a mistake." Briefly he put María into protective custody at a nearby inn and then returned her to Pachuca and slavery. The misadventures of María and Nicolás in Mexico City show them as provincials bemused by

the sluggishness of judicial processes and caught off guard by the deci-
siveness of don Antonio, who prevented María's suit, it seems, to keep her
as part of the inheritable estate. Yet they showed some familiarity with the
layout of the city and with legal procedures.[118]

Because the capital and the countryside were linked by a series of corridors, towns were linked directly to the metropolis, to a regional center
perhaps, and to towns en route, more than to each other. Mexico City
housed temporarily, and sometimes permanently, individuals and clusters
of people who themselves were fragments of distant tierras. However
remote their village, compatriots could be found there to exchange news
and gossip about each other and the affairs of home.

The Spaniard Juan Antonio Ramírez (ca. 1716), for example, spent most
of his early life in the fishing village of Alvarado and, as we have seen, went
to Mexico City after surprising his wife, María Valdivia, in the act of
adultery.[119] His sister-in-law, Magdalena Bravo (wife of Marcelo Bravo),
sent him a letter seven months later (in January 1734), so Juan claimed in
testimony he gave in 1741, with news that "the said [Juan's] wife had been
given such a bad wound in the breast that she had died of it. And this letter
was delivered by Pasqual Bravo, a brother of the said Marcelo, at the
corner San Bernardo. And because [Juan] does not know how to read he
went to the store in front of the said convent and begged the young lad
who was inside to read it."

About a month later, at the corner of San Felipe Neri, Juan ran into
another of his wife's relations, Manuel Bravo, who had come to Mexico
City to process an inheritance. Juan claimed that Manuel also confirmed
María's death. A third confirmation supposedly came from Joachín, a
mestizo native to Mexico City but resident for most of his life in Alvarado.
Joachín would have been a good source of information, if Juan's description of him, living "part of the time in the port [fishing] and part in this
city [peddling]," was true. Juan ran into Joachín in Mexico City's thieve's
market (baratillo) "a year before the epidemic,"[120] and there they discussed news of Alvarado; Joachín too stated that María had died of "fevers."[121] Two years later the two men met again in the same market,
where Joachín was selling black trousers. Juan took a pair on credit and, as
they chatted, found that Joachín had recently traveled from Alvarado with
Gregorio Zamudio, a vecino of the port. Juan then looked up Gregorio
and confirmed María's death a fourth time.

Juan's repeated corroborations of María's death (if indeed he made them
as he claimed) gave him plausible grounds for marrying a second time (in
1737).[122] Except for one thing. The inquisitors checked his story and in

Puerto de Alvarado on August 22, 1741, took a deposition from Pasqual Bravo, the man who supposedly had delivered the letter to Juan. Pasqual testified that "he has never left this port. Not now or at any time has he seen Mexico City, Puebla, Orizaba, or Córdoba because his work is to make trips by canoe and fish and always he has stayed in this port and the only other place he has been is the pueblo of Tlaliscoya [Nueva Veracruz] to drop off a load."

Pasqual's statement ruined Juan's defense, and the inquisitors found him guilty of bigamy and sentenced him to a typical penalty: abjuration and penance, two hundred lashes, banishment from Mexico City for ten years, and penal servitude for six years in "the plaza or castle of Vera Cruz."

Did Juan make up his elaborately circumstantial account? If he did he layered it masterfully with believably ordinary settings, meetings, exchanges, and characters. Possibly it was true except for the mistaking of somebody else for Pasqual Bravo.[123] For our purposes, however, Juan's story, assuming the easy accessibility of a Mexico City to others from his tierra, residing as well as sojourning, was at the very least plausible. It therefore shows how people from one locale (even a small, isolated, and unimportant coastal village such as Alvarado) could have kept track of a compatriot in the viceregal capital and vice versa. Resulting meetings and conversation, whether purposeful, as when Ramírez sought out Gregorio, or desultory, as when he chatted with Joachín at the market, focused inevitably, if not exclusively, on the home village.

Moreover there can be no doubt that on returning to Alvarado, Joachín, Gregorio, and the others would have passed on news of Juan in Mexico City. Towns and villages received news of their own through periodic contact with information available in the metropolis. The process by which information flowed back to the provinces from Mexico City, inferred in the case of Juan, can be documented in that of the mestizo Joseph Antonio Rozete (born ca. 1733).[124] In 1766 Joseph ran into María de los Dolores, a former neighbor from Chiautla (an alcaldía mayor, now in Puebla state), at the church of San Francisco. He had not seen her for five years, because she had moved to Piastla (jurisdiction of Acatlán, now in the hill country of southern Puebla state), some fifty miles to the east, while, at the same time, he had moved to Teguacan.[125] Their meeting occurred by chance in Mexico City when each came for the festival of Guadalupe. María, testifying on January 3, 1767, recalled that to her question as to "who had he come with," Joseph answered with the apparent non sequitur that "he had come on foot and was married to Antonia Navarro." The last startled her because Joseph had once been married to a woman in Chiautla. Back in Piastla she told friends and neighbors the story of her trip and meeting Joseph. Pablo Marcelino, a vecino of Teguacan, was present and became interested because in Teguacan he had known Joseph for four years as a married man. On returning he denounced Joseph to agents of the Inquisition.

In this way, through direct contact with a compatriot, news and gossip worked its way from Mexico City out to the towns. Once in the towns, the information was elaborated and interpreted by the oral network of the region. Although each of these places was small and isolated (Chiautla and Piastla of course much more so than Teguacan), information from each came together at the node of María's house, where María and her friends rehashed it, interpreted it, and then carried it away to repeat to others.

The key, then, was Mexico City drawing pilgrims from a large hinterland, in this instance for the festival of Guadalupe, so that former neighbors met after five years. Another variant, one that surely exemplifies a common behavior, can be seen in the conduct of the Spaniard Christóbal Hernández (born in the 1550s) in checking the mail drop at the cathedral.[126] He appeared before the Inquisition on August 20, 1615, and declared himself "more than sixty," born in Medina del Campo, resident for five years or so in the mining camp of Sombrerete (an alcaldía mayor, now in northwest Zacatecas state), and now a vecino of Mexico City.

> On Tuesday, August 18, this witness found two letters in the cathedral of this city on a small box next to the font of holy water. One was open, the other sealed. The first was addressed 'To my son Antonio Rodríguez Bezerra, may God protect, in New Spain, postage one *tostón*'; the second, 'Antonio Rodríguez, may God protect, in the Indies in New Spain, postage one *tostón*'. And because this witness knows and is a friend of the said Antonio Rodríguez [in Sombrerete] he took them to forward them at the first opportunity.

On reading the letter already opened, Christóbal learned that Antonio's wife in Moguer (province of Huelva) had given birth to a son on October 24, 1614. This jarred him, for he knew that Antonio also had a wife in Sombrerete, where he was "vecino and resident." He therefore reported Antonio to the Inquisition and submitted the letters as evidence.[127] The unremarkable little incident puts us inside an ordinary process, the picking up and interpreting of information waiting to be found at a standard meeting place. Similar occurrences must have been common everywhere, but in Mexico City more traffic, drawn from a wider range of places and renewed more frequently, permitted more and faster connections.

Mexico City also attracted pilgrims and sojourners in search of missing relatives. Thus the wife of the Spaniard Alonso Guerra (born ca. 1544 in Bohadilla de Rioseco, province of Palencia), missing for twelve years in the Indies, asked Pedro Rodríguez, her uncle and a merchant stationed in Cartagena, to search for him.[128] Pedro had no luck in Cartagena, but eventually traveled to Mexico City to sell a group of slaves. There he found Alonso, and his denunciation, dated June 16, 1599, recounts how.

About a month ago this witness saw, completely coincidentally, three men in capes in the portals of the main plaza. Because they appeared to be rural types, and because this witness understood that the said Alonso Guerra was dealing in cattle, he asked after him. They said that he lived in Mexico City toward Santa Anna.

Later Pedro spoke to a carter delivering fodder who told him that Alonso was his master's compadre (as godfather of one of his children). The carter, chatting on, added that Alonso too was a carter, "although in his tierra he had been a scribe." This final detail convinced Pedro that he had found the missing husband. Of course Pedro's account leaves out details of the unsuccessful inquiries he made, and on first reading we might think that the presumed connection between Alonso and the men in capes was a tenuous one. Yet the direction of his approach, to ask men in Alonso's general line of work, is clear. It shows how small even Mexico City could be, once men were placed in terms of their probable networks.

The volume of information in Mexico City and the rate at which it circulated made it a place to find information, yet it also allowed for some anonymity. Fugitives could hide or operate with a made-up identity, but only for so long. Eventually travelers from even the most obscure and far-flung towns passed through the city to recognize and greet their compatriot as the person they had known at an earlier time. Take María Guadalupe Delgadillo (born ca. 1760 in Tezcuco), who, as we have already seen, twice went to Mexico City to escape an unhappy marriage with José de los Santos of Tepexpan (jurisdiction of San Juan Teotiguacan, now in Mexico state).[129] In her autobiographical statement of May 3, 1780, she spoke of her time in the city and how she was discovered. "She subsisted for five months in the convent of San Lorenzo [on the first stay] serving mother Gertrudis Gil and having gone out to the street to take a treatment [for an ailment?] she met some relatives of her said husband three days later."

They forced her to return to José, as we have already seen, but she did so for only nine months and then ran away again to Mexico City. This time she served four different employers, three of whom were sisters in the Balbanera, San Juan de la Penitencia, and Santa Isabel convents; the fourth, Micaela Bueno, employed her before and after she served the sisters. In this way María remained undetected for five years or so. Then with grave consequences, she called attention to herself by contracting a second marriage. She took this step, she said, after she "asked some Indians from Tepexpan selling chickens at the Palace Fountain—she does not remember their names—for the said José Antonio and they said that he died."

So information direct from her husband's town lured María from hiding and into a public marriage. For her Mexico City was a place to hide or to be found. And whether one was lying low or searching, it acted as a vantage point from which to glean news from home villages, choosing informants with discretion, if necessary, so as to remain inconspicuous. The trick for a woman, perhaps, was to remain cloistered as much as possible, stay off busy streets, and be watchful, behavior that in any case was prescribed for 'respectable' women. Shrouding oneself in a *rebozo* surely made it easier to keep an eye on others while shielding one's own features from view. María's five years of seclusion from José and his relatives shows what could be done.[130]

Outlying Centers

Other points in the information network (improbable, isolated places with little traffic) functioned much as Mexico City did, but on a smaller scale. They too became meeting places, where carriers and receivers found their common ground and exchanged news. Gerónimo de Rivera, for example, married María de Jesús in Seville about 1591 and then left almost immediately for the Indies.[131] In Mexico he joined the Oñate expedition, to go "six hundred leagues to the north to discover the great population," and in 1600 he married a second time, in Apaseo (Celaya). He assumed that María had died, he said, because "he left when she was on her last legs and he did not receive any answers to the many letters he wrote to her." He testified (on November 22, 1603[132]) that she had been alive

about a year and a half ago [when] this witness was at Cuencamé [an alcaldía mayor in Nueva Vizcaya, now in Durango state] which is about fourteen leagues from the house of Rodrigo del Río, and a merchant vecino there who in Seville used to be known as something or other Morales—he said that he had changed his name—remarked that his first wife was still alive in Seville, news he had received from [Gerónimo's] brother.

In fact mining camps could be alive with information because transients frequently chose them as destinations. But because the amount of information arriving at smaller places was still limited, compared to Mexico City for example, they absorbed news and gossip all the more thoroughly. At least the unmarried Spaniard Juan Joseph de Ortega (born ca. 1715), who at fifty-eight had spent nearly his whole life in Guadalcázar, suggests this.[133] He testified (on July 5, 1773) that

> from his childhood he has had a fixed residence in this camp in which time it has had lots of bonanzas, so that hordes of people from every walk of life have come here, and he has known most of them from working as a miner and from being mayordomo of the confraternity of San Joseph, a position he has held for eight or ten years. He collects contributions from the faithful, not only in the camp itself, but in the whole of its jurisdiction.

When the time came, the Inquisition called upon Ortega's knowledge of the region, which extended even to an obscure coyote (a husband of a woman being investigated for bigamy), resident only a few years on an outlying ranch.

People in small, out-of-the-way places with few distractions and a slow pace snatched at scraps of information, whether generated locally or from afar. Those with something to hide might keep their secrets for a time in such outposts, but in the long run their true identities were likely to become known. San Miguel de Panzacola, a distant presidio in the province of Florida on the very edge of the viceroyalty, was the setting for one such unmasking. Francisco Xavier Ponce de León had been there for ten years when he injured a vertebra and returned to central Mexico.[134] At the presidio he had known his compadre Joseph Miguel Reyes (born ca. 1730) of Calpulalpa (jurisdiction of Tezcuco, now in the state of Mexico), formerly a soldier who turned to storekeeping after suffering a bone fracture, as married and with two children. All of this was normal enough and no cause for suspicion, as long as his earlier marriage remained unknown. However, as Ponce de León passed through the village of Calpulalpa, he learned that the village storekeeper shared the surname of his storekeeper compadre in Panzacola. Ponce de León remarked upon this and discovered that the two men were brothers. And so they had a topic. Soon the storekeeper found out that his brother had married again and Ponce de

León that he was already married in Calpulalpa. Ponce de León verified the information by speaking to the alleged wife, and then proceeded to Mexico City, where he denounced Joseph to the Inquisition.

Only by chance did Ponce de León learn of Joseph Miguel's other life in Calpulalpa. Yet the way in which apparently innocuous information about Joseph moved from a small presidio in the north to an insignificant village in the center of New Spain cannot be atypical. In these places the exchanges were more meandering, more leisurely, and consequently more exploratory, because fewer travelers to such places meant fewer distractions and a slower turnover of information. Thus assuming curiosity about people a constant, the attention given to information related inversely with the size of a place and the volume of traffic passing through it, rough indicators of the amount of information introduced or generated. A resident of Calpulalpa or Panzacola was far more likely to have complete knowledge of the people of his or her district and be more avid to piece together new information about them than, say, a resident of Mexico City. In December 1614 Catalina Rodríguez, resident most of her life in Dominican haciendas around Las Amilpas (an alcaldía mayor, formerly part of the marquesado, but escheated to the crown in 1583, now in Morelos state), told inquisitors that the mulatto Juan Luis could not possibly be married "because if he were she would have known it, having always been in contact with him, with his pueblo of Iguala [an alcaldía mayor, now northern Guerrero state], and with other places where he goes."[135] In July 1553 the seventy-year-old Spaniard Miguel de Montoya made the same kind of negative inference: "He knows for sure that if [María Hernández] were dead it would have been public knowledge in the said village of Cantillana [province of Seville], where her father and brothers live."[136]

Within regions, even very isolated ones such as Nuevo Santander, gossip about the people living in the small network of pueblos circulated more quickly than one might have expected. In 1784 the mulatto Joseph Laureano de la Cruz married the Indian María Silveria Delgado in Hoyos (jurisdiction of Santander, now in Tamaulipas state).[137] Almost immediately, however, "the reports began to circulate" that he was also married in Santa Bárbara (also in the jurisdiction of Santander), thirty leagues or so to the south. María confronted Joseph and he tried to cover up, saying that he had not married but had only run off with the woman in question. This excuse served only a short time, because the reports continued and gradually undermined the plausibility of Joseph's version.

We can see how a part of the sparsely populated north constituted itself as a 'region' by following the Spaniard Juan Antonio Mascareñas who, after marrying a second time, traveled about or received messages from various places, mostly in Nueva Vizcaya.[138] As he recounted it (in his autobiographical statement of January 8, 1737), the story began with his marriage at the presidio of Cerro Gordo (a military jurisdiction, now in north Durango state) in March 1734. After about a year, fellow soldier Joseph Flores, a native of Querétaro, told Juan that he had been in Sinaloa and had seen his first wife. Juan got a pass, intending, he said, to go to Guadalajara and turn himself in to the Inquisition. His actual movements, however, show him double-checking Joseph's report. He went 30 miles or so to the southwest, to the mining camp of Indé (an alcaldía mayor originally with jurisdiction over all of northern Nueva Vizcaya, now in northern Durango state) and then 400 miles to the southwest, to the mining camp of Canelas (jurisdiction of Topia and San Andrés de la Sierra and then Siánori, now in western Durango state), asking in each place for news of his wife. Then he doubled back 150 miles toward the northwest to reach the Huichol village of Guaxuquilla (jurisdiction of Colotlán, now in Zacatecas state), where his father-in-law, Leonisio Núñez, told him that in a mail run he had just made to Chihuahua (about 130 miles north of Guaxuquilla), he heard that the first wife was alive. This report became the final link that convinced Juan that he had indeed committed bigamy. Thus for Juan's purposes, the 'region' centered in Cerro Gordo, and he personally reconnoitered its core while also receiving key reports from far to the southwest, Sinaloa, and from the north, Chihuahua.

The assumption that a 'region' was knowable was even more pronounced when defined as an axis and two important centers. The inquisitors expected this of Lorenzo de Otalora Carbajal when they found fault with him for not properly verifying his wife's death.[139] Neither did his status as a slave excuse him. Listen to the inquisitor's question, asked during Lorenzo's hearing of July 20, 1664: "With Guatemala [where his wife was] so close to Oaxaca and with the two cities having so much communication between them, why didn't you make more effort to know if it were true that the said mulatto Blas had killed . . . your wife?"

Points of Entry

We have seen some examples of the central place of Mexico City in the network and how it interacted with other centers in the movement of information. We have also noticed that relatively isolated districts seized on news and gossip coming in, as they also kept track of each other locally. It remains to mention the points of entry into the network as a whole, for it was not a closed system.

Veracruz, of course, served for the entire colonial period as the most important and predictable portal to the outside world. Information carried from Spain touched there first. Its place may be illustrated by the ruminations of don Juan Gómez Franco, who in 1728 left his wife Inés María de Escobar and their daughter in San Lúcar de Barrameda and went to New Spain.[140] He testified (in his autobiographical statement of March 13, 1755) that he had presumed them dead and therefore married a second time because he had not received news of them for eighteen years. But he had never verified the death and remained troubled. In confession he admitted this to don Gregorio Toribio, a priest of Córdoba, who saw it as a straightforward matter of simply making "inquiries in Vera Cruz to find out if his wife were alive or dead." In fact Juan had done this before he married a second time, he claimed, going "from his home in Córdoba whenever ships were in [Veracruz] . . . to seek information."

Finally he received conflicting reports, both from men of San Lúcar who might very well have known his wife. One said that his wife had married a farmer, the other that she was dead. Much hinged on which was correct, and Gómez became anxious. He testified that "intermittently [this caused] so much turmoil that at times he seemed to be out of his senses and one time his wife—the one he was living with then—asked him what was wrong or what was causing this." All of this, however, came after the fact, and the inquisitorial prosecutor insisted that Juan's inability to secure sure information before marrying a second time constituted a "frivolous excuse . . . when to investigate the truth . . . in Vera Cruz where so many people arrive from his home region was a simple matter while for his wife [in Spain] it was more difficult because she did not know where her husband was after so many years without news."

To the prosecutor, then, the point of entry to the network had accessible, ample, and reliable information that Juan should have taken advantage of before marrying a second time. There could be no excuses for failing to do so. In Córdoba, moreover, even without going to Veracruz, Gómez was on a main route to Mexico City. He had access not only to the port itself but also to virtually all recent arrivals from Spain.

Because Veracruz was so highly regarded as a place where information could be found, affidavits taken there carried an extra measure of authority. The Spaniard Juan Antonio Chacón Gayón (born ca. 1661) tried to exploit this to counterfeit a report.[141] From Puebla he went to Veracruz to have fraudulent testimony drawn up from witnesses who alleged that they had seen the death and burial of his wife in Spain. Although the inquisitors were not fooled (the document was clumsily executed), Chacón's use of

Veracruz as a dateline coincided closely with assumptions shared by the judges as to its importance.[142]

The links between the main ports of the Indies and Seville (and later Cádiz and other ports) are of course a given. At the Seville end, information that eventually traveled to the Indies frequently reached there after an already complex journey from peninsular hinterlands.[143] In chapter 4, for example, we observed Catalina Rodríguez searching for news of her husband at the inns of Seville.[144] She knew that he was in Veracruz and found it fairly easy to get reports about him and to send messages to him, even though he was trying to avoid her. Magdalena de Urra also drew on the information network of Seville to search for her husband, Manuel.[145] She relied not on letters, she said, but on "reports of some of the people that come and go from Mexico," for Manuel had not written once in the fourteen years he had been away.

Distance and infrequent traffic between Acapulco and Manila made it more difficult to get information about people there. Particularly frustrating, perhaps, were instances in which two apparently reliable informants contradicted each other. In 1566 or 1567, the mulatto Ana de Aspitia married the Spanish tailor (from the Canary Islands) Juan López de Sosa in Mexico City, but as Ana testified in 1582, he never lived a proper married life with her.[146]

It will be about seven or eight years ago that the said Juan López . . . went to China with Captain Herrera and before and after [Ana] married the said Diego Hernández [her second husband], she heard that [Juan] was dead [because] Captain Herrera and another soldier having recently returned from the Philippines swore [to this] before the priest Miguel Izquiera.

But Agustín Ordiales denounced Ana (he had come from Manila only four months before), saying that he had known Juan well there for four years and had "never heard that he was dead." This, of course, is not quite the same as testifying that he was alive. Nevertheless it presumes that the death of an acquaintance could not have occurred without his notice. By 1582 Ana and Diego, a mulatto vaquero, had been married for five or six years and were living on "an estancia of don Juan de Guevara in the Chichimecas." It is not clear how and why Ana's life in the Chichimecas became an issue for Agustín, but Ana's predicament, and the Inquisition's, illustrate how slowness, delays, and conflicting reports in the network forced people constantly to assess the reliability of messengers.

CONCLUSION

The flow of information patterned itself in certain ways, while also retaining a random and capricious character. Curiosity—the appetite of people to know about each other and to expand and refine what they knew through soundings based on tierra, mutual acquaintances, relatives, and neighbors—animated the process. Neighbors and strangers passed on the news about each other: what they were doing and how they were getting on, where they were going and where they had been, who their spouses and who their paramours were, who they were working for and who with. This constantly needed to be renewed and recast (to reinforce stereotypes, to dramatize oneself as a protagonist, to highlight conflict, to deplore villainy), and so the narratives were constantly revised. As people passed along the startling and the commonplace, they affirmed shared values in a common world but also stood out as individuals and agents in their worlds, however small the settings in which they exercised some control.

It is clear that, in spite of some joking, individuals did not attack the church directly. And to a degree they made church norms their own, for when something discrepant emerged, they noticed it, checked it, passed it on, and filled in details, sometimes to confront miscreants directly, sometimes to speak directly to an official or to the Inquisition. Plebeians policed one another by exercising their curiosity and enjoying daily rations of gossip and news. They watched members of their own families most closely, especially in-laws, as did masters who oversaw the behavior of their servants and clients. We do not know how often they noticed, then turned a blind eye to, 'discrepancies,' but those who did merely delayed rather than stopped the spread of information. For few could pass up the chance to gossip with their peers, and sooner or later came a denunciation. If this led to the uncovering of bigamists, that result came mostly as an 'accidental' by-product of people doing what they would have done anyway: keep detailed mental notes about each other.

We have learned enough to wish that we had more. The banal exchanges and situations so briefly sketched by witnesses before the inquisitors remain one of the few windows we have on the dynamics and content of everyday conversations in a world now lost to us. Yet fragmentary as it is, the material is rich enough to merit close attention. A final fragment, for example, takes us to the hearth of a man and his wife speaking of a central concern of everyday life. It comes from Juana Pérez, whose husband, Francisco Macías, was accused of bigamy.[147] Testifying before the inquisitors on June 21, 1734, Juana searched her memory for what she could say about a possible second wife and came up with this: "He used to say that María Montaña, his ex-wife who died, used to make beautiful *tortillas* to eat."

Her wording "he used to" seems to indicate that Juana had heard Francisco say this many times. But on what occasions and to what purpose? Would they have been 'literal' occasions, when he found something amiss in the taste, texture, or consistency of María's tortillas? Or 'metaphorical' ones, moments of nostalgia for a former domestic life? We cannot know. Yet the comment implies a comparison of two wives as if the tortilla was a metonymy for them. Francisco thus conflates married life with the staple food on his table. His choice of words—not the all-purpose *good*, not the precise *tasty*, but the lyrical *beautiful*—point to an imagined former golden age with another woman.

Because Francisco made these remarks more than once, we may take them as a theme (not less complete for their brevity) that puts before us a central concern of everyday life. It is intriguing to think that in their households and in public places, men talked of how well their women made tortillas. Talk about their taste, texture, and appearance, metonimically sized up women: how well they ran households and how well they looked after the heads of them. This, a kind of measure of domestic contentment, mattered personally, of course, but it also constituted part of the male persona in his community.

CONCLUSION

✛ It is important to step back and remember what proponents of the Inquisition thought they would achieve by establishing a tribunal in Mexico. Writing from Taximaroa in September 1554, audiencia judge licenciado Lorenzo Lebrón de Quiñones expressed a representative view.

> The need for an Inquisition in this land is extremely great because crimes and acts of irreverence are so numerous . . . and neither the secular nor ecclesiastical justice metes out the appropriate punishments and [the problem] is going to increase because the ease or the dissembling of the penalty will give a new boldness and daring to sin.[1]

An Inquisition, then, would order and control crime, irreverence, and sin (there was not much to differentiate between them), in a way that existing institutions could or would not. In this light it is of interest to note what doctor don Pedro Moya de Contreras, Mexico's first inquisitor, thought he had accomplished in the first auto de fe, held on February 28, 1574. Writing to Juan de Ovando, president of the Council of the Indies less than a month later (March 24, 1574), Moya briefly refers to "an infinity of people" in attendance, "Spaniards as well as natives," whose presence "increased the authority of the act."[2] We note his satisfaction, then, that the authority of the Inquisition had been established and that it had been done with the support and enthusiasm of the Mexican populace. This must have seemed a fulfillment of his original design, as described in his letter of May 24, 1572, which expressed the hope that the people would learn to "censor and denounce each other with very Christian zeal." Mo-

ya's model, then, involved a hegemonic incorporation of the people, so
that they would control each other.[3] It was not a simple top-down view of
social control but rather an interactive one as basic Christian teachings,
suspect behaviors and acts listed in the edicts of faith, and the exemplary
punishments of autos de fe showed people what to do and how to do it.
Below I should like to explore the degree to which Moya's hopes were
fulfilled, as far as we can judge by bigamy cases.

Religious Practice

There can be no doubt, if one wants to put it this way, that the church
transmitted its 'ideology' to ordinary people.[4] But how completely and
with what distortions? As might be expected, results varied in levels of
piety and comprehension of doctrine, as the transmitters (priests and friars
in the parishes and doctrinas) contended less with outright disbelief or
rejection than lethargy, doctrinal accretions, and daily preoccupations. We
can see an example of the problem in the Spaniard Santiago Pantaleón,
accused of being a "superstitious healer" and a bigamist.[5] The prosecutor's arraignment in 1782 assumes an acceptable grounding in the faith,
surmising that his "Catholic parents . . . would have given him a medium
education, instruction in Christian doctrine . . . [and] sent him to primary
school." Santiago did not confirm, deny, or clarify how well he had been
indoctrinated, only that he had fallen away because of day-to-day concerns: "After giving himself to the work of cultivating the land, he forgot
his Christian doctrine completely."

If Santiago had forgotten some sort of Christian formation, Eusebia
Sánchez de los Santos claimed never to have had one.[6] In her hearing
before the inquisitors in 1789, she said that her "parents, poor rustics that
they were, did not teach her to read or the Christian doctrine. Maybe they
were ignorant themselves. But neither did her confessors or the priest's
assistant who married her . . . This is why she is now so backward in the
mysteries of our holy Catholic faith." Thus Eusebia traces her sin to her
ignorance and also implicates the church in it, for the parish failed, given
her parents' ignorance, to catechize her. This was a good tactic, for the inquisitors had to assume the basic indoctrination of parishioners ("the
principal prayers, the Articles of Faith, the Commandments of God, the
sacraments, the works of mercy, the deadly sins"), content that was common to Indian and Hispanic parishes alike.[7] We see a typical list of the
doctrine ordinary people were supposed to know in the questions the

tribunal posed to the loba Bárbara Martina in January 1771:[8] "Who is God? Who of the three divine persons became man? Who is in the holy sacrament? When will our Lord Jesus Christ come to judge the living and the dead? Where do those who die in grace go and where those who die in mortal sin?"

Following the usual pattern, the scribe did not record Bárbara's answers, only the inquisitors' assessment of them: "In substance correct in our common Spanish, although she left out or added one or another word." Satisfactory, then, but an exactly memorized recitation would have pleased them more.

In 1782 the mulatto Juan de Santa Ana Izquierdo passed his test in much the same terms, but we have a more complete listing of what he was asked.[9] The notary recorded that "He crossed himself and in Spanish said the Lord's Prayer, Ave María, Creed, Salve, the Commandments of the Law of God and of the Church, the Holy Sacraments, and other things of Christian doctrine that he was asked by the commissioner, in substance answering well to everything."

We could cite other assessments. For example that of the Spaniard Mariana Monroy, who in 1678 said the basic prayers "very well in Romance" and "gave a sufficient account of Christian doctrine."[10] Slight variations in positive evaluations ("in substance answering well," "in substance correct," and "a sufficient account") are too much alike to make distinctions.

The inquisitors also asked questions to elicit whether accused persons were practicing Christians as well as indoctrinated ones. A typical example would be, "Are you a baptized and confirmed Christian, do you hear mass, confess, and take communion at the times ordered by the Holy Mother Church?"

To build a picture of the religious practice of accused bigamists, inquisitors also relied on the corroboration of third parties. In Oaxaca, for example, we saw that Juan López came under review in 1561 because he married Ana Hernández, an alleged bigamist.[11] Alonso Portuguese, who had known Juan for more than fourteen years and had lodged him in his house for a year and a half, appeared as a character witness, testifying that he

> takes Juan López for a good Christian although there would be some weakness in the said Ana Hernández in that she is a woman. He knows that [Juan] goes to hear the mass every day to the cathedral, the churches of Santa Vera Cruz and Santo Domingo, and the hospital of Our Lady . . . He also gives

alms, even leaving them at the house when he goes out so that they can be given to whomever comes to solicit them.[12]

The mulatto María Jesús de la Encarnación, lacking Juan's resources to dispense in charity, nevertheless showed herself to be well grounded in the essentials. In her hearing of November 1781, she demonstrated a knowledge of the Lord's Prayer, Ave María, creed, confession, and commandments, but only "responded with fairly good understanding to doctrinal questions."[13] The disparity between her control over devotional and lack of it over doctrinal materials suggests, perhaps, her regular attendance at mass but a weak catechistic grounding. She declared to the inquisitors that she was "a Christian and, according to her mother, baptized; she was confirmed, she hears the mass, and has confessed and taken communion; the last time was Easter at the house of reclusion for women in Valladolid."

Others functioned at a lower level. The mestizo Pedro Mateo, claimed in 1666 that he attended the mass regularly but, as noted by the notary, "did not know the confession because he said he forgot it; neither does he know anything else about Christian doctrine, claiming that as a poor miserable he had no one to teach him."[14] Although it probably did not count against him, he also had no current "bull of the Holy Crusade" (an indulgence preached every two years and priced according to an individual's capacity to pay), explaining that he "did not see them offered and anyway he had no money to give as an alm."[15]

Francisco Macías and José Francisco Ortiz also showed low levels of cultic practice.[16] Francisco had gone through the usual religious rites of passage (baptism and confirmation in Aguascalientes), but in 1734, at fifty, he testified that "he is too busy with his work" to manage more than the minimal once-a-year confession, which would have been at Easter. José also adhered to a minimal cultic practice, it seems, for in March of 1781 he stated that he had last confessed and taken Holy Communion about a year before, "last Easter in Guanajuato."[17] He thought he had been baptized, but did not know if confirmed. Probably he had not, for the notary recorded that he showed "almost no understanding of Christian doctrine."

So levels of indoctrination ranged from virtually no understanding to "very good," and devotional practice, from rare attendance at mass, not even the prescribed minimum of once per year, to daily attendance. Those who did not measure up to church standards voiced extenuating circumstances (they had forgotten, had been too busy working, had grown up as poor miserables without indoctrination) rather than doubts as to the truth and value of the faith itself. They sat well within the boundaries of the Christian fold and seemed to have a basic idea of heaven and hell, sin and salvation, this life and the next.

But this hardly qualified them as the zealous guardians of faith and morals envisaged by Moya. Whatever piety they had, in fact, probably came to the fore most strongly when death appeared on the horizon and the church's monopoly of the means of grace, never doubted in the abstract, engaged them more urgently. Whether one's grasp of Christian teachings was rudimentary or developed, this was the time to put aside apathy or bravado. Diego de Villareal, for example, left his wife in Spain, and in New Spain he had lived for a time in concubinage with at least two women.[18] His appropriately somber, if formulaic, reference to finding out that his first wife "was dead and had passed from this present life" prefaced his central concern, to put his own moral house in order, which in practical terms meant marrying Juana de Torres "in order to be in the service of Our Lord and not to be in mortal sin."[19]

The perilousness of mortal sin in popular discourse can be seen in the solemn council of Captain Olmeda, master of the muleteer Francisco Catalán, when Francisco asked what he should do after finding out that he was a bigamist.[20] "He commended him to God and to the Virgin of Rosario to guide him in what he would have to do so that he would not lose his soul, and his said master gave him letters to a priest named don Pedro de Esquivel who lives on the bridge of Santa Catalina Martir."[21]

Thus we can understand Manuel Domínguez's uneasy conscience about marrying a second time to free himself from the authorities who arrested him for having an "illicit friendship" with Petra Eugenia Velasco, a widow of Guadalajara.[22] He fled immediately after the marriage, but his initial anxiety receded, and over a ten-year period he resumed regular contact with Petra. On falling sick, Manuel confessed his bigamy to a friar who ordered him to denounce himself to the Holy Office. Yet as the sickness passed, so too did Manuel's sense of urgency to receive the absolution, penance, and reconciliation of the Inquisition, and he was actively evading the Inquisition when their agents arrested him 1763. Antonio Piñero, in much the same way, responded appropriately in a moment of great danger.[23] Finding himself in the midst of a violent storm at sea, he determined to remove himself from a state of mortal sin by promising to marry his mistress, Francisca Cabrera. Yet once safely in port, he returned to his procrastinating ways.

Antonio and Manuel both feared eternal damnation but tried to hedge their bets by carrying on with their lives once danger had passed. The mestizo Pedro Manuel Galindo fits the same profile: a man worried about hiding his sin and also about the punishment that would come on revealing it. Five years after contracting an illicit marriage (in 1744), he admitted that it was

> certain that he kept silent to his confessors because he was afraid of the punishment of this Holy Office. Nevertheless he recognized the wrong he was doing and that he would not be able to save himself unless he got out of his illicit state, but the demon hobbled him and scared him so that he did not dare leave his illicit state for fear of the penalty referred to. He knew that his confessions were sacrilegious, but even so he did not have a bad opinion of the holy sacrament of the penance of the Eucharist or of matrimony.[24]

So Pedro Manuel tried to carry on as if all was normal but experienced a conflict (for purposes of his confession, personified as caused by the demon) that he did not or could not resolve. As long as a final accounting remained distant, he could live with the tension, waiting perhaps until he was sick, old, or in danger before clearing himself of mortal sin.

Unlike Pedro Manuel, Francisco Antonio García stopped going to confession after he married a second time, in 1746.[25] In a self-reflective statement before the inquisitors in May 1751 (just seven months before this thirty-year-old *mestizo* was to die), he explained how he had lived with an uneasy conscience. He said that even though "he knew and believed that with a first wife still alive one could not have a married life with a second, he [nevertheless] persuaded himself that this was licit." As an out Francisco seized upon a bit of folk theology that "he had heard from some muleteers [that] if you do not have a nuptial blessing within seven years a wife becomes only a mistress." In fact this was a kind of fallback position, not an actual rejection, of church teachings, a way to give himself a plausible excuse if required, for he had not tested it in the confessional.

Avoiding confession could be a telltale sign, in fact, as when the lobo Juan Lorenzo del Castillo, after abandoning his wife in 1702, also dropped his religious practices.[26] In his first hearing before the inquisitors (in 1708), he said that he had "not heard the mass, confessed, or taken communion at the times ordered by the Holy Mother Church since he left the said his wife, Teresa de la Cruz."[27] The sacrament of penitence, based on confession, required parishioners to reveal the truth. But confession meant punishment and the breakup of their new lives. At the same time, to conceal the truth amounted to a fearful sacrilege.[28]

The plea of ignorance, as we have already seen, was an argument for a mitigating circumstance, especially when used by people who presented themselves as rustics. We might be surprised, therefore, to see a wily Spaniard such as Miguel de Herrera (born 1695 in Havana) using it.[29] Listen as he summarizes in 1722, with due contrition and yet with a certain aplomb, points he had covered earlier: "He did not realize that it [bigamy] was a great sin until his confessors told him. Once he realized its gravity, he tried to go to the tribunal for help . . . and although he did not succeed it is certain that this was his intention. And now that he was not able to denounce himself he now does it in this confession."

Of interest here is Miguel's self presentation: an ignorant man who thought bigamy merely a small sin, but one he nonetheless had duly reported to his confessor. When he learned that it was serious, he acted responsibly and correctly but was the victim of some bad luck. As he portrayed it,

> he arrived at his wife's house on a Thursday at five in the afternoon and the next morning he consulted with the provincial of the Mercedarian monastery who said that it was too late to go to the tribunal that day, for it was already nearly noon, and that he should present himself to them on another day. But he could not because Saturday was a day of fiesta and thus, in readiness to go at the first opportunity, he was arrested on Saturday night.

The inquisitors doubted this version of events. They checked with the provincial and, finding him unable to remember the conversation he allegedly had had with Miguel, assumed that it had not taken place. As for the so-called day of fiesta, the notary wrote in the margin, "it was not, but a regular day of the Tribunal." So much for Miguel as an ignorant man but well-meaning and sincerely subservient to the church. Later he undermined this impression further by stressing that when seducing women, "he was scrupulous to only promise to marry them but never intended to actually do so."[30]

The mulatto Laureano de la Cruz also pleaded ignorance and, once in custody, presented himself as penitent because by then he had been properly instructed.[31] His statement comes in response to a clause of the prosecutor's arraignment (March 31, 1788) that he married a second time "presenting himself as unmarried, maliciously believing that he was only committing a venial sin that he hoped to correct later with God's pardon." This portrayal has Laureano as ignorant (of the difference between venial and mortal sin), but also cynical and manipulative of the sacrament of penitence. Laureano replied that he "now knows the seriousness of the crime although, at the time he committed it, he did not know it was against our holy faith. In a way, he has lived as a bad Christian in living incontinently with a woman." Thus Laureano paraphrases the formal charge but tries to remove the attribution of maliciousness in his motivation. He agrees in substance that he has "in a way" lived as a bad Christian but nonetheless a Christian.

So far, then, we have seen that bigamists accounted for their behavior in the language of penitents and no doubt genuinely dreaded the state of mortal sin. But not more so, perhaps, than they feared the punishments the Inquisition might impose. At the next stage, in custody and as they spoke in the dock, they had to make the best of it, and this meant assuming the stance of sinners in the confessional. They admitted guilt, pleaded for mercy, and argued that extenuating circumstances (most commonly ignorance, false reports, or temporary bedevilment) had caused their downfall. Such excuses, before the Inquisition became involved, stood people in good stead except, perhaps, when death seemed near.[32]

After all, as Pedro Pérez pointed out in 1621, disease and sickness were "given by God" and meant to be signs.[33] The state of one's body often pushed people to confession and the sacrament of Holy Communion so as to be ready for the worst. The twenty-nine-year-old Spaniard Mariana Monroy, whose first hearing before the inquisitors was in 1678, said (on March 3) that she "confessed [sacramentally] yesterday when she was gravely sick."[34] The mention of her grave condition in conjunction with her religious observances charges these with a special intensity but otherwise fits within her normal pattern of careful practice. Don Manuel del Alamo, on the other hand, who had not been practicing his faith, had to make a complete turnabout.[35] He testified (in 1788) that he had begun well,

> baptized in the parish of San Juan de Málaga and confirmed at a young age. In Spain he always heard the mass on the days prescribed and on most of those that were not, confessing and taking communion each week, fortnight, and only rarely [as infrequently as] once a month because he lived an orderly and Christian life in fear of God.

Once don Manuel got to New Spain, however, his conduct changed, as he fell in with "subjects of vicious conduct" and

> stopped hearing the mass on some prescribed days, when he was gambling for example, so as not to leave the game, and other times when he did not bother

to hear it because he was involved with some other diversion. But this was never out of contempt and he knew very well that he was sinning mortally. And in the same way his vicious passions dragged him down and he stopped confessing and taking communion.

Until his return to regular observance, don Manuel recalled, he had taken the sacrament only three times in the ten or eleven years he had been in New Spain:

> In Vera Cruz when he arrived from Spain; in this monastery of San Diego seven years ago; and last year in Apan [an alcaldía mayor, together with Tepeapulco, now in southeast Hidalgo state] with fray Joseph Manuel Arpide when he was bedridden and gravely ill. There he came to recognize his depraved life and tried to make amends with a firm spirit, resolving to continue his confessions if God would take away his sickness . . . and while he was sick he bought an indulgence for two reales.

Don Manuel's illness drove him back to the church, but his lapse in religious practice had not been a rejection of Christian faith. Being in mortal sin, he seemed to think, was temporary and correctable. The trick would be to pay attention to the signs (his illness, as it turned out), when they came. And he did, proving adept at 'leaving the game' in good time.

So because one's accountability for this life determined one's fate in the next, bigamists could be at war with themselves, caught between their life instincts and their dread of eternal damnation. After a long struggle with the problem, Marcos de la Cruz surrendered to the authority of the church.[36] He had fallen "into this misery," he said in 1671, (in answer to the inquisitor's question as to why he married a second time),

> dragged down and conquered by the love that he had for the said Juana Montaño. . . . For fourteen years he received the Holy Sacrament sacrelially, because in hiding his second marriage from his confessors, he was aware that he had not confessed completely. He meant no disrespect for the Holy Sacrament but was afraid of being discovered. Even though his conscience accused him constantly, he could not leave Juana.

We do not know if Marcos and Manuel found peace, but their confessions suggest that they had run out of ways to evade the inevitable, which for most amounted to the same thing. In that sense they were fortunate, for one could not absolve oneself, and few indeed were ready to pass from this life without absolution.

Yet the untimely death of the mulatto Pedro Domínguez reminds us that some missed their chance for a final reconciliation. Pedro, in the Holy Office's custody and known to be ill, was found dead, at thirty-one, on April 29, 1786.[37] "I certify that in the house that was Colegio de San Juan [wrote the notary Diego de Cosío] and is now used as a hospital for sick prisoners, I found the body of Pedro Antonio Domínguez. I called his name several times, but he did not answer, so I knew that he was truly dead."

We may assume a better passing for the thirty-year-old mestizo Francisco Antonio García, who had sufficient time for the last rites.[38] Antonio was apparently in good health, when agents of the Inquisition arrested him in Izúcar in April 1750. But eighteen months later, his health was failing rapidly. Listen to the doctor's report of October 27, 1751, after his examination of Antonio in the prison in Mexico City: "Prisoner number six has become gravely ill of the sickness called diarrhea. He now is having frequent attacks and they're coming more and more frequently, and his condition is aggravated because it is so damp in the said cell." Two days later the judges ordered Francisco hospitalized at San Juan de Diós. We have no further reports on his condition until December 8, when he died. Presumably the intervening weeks of inexorable decline allowed everyone to anticipate the end.

More difficult, but not less common, were the many prisoners who suffered mental illnesses and depression, as manifested in suicides, psychosomatic illnesses, and psychotic behavior that pointed to the breakdown of the personality.[39] Consider for example the case of the twenty-nine-year-old mulatto Juan Lorenzo de Castillo, whose manic-depressive mood swings baffled diagnosis. Dr. don Juan Joseph Brozuela, physician of the prisoners, filed a long report on Juan, dated August 12, 1709. In an assessment mixing certainty with tentativeness, he wrote that

> the prisoner in number eleven gives sufficient symptoms on which to base a probable judgment that he is truly demented. At the beginning of his imprisonment he suffered periods of great sadness accompanied by the silent refusal to take necessary nourishment. When the jailers punished him, wounding him in the head, he gave no indication that he felt it. And after the dementia, he became completely free of his former sadness . . . and instead of fear and silence, he became in equal measure daring and talkative, and from his old lack of appetite suddenly he is insatiably and extraordinarily voracious,

gulping and devouring as much as is put in front of him. As a result the said prisoner is now not only healthy but quite robust and in possession of all of his strength, except that he still is not directly in touch with his mind . . . [inferred] by the disposition and movements of his eyes and his [continued] insensitivity to the wound on his head . . . The witness judges, then, that the prisoner is unmistakably insane . . . and his madness will be difficult to cure because it does not admit or depend on natural principles but rather is an affliction of the spirit.

Nothing more is known of Juan until he abjures his error publicly in September 1718, nine years later. Apparently because of his fragile mental condition, the judges excused him from the normal public flogging and instead ordered him to confess on each of the next three Easters, to say the Rosary of Our Lady every Saturday for one year, and to resume married life with his first wife. Juan had been beaten by his jailer, examined by a perplexed doctor, and kept in the Holy Office's prison for ten years, but was reinstated to the fold and the sacraments and was therefore, at least for the time being, no longer in mortal sin. If all went well, he would die in a state of grace.

After a longer life and a shorter ordeal, the escaped slave and bigamist Sebastián de Loaysa managed to do the same, no mean feat given his circumstances.[40] Ignacio de Villalobos, a muleteer of Teguantepec (an alcaldía mayor in the marquesado, now in southeast Oaxaca), was taking Sebastián from Guatemala to Mexico City in chains. On the way, in the pueblo of Sanatepec (jurisdiction of Teguantepec), Sebastián died. It was a quick death and, thanks to fray Juan de Saavedra, a Dominican who administered the last rites, most likely a peaceful one.

I certify on the word of a priest [wrote fray Juan] that today, June 23, 1675, Sebastián de Loaysa—mulatto, bald, branded, age sixty to seventy—died in this pueblo . . . I attest that he died wearing manacles and chains, which I had removed in order to bury him on consecrated ground, treatment he was worthy of because he died with all of the Holy Sacraments.

INDIVIDUALS AND NORMS

Sebastián can stand for the complexity of the bigamists who came before the Inquisition, for none of the categories used to define him truly did: a slave, he passed as free; a skilled blacksmith, he practiced his trade sporadically and only at the behest of his owner; a mulatto, he was "very ladino"; a married man, he posed as unmarried to marry again; a renegade, he died in the arms of the same Mother Church that had chained him and ordered him to Mexico City for discipline. He represents, therefore, the disparity between society's labels and life. He, along with the other bigamists, collaborated with the efforts of church and state to impose a hegemonic model of comportment and ideology but selectively, imperfectly, and mostly on his own terms. There is little reason to think that he and the populace in general had an interest in morality in any abstract sense (especially as it touched on sexual behavior) and equally little reason to think that they had an interest in church doctrine except, possibly, as it might have helped them avoid pain, suffering, and misery and to gain some measure of comfort, security, and well-being. In simple terms, that meant avoiding hell and getting to heaven.

As in all hierarchical societies, bigamists in New Spain deferred to those in authority over them—or at least they pretended to. Yet Moya's dream of incorporating them as active partners in their own control was too optimistic. More realistically, as we already saw, Lebrón de Quiñones's thought that control came from giving out "the appropriate punishments." Sebastián would have understood. As a slave he knew his place at the bottom of society: the mark burned on his cheek by the branding iron served as a reminder; and if he forgot, there was always the lash. Yet he too carried on with his life and sidestepped many parts of the model, as he entered into illicit liaisons, married twice, worked on the side to accumulate some property, ran away, and practiced his religion in a perfunctory way.

If identities are difficult to categorize, so too are behaviors. Even apparently simple acts involved a political calculation, which meant that what was said and done would change, depending on whether it was to or in the presence of an equal or a superior. This politics of dominance-subservience was a matter of degree and circumstance, not a simple polarity. It framed the content and tone of behavior, which consisted of an interplay between folk beliefs (the taken-for-granted web of everyday lore, rituals, ideas, and "popular religion" that accompanied daily life[41]) and, however imperfectly grasped, the teachings of the church. In the main people concerned themselves with coupling, getting along, raising children, fitting into clienteles, finding work, and keeping track of each other. In this they were the agents and protagonists of their own lives. They worked like dogs, preyed on those they could victimize, and in a cut-throat world, in turn became victims of those more powerful than they; those who fell into debt wandered near and far in search of a job or, better yet, easy money. They scrambled not only to make a living but to make a life, although they would not have differentiated between the two.

It is of course true that people flocked to see the spectacle of punishment and reconciliation of Mexico's first auto de fe, which Moya supposed had established the authority of the Inquisition. And they would continue to do so. They also collaborated with the Inquisition by denouncing each other and sometimes themselves. Yet attending a spectacle in early modern times did not necessarily imply support for or even understanding of the ideology it represented, as if endorsing the program of a political faction at a rally. To think this presumes that the event held the same significance for the mulatto shoemaker, the Spanish merchant, the Franciscan friar, the Indian pulque supplier (perhaps from the outlying pueblo of Coatitlán), and the mestizo tamale vender as it had for Moya and his colleagues. And neither should we think, ipso facto, that people who reported each other as fornicators, as bigamists, and as engaged in illicit friendships did so strictly or even mainly to eradicate scandal, immorality, and sin. That would again presume too simplistic a fit between official ideology and the behavior in question. It is true that denouncers used the language of official ideology, but that does not mean that this is what denunciations were about. Instead they should be seen as coming out of the complex interplay of in- and out-group dynamics, supporting one's own and distrusting outsiders. People did keep track of each other, but as we have seen, conversations always worked their way back to networks and connections held in common. When these resulted in denunciations, they did so within the terms of reference of family, neighborhood, work, and clientele groupings.

We should remember that people primarily carried on with their own lives more than they observed those of their associates. And if forced to answer for their actions, they justified themselves with a mix of church teachings, folk wisdom, and common sense. Love, anger, lust, fear, pride, jealousy, friendship, concern for honor, ambition, opportunism, boredom, or depression cropped up in a thousand different ways and combinations, as people went about their business at home, in the streets, in the fields, and in distant places. These passions, emotions, and compulsions had a place amidst the most ordinary of daily routines. They also played their part in the complex event called "bigamy," which as marriage, moves us into the arena of private life; as sin and crime, to dynamics of social control by church and state; and, as 'mistake,' to the situational and fortuitous mix-ups and contingencies of everyday life.

With a sense of irony, perhaps, we should stress that bigamists complied with the norms of their church and society about as much as they avoided them. But in their own ways and, at least in part, on their own terms. Yes they married a second time, but as part of the logic of their living rather than to defy the official model of comportment to which, in its details, they were largely oblivious anyway. In instances of a clash, they deferred to or worked around, but rarely defied directly the prescribed comportment. They appear as, in the main, conventionally religious, deferential to authority, and driven by the opinions of their peers. Their new worlds were quite a bit like their old ones. How they created or drifted into them provides a view of the circumstances, agency, and self-reflections of small people in colonial society.

Possibly the most extraordinary aspect of bigamists' lives was that they became entangled with a fearful, powerful, and often corrupt institution, the Holy Office of the Inquisition. We should not understate what this cost them. Bigamists suffered arrest, confiscation of property, imprisonment, and terrible psychological stress; and in their trials and reconciliations, hardship, violence, and humiliation. We can only imagine the effects of a typical seventeenth-century punishment for bigamy: an agonizing and seemingly endless one or two hundred lashes, as one was paraded through the main streets of Mexico City, with a crier shouting out one's crime. Afterward came a long and brutalizing confinement of galley servitude for a term of five to seven years—if one survived.

Yet none of the bigamists ended up on a burning pyre; most were "reconciled" and returned to church and society; and many, perhaps more than we normally imagine, escaped the clutches of the Holy Office altogether. In the end the bigamists who constructed new worlds in the Indies should be seen not mainly as victims, heroes, or martyrs, but as ordinary folk making choices and carrying on day by day. In this they stand for countless others of their time and place, whose worlds have receded completely from our view.

Appendix

SAMPLE OF 216 BIGAMY FILES
FROM MEXICO'S NATIONAL ARCHIVE

Names	Birth-date	Date of First Marriage	Date of Second Marriage	Sex	Length of 1st Marriage in Years
Acosta, Miguel de, alias Sagualtipam	1745	1764	1774	Male	7
Aguila, Francisco de	1498	1558	1558	Male	
Aguirre, María de	1517	1529	1550	Female	15
Alamo, don Manuel del, alias don Josef Tribaldo	1747	1772	1783	Male	4
Albertos, Francisco	1607	1631	1660	Male	26
Alemán, Juan Bautista, alias Alegna	1700	1720	1735	Male	5
Alexo, Francisco, alias Antonio	1658	1681		Male	4
Alonso, Miguel	1549	1572	1586	Male	7
Alvarado, Alonso de	1651	1664	1678	Male	14
Amador y Frias, Phelipe de		1679	1684	Male	
Aranda, Juan de	1549	1566		Male	3
Araus, Nicolás Antonio de	1711	1735	1737	Male	0.5
Aspitia, Ana de	1547	1566		Female	8
Avila, Joana de				Female	
Ayala, Christóbal de	1545			Male	
Azacar, Juan López de		1568	1573	Male	
Azevedo, Antonio de		1571	1583	Male	10
Balencuela, Juana María	1753	1768	1779	Female	7
Baraona, Antonio de	1676	1695	1704	Male	5
Barrera, Juan de	1648	1672	1685	Male	5
Barrios Valderrama y Navera, Domingo	1746	1764	1766	Male	0.5
Benavides, Gerónimo de	1532	1543	1565	Male	0.1
Berástegui y Gordillo, don Julian de		1733		Male	
Biscarra, José Francisco	1751	1764	1776	Male	4
Blasa de la Candelaria, María	1720	1736	1741	Female	2
Buscarones, Ygnacio, alias don Ygnacio Bucareli	1718	1737	1744	Male	
Bustinca, Pedro de	1540	1554	1567	Male	3
Calderón, Marcos	1711	1734	1749	Male	2
Calderón, Sebastian, alias Andrade	1706	1734	1745	Male	5
Campuzano Palazios, Manuel de	1694	1713	1732	Male	16
Cañada, Pedro	1535		1581	Male	
Canto y Morales, don Salvador de	1714	1748	1751	Male	0.1
Castellón, Salvador	1741	1773	1778	Male	4
Castillo, Isidro del	1688	1708	1725	Male	8
Castroverde, Christóbal de	1576	1591	1611	Male	5
Catalán, Francisco	1614	1652	1654	Male	
Cavallero y Basave, Joseph	1741	1758	1767	Male	7
Cavallero, Juan Manuel, alias Castellanos Alvarado	1714	1729	1736	Male	3
Cavallero, Juan Manuel, alias Manuel Castellano Alvarado	1701	1729	1736	Male	3
Cervantes, María Ignacia	1753	1767	1787	Female	16
Chacón Gayon, Juan Antonio, alias Antonio Pérez Chacón	1661	1672	1697	Male	1.5

Length of 2nd Marriage in Years	Race	Race of First Spouse	Race of Second Spouse	Archival Reference
3	Creole	Mulatto	Indian	AGN, Inq., vol. 1156, exp. 13, fs. 309ff.
0.1	Spaniard	Spaniard	Creole	AGN, Inq., vol. 24, fs.13-16v; 27-28; 60-81.
8.5	Spaniard	Spaniard	Spaniard	AGN, Inq., vol. 25, exp. 4 and 5.
4	Spaniard	Spaniard	Creole	AGN, Inq., vol. 1214, exp. 11, fs. 126-245.
1	European	European	Creole	AGN, Inq., vol. 580, exp. 4, fs.486-734.
11	Slave	Slave	Mulatto	AGN, Inq., vol. 819, exp. 8, fs. 21-60.
	Slave	Slave	Unknown	AGN, Inq., vol. 648, exp. 7, fs. 497-593.
3	Spaniard	Spaniard	Creole	AGN, Inq., vol. 137, exp. 11.
8	Mulatto	Mulatto	Mulatto	AGN, Inq., vol. 524, fs. 190-257.
	Mulatto	Unknown	Unknown	AGN, Inq., vol. 526, fs. 360-380.
	Spaniard	Spaniard	Unknown	AGN, Inq., vol. 108, exp. 3.
4	Mestizo	Indian	Indian	AGN, Inq., vol. 1139, fs. 82-186.
	Mulatto	Spaniard	Mulatto	AGN, Inq., vol. 135, exp. 1.
	Unknown	Unknown	Unknown	AGN, Inq., vol. 90, exp. 31, fs. 359.
	Mulatto	Mulatto	Mulatto	AGN, Inq., vol. 26, exp. 4, fs. 83-114.
	European	Mulatto	Creole	AGN, Inq., vol. 134, exp. 6.
1	Spaniard	Spaniard	Unknown	AGN, Inq., vol. 135.
6	Mestizo	Mulatto	Mestizo	AGN, Inq., vol.1301, exp. 4, fs.22-94.
1.7	Mestizo	Mestizo	Unknown	AGN. Inq., vol. 547, exp. 6.
0.1	Spaniard	Creole	Creole	AGN, Inq., vol. 523, fs. 131-257.
0.8	Spaniard	Creole	Creole	AGN, Inq., vol. 1066.
12	Spaniard	Spaniard	Unknown	AGN, Inq., vol. 108, exp. 2.
	Creole	Creole	Unknown	AGN, Inq., vol. 964, fs. 376-405.
0.1	Mulatto	Indian	Mulatto	AGN, Inq., vol.1104, exp. 7, fs. 143-191.
8	Mestizo	Unknown	Mulatto	AGN, Inq., vol. 919, exp. 1 and vol. 918, exp. 3, fs. 41-50.
0.3	Creole	Unknown	Creole	AGN, Inq., vol. 918, exp. 21, fs. 330ff.
5	Spaniard	Spaniard	Unknown	AGN, Inq., vol. 91, exp. 6.
	Mestizo	Unknown	Unknown	AGN, Inq., vol. 933, exp. 7.
1	Mulatto	Mulatto	Mulatto	AGN, Inq., vol. 1138, fs. 211-341.
3	Spaniard	Spaniard	Creole	AGN, Inq., vol. 1234.
4	Spaniard	Unknown	Unknown	AGN, Inq., vol. 136, exp. 9.
0.1	Spaniard	Spaniard	Spaniard	AGN, Inq., vol. 933, exp. 8.
4	Mulatto	Indian	Unknown	AGN, Inq., vol. 1364, exp. 15, fs. 370v-418.
4	Mestizo	Mulatto	Mestizo	AGN, Inq., vol. 814, exp. 4, fs. 390-482.
4	Mulatto	Mulatto	Unknown	AGN, Inq., vol. 310, exp. 7.
13	Mestizo	Indian	Mestizo	AGN, Inq., vol. 606, exp. 10 and 11, fs. 578-613.
9	Spaniard	Spaniard	Creole	AGN, Inq., vol. 1161, fs. 1-141.
8	Creole	Mulatto	Mestizo	AGN, Inq., vol. 1387, exp. 1, fs. 1-121.
3	Creole	Mulatto	Unknown	AGN, Inq., vol. 1387, exp. 1, fs. 1-121.
1	Mulatto	Mestizo	Zambo	AGN, Inq., vol. 1214.
0.1	Spaniard	Unknown	Unknown	AGN, Inq., vol. 699.

Names	Birth-date	Date of First Marriage	Date of Second Marriage	Sex	Length of 1st Marriage in Years
Chamorro, Nicolás		1524	1537	Male	
Chavarría, Joseph Francisco de	1706	1721	1735	Male	6
Christóbal, Bernabé. alias Mavekp	1696	1715	1728	Male	3
Contreras, Phelipe, alias Bartolomé de Peralta	1707	1720		Male	
Cortés, Diego	1504	1521	1527	Male	
Cortés, Mathias	1665	1691	1704	Male	7
Cruz Malagón, Gregorio de la	1710	1731	1734	Male	0.1
Cruz, Andrés de la, alias Acevedo	1622	1647	1661	Male	6
Cruz, Antonio de		1706	1724	Male	0.5
Cruz, Baltasár de la			1618	Male	3
Cruz, Juan Laureano de la	1748	1761	1784	Male	
Cruz, Lorenza de la	1661	1678	1691	Female	4
Cruz, Marcos de la, alias de Tobar	1625	1648	1657	Male	7
Cruz, Matheo de la	1627	1644	1660	Male	3
Cruz, Nicolás de la	1609	1628	1632	Male	0.1
Delgadillo Hernández, María Guadalupe, alias Tres Palacios Hernández	1760	1772	1777	Female	1
Díaz, Ana	1519	1554	1558	Female	1.5
Díaz, Francisco	1549	1565	1587	Male	0.1
Encarnación, María Jesús de la, alias María Filomena Tavares	1749	1768	1777	Female	7
Espinosa, Inés de		1538	1579	Female	3
Figueroa, María de	1610	1621	1624	Female	0.5
Fragoso, Manuel		1562		Male	9
Francisco, Juan	1588	1612	1615	Male	0.5
Gachupín, Joseph el		1671	1699	Male	12
Galdos, Don Juan de				Male	
Galindo, Pedro Manuel	1709	1726	1744	Male	6
García Bullones, Pedro		1528		Male	0.1
García de Hoyos, Diego	1577	1584	1596	Male	
García, Francisco	1523	1551	1577	Male	3
García, Francisco Antonio	1720	1738	1746	Male	0.2
García, Joseph Manuel Antonio, alias Joseph Manuel Marrufo, el cocoliste		1750	1760	Male	3
García, Miguel	1522		1569	Male	
Gómez Franco, don Juan	1700	1721	1751	Male	7
González Alvarez, Domínguez	1544			Male	
González Carmona, Diego	1556	1574	1607	Male	2
González, Antonio	1541	1570		Male	11
González, Beatriz			1536	Female	
González, Joseph, alias Memela				Male	9
González, Lucía				Female	
Griego, Nicolás, alias Pérez	1539	1570		Male	
Guerra, Alonso	1544	1573	1585	Male	11
Guerra, Gerónimo	1554	1582	1585	Male	8

Length of 2nd Marriage in Years	Race	Race of First Spouse	Race of Second Spouse	Archival Reference
0.7	Spaniard	Spaniard	Spaniard	AGN, Inq., vol. 22, exp. 11.
3	Mulatto	Mulatto	Slave	AGN, Inq., vol. 794, exp. 24, fs. 226-322.
1.5	Mulatto	Mulatto	Mulatto	AGN, Inq., vol. 834, exp. 24, fs. 410-491.
	Mestizo	Creole	Unknown	AGN, Inq., vol. 969, exp. 17, fs. 210-294.
	Spaniard	Spaniard	Spaniard	AGN, Inq., vol. 22, exp. 5.
2	Mestizo	Mestizo	Mestizo	AGN, Inq., vol. 547, exp. 8.
5	Slave	Mulatto	Mulatto	AGN, Inq., vol. 794, exp. 1, fs. 1-39.
4	Zambo	Indian	Mestizo	AGN, Inq., vol. 592, exp. 3, fs. 271-377.
2	Unknown	Creole	Unknown	AGN, Inq., vol. 814, exp. 5 and 6, fs. 289-389.
6	Mulatto	Indian	Mulatto	AGN, Inq., vol. 347, exp. 3.
2	Mulatto	Unknown	Indian	AGN, Inq., vol. 1277, fs. 1-111.
1	Mulatto	Mulatto	Mulatto	AGN, Inq., vol. 526, exp. 2, fs. 37-151.
14	Creole	Unknown	Unknown	AGN, Inq., vol. 608, exp. 3, fs. 216-99.
3	Indian	Mestizo	Indian	AGN, Inq., vol. 586, exp. 9, fs. 502-72.
2	Mulatto	Black	Black	AGN, Inq., vol. 381, exp. 7.
1	Creole	Mestizo	Creole	AGN, Inq., vol. 1192, fs. 1-85.
12	Spaniard	Spaniard	Unknown	AGN, Inq., vol. 36, exp. 11, fs. 500-75.
6	Spaniard	Spaniard	Mestizo	AGN, Inq., vol. 138, exp. 6.
4	Mulatto	Mulatto	Indian	AGN, Inq., vol.1292, exp. 7, fs. 1-101.
0.6	Unknown	Unknown	Unknown	AGN, Inq., vol. 134, exp. 7.
0.1	Creole	Creole	Mulatto	AGN, Inq., vol. 370, exp. 3, fs. 307-20.
	Spaniard	Spaniard	Mestizo	AGN, Inq., vol. 136, exp. 7.
0.5	Spaniard	Spaniard	Creole	AGN, Inq., vol. 312, exp. 73, fs. 428-93.
3	Slave	Slave	Mulatto	AGN, Inq., vol. 544, exp. 23, fs. 463-481.
	Unknown	Unknown	Unknown	AGN, Inq., vol. 1371, exp. 9, fs.1-38.
3	Mestizo	Mestizo	Mulatto	AGN, Inq., vol. 921, exp. 29.
0.4	Spaniard	Spaniard	Indian	AGN, Inq., vol. 22, exp. 2.
	European	Spaniard	Unknown	AGN, Inq., vol. 250, fs. 238-44.
2	Spaniard	Spaniard	Unknown	AGN, Inq., vol. 108, exp. 7.\
4	Mestizo	Mestizo	Mulatto	AGN, Inq., vol. 922, exp. 1.
2	Mulatto	Slave	Mulatto	AGN, Inq., vol. 1231, exp. 6, fs. 28-103.
	Spaniard	Spaniard	Unknown	AGN, Inq., vol. 135, exp. 4.
4	Spaniard	Spaniard	Spaniard	AGN, Inq., vol. 972, exp. 1.
	Spaniard	Spaniard	Unknown	AGN, Inq., vol. 136, exp. 3.
7	Spaniard	Spaniard	Unknown	Huntington Library
	Spaniard	Unknown	Unknown	AGN, Inq., vol. 134, exp. 12.
2	Spaniard	Spaniard	Spaniard	AGN, Inq., vol. 22, exp. 12.
	Mestizo	Unknown	Creole	AGN, Inq., vol. 524, fs. 468-595.
	Spaniard	Spaniard	Unknown	AGN, Inq., vol. 137, exp. 5
	European	Black	Unknown	AGN, Inq., vol. 108, exp. 1.
	Spaniard	Spaniard	Spaniard	AGN, Inq., vol. 256, exp. 5.
1	European	Mestizo	Creole	AGN, Inq., vol. 135, exp. 6.

Names	Birth-date	Date of First Marriage	Date of Second Marriage	Sex	Length of 1st Marriage in Years
Guizával, Alonso de	1654	1675	1681	Male	3
Gutiérrez de Estrada, Juan de	1568	1586	1597	Male	2
Gutierrez, Francisco	1520	1558	1559	Male	1
Guzmán, Juan de	1576			Male	
Hermenegildo Hidalgo, Nicolás, alias Nicolás Cervantes		1754	1764	Male	3
Hernández de Hermosilla, Gonzalo	1559	1582	1588	Male	
Hernández, Ana, alias la serrana	1516			Female	
Hernández, Diego		1571		Male	6.5
Hernández, Gonzalo	1533	1550	1580	Male	2
Hernández, Pedro	1523			Male	
Hernández, Ynés, alias Florentina del Río		1524	1525	Female	0.4
Herrera, Miguel de	1695	1712	1721	Male	3
Hojeda, Diego de	1558	1575	1579	Male	1
Hortiz, Bartolomé, alias Manuel de Chanaquicia y Arteaga	1695	1717	1721	Male	0.5
Hoz, Agustín de	1546	1561	1573	Male	9
León, Gómez de	1542	1558	1571	Male	7
Lipona, Manuel de, alias Manuel de los Reyes Hernández	1715	1727	1738	Male	10
Lizarzaburo, Juan de	1640	1674	1677	Male	
Loaysa, Sebastián de	1614	1641	1659	Male	16
López de Utiel, Juan	1514			Male	9
López, Joseph Laureano	1743	1759	1765	Male	3
Lorenzo del Castillo, Juan	1680	1693	1706	Male	5
Lorenzo, Juan, alias Lorenzo Ramírez, alias Phelipe de Santiago	1677	1694	1704	Male	10
Luis, Juan	1585			Male	
Luis, Juan, alias Ruíz, alias de la Cruz		1641	1656	Male	1.5
Luis, Martín, alias Nicolás Rico	1561	1585	1587	Male	2
Macias, Francisco, alias el flaco		1714	1718	Male	1
Maldonado, Rosa, alias Rosalia del Carmen Maldonado	1742	1759		Female	
Martina, Barbara, alias María Estephanía	1745	1760	1766	Female	5
Mascarenas, Juan Antonio, alias Juan Antonio de Armenta	1700	1718	1734	Male	12
Matheo, Pedro, alias Pedro de Moya	1642	1660	1665	Male	1
Mayorga, Nicolás	1692	1727	1740	Male	1
Melendez, Hieronimo	1585			Male	
Méndez, Juan				Male	
Mendiola, Manuel de	1640	1662		Male	15
Miguel, Joseph, alias Miguel Antonio	1713	1738	1751	Male	6
Molina, Joseph de	1560	1586	1593	Male	0.2
Molina, Joseph Manuel	1725	1743	1772	Male	17
Monroy, Mariana	1649	1663	1676	Female	2

Length of 2nd Marriage in Years	Race	Race of First Spouse	Race of Second Spouse	Archival Reference
	Mestizo	Indian	Zambo	AGN, Inq., vol. 642, exp. 1, fs. 1-97.
3	Spaniard	Mulatto	Mestizo	AGN, Inq., vol. 261, exp. 3.
	Creole	Unknown	Unknown	AGN, Inq., vol. 23, exp. 8, fs. 69-153.
2	Spaniard	Spaniard	Unknown	AGN, Inq., vol. 308, fs. 162r-162v.
0.2	Creole	Mestizo	Unknown	AGN, Inq., vol. 1073.
1	Spaniard	Unknown	Unknown	AGN, Inq., vol. 138, exp. 7.
	Spaniard	Spaniard	Spaniard	AGN, Inq., vol. 24, exp. 6, fs. 157-249.
2	Unknown	Mestizo	Unknown	AGN, Inq., vol. 134, exp. 9.
5	Mulatto	Unknown	Indian	AGN, Inq., vol. 137, exp. 6.
	Spaniard	Spaniard	Unknown	AGN, Inq., vol. 24, exp. 3, fs. 109-126v, 143-155.
	Spaniard	Spaniard	Spaniard	AGN, Inq., vol. 22, exp. 3.
0.1	Creole	Creole	Creole	AGN, Inq., vol. 796, exp. 52, fs. 506-514.
0.5	Mulatto	Indian	Black	AGN, Inq., vol. 134, exp. 8.
0.3	Creole	Creole	Mestizo	AGN, Inq., vol. 790, exp. 1, fs. 1-200.
4	Spaniard	Spaniard	Spaniard	AGN, Inq., vol. 136, exp. 10.
0.1	Spaniard	Spaniard	Unknown	AGN, Inq., vol. 91, exp. 5.
8	Mestizo	Indian	Mulatto	AGN, Inq., vol. 1305, exp. 2, fs. 1-86.
	Spaniard	Unknown	Unknown	AGN, Inq., vol. 657, exp. 3, fs. 300-23.
12	Mulatto	Mulatto	Mestizo	AGN, Inq., vol. 595, exp. 20, fs. 456-538.
	Spaniard	Spaniard	Unknown	AGN, Inq., vol. 36, exp. 10, fs. 402ff.
3	Mestizo	Mestizo	Unknown	AGN, Inq., vol. 1062.
0.1	Mulatto	Mestizo	Mestizo	AGN, Inq., vol. 548, exp. 4.
0.2	Slave	Slave	Indian	AGN, Inq., vol. 548, exp. 5.
	Mulatto	Unknown	Indian	AGN, Inq., vol. 310, exp. 3.
6	Mestizo	Indian	Mestizo	AGN, Inq., vol. 594, exp. 9, fs. 534-619.
2	Spaniard	Spaniard	Mestizo	AGN, Inq., vol. 138, exp. 5.
3	Mestizo	Spaniard	Zambo	AGN, Inq., vol. 1246.
6	Mulatto	Mulatto	Mulatto	AGN, Inq., vol. 1180, fs. 14-98
3	Mulatto	Unknown	Mestizo	AGN, Inq., vol. 1089, exp. 1, fs. 1-108.
2	Mestizo	Unknown	Unknown	AGN, Inq., vol. 824, exp. 12, fs. 74-197.
0.3	Mestizo	Indian	Mestizo	AGN, Inq., vol. 605, exp. 2, fs. 189-278.
2	Creole	Mulatto	Mulatto	AGN, Inq., vol. 1139, fs. 187-287.
	Spaniard	Unknown	Unknown	AGN, Inq., vol. 308, fs. 140-140v.
0.1	Mestizo	Indian	Mestizo	AGN, Inq., vol. 26, exp. 2, fs. 12-27.
	Spaniard	Spaniard	Unknown	AGN, Inq., vol. 526, exp. 7, fs. 380-398.
3	Black	Slave	Indian	AGN, Inq., vol. 978, fs. 59-188.
7	Mestizo	Indian	Mestizo	AGN, Inq., vol. 262, exp. 3.
10	Zambo	Zambo	Mulatto	AGN, Inq., vol. 1102, exp. 1, fs. 1-130.
2	Creole	Spaniard	Spaniard	AGN, Inq., vol. 441, exp. 2, fs. 356-411v.

Names	Birth-date	Date of First Marriage	Date of Second Marriage	Sex	Length of 1st Marriage in Years
Monterroso, Diego de	1656		1684	Male	
Mora y Arellano, José de	1720	1750	1777	Male	5
Morales, Domingo, alias Hernández, alias Santos	1677	1703	1705	Male	2
Moxica, Sebastian de, alias Domingo Moxica	1667	1693	1698	Male	2
Muca, Pedro de la			1586	Male	
mungia, Sebastián Domingo de	1587	1624		Male	
Muñoz de Sanabria, Joseph	1686	1705	1720	Male	3
Muñoz Palomir, Pedro		1707	1718	Male	0.1
Muñoz, Isabel	1568	1585		Female	
Muñoz, Ysavel, alias la muñoza	1512	1522	1532	Female	
Ortega, Melchior, alias Melchior de León Ortega	1532	1560	1573	Male	2.5
Ortíz, José Francisco, alias Charco de la piedra	1740	1773	1778	Male	5
Ortiz, Pedro, alias Martín Ortiz	1533	1569	1573	Male	1
Orvel, Favian	1726	1748	1764	Male	2
Otalora Carvajal, Lorenzo de	1626	1653	1659	Male	1
Ovando, Christoval	1735	1752	1780	Male	16
Pabón, Juan Antonio	1680	1701	1711	Male	1.5
Pacheco, Juan Estebán	1721	1734	1758	Male	
Palomino Arias, Nicolás, alias García Espinosa	1672	1713	1720	Male	2
Pan y Agua, Joseph María	1716	1736	1740	Male	0.8
Panizal, Pedro de, alias Pedro Cortés	1548		1576	Male	
Pantaleón, Santiago	1742	1768	1779	Male	5
Pérez de Gardea, Joseph	1731	1750	1751	Male	2
Pérez de Othaeugui, Joan		1562	1581	Male	
Pérez Escandon, Joseph Antonio		1752	1763	Male	9
Pérez, Ana				Female	7
Pinero, Antonio			1608	Male	
Pinto Maldonado, Antonio	1544	1564	1581	Male	11
Pisa, Antonio de	1705	1726	1742	Male	5
Pisano, María Manuela	1747	1764	1781	Female	
Puerto y Arriola, Francisco del	1670	1692	1702	Male	6.5
Quesada, Agustín de	1711		1746	Male	
Quiñones, don Francisco del, alias don Alvaro de Quiñones	1577	1595	1607	Male	5
Quintero de los Sanctos, Joan		1582	1586	Male	0.3
Quintero Pastor, Joan	1539	1569	1583	Male	2
Quintero, Christobal				Male	
Rabelo, Manuel	1551			Male	
Ramírez, Andrés	1712	1735	1738	Male	2
Ramírez, Beatriz	1549	1560	1569	Female	2
Ramírez, Juan Antonio	1716	1733	1737	Male	0.5
Rangel, Francisco		1630	1666	Male	1
Reyes, Joseph Miguel	1730	1750	1757	Male	2
Reyes, Mariana de los	1565		1585	Female	
Reyes, Pascual de los	1712	1730	1743	Male	

Length of 2nd Marriage in Years	Race	Race of First Spouse	Race of Second Spouse	Archival Reference
7	Mestizo	Indian	Mestizo	AGN, Inq., vol. 526, exp. 1, fs. 1-36.
0.8	Creole	Mulatto	Mulatto	AGN, Inq., vol. 1145, exp. 19, fs. 192-282.
1.3	Mulatto	Zambo	Slave	AGN, Inq., vol. 796, exp. 1, fs. 1-101.
7	Mulatto	Mulatto	Mulatto	AGN, Inq., vol. 1258, exp. unnumbered, fs. 1-89.
2	Spaniard	Spaniard	Unknown	AGN, Inq., vol. 138, exp. 1.
	Slave	Slave	Slave	AGN, Inq., vol. 399, exp. 2.
6	Mestizo	Mestizo	Unknown	AGN, Inq., vol. 815, exp. 1, fs. 1-133.
	Spaniard	Spaniard	Unknown	AGN, Inq., vol. 797, fs. 234-354.
3	Mestizo	Mestizo	Unknown	AGN, Inq., vol. 137, exp. 10.
	Spaniard	Spaniard	Spaniard	AGN, Inq., vol. 22, exp. 4.
14	Spaniard	Spaniard	Creole	AGN, Inq., vol. 137, exp. 9.
3	Indian	Indian	Indian	AGN, Inq., vol. 1194, exp. 1, fs. 1-102.
4	Spaniard	Mestizo	Unknown	AGN, Inq., vol. 134, exp. 13.
23	Creole	Creole	Mestizo	AGN, Inq., vol. 1231, exp. 9, fs. 171-287.
	Slave	Indian	Mestizo	AGN, Inq., vol. 610, exp. 11, fs. 233-384.
4	Spaniard	Spaniard	Creole	AGN, Inq., vol. 1199, exp. 29, fs. 214-62.
14	Mestizo	Mestizo	Indian	AGN, Inq., vol. 815, fs. 456-573.
0.3	Zambo	Unknown	Unknown	AGN, Inq., vol. 1088, fs. 211-74.
1	Mulatto	Mulatto	Mestizo	AGN, Inq., vol. 796, exp. 53, fs. 515-523.
2	Creole	Creole	Unknown	AGN, Inq., vol. 816, exp. 35, fs. 315-90.
6	Spaniard	Spaniard	Unknown	AGN, Inq., vol. 136, exp. 4.
3	Creole	Mestizo	Mulatto	AGN, Inq., vol. 1242, exp. 19, fs. 262-316.
0.2	Mestizo	Mestizo	Mulatto	
4	Spaniard	Spaniard	Unknown	AGN, Inq., vol. 137, exp. 3.
5	Zambo	Indian	Indian	AGN, Inq., vol. 1145, exp. 27, fs. 377ff.
1	Spaniard	Spaniard	Spaniard	AGN, Inq., vol. 22, exp. 8.
1.5	Spaniard	Spaniard	Mestizo	AGN, Inq., vol. 317, exp. 1.
3	Spaniard	Spaniard	Mestizo	AGN, Inq., vol. 136, exp. 5.
2	Mulatto	Mestizo	Mulatto	AGN, Inq., vol. 1336, exp.14, fs. 1-70.
3	Zambo	Unknown	Mulatto	AGN, Inq., vol. 1234, exp. 1, fs. 1-37.
5	Spaniard	Spaniard	Creole	AGN, Inq., vol. 548, exp. 3.
1.4	Spaniard	Spaniard	Creole	AGN, Inq., vol. 820, exp. 1, fs. 1-52.
8	Spaniard	Spaniard	Creole	AGN, Inq., vol. 308, fs. 99rff.
3	Spaniard	Spaniard	Mestizo	AGN, Inq., vol. 138, exp. 4.
6	Spaniard	Spaniard	Mulatto	AGN, Inq., vol. 138, exp. 3.
	Black	Spaniard	Unknown	AGN, Inq., vol. 23, exp. 5, fs. 23-29.
	Spaniard	Spaniard	Unknown	AGN, Inq., vol. 135, exp. 2.
5	Mestizo	Indian	Mulatto	AGN, Inq., vol. 964, exp. 4, fs.211-302.
6	Mulatto	Indian	Black	AGN, Inq., vol. 134, exp. 3.
3	Creole	Mulatto	Creole	AGN, Inq., vol. 1341.
0.5	Mestizo	Unknown	Mestizo	AGN, Inq., vol. 606, exp. 4, fs. 381-414.
6	Mestizo	Indian	Mestizo	AGN, Inq., vol. 1013.
	Mulatto	Black	Mestizo	AGN, Inq., vol. 137, exp. 2.
1	Slave	Slave	Indian	AGN, Inq., vol. 918, exp.19, fs. 247-313.

Names	Birth-date	Date of First Marriage	Date of Second Marriage	Sex	Length of 1st Marriage in Years
Riberos, Francisco de	1576	1606	1612	Male	0.4
Rivera, Gerónimo de	1570	1591	1600	Male	
Robles Quiñones, Cosme de	1586	1604	1609	Male	1
Rodríguez, Jhoan	1553	1575	1591	Male	0.3
Rodríguez, Luis, alias Luis Ramírez	1556	1576	1578	Male	0.3
Rodríguez, Manuel de la Trinidad, alias Chauca	1714	1734	1739	Male	7
Rodríguez, Pedro Pablo	1721	1742	1748	Male	4
Romano, Manuel	1559	1577	1577	Male	0.3
Rosas, Hernández de	1575	1599	1618	Male	18
Ruíz, Catalina				Female	
Ruíz, Petronila	1555	1572		Female	0.1
Sánchez de los Santos, Eusebia	1752	1765	1786	Female	3
Sánchez Matheus, Pedro	1545	1558	1582	Male	24
Sánchez Navarro, Alonso, alias Pedro Navarro	1533	1551	1563	Male	12
Sánchez, Martín	1529	1556	1569	Male	6
Sanctabaya, Alonso de	1549	1567		Male	5
Santana Izquierdo, Juan de	1743	1775	1779	Male	6
Sebastián, Nicolás, alias Sebastián López	1651	1671	1672	Male	0.1
Serna, Alonso de la	1511	1530		Male	
Serrano y Mora, don Joseph	1730	1760	1772	Male	0.3
Soriano y Galbes, Joseph Antonio, alias Joseph Antonio Roquete	1733	1752	1763	Male	1
Sotomayor, María de			1537	Female	10
Ulloa, don Juan Antonio	1649	1667	1680	Male	11
Valencuela, Pedro de, alias Pedro de Pineda, alias don Pedro de Valencuela, alias don Pedro	1581	1600	1604	Male	2
Valle, Francisco del	1616	1647	1654	Male	7
Valles, Vincente del	1727	1748	1759	Male	11
Vargas, Gerónimo de	1518	1537	1547	Male	2
Vargas, Luisa de	1545	1556	1569	Female	
Vázquez Borrego, Manuel Antonio	1729	1762	1776	Male	7
Vázquez, Juana	1505	1522	1530	Female	10
Vega, Catalina de	1550	1562	1563	Female	0.1
Velásquez, Francisco	1706		1742	Male	
Villagrán, María de	1552	1566	1582	Female	6
Villar, Anna María de, alias la Xixona, alias buen rostro	1713	1726	1746	Female	5
Villareal, Diego de	1523	1540	1547	Male	1
Zapata, María Ignacia	1765	1777	1786	Female	1.5
Zavala, Joseph Eugenio	1740	1758	1768	Male	5
Zúñiga, Bartolomé de	1663	1677		Male	4

Length of 2nd Marriage in Years	Race First Spouse	Race of First Spouse	Race of Second Spouse	Archival Reference
1	Spaniard	Spaniard	Spaniard	AGN, Inq., vol. 325, exp. 6.
3	Spaniard	Spaniard	Unknown	Huntington Library-12-HM35106-Pt. 2.
0.1	Creole	Mulatto	Unknown	AGN, Inq., vol. 508, exp. 1, fs. 1-76.
10	Spaniard	European	Indian	AGN, Inq., vol. 272, exp. 1, and vol. 262, exp. 6.
	Spaniard	Spaniard	Spaniard	AGN, Inq., vol. 137, exp. 4.
9	Mestizo	Indian	Mulatto	AGN, Inq., vol. 942, fs. 1-100.
20	Mulatto	Mulatto	Mulatto	AGN, Inq., vol. 1166, exp. 7, fs.172ff.
1.5	Spaniard	Indian	Mulatto	AGN, Inq., vol. 108, exp. 5.
2	Spaniard	Unknown	Unknown	AGN, Inq., vol. 333, exp. 29.
	Spaniard	Unknown	Unknown	AGN, Inq., vol. 134, exp. 1.
	Mulatto	Unknown	Mulatto	AGN, Inq., vol. 134, exp.10.
2	Mulatto	Unknown	Mulatto	AGN, Inq., vol. 1266, exp. 8, fs. 246r-311v.
3	Spaniard	Spaniard	Spaniard	AGN, Inq., vol. 137, exp. 1.
18	Spaniard	Spaniard	Spaniard	AGN, Inq., vol. 135, exp. 3.
11	Spaniard	Spaniard	Spaniard	AGN, Inq., vol. 134, exp. 11.
	Spaniard	Spaniard	Unknown	AGN, Inq., vol. 136, exp. 8.
1.3	Mulatto	Mulatto	Mulatto	AGN, Inq., vol. 1279, exp. 13, fs. 1-99.
20	Mulatto	Slave	Unknown	AGN. Inq., vol. 525, exp. 51.
	Spaniard	Spaniard	Unknown	AGN, Inq., vol. 22, exp. 6 and 10.
1	Spaniard	Spaniard	Creole	AGN, Inq., vol. 1128
5	Mestizo	Indian	Mulatto	AGN, Inq., vol. 1062, exp. 2.
1.3	Spaniard	Spaniard	Spaniard	AGN, Inq., vol. 36, exp. 6, fs. 199-311.
1.5	Spaniard	Spaniard	Spaniard	AGN, Inq., vol. 657, exp. 1, fs. 125-75.
0.1	Spaniard	Spaniard	Unknown	AGN, Inq., vol. 466, exp. 14, fs. 329-82.
0	Creole	Creole	Creole	AGN, Inq., vol. 563, exp. 16, fs. 413-633.
0.3	Spaniard	Spaniard	Creole	AGN, Inq., vol. 1066.
0.5	Spaniard	Spaniard	Unknown	AGN, Inq., vol. 134, exp. 5.
	Unknown	Unknown	Unknown	AGN, Inq., vol. 29, exp. 11, fs. 102-412.
7	Spaniard	Creole	Creole	AGN, Inq., vol. 1207, exp. 6, fs. 118-257.
8	Spaniard	Spaniard	Spaniard	AGN, Inq., vol. 22, exp. 16, fs. 235-276.
10	Spaniard	Unknown	Unknown	AGN, Inq., vol. 91, exp. 9.
	Indian	Indian	Unknown	AGN, Inq., vol. 919, exp. 8.
4	Mestizo	Mulatto	Indian	AGN, Inq., vol. 137, exp. 5.
7	Indian	Unknown	Unknown	AGN, Inq., vol. 964, fs. 1-168.
	Spaniard	Black	Unknown	AGN, Inq., vol. 23, exp. 10, fs. 166-226
1	Creole	Mestizo	Mulatto	AGN, Inq., vol. 1275, exp. 16, fs. 1-110.
2	Creole	Creole	Slave	AGN, Inq., vol. 1102, exp. 3, fs. 135-190.
	Spaniard	Creole	Unknown	AGN, Inq., vol. 543, exp. 11, fs. 141-75.

Notes

Introduction

1. John Bossy, "The Mass as a Social Institution," *Past and Present* 100(August 1983):39.

2. "For a good part of the hope of salvation (*salutis*)," in the commentary of the fifteenth-century canonist Gabriel Biel, "is the hope of evading the machinations of one's enemies." Cited in Bossy, "The Mass," p. 39.

3. Pescador, for example, characterizes the mosaic of marriage markets in the barrios of late colonial Mexico City as "pequeños y localizados circuitos independientes que sólo esporádicamente encuentran un intercambio muy marginal y más bien fragmentado." In spacial terms, then, he views Mexico City as a kind of "conjunto de pequeños pueblos . . . marcadas por la división de sus grupos raciales y por sus esferas parroquiales." Juan Javier Pescador, *De bautizados a fieles difuntos: Familia y mentalidades en una parroquia urbana: Santa Catarina de México, 1568–1820* (Mexico City: El Colegio de México, 1992), pp. 239–40.

4. In the Bajío, for example, where the "intersection of commercial expansion and population growth" led to particularly acute insecurities and subsistence crises. John Tutino, *From Insurrection to Revolution in Mexico: Social Bases of Agrarian Violence, 1750–1940* (Princeton: Princeton University Press, 1988), p. 61.

5. 'Unskilled' is a conventional but not very accurate characterization of the manual labor associated with ranching, farming, transport, and some tasks connected with mining. Such work in fact required considerable skills. It was work that was intensely physical, however, done at the behest of and under the supervision of others, and usually with an employer's equipment or on his land. On the other hand, it required no particular training or certification, mainly a strong back, endurance, and perhaps some manual dexterity, although experience surely counted.

6. E. P. Thompson, "Patrician Society, Plebeian Culture," *Journal of Social History* 7(1)(Fall 1973):383.

7. Braudel associates the vagabond type, men or women without masters, to the "undercover modernization" of the "traditional sector" in the seventeenth-century French countryside, which pushed "thousands of peasants . . . on to the roads." The enclosures in England had the same effect. Fernand Braudel, *The Wheels of Commerce: Civilization and Capitalism, 15th–18th Century*, trans. Siân Reynolds (New York: Harper and Row, 1982) 2:510. The Spanish picaresque novel shows us the type as a kind of antihero from the sixteenth century.

8. The Inquisition section of Mexico's national archive (Archivo General de la Nación) has 1,553 volumes in it; in 1982, however, Dr. Miguel Civeira Taboada made the astonishing claim that 3,490 additional volumes, consisting of 20,000 cases, still have not been made available to researchers. These would be located, one might suppose, in the former Ramo de Indiferente, which as of Richard Greenleaf's report of 1974, has 21,950 volumes, 6,000 of which have gone into a provisional archive. Greenleaf has examined thirty-four boxes of this material and gives brief descriptions of their contents. Richard E. Greenleaf, "The Archivo Provisional de la Inquisición (México): A Descriptive Checklist," *The Americas* 31(2)(October 1974):206–11.

The archive of the tribunal of Cuenca, with 8,000 trial records, is comparable in its completeness to Mexico's. Gustav Henningsen, "The Archives and the Historiography of the Spanish Inquisition," in Gustav Henningsen and John Tedeschi, eds., *The Inquisition in Early Modern Europe: Studies on Sources and Methods* (Dekalb, Ill.: Northern Illinois University Press, 1986), pp. 71–72n, 59–60.

9. Criminal trial records are in some ways comparable. William B. Taylor, for example, has pointed out that they record aspects of "behavior as well as the voices of the peasants themselves speaking of the world in which they lived." Taylor listened well and produced a notable book, but he did not present the voices of his peasants directly as *individual* voices; as he states in his introduction, he concerned himself mainly with "patterns of social behavior." William B. Taylor, *Drinking, Homicide, and Rebellion in Colonial Mexican Villages* (Stanford: Stanford University Press, 1979), p. 3. Another work based on criminal records, Michael C. Scardaville's "Crime and the Urban Poor: Mexico City in the Late Colonial Period" (Ph.D diss., University of Florida, 1977), is similar in tone to Taylor's *Drinking*, although he briefly summarizes some of the circumstances relative to given crimes.

Patricia Seed, in her *To Love, Honor, and Obey in Colonial Mexico: Conflicts over Marriage Choice, 1574–1821* (Stanford: Stanford University Press, 1988), also decided that she could include "only a few" actual cases in the body of her text; she summarizes the rest statistically or in notes (p. 13). Her study rests on a massive documentation—virtually all the extant marriage applications and prenuptial disputes. (Marriage applications are also frequently copied out for inquisitorial bigamy investigations as well.) Silvia M. Arrom transcribed and published some material relative to divorce cases separately (*La mujer mexicana ante el divorcio eclesiástico (1800–1857)* (Mexico City: Secretaría de Educación Pública, 1976)

NOTES TO PAGE 5

from her major work, a more synthetic treatment dealing with some of the same subject matter, *The Women of Mexico City, 1790–1857* (Stanford: Stanford University Press, 1985).

Notary records also contain a wealth of details for patient researchers with the stamina to piece them together, as James Lockhart demonstrated years ago in drawing up a remarkably vivid picture of the society of early Peru. Later he used them to show the social and economic links of a provincial center, Toluca, to Mexico City. Yet notary materials seem best used in conjunction with other materials, to explain processes, functions, and linkages between types, more than to focus on individuals as such. James Lockhart, *Spanish Peru, 1532–1560: A Colonial Society* (Madison: University of Wisconsin Press, 1968); "Spaniards among Indians: Toluca in the Later Sixteenth Century" and "The Magistrate of Zacualpan," both in James Lockhart, *Nahuas and Spaniards: Postconquest Central Mexican History and Philology* (Stanford, 1991), pp. 202–61; and "Capital and Province, Spaniard and Indian: The Example of Late Sixteenth-Century Toluca," in *Provinces of Early Mexico: Variants of Spanish American Regional Evolution*, Ida Altman and James Lockhart, eds. (Los Angeles: UCLA Latin American Center Publications, 1976), pp. 99–123.

Nevertheless Lockhart proved the value of fragmentary, unsynthesized materials and so did Richard Cobb, using a more homogenous source. In Paris Cobb found a box of *procès-verbaux de mort violente;* the records, dating from 1795–1801, contain "the particulars of 404 persons . . . who met violent deaths through suicide, accidents, murder, and natural causes" (p. 3), collected by the *juges de paix* of the old Châtelet quarter. From bits and pieces of testimony, he evokes a surprisingly immediate picture of the down-and-out of revolutionary Paris. Richard Cobb, *Death in Paris, 1795–1801* (Oxford: Oxford University Press 1978).

10. Cited in Edward Muir and Guido Ruggiero, eds., *Microhistory and the Lost Peoples of Europe*, trans. Eren Branch (Baltimore and London: Johns Hopkins University Press, 1991), p. xii. See Eric Van Young's exploration of some implications of postmodernism for the historian, "The Cuautla Lazarus: Double Subjectives in Reading Texts on Popular Collective Action," *Colonial Latin American Review* 2(1–2)(1993):4: "There must always be a certain amount of epistemological hand-wringing," he says, in trying to sort out "the puzzle of the trialogue among intended meaning, preconscious/unconscious meaning, and [the] imputed meaning" of our sources. By now it is clear, as Howard Kaminsky has pointed out, that "grand, authoritative, unquestioned abstractions" cannot be overlaid on information and representations we find in the sources. Howard Kaminsky, "From *Mentalité* to Mentality: The Implications of a Novelty," in Mark D. Szuchman, ed., *The Middle Period in Latin America: Values and Attitudes in the 17th–19th Centuries* (Boulder and London: Lynne Rienner Publishers 1989), p. 28. In my own attempt to come to terms with a postmodernist critique of narratives and whether they represent what happened or simply themselves, I find Tzvetan Todorov's stress on a diologic relation with sources useful. Todorov, *The Conquest*

of America, trans. Richard Howard (New York: Harper and Row, 1987), p. 250. Richard Boyer, "The Inquisitor, the Witness, and the Historian: The Document as Discourse," unpublished paper, meeting of Canadian Association of Hispanists, Carleton University, Ottawa, Ontario, May 31, 1993.

11. Inquisition records have become associated with the study of individuals and mentalities. Emmanuel Le Roy Ladurie's *Montaillou*, with its details of the daily life and the web of interrelationships of late-thirteenth-century Occitan villagers in southern France, is a well-known example. Emmanuel Le Roy Ladurie, *Montaillou: The Promised Land of Error*, trans. Barbara Bray (New York: George Braziller, 1978). However, the work also has been criticized, most notably by Leonard E. Boyle, O.P., who pointed out inaccuracies in Le Roy Ladurie's transcription of testimony from Bishop Fournier's register. See his "Montaillou Revisited: *Mentalité* and Methodology," in *Pathways to Medieval Peasants*, ed. J. A. Raftis, Papers in Medieval Studies (Toronto: Pontifical Institute of Mediaeval Studies, 1981) 2:119–40. Another critic, Renato Rosaldo, charges that Le Roy Ladurie ignores the 'politics' of how his source was created. Le Roy Ladurie's admission that the information found in the inquisitorial registers was extracted in an "unequal dialogue" becomes a mere formality, not reflected in the way he uses the register in the rest of the book. Instead he "closes this opening to the interplay of power and knowledge by stressing . . . the scrupulous will to truth that drove [Bishop] Fournier." Renato Rosaldo, "From the Door of His Tent: The Fieldworker and the Inquisitor," in *Writing Culture: The Poetics and Politics of Ethnography*, James Clifford and George E. Marcus, eds., (Berkeley and Los Angeles: University of California Press, 1986), p. 80.

Carlo Ginzburg has given us an equally celebrated work drawn from Inquisition records. His study of a single individual of sixteenth-century Friuli, Domenico Scandella, who was burned at the stake for his heretical cosmology, gives us a feel for the complex interplay between popular and high culture (or at least that drawn from books). Carlo Ginzburg, *The Cheese and the Worms: The Cosmos of a Sixteenth-Century Miller*, trans. John Tedeschi and Anne Tedeschi (Baltimore: Johns Hopkins University Press, 1980).

12. Le Roy Ladurie, *Montaillou*; Ginzburg, *The Cheese and the Worms*.

13. I am thinking here of the "cumulative effects in the matter of marriage choice" found by Patricia Seed (*To Love, Honor, and Obey*, p. 6) because of "incremental and irregular[ly] pace[d] . . . cultural and institutional change" through the period. At least for the transition from "honor as . . . moral worth" to "honor as a standard of class and property" (p. 240), the argument seems to depend on evidence drawn from the upper orders, which generated most of the relatively few parental oppositions to marriages desired by their children (less than 1 percent in the mining zone of Parral between 1770 and 1814, according to McCaa, and surely not much higher elsewhere). Robert McCaa, "Gustos de los padres, Inclinaciones de los novios y reglas de una feria nupcial colonial: Parral, 1770–1814," *Historia Mexicana*, 40(4)(1991):392. That does not invalidate Seed's point, but it does invite

us to examine how and with what variations the new ethos spread to the population in general. See also Patricia Seed, "Marriage Promises and the Value of a Woman's Testimony in Colonial Mexico," *Signs* 13(2)(Winter 1988):253–76. One continues to find, of course, continuities (or apparent continuities) in matters touching on marriage, family, and sexuality in Mexican society that reach back to patterns of the colonial era. See "Foro de Ideas," *Excelsior*, 7 de Mayo de 1993, sec. I:1–4). As for bigamy, from an analysis of the 1970 census, Benavente concludes that one in six men in contemporary Mexico is a bigamist. Olivia Benavente, "La biginia/bigamia en México," *Fem: Publicación feminista trimestral* 2(7)(abril–junio 1978): 64–65.

14. As opposed to indirectly, through *principales*, a process more or less complete in Tlaxcala by the end of the sixteenth century and the result, mainly, of the increasing numbers of Spaniards in relation to Indians. Charles Gibson, *Tlaxcala in the Sixteenth Century* (Stanford: Stanford University Press, 1967 [1952], pp. 192–94. For the population ratios in Mexico City, Charles Gibson notes that at midsixteenth century, Indians outnumbered Spaniards by ten to one. This changed by the end of the eighteenth century to three to one in favor of Hispanics, if the "intermediate classes" are grouped with Spaniards. Charles Gibson, *The Aztecs under Spanish Rule: A History of the Indians of the Valley of Mexico, 1519–1810* (Stanford: Stanford University Press, 1964), p. 380. Pescador notes, from detailed parish censuses taken in Santa Catarina in Mexico City between 1778 and 1788, that 'border' zones, where Indians lived in the Spanish-casta zone and vice versa, were noted by the enumerator. Pescador, *De bautizados*, p. 202.

15. Peter Laslett, *The World We Have Lost* (London: Methuen and Company, 1965 [1970]), p. 53.

16. Pierre Chaunu, "Inquisition et vie quotidienne dans l'Amérique Espagnole au XVIIe siècle," *Annales E.S.C.* 11(2)(1956):230. More recently Jean-Pierre Dedieu has made the same point, stressing the value of Inquisition documentation for "historical anthropology." Jean-Pierre Dedieu, "The Archives of the Holy Office of Toledo as a Source for Historical Anthropology," trans. E. W. Monter, in Henningsen and Tedeschi, eds., *The Inquisition*, pp. 158–89.

17. Richard E. Greenleaf, *The Mexican Inquisition* (Albuquerque: University of New Mexico Press, 1969), pp. 1–2. In all of his work, Greenleaf's careful abstracts of cases preserve much of this ambiance of daily life that he speaks about. See also his *Inquisición y sociedad en el México colonial* (Madrid: J. Porrua Turanzas, 1985), a collection of his essays. "The Great Visitas of the Mexican Holy Office 1645–1669," *The Americas* 44(4)(April, 1988):399–420, anticipates his forthcoming volume, *The Mexican Inquisition in the Seventeenth Century*. In "The Mexican Inquisition and the Indians: Sources for the Ethno-Historian," *The Americas* 34(January 1978):315–37 and "The Inquisition Brotherhood: Cofradía de San Pedro Mártir of Colonial Mexico," *The Americas* 40(2)(October 1983):171–207, he demonstrates the value of Inquisition records for writing social history.

Other scholarship has focused on the trials of crypto-Jews in the late sixteenth and midseventeenth centuries. For example Seymour B. Liebman: *The Jews in New Spain: Faith, Flame, and the Inquisition* (Coral Gables: University of Miami Press, 1970); "The Great Conspiracy in New Spain," *The Americas* 30(1973):13–81; and his translation of the Jesuit Mathias de Bocanegra's account of the auto de fe of 1649, *Jews and the Inquisition of Mexico 1649* (Lawrence, Kansas: Coronado Press 1974); José Toribio Medina, *Historia del Tribunal del Santo Oficio de la Inquisición en México*, 2d ed., ampliada por Julio Jiménez Rueda (Mexico City: Ediciones Fuente Cultura, 1954); Genaro García, ed., *Autos de fé de la Inquisición de México con extractos de sus causas 1646–1648* (Mexico City: La viuda de C. Bouret, 1910). Stanley M. Hordes is using the files collected on crypto-Jews to flesh out their place in the economic and social life of New Spain. Stanley M. Hordes, "The Inquisition as Economic and Political Agent: The Campaign of the Mexican Holy Office against the Crypto-Jews in the Mid-Seventeenth Century," *The Americas* 39(1982):23–38 and "The Crypto-Jewish Community of New Spain, 1620–1649: A Collective Biography" (Ph.D diss., Tulane University, 1980).

Since 1979 the members of the "Seminar on the History of *Mentalité* and Religion in Colonial Mexico," based at the Instituto Nacional de Antropología e Historia (INAH, in Mexico City) have been working with Mexican Inquisition archives within the framework of the multidisciplinary tradition of European *mentalité* historiography. Sergio Ortega, its former director, has published statements describing their assumptions and approach, but the published work of those participating in the seminar, especially that of Serge Gruzinski and Solange Alberro, goes beyond any brief methodological statement. See citations to their work below and in the bibliography. Sergio Ortega Noriega, "Introducción a la Historia de las Mentalidades: Aspectos metodológicos," *Estudios de Historia Novohispana* 8(Mexico City: UNAM, 1985):127–38 and "Seminario de historia de las mentalidades y religión en México colonial," in *Familia y Sexualidad en Nueva España* (Mexico City, Fondo de Cultura Económica, 1982, pp. 100–18), a collection of papers given at the seminar's first symposium. Richard Boyer, "Escribiendo la historia de la religión y mentalidades en Nueva España" (*Ibid.*, pp. 119–137) comments on the seminar's project. Other publications of the seminar include *Introducción a la historia de las mentalidades*, Cuadernos de trabajo, no. 24 (Mexico City: INAH, 1979); *Seis ensayos sobre el discurso colonial relativo a la comunidad doméstica*, Cuadernos de trabajo, no. 35 (Mexico City, INAH, 1980); *La memoria y el olvido: Segundo simposio de historia de las mentalidades* (Mexico City: INAH–SEP Cultura, 1985); Sergio Ortega, ed., *De la santidad a la perversión o de porqué se cumplía la ley de Dios en la sociedad novohispana* (Mexico City: Grijalbo, 1986); and *El placer de pecar y el afán de normar: Ideologías y comportamientos familiares y sexuales en el México colonial* (Mexico City: Editorial Joaquín Mortiz, 1987). Members of the seminar, in addition to their chapters in the edited works cited above, also have made more complete statements of their research in unpublished theses. Dolores Enciso Rojas, "El delito de bigamia y el Tribunal del Santo Oficio de la Inquisición en Nueva España, siglo

XVIII," thesis for the title of Licenciado en Historia, Facultad de Filosofía y Letras, Universidad Nacional Autónoma de México, 1983; María Elena Cortés Jácome, "El grupo familiar de los negros y mulatos: Discurso y comportamientos según los archivos inquisitoriales, siglos XVI–XVIII," thesis for the title of Licenciado en Historia, Facultad de Filosofía y Letras, Universidad Nacional Autónoma de México, 1984; Jorge R. González, "El delito de solicitación en el obispado de Puebla durante el siglo XVIII," thesis, Escuela Nacional de Antropología e Historia, Mexico City, 1982.

18. James Lockhart, review of *Reliving the Past: The Worlds of Social History*, ed. Olivier Zunz, *Hispanic American Historical Review* (hereafter HAHR) 67(3)(August 1987):500. Lockhart is referring to work in European history, but the point applies to Latin American history as well.

19. Enciso Rojas, "El delito de bigamia," pp. 80–81. Her figures for the sixteenth and seventeenth centuries are taken from Solange Alberro, *La Actividad del Santo Oficio de la Inquisición en Nueva España 1571–1700* (Mexico City: INAH 1981), pp. 233–34; the eighteenth century tabulations (p. 104) are her own.

20. For a discussion of the problem of index entries not always representing actual cases (or crimes), see Alberro, *La Actividad*, pp. 15–17.

21. The average length of second marriages in my sample is slightly over four years (4.06) for women (n = 25) and slightly under it (3.96) for men (n = 143). I compile the 'end' of the married life of a couple by using the date of inquisitorial or secular intervention or by using the approximate date when one spouse abandoned the other.

22. Enciso Rojas, "El delito de bigamia," p. 96.

23. Once again there is a slight difference in what we are comparing. The racial designation taken from the index might not represent what the accused or others would have said. For a definition of *calidad*, I follow Robert McCaa, "Calidad, Class, and Marriage in Colonial Mexico: The Case of Parral, 1788–90," HAHR 64:3(August 1984):77.

24. Alberro, *La Actividad*, p. 257.

25. Enciso Rojas, "El delito de bigamia," pp. 112–13.

26. I borrow the term "pointillism" from Le Roy Ladurie's, *Montaillou*, p. 10; the comment is omitted from the English edition. In briefer format, Solange Alberro also produced arresting sketches of a similar kind from Mexican Inquisition files. See Solange Alberro, "Juan de Morga and Gertrudis de Escobar: Rebellious Slaves," and "Beatriz de Padilla: Mistress and Mother," in David G. Sweet and Gary B. Nash, eds., *Struggle and Survival in Colonial America* (Berkeley and Los Angeles: University of California Press, 1981), pp. 165–88, 247–56. Roland Barthes says that the "superfluous detail" of novelistic technique "rounds out" the world, but in his view only as a rhetorical device to give historical narratives authority. Michal Glowinski, "Document as Novel," *New Literary History* 18(2)(Winter 1987): 394–95; Raphael Samuel, "Reading the Signs," *History Workshop* 32(Autumn 1991):93.

27. After Todorov (see n10) I have tried to maintain a dialogic, rather than authoritative, stance, to search as best I can for their intent and meaning and to have my say as well.

28. Le Roy Ladurie (*Montaillou*), Jean-Pierre Dedieu, and Jean Duvernoy have all transposed Inquisition files from reported to direct speech in this way. Duvernoy, for example, says that he made "a literal translation to the degree that it is possible," omitting "repetition of words in the same sentence" and using "the style of direct speech," in order to avoid "an avalanche of subordinate clauses." Jean Duvernoy, *Inquisition à Pamiers: Interrogatoires de Jacques Fournier, 1318–1325 choisis, traduits du texte latin et présentés par* . . . ([Toulouse]: Editions Edouard Privat, 1966), p. 7. Examples of Dedieu's transpositions can be seen in his "The Archives of the Holy Office," pp. 158–89. Dedieu has now changed his position slightly: "I should not do it now [i.e.] . . . use the first . . . person to transcribe declarations of the defendant when he is talking about himself in a strictly scientific and specialized publication, or if my point were to study the value of the inquisitorial sources. I should otherwise accept it, for immediateness sake" (personal communication, January 23, 1989). In Dedieu's major work, *L'Administration de la Foi: L'Inquisition de Tolède (XVIe–XVIIIe Siècle)* (Madrid: Casa de Velázquez, 1989), he quotes testimony in the third person. Nevertheless he clearly signals the view that depositions are the 'voice' of the witness (rather than the notary). Here are some examples of his lead-ins to quoted testimony: "Une femme de son village raconte:" (p. 42); "Comme le disait ce meunier:" (p. 45); "Laissons parler l'intéressée:" (p. 103); "Ecoutons le bachelier Juan de Salinas" (p. 311); "Laissons parler les témoins:" (p. 340). For the same style, see as well Jean-Pierre Dedieu, "Le Modèle Sexuel: La Défense du Mariage Chrétien," in Bartolomé Bennassar, ed., *L'Inquisition Espagnole XVe–XIXe Siécle* (Paris: Hachette, 1979), pp. 313–38. Richard L. Kagan, in a work based on an inquisitorial trial record and a register of a Spanish woman's dreams, says "occasionally I have transposed material reported in third person . . . into Lucrecia's voice . . ." Richard L. Kagan, *Lucrecia's Dreams: Politics and Prophecy in Sixteenth-Century Spain* (Berkeley, Los Angeles, Oxford: University of California Press, 1990), pp. xiii and 59–62. On the high quality of Inquisition transcripts, see Eric Van Young, "The Cuautla Lazarus," p. 11, and his "Millennium on the Northern Marches: The Mad Messiah of Durango and Popular Rebellion in Mexico, 1800–1850," *Comparative Studies in Society and History* 28(1986):390n.

Le Roy Ladurie's and Duvernoy's transpositions of Bishop Fournier's register are noteworthy, given the problematic nature of it as repository of direct speech. Testimony given by witnesses in their vernacular Occitan was 'recorded' by notaries in Latin, read back for confirmation in 'instant translation,' and then later translated once again by Le Roy Ladurie and Duvernoy (independently) into French. Leonard Boyle discusses these and other methodological problems of *Montaillou* (Leonard Boyle, "Montaillou Revisited," pp. 119–40). Natalie Zeman Davis says that rendering Occitan into Latin constitutes "two modes of discourse," but generally approves of Le Roy Ladurie's use of his source. N. Z. Davis, "Les conteurs de Montaillou," *Annales: ESC* 34(1)(1979):69. In the Mexican tribunal, notaries recorded spoken testimony in Spanish, the language in which it was given. In a few cases (noted as we go) a translator rendered spoken Nahuatl into Spanish and then the notary recorded it. Lockhart warns that such translations represent "mutilation through paraphrase and [the] use of Spanish narrative convention." Lockhart, *Nahuas and Spaniards*, p. 75; see also p. 106. Duvernoy points out that by the fourteenth century, "le progrès juridique est néanmoins un fait acquis, et, dans l'ensemble, *les réductions des notaires sont plus longues et plus circonstanciées qu'auparavant. Le Registre de Geoffroy* (1308–1309) contient déjà des narrations savoureuses" (Duvernoy, *Inquisition, p.* 10; emphasis added). This seems to suggest a shift from the midthirteenth century when, according to Walter L. Wakefield, scribes still recorded testimony "in standardized phrases which incorporated the essential points," rather than verbatim. These depositions were then copied into registers, rearranged as necessary to bring together those which had some affinity . . ." Walter L. Wakefield, *Heresy, Crusade and Inquisition in Southern France, 1100–1250* (Berkeley and Los Angeles: University of California Press, 1974), p. 175.

In *Fiction in the Archives: Pardon Tales and Their Tellers in Sixteenth-Century France* (Stanford: Stanford University Press, 1987), an analysis of "letters of remission" as 'fictional' narratives (fictional in the sense of crafted for a given purpose and audience and reflective of cultural common ground) addressed to the king in order to secure a pardon, Natalie Zemon Davis also struggles with the degree to which the letters record individual voices or notarial formulae. Although, they were "collaborative efforts," she also concludes that "they gave much greater scope to the person to whom the notary was listening" than does, for example, testimony given in a criminal proceeding which was "directed at every moment by the judge" (pp. 4–6). The notary's rendering of stories into the third person was to properly present "the actor . . . [as] supplicant," so as "not [to] recount . . . adventures as though . . . a hero in a folktale showing his strength" (p. 57). As for the internal evidence of the stories themselves, colloquial language, settings, and motivations vary with gender, class, and setting. Moreover in the finished letters (the product of a rough transcription, a reading back for additions or corrections, and the writing of a final version), Davis's reading of some five thousand of them leads her to judge that they "have a variety about them that seems impossible to attribute merely to the talents of a limited number of notarial hands" (p. 23).

Giulia Calvi, in her *Histories of a Plague Year: The Social and Imaginary in Baroque Florence*, trans. Dario Biocca and Bryant T. Ragan Jr. (Berkeley and Los Angeles: University of California Press, 1989), has used a differently structured source, criminal trial records of the Florentine Public Health Magistracy, for a comparable purpose. She sees these unfolding as a kind of "oral theatricality" in "the encounter between defendant and judge." It was concerned with "details, differences, and circumstances, [and thus] penetrated beyond generalized masks [of characters found in literary texts] and reconstructed, albeit fragmentarily, the actors' profiles," which reveal "a society of people who have power despite all their hardship" (pp. 56–58).

In cases of marriage oppositions found in the archdiocesan records of New Mexico (and in the Matrimoniales section of the AGN), notaries recorded some testimony as direct speech. Ramón A. Gutiérrez has used this material to good advantage in his "From Honor to Love: Transformations of the Meaning of Sexuality in Colonial New Mexico," in Raymond T. Smith, ed., *Kinship Ideology and Practice in Latin America* (Chapel Hill and London: University of North Carolina Press 1984), pp. 237–63, and in his "Honor Ideology, Marriage Negotiation, and Class-Gender Domination in New Mexico, 1690–1848," *Latin American Perspectives* 12(Winter 1985):81–104. To judge by the passages Gutiérrez quotes, transcripts of direct speech (except for verb tense) are no different from those of reported speech found in Inquisition records. The similarity suggests to me that notaries wrote down what they heard, as they were supposed to.

In his recent translation of the journal of Columbus, Robert H. Fuson, without giving the kind of detailed justification that we might like, notes simply that "the first person is restored where Las Casas and Fernando [Colón] switch to third person . . ." Robert H. Fuson, trans., *The Log of Christopher Columbus* (Camden, Me.: International Marine Publishing Company, 1987), p. 11.

29. Archivo General de la Nación, Mexico [hereafter AGN] Inquisición, tomo 642, exp. 1, f. 75v. This is an unusually short response to a question that sometimes elicits narratives that ramble on for four or five pages.

30. In some instances, in fact, the title page of the file includes a kind of table of contents.

31. Some readers might want to use the index to follow more sequentially the pieces of the stories of individuals distributed through the chapters. These stories are worth preserving, for few have otherwise survived in which plebeian protagonists take center stage. A distinction can be made between my attempt to piece together over two hundred cases and the inevitably more coherent, focused register used by Le Roy Ladurie. Even more 'coherent' can be reconstructions of single cases, such as that of Ginzburg's Friulian miller Domenico Scandella, in *The Cheese and the Worms*. Richard Boyer, "Juan Vázquez, Muleteer of Seventeenth-Century Mexico," *The Americas* 37(1981):421–43, also sketches the life of a single individual, a less-articulate but possibly more representative one.

CHAPTER ONE

1. AGN, Inq., t. 1038, fs. 1–78. This paragraph is drawn from various sections of the file: the first *audiencia de oficio* of the inquisitors with Andrés, the description made of him when he was put in the inquisitorial jail, and the certified copy of the record of this marriage in the parish register of Escuintla.

2. Apparently San Gerónimo was still owned by the Dominican convent of Guatemala City, as it was in Thomas Gage's day. Gage places it in the valley of San Nicolás (so-named "from an estancia called San Nicolás belonging to the Dominicans' cloister of Cobán") near the Quiché Maya settlement of Rabinal, a town "of at least eight hundred families, which hath all that the heart can wish for pleasure and life of man." Gage says that San Gerónimo produced more sugar (sent by mule back to Guatemala) and had more slaves ("under the command of two friars") than the three Dominican sugar farms in the valley of Amatitlán. It was also known for the horses bred there, "incomparably the best of all the country of Guatemala for mettle and gallantry." J. Eric S. Thompson, ed., *Thomas Gage's Travels in the New World* (Norman: University of Oklahoma Press, 1958), pp. 205, 210–11. Little is known of sugar production in Guatemala, but MacLeod notes that by the mideighteenth century, Dominicans and Jesuits had "some half dozen large enterprises." Murdo J. MacLeod, "Ethnic Relations and Indian Society in the Province of Guatemala, ca. 1620–ca. 1800," in M. MacLeod and R. Wasserstrom, eds., *Spaniards and Indians*, p. 197.

3. Andrés and Manuela had had eight children, three of whom had died by the time of his hearing before the inquisitors in 1768.

4. Andrés's motive for leaving the sugar hacienda comes from his autobiographical statement, given to the inquisitors on December 13, 1768. The south coast refers to the coastal zone of Soconusco, today Chiapas state.

5. Andrés had been confirmed and had lived a sacramental life: taking Holy Communion "at the times the holy mother church orders," he said, and regularly hearing the mass. As well he "responded well to all the rest of [the questions about] Christian doctrine."

6. Probably Andrés's first choice would have been to seduce Paula rather than marry her but, as we shall see in chapter 3, marriage was often a precondition for sexual relations. In his interview with the Guatemalan commissioner, five weeks after he was arrested (December 17, 1762), Andrés said that he married the second time because of a "moral lapse" (*fragilidad*).

7. Encisco Rojas ("El delito de bigamia," p. 133) makes this point more generally for bigamists.

8. Note, then, that cohabitation began about a week before the marriage.

9. Andrés would have needed help handling the livestock. He probably promised Ignacio a share of the proceeds rather than a wage.

10. Ignacio was a cousin of Paula's mother.

11. Today Salamá, ten miles or so east of Rabinal.

12. Jaime Contreras and Jean Pierre Dedieu, "Geografía de la Inquisición española: La formación de los distritos, 1470–1820," *Hispania* 40(1980): 40–42.

13. Edward Peters, *Inquisition* (Berkeley and Los Angeles: University of California Press, 1989), p. 84.

14. Jaime Contreras, "Aldermen and Judaizers: Cryptojudaism, Counter-

Reformation, and Local Power," in Cruz and Perry, eds., *Culture and Control*, pp. 93–123.

15. Contreras and Dedieu, "Geografía de la Inquisición," pp. 40–42.

16. Jaime Contreras and Gustav Henningsen, "Forty-Four Thousand Cases of the Spanish Inquisition (1540–1700): Analysis of a Historical Data Bank," in Henningsen and Tedeschi, eds., *The Inquisition*, pp. 113–14. Spanish zeal to catechize the population began well before the Council of Trent, and Spain was at least a hundred years ahead of France in getting firm results among the populace in general. Jean-Pierre Dedieu, "'Christianization' in New Castile: Catechism, Communion, Mass, and Confirmation in the Toledo Archbishopric, 1540–1650," in Cruz and Perry, eds., *Culture and Control*, pp. 2–6, 21.

17. And with considerable energy, especially from the mid-1550s, when Alonso de Montúfar arrived. Richard E. Greenleaf, *Zumárraga and the Mexican Inquisition 1536–1543* (Washington, D.C.: Academy of American Franciscan History, 1962), pp. 3–25; Greenleaf, *The Mexican Inquisition*, pp. 7–8.

18. Contreras and Henningsen, "Forty-Four Thousand Cases," p. 115. The compilation made by Contreras and Henningsen, about half-completed now, charts for the first time the overall shape of Inquisition concerns by cataloguing the *relaciones de causas*, summary reports sent to the Supreme Council of the Inquisition (*Suprema*) by district tribunals. Henningsen's earlier report, "El Banco de datos: Las relaciones de causas de la Inquisición española (1550–1700)," *Boletín de la Real Academia de la Historia* 174(1977):547–70, is now incorporated in the work cited above.

19. Charles V's cedula of 1538 placed Indians under the jurisdiction of the viceroy rather than the Inquisition. Greenleaf says that this order was not "effectuated" and their exclusion came only in December 30, 1571, as decreed by Philip II. Greenleaf, *Zumárraga*, p. 74 and 68–74, *passim*. Lesley Byrd Simpson, in *Many Mexicos*, 4th rev. ed. (Berkeley and Los Angeles: University of California Press, 1966), pp. 187, 194, implies that the early decree was followed.

20. Greenleaf, *Zumárraga*, pp. 17–18, 68, 74; Solange Alberro, *Inquisición y Sociedad en México, 1571–1700* (Mexico City: Fondo de Cultura Económica, 1988), pp. 21–22; Robert Ricard, *The Spiritual Conquest of Mexico*, trans. Lesley Byrd Simpson (Berkeley, Los Angeles, London: University of California Press, 1966), pp. 272–73; Serge Gruzinski, *Man-Gods in the Mexican Highlands*, trans. Eileen Corrigan (Stanford: Stanford University Press, 1989), p. 197n.

21. From a chart prepared by Yolanda Mariel de Ibáñez of inquisitorial activity in the sixteenth century and reproduced as Appendix 31 in M. Ballesteros Gaibrois, "Los fondos inquisitoriales americanísticos," in *Historia de la Inquisición* 1:132. Don Pedro Moya de Contreras arrived in Mexico City on September 12, 1571, and the public ceremony in which secular officials and the people of Mexico swore to uphold the faith and to denounce heretics took place on November 4, 1571. Thus the twelve Judaizers that Ibáñez lists for 1571 must have been dealt with before

Moya took over. From 1572 to 1594, only twenty-two Judaizers came before the Mexican tribunal, although another forty-nine appear in the five years 1595–99. Medina mentions twenty-seven bigamists and five cases of fornication in Mexico's first auto de fe, held on February 28, 1574; in the second auto de fe (March 6, 1575), twenty-five of the thirty-one prisoners were charged with bigamy, polygamy, or instances of giving false testimony to marry a second time illegally. Medina, *Historia del Tribunal,* pp. 38–40, 61, 72–73.

22. Bennassar, ed., *L'Inquisition espagnole* pp. 326–36, and cited in Dedieu, "The Archives," p. 59; Henningsen, "The Archives," p. 67. In Mexico concubinage was handled mostly by church courts. In Europe, however, it seemed to have been a strong concern of the Holy Office. See also Alberro, *La Actividad,* p. 68.

23. This would be, as Alberro estimates, about 20 percent of the total population, because Indians were excluded from prosecution and because their "sociocultural context" had the practical effect of excluding them from playing the role of denouncers of others. Alberro, *Inquisición y sociedad,* p. 26.

24. The "Instrucciones del Ilustrísimo Señor don Diego de Spinoso, Inquisidor general, para la plantación de esta Inquisición," dated Madrid, August 18, 1570, are printed in Archivo General de la Nación, México, *Catálogo del Ramo Inquisición (1),* revisado y corregido por Guillermina Ramírez Montes, Serie: Guías y Catálogos 42 (Mexico City: Publicaciones del Archivo General de la Nación, 1979), pp. 12–21; and in Alberro, *Inquisición y sociedad,* pp. 199–202. A great deal of attention is paid to record keeping in these directives.

25. Alberro, *La Actividad,* p. 18. This has not yet been worked out in detail, because modern scholarship has shown little interest in institutional procedures and their juridical context as such. John Tedeschi makes this point for the Roman Inquisition but, as Jean-Pierre Dedieu points out, it also holds for the Holy Office in general. John Tedeschi, "Preliminary Observations on Writing a History of the Roman Inquisition," in F. Forrester Church and Timothy George, eds., *Continuity and Discontinuity in Church History* (Leiden: E. J. Brill, 1979), p. 234; Jean-Pierre Dedieu, "L'Inquisition et le Droit: Analyse Formelle de la Procédure Inquisitoriale en Cause de Foi," *Mélanges de la Casa de Velázquez* 23(1987):227. In addition to the work in progress by Tedeschi and the helpful sketch by Dedieu, one should also mention the previously cited work by Edward Peters (*Inquisition*). Henry Charles Lea, *A History of the Inquisition of Spain,* 4 vols. (New York: AMS Press, 1966 [1906–7]), still has the most detailed summary of trial procedures (2:457–586 and 3:1–230). For an authoritative but brief summary, see Gustav Henningsen, *The Witches' Advocate: Basque Witchcraft and the Spanish Inquisition (1609–1614)* (Reno: University of Nevada Press, 1980), pp. 37–46. A useful lexicon of terminology used by the Holy Office, mostly drawn from Juan Antonio Llorente, can be found in M. Jiménez Monteserin, "Léxico inquisitorial," in *Historia de la Inquisición* 1:184–217.

26. María Paz Alonso Romero, *El Proceso Penal en Castilla (siglos XIII–XVIII)* (Salamanca: Ediciones de la Universidad de Salamanca, 1982); Dedieu, "Analyse Formelle," p. 250.

27. Alonso Romero, *Proceso Penal*, p. 208. The basis for such a view stems from Saint Augustine's definition that "sin is all action, word, or deed opposed to the eternal law," which Delumeau points to as fixing on Christian theology "a new dimension." Jean Delumeau, *Sin and Fear: The Emergence of a Western Guilt Culture, 13th–18th Centuries*, trans. Eric Nicholson (New York: Saint Martin's Press 1990), pp. 191–92.

28. L. Suárez Fernández, "Los antecedentes medievales de la Institución," in *Historia de la Inquisición* 1:266–67; J. Contreras, "Las adecuaciones estructurales en la Península," Ibid., pp. 754–59.

29. Contreras quotes the warnings from a "Juramento que ha de leer el pueblo antes de que se lea el Edicto de fe" [undated but most likely from the second half of the sixteenth century], in "Las adecuaciones," p. 755. More useful for our purposes, perhaps, is the edict of faith published in Mexico in November 1571, to coincide with the installation of the Mexican tribunal. Although it calls for denunciations and specifies kinds of behavior to denounce, noncompliance is threatened with an unadorned but deadly "so pena de excomunicación." Lea, *A History of the Inquisition* 2:589; this work also contains a copy of this edict, pp. 587–90. To date 281 edicts of faith promulgated in Mexico between 1576 and 1819 have been located in the Mexican archives. Of these, 20 came from Spain or Rome and the rest originated in Mexico. Alberro, *Inquisición y sociedad*, pp. 75n, 76n.

30. Cited in Julio Jiménez Rueda, *Don Pedro Moya de Contreras: Primer Inquisidor de México* (Mexico City: Ediciones Xochitl, 1944), p. 49; and in Medina, *Historia del Tribunal*, pp. 47, 52. The first edict, authored by Moya, was published on November 4, 1571. Alberro, *Inquisición y sociedad*, p. 128.

31. Defined by the Council of Trent as contrition, confession, and satisfaction. J. Donovan, trans., *The Catechism of the Council of Trent* (Dublin: Richard Coyne; London: Keating and Browne, 1829), pp. 262–72.

32. Medina, *Historia del Tribunal*, p. 47.

33. Alberro, *Inquisición y sociedad*, pp. 75–77.

34. Cited in Ruth Behar, "Sex and Sin, Witchcraft and the Devil in Late-Colonial Mexico," *American Ethnologist* 14(1)(February 1987):50.

35. Medina, *Historia del Tribunal*, pp. 65–66. The high fascination focused on the English corsairs of John Hawkins, who were captured off San Juan de Ulúa in 1568. The first auto served, as this self-congratulatory report might suggest, to reinforce the need for the tribunal in Mexico, but probably nobody doubted this anyway, and before it even took place Moya had been promoted to the position of archbishop of Mexico, as of June 17, 1573. A. Huerga, "El Tribunal de México en la época de Felipe II," in *Historia de la Inquisición:* 1:950n.

36. Torquemada, of course, drew upon procedures developed by the medieval Inquisition, most notably the handbook of Nicolas Eymericus (*Directorium inquis-*

itorum), which, in turn, was an adaptation of the inquisitorial methods of Roman law. This larger backdrop is summarized by Peters, *Inquisition*, pp. 1–74. This paragraph is based on that work, pp. 75–104.

37. Lea, *A History of the Inquisition* 3:37. Lea stresses the uniformity of procedures; Tedeschi ("Preliminary Observations") and Dedieu ("L' Inquisition") have both reopened the question of *how* uniform they actually were. Within a range, however, I am inclined to see the procedures as following a pattern, especially in trials of one type, such as those used for this study. For the work patterns and atmosphere of the Suprema see Henningsen, *The Witches' Advocate*, pp. 360–62. Greenleaf stresses that Spanish procedures, "modified to meet the problems of the New World," obtained in the period of the episcopal Inquisition, but with many abuses. In the 1550s and 1560s, therefore, many petitioners asked that a regular tribunal institutionally answerable to the Suprema in Madrid be established in Mexico. Greenleaf, *Zumárraga*, pp. 17–19, 21–22. The instructions sent with Mexico's first inquisitor, Pedro Moya de Contreras, outline some of the differences in the operating of an American tribunal. For a summary see A. Huerga, "La implantación del Santo Oficio en México," in *Historia de la Inquisición* 1:727–28. Also see references cited in n24. Tambs sketches institutional developments in the eighteenth century and stresses the continuity of concerns and procedures, except for the tendency to use the tribunal more overtly in the second half of the eighteenth century in the service of the regalist state. Lewis A. Tambs, "The Inquisition in Eighteenth-Century Mexico," *The Americas* 22(2)(October 1965):167–81.

38. On this complex point Alberro is essential (*Inquisición y sociedad*, p. 79 and pp. 30–79). For the structures of prison life consult the section "El descenso a los infiernos," pp. 223–280; for the lower standards in the frontier, see her discussion of cases of Zacatecas, pp. 379–413; however, the theme recurs throughout her book.

39. Moya's instructions specify in great detail how records are to be kept in the new tribunal. See n24.

40. Donovan, *Catechism*, p. 278.

41. Peters, *Inquisition*, p. 87. See Le Roy Ladurie (*Montaillou*, p. xiii) on the skill and persistence of Jacques Fournier in drawing out information from witnesses. The rise of the confessional might be dated to the late eleventh century, when Anselm of Canterbury made the fundamental distinction between sins committed voluntarily and those out of ignorance. Le Goff says that once this distinction was fixed, "all spiritual and moral life centered on the search for intentions . . ." and clerics became expert in eliciting this kind of introspection from laymen in the confessional. Jacques Le Goff, *The Birth of Purgatory*, trans. Arthur Goldhammer (Chicago: University of Chicago Press, 1981), pp. 214, 213–17.

42. Often a pointed question or two follows a lengthy, rambling statement.

43. With regard to the Spanish Inquisition, Peters (*Inquisition*, p. 92) notes that notaries "carefully recorded . . . all of the information collected in the confessions and denunciations." On the general point of the notary in inquisitional judicial

procedure, he stresses that trials "had to be recorded in writing in full" and that "the recording of trials appears to have been extremely conscientious" (p. 66).

44. Pierre Goubert, *The Ancien Régime: French Society, 1600–1750*, trans. Steve Cox (New York: Harper and Row, 1973), p. 267.

45. AGN, Inquisición, vol. 657, leg. 3. About 1600 Melchor Rodríguez, a vecino of Puebla, said something similar, calling the commissioner of the Inquisition in Puebla "a little Jewish dog." Medina, *Historia del Tribunal*, p. 169.

46. Seventeenth-century Florentine notaries in criminal courts did the same, "even to the point of reporting improper speech and dialects." This for Calvi suggests the same point—that notaries transcribed testimony accurately. Calvi, *Histories of a Plague Year*, p. 56.

47. AGN, Inquisición, vol. 1038, fs. 1–78. For trial procedures I have found the works by Lea, Dedieu, and Jiménez Monteserin cited in n25 useful. Adelina Sarrión Mora also discusses trial procedures in her "El médico y la sociedad rural del siglo XVII: El proceso inquisitorial de Francisco Martínez Casas," in *Inquisición Española: Nuevas Aproximaciones* (Madrid: Centro de Estudios Inquisitoriales, 1987), pp. 297–321. Greenleaf, *Zumárraga*, p. 21n summarizes procedures in Mexico from the Zumárraga period.

48. The notary inserts that don Juan was "gravely ill and close to death," which may account for the five-week delay between Andrés's arrest and hearing.

49. The wording here and the lack of a separate commission in the file to collect testimony in Escuintla makes it appear that don Juan Falla was supposed to look after that but had not. From the material that follows, however, I think it possible that a separate commission had earlier been sent to the commissioner in Ciudad Real but had not been carried out.

50. This from a letter by dr. don Christóbal Fierros y Torres, for the tribunal in Mexico City, dated August 1, 1764, commissioning dr. don Simón Joseph de Matos y Oliva, archdeacon of the cathedral, rector of the archdiocesan *colegio seminario*.

51. The last item in the file from Matos y Oliva is dated January 2, 1765, and the first item from his successor, September 25, 1766. Assuming a gradual weakening through ill health and an interval before a new commissioner was appointed, Chacón went for about nine months with no one to spur him or direct him.

52. I infer this timing because of the October date of the *escrito de clamosa*, which would have been dated shortly after the Escuintla testimony had arrived.

53. The document cites the "long distance between the kingdom of Guatemala and the capital," the savings in the expenses to conduct him to Mexico City, the reduction of the risk of his escaping, and adds that "it is the custom that cases of this kind occurring in Guatemala be continued by the commissioner of this Holy Office." In fact from the files that I have seen, this was not a customary procedure. Most cases, as already suggested, receive their definitive hearings in Mexico City.

54. This means that the court was prepared to hand down a sentence without reviewing the transcripts of direct testimony from the accused and the witnesses,

but only as summarized by court notaries at the service of the prosecutor. From my standpoint these materials are the least informative in the files, as they tend to be more formulaic and condensed for purposes of prosecution. On the other hand, the bases for these summaries (depositions of witnesses and statements made by the accused) are the most valuable material in the files.

55. Regulations called for the completion of the three hearings within ten days of the arrest. Henningsen, *The Witches' Advocate*, pp. 40, 456–57n.

56. Some major revisions occasionally appear in second and third hearings, but normally only small additions emerge. Yet slight emendations and rephrasings can provide significant clarifications of prisoners' stories and reveal glimpses of their states of mind as imprisonment drags on. Sometimes prisoners used these hearings or asked for special ones to plead for mercy, to complain of dampness in the cell, to request reading material, or to petition that the trial be sped up.

57. In this case the *acusación* is dated December 19 but was read to Andrés on January 19. The prosecutor, therefore, must have drawn it up immediately after Andrés's third hearing.

58. Sometimes only at this moment did prisoners discover why they had been arrested and brought to trial. Responses to the articles of the accusation and to the summary of testimony can be very useful for clarifying the point of view and motivation of the accused.

59. In editing the summaries to conceal the identity of witnesses, there was no such thing as unnecessary detail, only identifying detail. Note however that at the very outset of this case, the deputy alcalde mayor failed to hide the identity of a denouncer by sending Andrés and Ignacio to Guatemala together. The accused and his lawyer also had the right to a transcript of the witnesses' testimony.

60. The ordinary represented the bishop within whose jurisdiction the crime took place.

61. The judges were don Francisco Xavier Gamboa and don Francisco Leandro de Viana, *alcaldes de crimen*.

62. In this case a *sentencia con méritos*, which was a summary of the trial together with the verdict. Rarely were such judgments read behind closed doors.

63. It may have been that the kinds of judicial irregularities noted by Alberro and José Toribio Medina apply mainly to cases involving wealthy Jews, when "ideological considerations" became subordinated to patterns of complicity or factionalism taking place within the wealthy and powerful strata of society. Certainly Medina pays little attention to bigamists and to other minor crimes. See Alberro, *Inquisición y sociedad*, p. 47. Note, however, that in Andrés's case the inquisitors would have been content to pass sentence on the basis of a summary of evidence (the accusation and the publication of witnesses), which of course was biased in favor of the prosecution. The historian, if not the accused, benefits from the fact that the raw and more discursive views of witnesses and of the accused are also in the files. Yet even the summaries ramble on to a surprising degree, with extra material included that has little bearing on the case in the narrowest sense. Lea,

speaking of the public reading of the sentences, says that they "disseminat[ed] corruption" because unnecessary detail made them "an effective popular education in vice." For instance, citing the sentence of Ana de Cervantes, read in an auto de fe of January 1, 1651, Lea finds it "superfluous" that the public would hear that she had "tratado torpemente con otras mugeres como si esta fuese hombre, usando para ello un instrumento que llaman baldrés." Lea, *A History of the Inquisition* 4:510. *Baldrés* is an older form of *baldés*, a soft and supple animal skin ("piel curtida, suave y endeble que sirve para guantes y otras cosas"), which might have served as an artificial phallus. See *Diccionario de la Lengua Castellana*, 7th ed. (Madrid: La Academia Española, 1832), q.v. *baldrés, baldés*. If the summaries can be so circumstantial, it gives confidence that notaries indeed were doing their job in taking down the original depositions in careful detail. It appears that edicts of faith were also circumstantial enough that they at times even put dispersed and ill-informed Jews back in touch with their faith. Alberro, *Inquisición y sociedad*, p. 77.

64. Although the intent was to maintain high judicial standards, which can be seen as a kind of protection for the accused.

65. Northrup Frye, *Anatomy of Criticism: Four Essays* (Princeton: Princeton University Press, 1957), pp. 43–52.

66. The dramatistic structure of trial dossiers is, with few exceptions, also a chronological one. When it is not, there is a logic to the exception, as we have already seen, for example, in the placement of the *edicto de clamoso* (October 29, 1768), officially opening the trial, as the first item. This was followed by the original denunciation (November 10, 1762), the earliest dated document in the file, and commissioner Falla's examination of Andrés in Guatemala City. Letters *to* the Inquisition are filed by the date they are received, rather than that of their writing. Sometimes material is subclassified by region and then chronologically, as in this case are the reports from Chiapas and from Guatemala.

67. The Inquisition found bigamists among old Christians of every station. Solange Alberro's compilation of the activity of the Mexican tribunal catalogues 1,046 bigamy cases from 1522 to 1700, or 9 percent of all trials (n = 11,443). Only 7 percent of these were tried before 1570. Alberro, *La Actividad*, pp. 231–34. Contreras and Henningsen's tabulation of Mexican records in the Suprema (annual summary reports of trials) indicate how incomplete those records are. For the period 1560 to 1614, they tabulate only 699 cases, of which 132 (19 percent) were for bigamy, and from 1615 to 1700 a total of 251, of which 66 (26 percent) were for bigamy. For all tribunals from 1560 to 1700, they tabulate 2,468 bigamy trials, which is 5.8 percent of all trials. Contreras and Henningsen, "Forty-Four Thousand Cases," pp. 118–19.

68. Peters, *Inquisition*, p. 87.

69. I see bigamy as a legal more than a behavioristic category. It means that one had violated the sacrament of matrimony by contracting a second marriage when a first spouse was still alive.

70. Juan Vázquez, for example, a seventeenth-century muleteer, was openly

defiant in asserting to the court his 'moral' reasons for contracting a second (bigamous) marriage. Boyer, "Juan Vázquez," pp. 441–42.

71. Dedieu, "The Archives," p. 168. In saying this he seems to be referring more to summaries and statements by prosecutors than the unedited depositions of the trial records that I have seen. Nevertheless one is well advised to be careful with the written attributions when they directly touch upon lapses in orthodoxy.

72. 'Output' is more than the sum of 'input,' as the empirical tradition might suggest. The former varies with the narrator (who experiences, processes, and transforms something), the subject, and the audience. Thus recall varies with stimulus and context, not to say motivation. Noam Chomsky, "A Cartesian View of Language Structure," in C. P. Otero, ed., *Noam Chomsky: Language and Politics* (Montreal and New York: Black Rose Books, 1968), pp. 100–115. The Seminar on the History of Mentalities devoted their second symposium to the problem of memory. Serge Gruzinski, for example, showed how a "mutilated memory" can give a true idea of mentality. Serge Gruzinski, "La memoria mutilada: Construcción del pasado y mecanismos de la memoria en un grupo otomí de la mitad del siglo XVII," in Seminario de Historia de las Mentalidades, *La memoria y el olvido*, pp. 33–46. Alfredo López Austin argues that memory is a "dialectical interplay" between ideology and daily life, but an unequal one. The former, he says, "restrains [the merely] casuistical and anarchical assimilation" of the latter; the latter occasions the "conjuncture" that "gives a dynamic to [ideological] structures." Alfredo López Austin, "La construcción de la memoria," in Seminario de Historia de las Mentalidades, *La memoria y el olvido*, p. 76. Nancy Farriss reminds us that the linkage between popular culture (and behavior) and official ideologies is not a mechanical from-the-top-down imposition. The inarticulate "have values, ideas, and attitudes that are not necessarily mere impoverished versions of those held by the politically powerful." She defined her problem as trying to find a way to recover their "voice [which] is largely mute in the written record." Nancy Farriss, *Maya Society under Colonial Rule: The Collective Enterprise of Survival* (Princeton: Princeton University Press, 1984), p. 402.

73. Patricia Aufderheide found in her study of Inquisition confessions taken in Brazil that confessants distinguished between two worlds: that of the "vida práctica . . ." "in which [people] actually lived" and that defined by religio-legal codes and dogmas. In their vida práctica it was not expected that people would meet the high standards of the formal codes and dogmas, so a kind of double standard gave some slack to ordinary people. Patricia Aufderheide, "True Confessions: The Inquisition and Social Attitudes in Brazil at the Turn of the XVII Century," *Luso-Brazilian Review* 10(2)(Winter 1973):227–28.

Kenneth Burke makes the metaphor of "imposing" ideologies seem ridiculous by drawing it literally: "a spirit taking up its abode in a body: it makes that body hop around in certain ways; and that same body would have hopped around in different ways had a different ideology happened to inhabit it." His concern is to stress that individuals exercise agency, that what they do, say, and think should not be seen simply as a set of robotlike conditionings. Kenneth Burke, *Language as Symbolic Action* (Berkeley, Los Angeles, London: University of California Press, 1966), p. 6.

74. Ida Altman, *Emigrants and Society: Extremadura and Spanish America in the Sixteenth Century* (Berkeley, Los Angeles, London: University of California Press, 1989), p. 92.

75. On the impossible task of controlling sexuality see Asunción Lavrin, "Sexuality in Colonial Mexico," in Asunción Lavrin, ed., *Sexuality and Marriage*, pp. 47–92, and especially the general comment on p. 47.

76. Most of these were dropped, sometimes to be passed to other jurisdictions, unless they could be connected to heresy. Alberro, *La Actividad*, pp. 233–34.

77. Patricia Seed, *To Love, Honor, and Obey*, pp. 63, 266–67n.

78. Thomas Calvo, "The Warmth of the Hearth: Seventeenth-Century Guadalajara Families," in Lavrin, ed., *Sexuality and Marriage*, pp. 292–93, 297. Pescador cites illegitimacy rates of between 20 and 30 percent of all baptisms in the parish of Santa Catarina and Denis Valdés even higher than that for El Sagrario in Mexico City. Pescador, *De bautizados*, pp. 147, 149, 201; for Valdés I am using Pescador's citation of him in Denis Valdés, "The Decline of the Sociedad de Castas in Mexico City" (Ph.D diss., University of Michigan 1978), p. 33. McCaa's well-considered estimate for urban areas in late colonial Mexico is "at least one-quarter of total baptisms" in urban areas in the late-colonial era, which at least in part stems from highly imbalanced sex ratios that put women at such a disadvantage in the marriage market that they too easily believed whatever promises to marry seducers might offer up. Robert McCaa, "Marriageways: Courtship, Coupling, Cohabitation and Matrimony in Mexico and Spain, 1500–1900" (Paper prepared for the conference on Familia y Vida Privada: América, Siglos XVI a XIX, May 3–4, 1993, Mexico City), p. 13. Seed points to another, perhaps complementary aspect of the disadvantaging of women in the eighteenth century: the shift in association of status from virtue to wealth. A man's verbal promise to marry became increasingly devalued, often merely a ploy for seduction, with consequences, if any, of only a monetary payment for damages. Seed, "Marriage Promises," pp. 253–276, especially pp. 274–76. It is clear that illegitimacy rates for Indians were far lower than for Spaniards, castas, and blacks and lower as well for rural than for urban places. See, for example, Claude Morin, *Santa Inés Zacatelco (1646–1812)* (Mexico City: INAH, 1973), pp. 73–74.

79. Woodrow Borah and Sherburne F. Cook, "Marriage and Legitimacy in Mexican Culture: Mexico and California," *California Law Review* 54(1966):950–51. As a formal written contract, barraganía seems to have died out in the fifteenth century (McCaa, "Marriageways," p. 7), but stable forms of cohabitation informally imbedded in the culture continued to be a commonplace, as we shall see. Pilar Gonzalbo Aizpuru, *Las mujeres en la Nueva España: Educación y vida cotidiana* (Mexico City: El Colegio de México 1987), pp. 44–47.

80. Michael C. Scardaville, "Crime and the Urban Poor," pp. 167 and 164–74. Men who had deserted their wives would have had ample opportunity to find another woman to live with, for, to cite the figures from the 1811 census in cuartel 2 (which corresponds almost exactly with the parish of Santa Catarina), 70 percent of all women were living in households without men. Pescador, *De bautizados*, pp. 222, 243–44.

81. A few were forced to marry.

CHAPTER TWO

1. Elsa Malvido, "Algunos aportes de los estudios de demografía histórica al estudio de la familia en la época colonial de México," in Seminario de Historia de las Mentalidades, *Familia y sexualidad*, pp. 92–94.

2. Pescador, *De bautizados*, pp. 210, 202–12.

3. Ibid., p. 210. There is also a more idealized view, more reflective of pious accounts left behind by religious of both sexes, see Josefina Muriel, "La transmisión cultural en la familia criolla novohispana," in Pilar Gonzalbo Aizpuru, *Familias novohispanas*, pp. 113–22.

4. Carlo Ginzburg, "Clues: Roots of an Evidential Paradigm," in Ginzburg, *Clues*, pp. 114–15.

5. These usually proceeded with some formal schooling (reading, writing, arithmetic, and Christian doctrine for boys; reading, Christian doctrine, and sewing for girls), but it was superficial and extraneous to the real learning referred to above.

6. The first represents a kind of retrospective forecasting associated with the "Zadig Method," which in the late nineteenth century was applied to diachronic disciplines (history, archaeology, paleontology) that could not reproduce causes in a laboratory. See Ginzburg, "Clues," pp. 117, 210–11n. For causation from 'scene', see Kenneth Burke, *A Grammar of Motives* (Berkeley, Los Angeles, London: University of California Press, 1969 [1945]), pp. xv–xxiii, 3–20, 127–70. The process should not be confused with teleological attributions, mostly applied to motive, to the effect that because something happened, someone *wanted* it to happen.

7. AGN, Inq., vol. 134, exp. 11. Martín was born and spent his first six or seven years in Colmenar del Arroyo (province of Madrid), the next eight years in San Martín de Valdeiglesias (province of Madrid), and then moved to Cebreros. Martín's mother was from San Martín and his father from nearby Hoyos [del Espino].

8. By now, no doubt, Martín held the title of "master," for aside from examiners being more lenient with the sons of colleagues, the assumption was that daily contact with a father resulted in sufficient knowledge of the father's trade. Felipe Castro Gutiérrez, *La extinción de la Artesanía Gremial* (Mexico City: UNAM, 1986), pp. 75–76. The investigation of Martín established that he was not a bigamist, and the case was therefore suspended. As a result his file lacks full information on his family and has no information on how his father's estate was divided. Much of what

can be learned about Martín, as we shall see, comes from the testimony of his lifelong acquaintance Andrés.

9. Andrés at that time was fifty-four and a vecino of Mexico City, "at the hospital for syphilitics." He had known Martín for more than forty years in Cebreros (twelve years; Martín was twelve when his father and he emigrated from pueblo Hoyos to Cebreros), Seville, and Mexico City.

10. The six children were by his first wife; three survived and two went to the Indies. He also had three children by his second wife, but it is not clear whether in Seville or in Mexico. In the second marriage, Gerónimo Sánchez, a coworker in the mint (and possibly a relative?), acted as padrino, a point that shows us once again Martín's linkages to other men of his trade.

11. In Seville, "in the king's forges," Martín lost an eye when an iron filing flew into it. Andrés said that he had been "*calzando una yunque*," which might mean casting or shimming an anvil. Andrés places the accident *after* his leaving Seville, but I have taken Martín's version, that it happened in Seville, to be the correct one. Andrés also knew that Martín had been employed in the Mexico City mint for nine or ten years, five or six of which they were coworkers. Andrés goes on to confirm that Martín came with his wife and also tells us that he and Martín live in the same neighborhood: "He brought a daughter and son [to New Spain] from his first marriage and has two children by a wife here [the one he returned for when he immigrated]—the son is twenty, the daughter is married and gone to Peru—and [Martín] lives behind the syphilitic hospital."

12. Yet he could not name any of them, possibly because as a mint worker, he had little day-to-day contact with the blacksmith shops on the street.

13. The only clues pointing to why he moved consist of his mention of the 'pull' factors of Seville and then the Indies as destinations, which stand out by his failure to mention those that might have 'pushed' him—for example debt or an unhappy marriage, reasons that, as we shall see, figure in other accounts.

14. AGN, Inq., vol. 135.

15. Whether his schooling was full-time or not is not clear. However, later in New Spain, he commented expertly on different handwriting in letters sent from home.

16. The judgment as to the modesty of the enterprise comes from Mota y Escobar's estimates of the worth of merchants (perhaps not quite the same thing as the value of their stock and cash) in Guadalajara in 1603. Cited in Woodrow Borah, *Price Trends of Royal Tribute Commodities in Nueva Galicia, 1557–1598* (Berkeley, Los Angeles, Oxford: University of California Publications, 1992), p. 16. The operation seems comparable to the one described by Andrés García—a modest man who nevertheless "seems well on his way to lasting wealth" (p. 144)—in a letter to his nephew in 1571. James Lockhart and Enrique Otte, *Letters and People of the Spanish Indies: The Sixteenth Century* (London: Cambridge University Press, 1976), pp. 143–46. From the store in Oaxaca, Antonio must have delegated some of the actual peddling to petty traders (*viandantes*), taking con-

signments of goods on "one-term contracts." John Kicza defines the work of the *viandante*, the "marginal, itinerant, and petty regional" trader, as typically the following: he "usually approached the individual merchant and entered into a one-term contract to take his goods into the hinterland. . . . There the merchandise would be sold from muleback in small villages which could not support a full-time merchant." See John E. Kicza, *Colonial Entrepreneurs: Families and Business in Bourbon Mexico City* (Albuquerque: University of New Mexico Press, 1983), p. 96. If Kicza sees the *viandante* as a small-scale distributor of goods that might not otherwise reach out-of-the-way places, Rodolfo Pastor argues that he was a competitor and interloper, selling and buying in a market that the *alcalde mayor* of a district—together with his creditors, benefactors, and clients—expected to monopolize. "Por consiguiente, a menudo se persigue a estos competidores por medio del cobro riguroso (o 'excesivo') de las alcabalas y otros derechos." Rodolfo Pastor, "El repartimiento de mercancías y los alcaldes mayores novohispanos: Un systema de explotación, de sus orígenes a la crisis de 1810," in Borah, *El gobierno provincial,* pp. 215–16.

17. AGN, Inq., vol. 134, exp. 8. His father and grandfather, both *sederos,* were Spaniards from Medellín and members of the silk-workers' guild; on July 3, 1556, and again on January 11, 1557, Juan was named by the *cabildo* as inspector (*veedor*) of the silkworkers. Juan died in the spring of 1593, for on May 4 of that year, the *cabildo* reassigned his former [commercial] site (*sitio*) to Gerónimo Conde and granted to his widow "the site next to the pillar (*pilar*)." Edmundo O'Gorman, director, *Guía de las actas de cabildo de la ciudad de México, siglo XVI* (Mexico City: Fondo de Cultura Económica, 1970), pp. 318, 325, 774. His mother, Elvira, was a free mulatto. The presumption generally obtained that race mixing meant illegitimacy and, as in the next case, vice versa.

18. The sentence was pronounced in 1582 and also required Diego's appearance in the auto de fe, abjuration of his sin, and two hundred lashes in the streets.

19. For some patterns and variations, see Altman, *Emigrants and Society,* pp. 150–53.

20. AGN, Inq., vol. 508, exp. 1, fs. 1–76. Cosme was an *hijo natural,* the offspring of unmarried parents which was the least serious of the illegitimate categories. Had his parents ever married, he would automatically have been legitimated. More serious forms of illegitimacy were *adulterinos* (springing from adulterous unions) and *espurios* (children fathered by priests). Ann Twinam, "Honor, Sexuality, and Illegitimacy in Colonial Spanish America," in Lavrin, ed., *Sexuality and Marriage,* pp. 118–49, especially 119. For a broader definition of *spurii,* see Borah and Cook, "Marriage and Legitimacy," pp. 949–52. Malvido ("Algunos aportes," p. 93) also reviews categories of illegitimacy. Yet illegitimacy carried the suspicion of racial stigma, as can be seen by the shoemaker Lucas Roldán's comment "*el rostro le tiene [Cosme] como amestizado.*"

21. On the logic of racial intermarriage, as the Spanish jurist Juan Solórzano Pereira noted, "few Spaniards of honour . . . would marry an Indian or Negro

woman." A young man who petitioned to do so in nineteenth-century Cuba cited his "misfortune of being one of those men . . . cut off from society and in constant contact with the pardos." Verena Martínez-Alier, *Marriage, Class and Colour in Nineteenth-Century Cuba: A Study of Racial Attitudes and Sexual Values in a Slave Society*, 2d ed. (Ann Arbor: University of Michigan Press, 1989), pp. 64–65, 161n.

22. Alonso, together with "a dance master" of Puebla, danced at the wedding.

23. On the marginality of "non-encomendero farmers and stock growers," see Lockhart's comments in "Spaniards Among Indians: Toluca in the Later Sixteenth Century," in Lockhart, *Nahuas and Spaniards*, p. 209.

24. In the Puebla area Cosme worked at his trade for less than half of the four-year period following the marriage and again for a year and a half in Mexico City after he left Juana. Possibly he collaborated in some way with his brother Pedro Muñoz (who used his mother's surname), apparently a journeyman tailor; I infer this because he was "living in the house of Núñez Pérez," apparently as an employee in the shop and home of a master. Note that Pedro, plebeian though he was, had at least based his life in the middle of the Hispanic world of Mexico City; his standing in society is about what might have been expected for Cosme.

25. This time on his uncle's farm, near Ixtapa.

26. AGN, Inq., vol. 1013.

27. They too were probably married to Indian women from the town, although Joseph does not specify this. He does say that one sister was married to a French chemist in Tezcuco and another to Vicente [?] Alvarez, a weaver in Calpulalpa.

28. As a guess, he might have gambled away some of his wife's possessions, which did happen, as we shall see in chapter 4. For literary treatment of the vice of gambling within the context of Counter-Reformation Spain, see Anne J. Cruz, "La bella malmaridada: Lessons for the Good Wife," in Cruz and Perry, *Culture and Control*, p. 160.

29. It is more difficult to explain Cosme who, as we saw, grew up in Mexico City and learned silkweaving there but sporadically served in the countryside. Probably he worked as a *mayordomo* supervising others and therefore did not have to know directly about crops and animals.

30. AGN, Inq., vol. 1156. Depending on how one defines urban, 80 to 90 percent of Mexico's population was rural as late as the first half of the nineteenth century. Arrom, *The Women*, p. 325n.103.

31. Felipe could say the Lord's Prayer, Ave Maria, Salve, and Credo well and could recite the sacraments and commandments of the church correctly, but he crossed himself incorrectly and stumbled on the ten commandments. He did not learn to read or to write. Rural types, as we shall see in other cases, seemed to fare less well in their knowledge of religious doctrine. For a general comment, see Pilar Gonzalbo Aizpuru, "La ortodoxia imposible: Doctrina y práctica social en el

campo novohispano," in Sánchez, Van Young, and von Wobeser, *La ciudad y el campo* 2:857–66.

A comparable upbringing found the mulatto Juan de Santana Izquierdo (born 1743) remaining with his parents in Colima until he was thirty (AGN, Inq., vol. 1279, exp. 13, fs. 1–99). As with Felipe, Juan's 'schooling' consisted of absorbing the general complex of skills of country people, as he farmed and drove mules with his father. Later, on an hacienda near Zapotlán (Michoacán), he served as an ordinary laborer (*operario*).

32. AGN, Inq., vol. 972, exp. 1. The details below come from Juan's hearing of March 13, 1755.

33. "Teniente de milicias de infantería española de la villa de Córdoba."

34. A hint of the cost of such an end comes from his request, ten months before he died, to be allowed some time in the sun to relieve the pain in his feet caused by the dampness of his cell. The request comes on March 13, 1755, after his first audience with the judges and after a three-year imprisonment: "por hallarse enfermo de los piés y de relajación suplica se le permita salir al sol porque teme le ha de hacer mal la humedad de la carcel." Juan's linkage of dampness and problems with the feet suggests poor circulation, possibly gout, a form of arthritis. Juan died with his request denied.

35. ". . . por ausencia del reo en México, desde los principios de la siembra de dicho tobaco hasta se debió a mí industria, crédito, asistencia, y trabajo, su cultivo y beneficio hasta el conserviente [y] acotado de poder disponerse de dicha cosecha como efecto adquirdos durante el tiempo de la compañía que para mi lo fue legal como inculpable el engaño . . . [entonces quiere] algún razonable socorro del producto del dichos bienes secuestrados especialmente el valor de la cosecha de tobaco. (fs. 84r and v)

36. Dedieu, "'Christianization' in New Castile," pp. 3–6. Schooling in this form applied little to Indian communities. Friars preferred to work in the native languages, and native towns resisted the acculturative objectives associated with having schools in their communities. Adriaan C. Van Oss, *Catholic Colonialism: A Parish History of Guatemala, 1524–1821* (Cambridge: Cambridge University Press, 1986), pp. 143–46, 162. Parental rejection of schools once again underlines their merely supplementary place in raising children.

37. Gonzalbo, *Las mujeres*, p. 129.

38. Dedieu, "'Christianization' in New Castile," pp. 3–6; Gonzalbo, *Las mujeres*, pp. 92, 104–5, 127–47.

39. AGN, Inq., vol. 815, exp. 1, fs. 1–133.

40. In this Joseph may be contrasted with a man of the sixteenth century, Miguel Alonso (born 1549), who attended school to age thirteen in Ayamonte (Huelva), but at forty, having worked about ten years as a farm laborer in Huexocingo

(Tlaxcala), declared that he could neither read nor write. AGN, Inq., vol. 137, exp. 11.

41. AGN, Inq., vol. 1166, exp. 7, fs. 172ff.

42. AGN, Inq., vol. 526, exp. 2, fs. 37–151.

43. AGN, Inq., vol. 1089, exp. 1, fs. 1–108.

44. AGN, Inq., vol. 441, exp. 2, fs. 356–411v.

45. AGN, Inq., vol. 1275, exp. 16, fs. 1–110. The quotation is from María's hearing of May 6, 1788.

46. AGN, Inq., vol. 1214. Catechism and basic skills were the essential curriculum, and therefore María may have been more typical than our previous two cases. Girls "almost never" learned arithmetic, and only a few mastered writing (Gonzalbo, *Las mujeres*, p. 129). On comparative literacy rates from a sample of 659 marriage applications from the archdiocese of Mexico City, Seed, counting the ability "to put even a few letters together," found only 16 percent of women literate, as opposed to 46 percent of men. Seed, "Marriage Promises," p. 272.

47. But not conclusively, perhaps, from only one case and without a way to assess the affect of variables other than gender (for example, race and class). Yet our accounts do point to a gendered pattern, with parents restricting daughters to a narrow domestic world and setting them to chores associated with female work: food preparation, cleaning, and the care and making of clothing. Of course we would like to know a lot more about the complex of domestic routines, but because they were just that, routines familiar to everybody, they did not merit detailed description before the court.

48. AGN, Inq., vol. 108, exp. 2. From 1542 Perpignan was under siege by Francis I during the fourth in a series of wars (1542–1545) between Charles V and Francis I. In the early going, French armies had some successes on the frontiers of Spain, Flanders, and Savoy. The siege was unsuccessful, for several companies of Spanish veterans under captains Cervellón and Machicão sallied forth and immobilized French artillery. This plus the news that the Duke of Alva was coming with a relief column led to the French withdrawal. Gerónimo must have arrived shortly after this action had taken place. Don Francisco de Paula Mellado, et. al., *Diccionario Universal de Historia y de Geografía*, 7 vols. (Madrid, 1846), II, p. 180; VI, p. 72; Antonio Domînguez Ortiz, *The Golden Age of Spain, 1516–1659* (New York, 1971), p. 59.

49. Lockhart, *Nahuas and Spaniards*, p. 93.

50. Gerónimo's chronology is vague, but firm enough to present some problems in meshing it with Zorita's career, especially in Santo Domingo. Because Zorita was away from Santo Domingo for two and a half years (1550–52), when Gerónimo, according to his own chronology, would have established his relationship with him, one is tempted to place Gerónimo in Santo Domingo earlier (say in 1548 or 1549) or simply assume that the six months after Zorita returned to Santo Domingo (from May 1552) was the period when Gerónimo entered his clientele. Here is a brief summary of Zorita's movements in the Indies, according to Benjamin Keen:

Date	Work
6/1548	Arrives in Santo Domingo
6/1548–1/1550	Sails to New Granada to conduct residencia of Governor Miguel Díez de Armendáriz
5/1552	Returns to Santo Domingo
Spring/1553	Sails to Golfo Dulce on the Guatemalan coast, to take up judgeship in the Guatemala audiencia
8/1556	Arrives in Mexico City, to take up judgeship in the Mexican audiencia
1566	Returns to Spain
1585	Completes Lords of New Spain

Alonso de Zorita, *Life and Labor in Ancient Mexico: The Brief and Summary Relation of the Lords of New Spain*, trans. and with an introduction by Benjamin Keen (New Brunswick, New Jersey: Rutgers University Press, 1963), pp. 18–52.

51. The laws of the Indies specified three general categories of *escribanos:* public, royal, and enumerated. A royal scribe could work anywhere in the king's domain, except in places where enumerated scribes were given a monopoly. Bernardo Pérez Fernández del Castillo, *Historia de la escribanía en la Nueva España y del notariado en México* (Mexico City: Editorial Porrua, 1988), p. 55.

52. AGN, Inq., vol. 136, exp. 10.

53. Madrid was not officially the capital until 1561.

54. Don Juan Antonio Ulloa (born 1649) claimed a more illustrious lineage than Agustín but, because he was a younger son born of a second wife (whom his father married well after Juan was born), he was relegated to a secondary place in the family. Juan's father, don Luis de Ulloa Pereira, had been an alderman of Toro (Zamora), with entailed property in that city; his grandfather had been a knight of the order of Alcántara and alderman in Soria. Overshadowed by his older brother, don Diego de Ulloa, heir to the entail and knight of the order of Santiago, don Juan would later call upon don Diego's patronage when he followed him to Peru. Before that, however, he acted as his proxy in Toro, where he managed family properties and stood in as alcalde mayor and alderman.

A sketch of these background details puts what we know of don Juan's actual formation into context, for his own account of his early years, related to the inquisitors on August 4, 1686, is all too brief.

He was raised in his parents' house [in Toro] until he was two [in 1651]. Then they took him to Madrid, and he was there until he was sixteen, learning to read and to write and also a little grammar, with the masters that he referred to. Then he returned to Toro and married doña María Arias, daughter of sergeant major don Juan Arias de Yebra and doña Francisca Zenteno.

One witness described don Juan as a quarrelsome type ("*de natural bulliciosso*"), and it may have been in an altercation at the court in Madrid that he received the wound that left a prominent scar on the left side of his nose. In any case don Luis ended his son's formation promptly at sixteen, returned him to Toro, and married him to doña María. The marriage contracts had already spelled out the content of her dowry, and a promissory note guaranteeing it was signed by don Juan. Following the wedding the groom took his bride to reside in the family houses in Toro, and he began to fulfil the important, if secondary, role of stand-in for his absent brother.

In the arraignment the prosecutor said that don Juan had misrepresented his legitimacy, that in fact he was a "bastard son of the said don Luis de Ulloa," and that don Diego was therefore only his half brother. Nevertheless don Juan's birth must have counted for something, for his sentence was read behind the closed doors of the chamber, thus sparing him the pain of public humiliation. AGN, Inq., vol. 657, exp. 1, fs. 125–75.

55. "The majority of the wholesalers improved or maintained their social position when they married." Louisa Schell Hoberman, *Mexico's Merchant Elite, 1590–1660: Silver, State, and Society* (Durham and London: Duke University Press, 1991), pp. 65, 64–68. For elite marriages Muriel Nazarri shows how a pool of wealthy merchants in the São Paulo marriage market led to a shift in the institution of the dowry. Muriel Nazarri, "Parents and Daughters: Change in the Practice of Dowry in São Paulo (1600–1770)," HAHR 70(4)(November 1990): 639–65.

56. Alamo also administered the municipal common property (*propios*) in Málaga. AGN, Inq., vol. 1214, exp. 11, fs. 126–245.

57. AGN, Inq., vol. 1234. *Chalupas* are small, two-masted boats, fitted with six or eight oars on each side.

58. Among the notables were archbishop designate and future viceroy of New Spain, doctor don Juan Antonio de Vizarrón y Eguiarreta (1734–40), like Manuel a Basque, and several Inquisition judges as well.

59. The testimony here comes from Manuel's autobiography as he stated it in the dock six years later, on August 27, 1736.

60. Manuel says that he stayed in the houses of don Juan de Ladera y Palazios and of don Pedro Pablo de la Fuente Rosillo, possibly men from his *tierra*. For influential Basques in Chihuahua, see Phillip L. Hadley, *Minería y sociedad en el centro minero de Santa Eulalia, Chihuahua (1709–1750)*, trans. Roberto Gómez Coroza (Mexico City: Fondo de Cultura Económica, 1979), pp. 42–43, 46–47.

61. Cosihuiriáchic had "200 vecinos ca 1745"; at roughly the same time, San Felipe reportedly had a population of "2000 families of 'Spaniards' . . . in addition to an undisclosed number of mestizos and mulattoes." Peter Gerhard, *The North Frontier of New Spain* (Princeton: Princeton University Press, 1982), pp. 190, 200. There were other settlements as well within the district. The main centers, Santa Eulalia and San Felipe, counted 214 and 292 vecinos, respectively, in 1725. Hadley, *Minería y sociedad*, p. 33.

62. Probably selling to other mining camps in the district. He also had a five-month term as a bookkeeper (*rayador*) at San Felipe Real.

63. AGN, Inq., vol. 586, exp. 9, fs. 502–72. On the care with which the Jesuits looked after the spiritual life of their workers on haciendas, see Gonzalbo, "La ortodoxia imposible," p. 862.

64. Although the file does not state it explicitly, I infer that Juan Lázaro departed because he was part of the administrator's clientele.

65. He held other jobs too, discussed in chapter 5.

66. So Mateo said in his autobiographical statement, nearly twenty years later (November 23, 1666). He also claimed that his father-in-law later sent a letter reporting that María had died.

67. Mateo, claiming to be "sickly" (*achacoso*) and suffering from the cold of his cell, asked for a blanket after his first hearing. His discomfort, however, lasted but a short time, as the judges decided that he was an Indian and remanded him to the jurisdiction of "the ordinary of the Indians of this archbishopric."

68. AGN, Inq., vol. 374, exp. 11, fs. 146ff. The descriptive phrase comes from his genealogical statement.

69. One thinks of the comparably youthful, Diego Cortado and Pedro del Rincón, in Seville. Diego had learned the trade of tailoring from his father, but "gifted as I was," he said, "I went from cloth cutting to purse cutting" on quitting "humdrum village existence" and going to Toledo and then, with Pedro, to Seville. Miguel de Cervantes, "Rinconeta y Cortadillo," in *Six Exemplary Novels*, trans. Harriet de Onís (New York: Barron's Educational Series, 1961), 166.

70. Two of Baltasar's three brothers, an uncle, and a cousin also went to the Indies.

71. AGN, Inq., vol. 1341.

72. The family had consisted of both of Juan's parents, a maternal uncle, and a paternal aunt. The aunt had two sons and two daughters; one son was still single and the other was a priest; the daughters were both married to bakers, one with three children, the other he did not know about. In addition Juan's brothers, Joseph, Casimiro, and Miguel (all apparently older than Juan and therefore having benefited from longer parental contact) also based themselves in or near Puebla. Joseph followed the trade of his maternal uncle, gunsmithing, and married a woman of Puebla; Casimiro moved to nearby Acacingo, probably to farm and to marry (Juan did not know with whom); Miguel married a woman from Puebla but later moved to Mexico City. Because Juan moved between Alvarado, Vera Cruz, and Mexico City, he maintained regular contact with Miguel (the only brother whose children, three in this case, he knew about) in Mexico City but apparently not with Casimiro and Joseph.

73. Such placements were sometimes made by parents themselves, but with continued contact and supervision. Placing a boy with a tradesman did not always imply that the latter became a surrogate parent during the training period. In 1571 Alvaro Vao, pilot of the sandbar and in charge of artillery at the port of Villanueva

de Portimao, placed his son Martín Luis, then ten, with a shipwright. (AGN, Inq., vol. 138, exp. 5.) He limited the influence of Martín's master to the transmission of his technical skills and retained control over other aspects of his son's formation by keeping him in his own house until Martín went to sea, somewhat later. Manuel de Ovando, a farmer, blocked out his son Christóbal's (born 1735) formation in two stages: first he placed him with his brother, a priest of the same village, to learn to read and to write; then at age twelve, he apprenticed him with a tailor. AGN, Inq., vol. 1199, exp. 29, fs. 214–62.

74. In this he would have been a typical product of a parish school, where the object was to teach reading by means of printed prayers and catechisms. These would have been partly memorized anyway, so the 'reading' must have been a quasimnemonic aid. Probably the ability to read cursive writing depended on learning to write.

75. AGN, Inq., vol. 605, exp. 2, fs. 189–278.

76. AGN, Inq., vol. 834, exp. 24, fs. 410–91.

77. The first comes from his "confession," a statement taken on January 23, 1731, when he was arrested, the second from Bernabé's autobiography, in his hearing of September 3, 1731.

78. He also spent a year running a mule team out of Zacatecas.

79. In his midthirties he knew that his parents were dead and could say that he had known his maternal grandmother (Juana la Bautista, "Indian") and two maternal aunts ("Thomasa, married to Pedro, a slave; María, married to an *indio chino* tailor"). "He only had one sister, María de la Candelaria; he left her in Querétaro and knows nothing about her."

80. AGN, Inq., vol. 548, exp. 4. The racial description comes from Juan's first wife.

81. In early modern England, young servants changed masters "as the normal thing every few years." Laslett, *The World We Have Lost*, p. 7.

82. AGN, Inq., vol. 657, exp. 3, fs. 300–323.

83. AGN, Inq., vol. 523, fs. 131–257.

84. For this series I include Baltasar, who at seven ran away from his uncle; 'ten' could be ten to twelve, assuming that Pedro Mateo's "pretty big" might mean twelve or so.

85. In contrast, because running away from a marriage was not acceptable from the perspective of the court, but had to be explained; see chapter 4.

86. AGN, Inq., vol. 108, exp. 5.

87. AGN, Inq., vol. 523, fs. 131–257.

88. Another sixteenth-century Spaniard, Alonso Guerra, found himself no less disconnected from his family twenty-five years after going to the Indies. Going over his genealogy in the dock (in 1603), Alonso recounted that all six of his uncles had been sharecroppers or small farmers in Villa de Bohadilla de Rioseco (Extremadura), and none had left the village. But he had forgotten the names of wives and children (except for one cousin married to a deaf-mute farmer) and the Chris-

tian names of two maternal aunts. His hazy memory of his aunts contrasts with his sharper characterizations of their husbands, Martín García (a hazelnut farmer, father of the notary of the village) and Miguel Gordo (a farmer from a neighboring village). Alonso had three brothers, one who died young and two others who remained in the home village as farmers. Of four sisters, two had married by the time he left, one to a farmer, the other to a man whose work he did not specify. AGN, Inq., vol. 256, exp. 5.

89. AGN, Inq., vol. 135. Of his father's four brothers, one, it seems, remained in Tordesillas and a second, after a time in Mexico, returned there.

90. AGN, Inq., vol. 1089, exp. 1, fs. 1–108.

91. Tezontepec was an Augustinian doctrina from 1554, but by the middle of the eighteenth century it had been secularized. It was in the far south of the Pachuca jurisdiction. Peter Gerhard, *A Guide to the Historical Geography of New Spain* (Cambridge: Cambridge University Press, 1972), pp. 209–11. Bárbara mentions San Mateo Yxtlahuaca as her place of birth; Bustamante said it was Rancho Santa María.

92. AGN, Inq., vol. 605, exp. 2, fs. 189–278.

93. In this Pedro was not alone, for a parish census of Xalostotitlan in 1650 has more than a third of the pueblo's Indians not registered because they were on haciendas. Gerhard, *North Frontier*, p. 107.

The family of Andrés de la Cruz (born 1662) provides another example of the cultural drift that came from integration into the Hispanic world. His mother was Indian but "ladinized" and married to a mulatto slave who was foreman of a mine at Sultepec. When Andrés ran off, at age seven, he did not go to his mother's notable uncle, don Nicolás, the governor of a pueblo near Valladolid and a *curandero* who specialized in setting broken bones. Instead he went to Zacatecas, to serve fray Agustín. AGN, Inq., vol. 592, exp. 3, fs. 271–377.

94. Or in the case of the former slave Juana Robledo, an aged matriarch around whom the rest of the family clustered. Testifying at age thirty, Juan Lorenzo (born 1677) said he had been raised in San Luis de la Paz, sold to a master in Querétaro when he was twenty, and was a runaway at twenty-six. Juana, "now very old," still lived in San Luis, three of Juan's sisters with her, and two brothers, both married and both working as miners, in separate households. Two married uncles, brothers of his father, lived near San Luis, serving as mayordomos on a rancho. The important point here, however, is that the mother, then either freed or 'retired,' continued to be the central focus of the family. AGN, Inq., vol. 548, exp. 4.

95. AGN. Inq., vol. 547, exp. 6.

96. The proportions here assume a similar pattern for the Hispanic world and France. For the latter, Robert Wheaton has noted: "On the average between one-third and one-half of all children would die before they reached the age of five." Robert Wheaton, "Introduction: Recent Trends in the Historical Study of the French Family," in Wheaton and Hareven, *Family and Sexuality*, p. 13. McCaa, taking into consideration the death rates of late-eighteenth-century Nueva

Viscaya, concludes that "para la gran mayoría de jóvenes de ambos sexos el padre o tutor, es decir la patria potestad, no contó mucho en las cuestiones matrimoniales." McCaa, "Gustos de los padres," p. 591.

97. AGN, Inq., vol. 1199, exp. 29, fs. 214-62.

98. AGN, Inq., vol. 1214.

99. AGN, Inq., vol. 794, exp. 24, fs. 226-322.

100. AGN, Inq., vol. 310, exp. 7.

101. AGN, Inq., vol. 1292, exp. 7, fs. 1-101.

102. AGN, Inq., vol. 272, exp. 1, and vol. 262, exp. 6.

103. Arrom, *The Women*, p. 62.

CHAPTER THREE

1. Nancy F. Cott, "Divorce and the Changing Status of Women in Eighteenth-Century Massachusetts," *William and Mary Quarterly*, 3d ser., 33 (1976): 611-12; Arrom, *The Women*, pp. 65-79. In a nineteenth-century variant, John Stuart Mill characterized women as "bond servant[s]" of their husbands. Deborah Gray White, *Ar'n't I a Woman? Female Slave in the Plantation South* (New York: Norton and Company Inc., 1985), p. 15.

2. Fewer brides brought a dowry to a marriage than we might have thought. Calvo has found only forty notarized dowries for all of Guadalajara in the seventeenth century. Thomas Calvo, "Matrimonio, iglesia y sociedad en el occidente de México: Zamora (siglos XVII a XIX)," in Gonzalbo, *Familias novohispanas*, p. 107n. One has the impression that there were more of them in more-established areas, in Mexico City perhaps, and in the cities of Spain. Lavrin and Couturier seem to have found more dowries, or at least traces of them, from Guadalajara and Puebla, to indicate that they were more frequently a part of the marriage arrangement, if not recorded fully as legal instruments, than Calvo's figures suggest. Asunción Lavrin and Edith Couturier, "Dowries and Wills: A View of Women's Socioeconomic Role in Colonial Guadalajara and Puebla, 1640-1790," HAHR 59 (2) (May 1979):282. Altman (*Emigrants and Society*) gives some examples of commoner dowries as part of the patronage of masters to servants (pp. 70-72) and as adopted by prosperous artisans (pp. 96, 98).

3. Arrom, *The Women*, pp. 62, 67-68; Lavrin and Couturier, "Dowries and Wills," p. 282.

4. Muriel, "La transmisión," p. 109.

5. In part this can be seen as getting rid of the paradox established by Gratian, who said that "Marriages contracted in secret are not denied to be marriages" but are "prohibited, inasmuch as if one of the parties changes his mind, the judge cannot believe the . . . other." Quoted in Gottlieb, "The Meaning of Clandestine Marriage," in Wheaton and Hareven, eds., *Family and Sexuality*, p. 52.

6. Ibid., p. 51; Wheaton, "Introduction," p. 11. The *información matrimonial*, or

marriage application, preceded Trent and, after the Confesionario of fray Alonso de Molina (1569), consisted of the petition, the authorization to proceed by the vicar general, the testimony attesting to the unmarried status of the petitioners, the statement by the petitioners that it was their will to marry, and the granting of a license to marry. María de Lourdes Villafuerte García, "Casar y compadrar cada uno con su igual: Casos de oposición al matrimonio de la ciudad de México, 1628–1634," in Seminario de Historia de la Mentalidades, Del dicho, pp. 66–67.

7. Ramón A. Gutiérrez, When Jesus Came, the Corn Mothers Went Away: Marriage, Sexuality, and Power in New Mexico, 1500–1846 (Stanford: Stanford University Press, 1991), p. 243; Lavrin, "Sexuality in Colonial Mexico," p. 84n. The Council of Trent redefined "incestuous" from applying to marriages or sexual relations between people related to the fourth degree to applying to those between people related to the second degree. Susan M. Socolow, "Acceptable Partners: Marriage Choice in Colonial Argentina, 1778–1810," in Lavrin, ed., Sexuality and Marriage, p. 237n5. Or to dispense with one or another procedural requirement, most commonly the full cycle of three amonestaciones, or reading of the banns, to invite the community to declare any knowledge they might have of valid impediments to the upcoming marriage. In 850 applications from 1628–34 in Mexico City, Villafuerte found 115 requests (13.5 percent) to dispense with three readings of the banns. The reasons given, in order of frequency, were to speed the marriage before parents could actively oppose it (n = 79), to accommodate one of the petitioners who was close to death (n = 14), to allow for departures for business or work (n = 8), and various other reasons (n = 14), including that of "hiding a difference in calidades." Villafuerte, "Casar y compadrar," pp. 67–68.

8. Gutierrez, When Jesus Came, pp. 241–70, but especially pp. 267–68, for the sacramental rite in the church setting. This is a kind of ideal version. Often there was no nuptial mass, but only a nuptial blessing; often the marriage itself took place out of sight of the priest or with him present, but in a private home; often there was a long gap between marriage and the velación, or priestly blessing. Calvo, finding the marriage and blessing increasingly fused as one event from 1727, suggests that this represents a culmination in the long campaign of the church to supplant the social with the sacramental aspect of marriage. Calvo, "Matrimonio," pp. 105–6; see also his Poder, religión y sociedad en la Guadalajara del siglo XVII (Mexico City: Centre d'études Mexicaines et Centraméricaines 1992), p. 169.

9. For a description of how parish records were supposed to be kept and how they were actually kept, see Morin, Santa Inés Zacatelco, pp. 19–20.

10. Gutiérrez, When Jesus Came, pp. 254, 227–29; Gottlieb, "The Meaning of Clandestine Marriage," p. 70; McCaa, "Gustos de los padres," pp. 586–91.

11. The term clandestine, Gottlieb shows, could cover a wide range of practices objected to by the church ("The Meaning of Clandestine Marriage," pp. 53, 67, 71–72).

12. But, as Seed has shown, for church officials to annul a marriage on grounds

of clandestinity would normally require a woman to testify that "she had [not] willingly participated in the sexual act . . ." Thus the existence of the impediment seemed directed more to protect the consent of contracting parties than to alter procedures as such. In French law clandestinity equated with abduction rather than elopement, because *clandestinité* meant "without parental consent" rather than "without proper formalities." Patricia Seed, *To Love, Honor, and Obey*, pp. 255n9, 32–34, 89–90, 275n49. See also Charles Donahue, Jr., "The Canon Law on the Formation of Marriage and Social Practice in the Later Middle Ages," *Journal of Family History* 8(2)(Summer 1983):114–45.

13. Seed, *To Love, Honor, and Obey*, pp. 34–35, 254n6; G. L. Mosse, "Changes in Religious Thought," in *The New Cambridge Modern History*, vol. 4: *The Decline of Spain and the Thirty Years War, 1609–48/49*, ed. J. P. Cooper (Cambridge, Cambridge University Press, 1970), pp. 185–87. Church as well as states in early modern Europe contended with the inertia of customary law as each encroached on ancient usage and tradition. Resistance became widespread during "the general crisis" of the seventeenth century.

14. John Lynch, *Spain under the Habsburgs* (Oxford: Basil Blackwell, 1964) 1:258 and 236–270.

15. J. H. Elliott, *Europe Divided 1559–1598* (Glasgow: Fontana/Collins, 1968), p. 162.

16. Seed, *To Love, Honor, and Obey*, pp. 35–40. An analogous and even more radical intrusion into the hitherto private lives of parishioners came with the Tridentine reform of the sacrament of penance. Priests in the confessional were instructed to stress that "the act itself" mattered less in one's focus of contrition than the origins of the act in "the stirrings of . . . desire." The result, Michel Foucault argues, was to "transform sex into discourse," to convert the secrets of desire, sensation, and bodily pleasure into "the nearly infinite task of telling— telling oneself and another . . . everything." Michel Foucault, *The History of Sexuality, vol 1: An Introduction*, trans. Robert Hurley (New York: Random House, 1978), pp. 19–20. See, as well, his chapter 1, note 41 and text, linking inquisitorial interrogations to the ethos of confession and penance. For the use of penance and confession among the Nahuas, see J. Jorge Klor de Alva, "Sin and Confession among the Colonial Nahuas: The Confessional as a Tool for Domination," in Sánchez, Van Young, and von Wobeser, *La ciudad y el campo* 1:91–101; and Serge Gruzinski, "Confesión, alianza y sexualidad entre los Indios de Nueva España: Introducción al estudio de los confesionarios en lenguas indígenas," Seminario de Historia de las Mentalidades, *El placer de pecar*, pp. 169–215.

17. Martínez-Alier, *Marriage*, p. 104.

18. That many avoided such intervention is evident from the stories of those who did not. Some friendships, for example, formed, endured for a time, and then broke apart without reference to policing mechanisms; others endured for many years before they were deemed 'illicit.'

19. Seed (*To Love, Honor, and Obey*), by examining cases of contested marriages,

explains patterns and circumstances in which children judicially resisted parental attempts to veto their choice of marriage partner.

20. AGN, Inq., vol. 138, exp. 6.

21. Elsewhere he said eight days. Note that this adds precision to the bald statement, quoted above, that he had fled after the nuptial.

22. By 1589 Pedro de Vega was a farmer living in Chalco. In Seville Pedro had booked passage for himself and Francisco with a Captain Villaviciosa, and they were in San Lucar for final embarkation when, at the last minute, Francisco fell ill and remained behind. For a year he stayed in Seville, avoiding contact with anybody in Lepe while waiting for the next year's sailing. He contacted Villaviciosa once again, sailed as his cabin boy, and joined Pedro in New Spain. My chronology depends partly on data collected by the Chaunus. In 1560 the Santa Catalina, a 500-ton galleon owned by Juan de Villaviciosa but captained by Basco Bello, sailed for New Spain. It was commandeered to act as the flag ship for the return to Spain. We also have another possibility. Miguel de Villaviciosa was master of the San Salvador, a 120-ton ship which returned to Spain from Santo Domingo in 1562. There is no record of this ship going to the Indies, and Miguel makes no other appearances as master of a ship. Huguette Chaunu and Pierre Chaunu, *Séville et l'Atlantique (1504–1650)* (Paris: Librairie Armand Colin, 1955–56) 3:19, 20–21n, 32; 4:284.

23. AGN, Inq., vol. 441, exp. 2, fs. 356r–411v.

24. It is worth thinking about why it should matter, since Ayamonte is relatively close by, in the diocese of Seville. On Mariana's part, distinguishing between the two suggests the precision with which people fixed tierra. On Manuel's part, one can imagine reasons to subsume the smaller place in the larger one, because it was less important or because it had been his more recent place of residence.

25. As we shall see in chapter 4, Mariana later regretted the marriage, ran away from Manuel, and remarried.

26. AGN, Inq., vol. 918, exp. 21, fs. 330ff. Rita was an espurio, the lowest category of illegitimates in Hispanic society. Borah and Cook, "Marriage," pp. 950–951; Twinam, "Honor," p. 119.

27. Murdo J. Macleod, *Spanish Central America: A Socioeconomic History, 1520–1720* (Berkeley: University of California Press, 1973), p. 115.

28. Gutiérrez, *When Jesus Came*, pp. 190 and 176–226. In general in the Indies, the ordinary estates that in Spain would pay taxes were exempted from them; instead Indian and caste tributaries carried the burden. Cayetano Reyes G., "Expósitos e hidalgos, la polarización social de la Nueva España," *Boletín del Archivo General de la Nación*, ser. 3, 5(2)(16)(April–June 1981):4. In eighteenth-century Virginia, the planter aristocracy constructed honor in racial terms, to align poor whites with themselves instead of with blacks who, in class terms, were their natural allies. Edmund S. Morgan, *American Slavery, American Freedom: The Ordeal of Colonial Virginia* (New York: W. W. Norton and Company, 1975), pp. 326–28 and 316–37.

29. Note that nothing is said of the marriage as such, the moment when a man and woman clasped hands and promised to be man and wife.

30. Lavrin, "Introduction," p. 6, "Sexuality," pp. 62–63; Seed, "Marriage Promises."

31. AGN, Inq., vol. 797, fs. 234–354.

32. On the contractual basis of marriage as drawn from Roman law, see James A. Brundage, "Sexual Equality in Medieval Canon Law," in *Medieval Women and the Sources of Medieval History*, Joel T. Rosenthal, ed. (Athens and London: University of Georgia Press, 1990), p. 68; Lavrin, "Introduction," p. 6.

33. Cott, "Divorce," p. 599.

34. Gutiérrez, *When Jesus Came*, pp. 255; McCaa, "Gustos," p. 593; Pescador, *De bautizados*, pp. 150–75.

35. Gutiérrez, *When Jesus Came*, p. 231.

36. AGN, Inq., vol. 91, exp. 9. Don Bernardino was the first-born son of don Hernán Pérez de Bocanegro (died 1567), *conquistador* of New Galicia, *encomendero*, and sometime *alcalde ordinario* (1537, 1543) and *alcalde de mesta* (1538, 1544) of Mexico City and acting viceroy of New Spain while don Antonio de Mendoza was fighting in New Galicia. Don Hernán entailed his property in favor of don Bernardino in 1564, but the advantage came to naught. Before he could enter into his inheritance, he was implicated in the revolt of the marqués del Valle in 1566. The court sentenced him to death, a fate he escaped only in the eleventh hour, when the sentence was commuted to loss of all property, twenty years' service in the King's coast guard, and perpetual banishment from all territories of the Spanish crown. Bocanegro spent his last days in Orán, still serving his sentence. Guillermo Porras Muñoz, *El gobierno de la cuidad de México en el siglo XVI* (Mexico City: UNAM, 1982), pp. 391–94.

37. A "Thomé de Vega, escribano," was granted a building lot in Mexico City on January 19, 1569. Edmundo O'Gorman, *Guía*, p. 416. Vega must have been an escribano attached to the corregidor or his lieutenant because Indian notaries writing in Nahuatl handled wills, deeds, and other legal instruments, and they also wrote out the documents that recorded matters of town government. The corregidor would have handled "petty squabbles over lands, debts, thefts, and women" and dealt with blacks, castas, and Spaniards as well as Indians. Gibson, *The Aztecs*, p. 91; S. L. Cline, *Colonial Culhuacan, 1580–1600: A Social History of an Aztec Town* (Albuquerque: University of New Mexico Press 1986), p. 37, and for Indian notaries, pp. 43–47.

38. Her dowry had included the encomiendas of Cuzamala (jurisdiction of Tetela del Río, now in the state of Guerrero), and half of Teutenango (jurisdiction of Tenango del Valle, now in the state of Mexico). Tribute from the two towns brought in about 5,000 pesos per year. Doña Isabel was the daughter of captain don Francisco Vázquez de Coronado, governor and captain general of New Galicia and explorer of New Mexico. Porras Muñoz, *El gobierno*, pp. 205, 268.

NOTES TO PAGES 70–73

39. Peter Lombard, in the middle of the twelfth century, proposed an essential distinction between words of future consent, a betrothal, and words of present consent, a marriage. The distinction became permanently imbedded in canon law. Both were binding, but difficulties arose when, for example, a man betrothed to a woman with whom he had not had sexual relations promised to marry a second woman with whom he had. In her phrasing Francisca seems to indicate that she understood the difference. Seed, "Marriage Promises," pp. 255–58; Lavrin, "Introduction," pp. 4–6.

40. Gutiérrez, *When Jesus Came*, pp.177, 179.

41. Martínez-Alier, *Marriage*, p. 111; Twinam, "Honor," p. 127. We shall return to this theme below.

42. Lesley Byrd Simpson, *Many Mexicos*, p. 133.

43. Richard Boyer, "Absolutism versus Corporatism in New Spain: The Administration of the Marquis de Gelves, 1621–1624," *International History Review* 4(4)(November 1982):475–503, argues that society and politics must be understood in terms of the personalistic ties at all levels of society.

44. The marriage to Alonso might not have been entirely satisfactory, to judge from a long-standing liaison Catalina had with Blas Mexía, while married to Alonso. Blas, a vecino of Mexico City seventeen years older than Catalina (age forty when he testified in 1573) said that he "had Catalina de Vega as his mistress (*concubina*) for four or five years but left her two years ago out of fear of his conscience." This may have been possible only because Alonso had abandoned Catalina for long periods.

45. Yet clandestinity was prohibited in the Laws of Toro, where Spanish family law was codified in 1369 and "promulgated for general use in 1505." Lavrin and Couturier, "Dowries and Wills," p. 282. Thus the reason for the royal pardon of the "penas en que incurrieron conforme a la ley de Toro" issued in 1518 to Alonso de Avila and doña Elvira Guillén and the witnesses present at their marriage. Francisco del Paso y Troncoso, compiler, *Epistolario de Nueva España, 1505–1818*. (Mexico City: Antigua Librería Robredo, de José Porrúa e Hijos, 1939–42) 1:31–32. Tridentine reforms had a full impact in the Indies by the end of the sixteenth century, but not before (Lavrin, "Introduction," p. 7), as the contrast in Catalina between 1563 and 1596 might imply. The decrees of the Council of Trent were ratified in a papal bull of January 26, 1564. Philip pondered for "many months" over whether to publish them in Spain and eventually consented "with the proviso that they did not encroach on the rights and privileges of the Spanish crown, especially in appointments to benefices." Lynch, *Spain* 1:245.

46. AGN, Inq., vol. 24, fs. 13–16v, 27–28, 60–81.

47. See note 32, above.

48. As well, given Francisco's age, he may have been concerned to keep the wedding out of public view (thus not requiring two of the public announcements of it), to avoid the charivaris that customarily accompanied marriages between people with such a large age discrepancy. Natalie Zemon Davis, *Society and*

Culture in Early Modern France (Stanford: Stanford University Press, 1975), pp. 105, 301n35.

49. The petition appears as direct speech, as indicated by my translation.

50. AGN, Inq., vol. 36, exp. 11, fs. 500–575.

51. A similar report had surfaced earlier in Zultepec, during the marriage investigation; Carreño extracted such strong denials from Pedro that he allowed the marriage to proceed.

52. The notary records some of Ana's testimony as direct speech and some as indirect. In the translated passage, the two are intermixed, and I have used the third person because it is dominant.

53. As Eugene Genovese argues, a reciprocal dependence also obtained in United States slave regimes: masters depended on the love and respect of their slaves, slaves on the paternalism, kindness, indulgence, and even discipline of their "'good' masters." Eugene Genovese, *Roll, Jordan, Roll: The World the Slaves Made* (New York: Vintage Books, 1976), pp. 70, 70–112.

54. AGN, Inq., vol. 325, exp. 6.

55. AGN, Inq., vol. 332, exp. 7.

56. AGN, Inq., vol. 605, exp. 2, fs. 189–278. La Barca was an alcaldía mayor in the region of Guadalajara (now in Jalisco state); Pénjamo and Piedragorda were in the jurisdiction of León (now in Guanajuato state).

57. AGN, Inq., vol. 1145, exp. 19, fs. 192–282.

58. AGN, Inq., vol. 1139, fs. 82–186.

59. Joseph found Nicolás a place to live in the neighborhood of San Gregorio.

60. Even casual bystanders, not masters as such, seemed eager to arrange the marriages of their inferiors, as did two strangers in 1691. The matchmakers were Luis Antonio, "a *coyote*, native to Guadalajara and unmarried and Francisco Barajas, a Spaniard, at that time in prison." The groom-to-be was Diego de Sosa, also in prison (hence the connection with Barajas), a free mulatto in jail for a homicide; the bride was the mulatto Lorenza de la Cruz, at the time under detention (*depositada*) in a private house in Guadalajara, on suspicion of being an escaped slave. The jailer and his wife acted as padrinos. This summary, coming from Lorenza's testimony, does not explain how either Barajas or Luis Antonio knew about her. AGN, Inq., vol. 526, exp. 2, fs. 37–151.

61. Gutiérrez, *When Jesus Came*, p. 242; Lavrin, "Sexuality," pp. 52–54.

62. Gutiérrez, *When Jesus Came*, pp. 267–68.

63. AGN, Inq., vol. 136, exp. 10.

64. Although Agustín pretended to hidalgo standing, he nevertheless did not merit the honorific "don," a title reserved for very few in the sixteenth century. As we saw in chapter 2, Agustín enjoyed an elite upbringing. He married twice in Spain, both times to daughters of *hombres nobles*, or noblemen. In 1580 he went with Philip II's armies to invade Portugal as company standard-bearer.

65. The characterization of Mari comes from a letter in the file written by Antonio de Hamaniego. That fray Juan and Mari had the same surname suggests

that they were related, but we cannot be sure, given the number of Gómezes in New Spain.

66. A reference to the estancia, one of eighteen in the district of Tlazazalca in a census of the bishopric of 1631, indicates that by then it had changed owners but perhaps not the size of its herds from fifty years before: "la estancia de Ucacuaro de Ana de Chávez cría (ciento y veinte) doscientas mulas que hierran cada año y siembra tres o cuatro fanegas de maíz." The figure of 120 mules is changed to 200 in Bishop Francisco de Rivera's hand, which could mean that he corrected an understatement, made perhaps to minimize tithe payments, after a first-hand assessment. Ramón López Lara, ed., *El obispado de Michoacán en el siglo XVII: Informe inédito de beneficios, pueblos y lenguas* (Collección "Estudios Michoacanos," 3; Morelia: Fimax Publicistas, 1973), p. 102.

67. AGN, Inq., vol. 24, fs. 13–16v; 27–28; 60–81.

68. Gottlieb, "The Meaning of Clandestine Marriage," p. 69.

69. Martínez-Alier, *Marriage*, pp. 122 and 103–19.

70. AGN, Inq., vol. 91, exp. 5.

71. For an instance of the "alliance-making" between servant and mistress to facilitate the latter's love affairs ("a potent, if unreliable weapon in women's campaigns to blunt male power"), see Elizabeth S. Cohen and Thomas V. Cohen, "Camilla the Go-between: The Politics of Gender in a Roman Household (1559)," *Continuity and Change* 4(1)(1989):53–77. I am grateful to Asunción Lavrin for this reference.

72. Boyer, "Juan Vázquez," pp. 436–40.

73. AGN, Inq., vol. 586, exp. 9, fs. 502–72.

74. AGN, Inq., vol. 548, exp. 4.

75. AGN, Inq., vol. 608, exp. 3, fs. 216–99.

76. Gutiérrez, *When Jesus Came*, pp. 210–11.

77. In answer to the question, "do you think one can marry a second time when a first wife is alive?" Marcos replied: "no, porque el santo sacramento del matrimonio trae consigo unión entre los que lo contrahen de tal manera que sino es con la muerte del uno de los casados no puede el otro casarse otra vez."

78. Increasingly because this case falls well before the late eighteenth century when, according to Seed, a "semantic drift" took place in the meaning of the word *love:* from "attachment or will," based on reason, to "uncontrollable sexual passion." Seed, *To Love, Honor, and Obey*, pp. 118–20.

79. The kind of strong feelings that drove Marcos to marry pushed others as well. In this the Spaniard Antonio de Acevedo (born ca. 1550 in Tordesillos), who in Oaxaca married Elvira Rodríguez in 1583, reminds us of Marcos. A year after the marriage, he told the inquisitors that "with the ecstasy (*arrebatamiento*) of love and ardor he was blinded to what he was doing in marrying a second time." AGN, Inq., vol. 135.

80. AGN, Inq., vol. 605, exp. 2, fs. 189–278.

81. Martínez-Alier, *Marriage*, pp. 122.

82. Gutiérrez, *When Jesus Came*, pp. 213–14.

83. AGN, Inq., vol. 1305, exp. 2, fs. 1–86.

84. This account comes from the testimony of the Spaniard don Manuel Francisco de la Torre of Querétaro, who nearly twenty years after the event (in 1745), in order to denounce Manuel as a bigamist, told of how he had married Josepha. Don Manuel recounted (and the notary recorded) Manuel's speech in the first person, as is reflected in my translation.

85. ". . . por el capto voluntario que hizo Liçona de la dicha su hija . . ."

86. Manuel and Josepha settled into a married life that in eleven years produced four children. Then about 1738, Manuel went to San Luis Potosí, "deflowered" an eighteen-year-old servant in his supposed half-brother's household, and eloped with her.

87. AGN, Inq., vol. 108, exp. 2.

88. AGN, Inq., vol. 22, exp. 8.

89. The final phrase as the notary recorded it from Ana's testimony is, "tomó acceso carnal con esta declarante."

90. Cervantes's novella "La fuerza de la sangre" contrives to solve the problem of rape in a similar way, though with a more romantic twist. Twenty-two-year-old Rodolfo, "whose wealth, base instincts, illustrious lineage, excessive freedom, and bad companions had spurred him on to deeds ill-suited to his station," raped the beautiful and virtuous Leocadia, the sixteen-year-old daughter of an "old hidalgo" of Toledo. Later Rodolfo's parents arrange a meeting of their son and Leocadia, as part of a scheme to induce him to marry her. Rodolfo, at this point ignorant of the fact that Leocadia is the woman he violated eight years before, at table becomes the object of Leocadia's desire and vice versa. With thoughts that jar a modern sensibility, Cervantes reconstructed Leocadia's thoughts: "seeing herself so near him who was dearer to her than the light of her eyes . . . [she] began to turn over in her imagination what had happened between her and Rodolfo. In her heart, she felt her hopes of becoming his wife begin to wane; she considered how close she was to being happy or hapless forever . . ." The message seems to be that the rape itself was a minor consideration in the face of possible reconciliation and marriage, the recovery of one's honor, and thereby the securing of happiness. Miguel de Cervantes, "La fuerza de la sangre," in *Spanish Stories/Cuentos Españoles*, ed. Angel Flores (New York: Bantam, 1960), pp. 64–91. The quoted passages are from pages 65 and 85.

91. AGN, Inq., vol. 108, exp. 4, fs. 291–92.

92. AGN, Inq., vol. 563, exp. 16, fs. 413–633.

93. Don Francisco's sister was doña Ana del Valle y Avila, a widow formerly married to don Pedro de Candinas, who had held "oficios de justicia," according to don Francisco, and also occupied himself with "the farms that he had in the [nearby] provincias of Tepeaca and Guaxoçingo."

94. AGN, Inq., vol. 790, exp. 1, fs. 1–200.

95. Gutiérrez, *When Jesus Came*, pp. 250–51.

96. AGN, Inq., vol. 26, exp. 4, fs. 83–114. The attribution *muger del mundo*, to be seen again below, was a male tactic to counter the claim by a woman that betrothal had preceded seduction. Lavrin, "Sexuality," p. 59. I have not seen the variant *muger mundana*, but it had exactly the same connotations. For examples see McCaa, "Gustos," pp. 599, 601, and for a juxtaposition of the two variants used as synonyms, 602. Apparently on occasion the adjective *mundana* could stand alone, thus becoming the substantive signifying the two-word phrase. François Giraud, "La reacción social ante la violación: Del discurso a la práctica (Nueva España, siglo XVIII)," in Seminario de Historia de las Mentalidades, *El Placer de Pecar*, p. 330.

97. Lavrin ("Sexuality," p. 62) points out that records to indicate that the women of colonial Latin America "regarded sexual intercourse as a pleasurable act or a source of enjoyment" have not been found. Leonor's testimony, I think, comes close, but remains only an inference based on her earthy demeanor and the way that she seemed to initiate liaisons.

98. Inns dispensed large quantities of pulque or wine. Laws attempting to limit the number of such outlets in Mexico City date from 1579, 1585, and 1586. Taylor, *Drinking*, p. 37. In the sixteenth century, towns in the Valley of Mexico began to shift production from maize to pulque, to supply "taverns with pulque along the entire route to Mexico City by 1590." Gibson, *The Aztecs*, p. 318. For the eighteenth century see, in addition to Taylor, Juan Pero Viqueira Albán, *¿Relajados o reprimidos? Diversiones públicas y vida social en la cuidad de México durante el Siglo de las Luces* (México City: Fondo de Cultura Económica, 1987), pp. 169–219, and Michael C. Scardaville, "Alcohol Abuse and Tavern Reform in Late Colonial Mexico City," HAHR 60:4 (November 1980), pp. 643–671.

99. One wonders what Leonor said to him and how he reacted. I cannot imagine that he found the incident amusing.

100. Not, apparently, because she spoke no Spanish, but possibly "in the name of juridical unimpeachability" because Nahuatl was presumed by the court to be her first language. Lockhart, *Nahuas and Spaniards*, p. 106. This may mean, then, that Nahuatl was Leonor's mother tongue, and her designation as "mulatto" included part-Indian parentage.

101. AGN, Inq., vol. 796, exp. 52, fs. 506–14. This comes from his second hearing before the inquisitors and therefore was not admitted the first time around. Miguel was born in Havana.

102. The distinction comes in a hypothetical dialogue between a confessor and a penitent, as the former probes to refine his understanding of the motivation behind this sin in Corella's seventeenth-century manual for confessors. P Fr. Iayme de Corella, *Práctica de el confessonario y explicación de las 65 Proposiciones . . .* [Valencia: Imprenta de Iaume de Bordazar, 1689], pp. 105–6. I am grateful to Asunción Lavrin for calling my attention to this work.

103. Corella stressed that in these cases it should be determined whether a discrepancy existed between the calidad and wealth of the man and woman. In

cases of discrepancy, marriage was not required; it was in cases of no discrepancy. He also advised clerics to suspect women who in such a circumstance might be trying to maneuver themselves into an advantageous marriage. Men, therefore, would be protected from the consequences of "the bedazzlement of deceptive passion" ("para no alucinarse con las tinieblas de la pasión engañosa"). Corella, *Práctica de el confessonario*, pp. 105–6.

104. Lavrin, "Introduction," p. 6. For Blas López, another example of the type, who was "notorious for wooing women with promises of marriage," see Gutiérrez, *When Jesus Came*, pp. 237–38. And it apparently became more frequent during the eighteenth century. Seed, "Marriage Promises."

105. Martin Luther observed a similar problem in Germany: "Rascals travel about from town to town, and wherever one of them sees a wench who takes his fancy he gets hot and starts thinking how to get her, and proceeds to get engaged again." Cited in Gottlieb, "The Meaning of Clandestine Marriage," p. 78n.

106. Martínez-Alier, after legislation by the Council of the Indies in 1780, also distinguishes between "'elopements for reasons of marriage'" and "elopement with a view to premarital concubinage." Martínez-Alier, *Marriage*, pp. 103–19.

107. Edward Shorter, *The Making of the Modern Family* (New York: Basic Books, 1975), p. 73.

108. Gutiérrez, *When Jesus Came*, p. 231. The exception, as we have seen, might be foundlings or illegitimate daughters, whom parents expected to remain permanently in households as 'servants'.

109. AGN, Inq., vol. 137, exp. 10.

110. In coming from a base three leagues away, the young man was working a territory of over three hundred square miles (an indication of the range but not necessarily the outer limits) within which mating took place in a sparsely settled zone. Marriage registers can chart the movements of people but more intimate sources, such as autobiographies in bigamy records, would be needed to construct some sort of 'geography of mating.' See Michael M. Swann's analysis of parish marriage data for Santiago Papasquiaro and San Juan del Río, in *Tierra Adentro: Settlement and Society in Colonial Durango* (Boulder: Westview Press, 1982), pp. 117–27.

111. This paragraph comes from Isabel's autobiographical statement (October 29, 1588). The judge was licenciado Antonio Maldonado.

112. AGN, Inq., vol. 834, exp. 24, fs. 410–91.

113. AGN, Inq., vol. 137, exp. 11.

114. A trial that resulted because he buckled under the pressure and married Luisa.

115. As we saw above, when the relatives of doña Clara Ochoa restored her honor by isolating Francisco del Valle in Puebla and forcing him to marry her.

116. AGN, Inq., vol. 466, exp. 14, fs. 329–82.

117. Possibly he received news that the estate was not worth the journey.

118. Lavrin, "Sexuality," pp. 65–66; Seed, "Marriage Promises," pp. 267–68.

119. The judges spared him the humiliation of public flogging, the normal fate of mestizos and mulattoes, but nevertheless sent him to serve five years rowing in the galleys.

120. AGN, Inq., vol. 815, exp. 1, fs. 1–133.

121. From the valley of Santiago Papasquiaro (Nueva Vizcaya), to Guadiana (Durango), to the shepherd's camp of don Gregorio Macías de Mendiola (near the valley of Súchil), to San Felipe, and finally to Potosí del Saltillo and the hacienda of don Pedro Montes de Ocá.

122. To judge from the pointedly negative comments made in 1755 by the bishop of Durango, don Pedro Anselmo Sánchez de Tagle, the diocese lacked clerics with talent, commitment, and industry. Guillermo Porras Muñoz, *Iglesia y estado en Nueva Vizcaya (1562–1821)* (Mexico City: UNAM, 1980), pp. 193–94. The comment may also be read as the criticism of a friar (one apparently ministering to an Indian suburb of Sombrerete) of the secular clerics in charge of the mining camp's Hispanic parishes. Gerhard, *The North Frontier*, p. 131.

123. AGN, Inq., vol. 814, exp. 4, fs. 390–482. Joseph was native to Tenancingo, an alcaldía mayor about ten leagues south of Toluca, now in Mexico state.

124. For a similar example that came to the archbishop of Mexico from the priest of Sultepec in 1789, the attorney recommended regularizing a consensual relationship, otherwise "he will elope with her and their souls will be left without remedy." Quoted in Lavrin, "Sexuality," p. 77.

Associating vagabondage with marriage irregularities was not peculiar to Isidro. Church authorities repeatedly ordered people living apart from their spouses to resume the *vida maridable* or married life (Corella, *Prática de el confessonario*, p. 60). Similar initiatives came from the viceroys, who periodically ordered that single males with no fixed residence be rounded up, to check on their marital status. In one of these Viceroy Guadalcazar commissioned doctor Damián Gentil Parragas in 1615 "to round up the vagabonds" in the city and district of Antequera. A denunciation of Juan de Guzmán said that he had a wife in Seville and also one in Mexico City. In fact Guzmán had married Luisa Téllez of Mexico City only two years before. Gentil ignored the more serious charge of bigamy and ordered him back to the vida maridable in Mexico City within twenty days, on pain of two years of forced labor in the Philippines. AGN, Inq., vol. 308, fs. 162r–162v. See also Boyer, "Juan Vázquez."

125. AGN, Inq., vol. 108, exp. 5.

126. Corella, *Práctica de el confessonario*, p. 60.

127. As an argument it implies that he had not given his consent, but it failed. The judges found him guilty and sentenced him to two hundred lashes and six years rowing in the galleys.

128. AGN, Inq., vol. 942, fs. 1–100.

129. *Mala vida* can refer to immoral ways and, more commonly, to ill treatment, lack of support, and overwork in general. Richard Boyer, "Women, La Mala Vida, and the Politics of Marriage," in Lavrin, *Sexuality*, p. 284n38.

130. AGN, Inq., vol. 22, exp. 3.

131. Cited in Borah and Cook, "Marriage," p. 950 (emphasis added).

132. Pierre Bourdieu, "Marriage Strategies as Strategies of Social Reproduction," in Forster and Ranum, *Family and Society*, p. 140.

133. Gottlieb, "The Meaning of Clandestine Marriage," p. 67. This of course was the basis for their undoing.

134. Seed has shown that arguments within parental oppositions stressed the future contentment of their children. Seed, *To Love, Honor, and Obey*, pp. 120–21.

CHAPTER FOUR

1. John Bossy, "The Counter-Reformation and the People of Catholic Europe," *Past and Present* 47 (May 1970):60.

2. Ibid., p. 15; André Burguière, "Le rituel du mariage en France: Pratiques ecclésiastiques et pratiques populaires (XVIII siècle)," *Annales: Economies, Sociétés, Civilisations* (33)(3)(May–June 1978):644. For the diocese of Cuenca, Nalle estimates that 80 percent of the populace were effectively catechized in the last two decades of the sixteenth century. Sara Tilghman Nalle, "Religion and Reform in a Spanish Diocese: Cuenca, 1545–1650," (Ph.D. diss., Johns Hopkins University, 1983), pp. 228–32. See also her "Popular Religion in Cuenca on the Eve of the Catholic Reformation," in Haliczer, ed. and tran., *Inquisition and Society*, pp. 67–87; and Dedieu, "The Inquisition and Popular Culture in New Castile," in Haliczer, *Inquisition and Society*, pp. 129–46. For the diocese of Coria, one sees a remarkable anticipation of Tridentine reforms in the work of Bishop Francisco Mendoza y Bobadilla (1536–50). Yet a diocesan *visita* of 1591 revealed a parish clergy still badly in need of discipline and direction in the carrying out of their pastoral duties. Don Francisco San Pedro García, "La Reforma del Concilio de Trento en la diócesis de Coria," *Hispania Sacra* 10 (2 a semestre 1957): 273–99.

3. As the model applies, see François Giraud, "De las problemáticas europeas al caso novohispano: Apuntes para una historia de la familia mexicana," in Seminario de Historia de las Mentalidades, *Familia y sexualidad*, pp. 58–59. I also deal with this connection, in Boyer, "Women," pp. 252–55.

4. Giraud, "La reacción social," p. 340.

5. Shorter, *The Making of the Modern Family*, pp. 222 and 218–27, provides a general orientation to the rest of the paragraph. See also Davis, *Society and Culture*, pp. 97–123. Concerning local marriageable women, one thinks of the high rates of village endogamy found by French demographic historians in the seventeenth and eighteenth centuries. For a brief overview, see André Burguière, "La historia de la familia en Francia: Problemas y recientes aproximaciones," in Seminario de Historia de las Mentalidades, *Familia y sexualidad*, pp. 18–22.

6. Bossy, "The Counter-Reformation," p. 54.

7. For instance there were the implications for married life that marriage was a

contract, or the so-called "clean-hands rule," which said that a husband could not hold his wife to higher standards of sexual morality than he himself practiced. Brundage, "Sexual Equality," pp. 67–68.

8. See as well the case study of Francisco Noguerol de Ulloa, who was forced into an unwanted marriage and escaped to the Indies. Alexandra Parma Cook and Noble David Cook, *Good Faith and Truthful Ignorance: A Case of Transatlantic Bigamy* (Durham and London: Duke University Press, 1991).

9. AGN, Inq., vol. 466, exp. 14, fs. 329–82.

10. AGN, Inq., vol. 797, fs. 234–354.

11. AGN, Inq., vol. 108, exp. 4, fs. 291–92.

12. AGN, Inq., vol. 699.

13. AGN, Inq., vol. 134, exp. 10.

14. Petronila's testimony provides a rare instance in which the scribe records her testimony as direct speech.

15. AGN, Inq., vol. 918, exp. 19, fs. 247–313. In a comparable case, Nicolás Sebastián, married to a mulatto slave on the sugar estate of Archillaga in Guatemala, left her after a marriage of only twenty days, because he determined to run away from his master. AGN, Inq., vol. 918, exp. 19, fs. 247–313.

16. AGN, Inq., vol. 834, exp. 24, fs. 410–91.

17. AGN, Inq., vol. 605, exp. 2, fs. 189–278.

18. AGN, Inq., vol. 108, exp. 5.

19. AGN, Inq., vol. 134, exp. 3.

20. AGN, Inq., vol. 608, exp. 3, fs. 216–99.

21. AGN, Inq., vol. 1066, exp. 4, fs. 168–176.

22. The practice, perhaps, is to be traced to patterns established during the Reconquest, when "conditions . . . encouraged irregular matrimonial initiatives by both men and women so that abduction and elopement, together with seduction and even rape, developed into a specific type of medieval courtship procedure." Heath Dillard, *Daughters of the Reconquest: Women in Castilian Town Society, 1100–1300* (Cambridge: Cambridge University Press 1984), pp. 135–36. Also, as Ruiz Gaytán reminds us, "adultery and seduction," as well as rape, were "middle and upper class moral dramas" but never much of an issue when working class or servant women were so violated. Beatriz Ruiz Gaytán F., "Un grupo trabajador importante no incluido en la historia laboral mexicana (trabajadoras domésticas)," in Elsa Cecilia Frost, Michael C. Meyer, and Josefina Zoraida Vázquez, compilers, *El trabajo y los trabajadores en la historia de México* (Mexico City and Tucson: El Colegio de México and University of Arizona Press, 1979), p. 433; see also the more complete, extremely useful analysis in Giraud, "La reacción social."

23. AGN, Inq., vol. 814, exp. 5 and 6, fs. 289–389.

24. At first she thought she had been called by the Inquisition because of her concubinage.

25. AGN, Inq., vol. 608, exp. 3, fs. 216–99.

26. AGN, Inq., vol. 815, exp. 1, fs. 1–133. Homicide and adultery with the

promise to marry was an invalidating impediment. Corella, *Práctica de el confessonario*, pp. 120–21.

27. AGN, Inq., vol. 595, exp. 20, fs. 456–538.

28. AGN, Inq., vol. 796, exp. 52, fs. 506–14.

29. AGN, Inq., vol. 108, exp. 2.

30. AGN, Inq., vol. 26, exp. 4, fs. 83–114.

31. AGN, Inq., vol. 22, exp. 11.

32. I take Campomayor to be El Campo "in Trujillo's tierra," which at that time had ninety-seven vecinos. Both villages were in the province of Cáceres. Altman, *Emigrants and Society*, p. 103.

33. AGN, Inq., vol. 108, exp. 7.

34. This from a conversation with the shoemaker Francisco López, after she returned to El Campo. He reported it in a deposition made in June 1572 in Vera Cruz.

35. AGN, Inq., vol. 137, exp. 4.

36. Cited in Mary Elizabeth Perry, *Gender and Disorder in Early Modern Seville* (Princeton: Princeton University Press, 1990), p. 14.

37. AGN, Inq., vol. 135. She wrote from Tordehumos, diocese of Palencia, jurisdiction of Medina de Rioseco

38. AGN, Inq., vol. 22, exp. 12. The quotations come from Beatriz's testimony, recorded as direct speech, in 1538.

39. AGN, Inq., vol. 820, exp. 1, fs. 1–52. This case is dealt with in more detail in Boyer, "Women," pp. 252–86.

40. For a discussion of how abandoned women might have supported themselves, see Perry, *Gender and Disorder*, pp. 14–32.

41. AGN, Inq., vol. 933, exp. 8.

42. Ibid.

43. AGN, Inq., vol. 136, exp. 9. His testimony dates from 1584.

44. AGN, Inq., vol. 23, exp. 5, fs. 23–29. This file, an *información* rather than a *proceso*, does not indicate how long Catalina had been alone.

45. For two examples, the first a woman traveling with her sister and brother-in-law, the second with her daughter and son-in-law, see AGN, Inq., vol. 250, fs. 238–44 and AGN, Inq., vol. 137, exp. 9.

46. AGN, Inq., vol. 606, exp. 4, fs. 381–414.

47. AGN, Inq., vol. 548, exp. 3.

48. AGN, Inq., vol. 25, exp. 4 and 5.

49. However, he was not among the conquistadores who made representations to the first viceroys (1540–50) for rewards for services. This is probably because he had shifted his base to Peru. Francisco A. de Icaza, compiler, *Conquistadores y pobladores de Nueva España: Diccionario autobiográfico sacado de los textos originales*, 2 vols. (Guadalajara: Edmundo Aviña Levy, 1969 [Madrid, 1923]).

50. Juan Núñez de Prado left Potosí late in 1549 with seventy soldiers (one of whom must have been Diego) and arrived in the Tucumán area in the early 1550s.

In 1552 he moved the original foundation of Tucumán, El Barco, fifty leagues to the south, where Santiago del Estero is located. Roberto Levillier, *Nueva crónica de la conquista del Tucumán* (Madrid: Sucesores de Rivadeneyra, 1927–31) 1:183.

51. This testimony, dated 1562, is part of Diego's proof of service collected, by his son Pedro in Lima.

52. Rumors kept arriving that Diego was alive, and the issue generated much talk. As we shall see in chapter 5, the talk (dividing into those who believed the rumors and those who rejected them) reflected political divisions in the community.

53. AGN, Inq., vol. 134, exp. 7.

54. AGN, Inq., vol. 134, exp. 13.

55. AGN, Inq., vol. 333, exp. 29.

56. Huntington Library, HM 35159.

57. The fleet left Spain in the last two weeks of May 1600 and on arrival at Vera Cruz (the exact date is unknown), fourteen ships were lost, because they failed to navigate the sandbar. Diego was therefore lucky to arrive unscathed. Chaunu and Chaunu, *Séville et l'Atlantique* 4:92, 99n.

58. Another example, in part already sketched in chapter 2, is that of Francisco de Riberos. He had married his first wife, María Francisca, in 1603 and after five months left her at home, when he embarked for Angola, Brazil, and Cabo Verde. Two years later he returned, but after two months he again embarked, to Cabo Verde and Brazil and to "different places," a series of voyages that took seven or eight years. Captured and "robbed" by the Dutch at sea, Francisco was eventually released and made his way to Seville. Throughout those eight years he had had no news of María Francisca and, as we have seen, allowed his employer to engineer a second marriage for him, without traveling to Conde to check if she were alive. AGN, Inq., vol. 325, exp. 6. See also the cases of Manuel de Campuzano (AGN, Inq., vol. 1234), mentioned in chapter 2, and Manuel Caballero (AGN, Inq., vol. 1387, exp. 1, fs. 1–121).

59. AGN, Inq., vol. 824, exp. 12, fs. 74–197.

60. AGN, Inq., vol. 1166, exp. 7, fs. 172ff.

61. Emphasis added.

62. Possibly Valle de San Francisco, where the Alamos mining camp was located, in the jurisdiction of Charcas, now in San Luis Potosí state.

63. AGN, Inq., vol. 1194, exp. 1, fs. 1–102.

64. Jan Bazant, *Cinco haciendas mexicanas: Tres siglos de vida rural en San Luis Potosí (1600–1910)* (Mexico City: El Colegio de México 1975), pp. 30–34.

65. AGN, Inq., vol. 524, fs. 190–257.

66. AGN, Inq., vol. 548, exp. 3.

67. Cited in Glen Caudill Dealy, *The Latin Americans: Spirit and Ethos* (Boulder: Westview Press, 1992), p. 36n35.

68. AGN, Inq., vol. 441, exp. 2, fs. 356–411v. Mariana was a creole Spaniard.

69. Manuel, who surely was anxious to resume control over his wife, probably

devised the plan that brought Mariana from safety. He enlisted the help of Mariana's friend, Francisca de Garibay, who (as Mariana recounted it) went to the convent and told [Mariana] to go back to her house and she would give her whatever she needed. She was not to be afraid, because Manuel had fled after [Francisca] complained to the viceroy, the marqués de Mancera, telling him that Manuel Figueroa had given her the mala vida and abusive treatment, [because] he was going to send Manuel to China [that is, the Philippines].

70. Cott, "Divorce," pp. 611–612.

71. In a later period (1800–1857), Arrom found that twenty-one of forty-nine men who made petitions or countercharges in divorce cases "held in-laws responsible" for their marriage problems, and four of these even "threatened to kill their mothers-in-law." Yet only two in a sample of eighty-one (women initiated sixty-nine cases and men initiated twelve) cited in-laws as the problem. Perhaps an additional five cases, in which marital discord was linked to couples living with parents, could represent instances of women in conflict with mothers-in-law. Arrom, *The Women*, pp. 247–49 and appendix C.

72. AGN, Inq., vol. 1336, exp. 14, fs. 1–70. Córdoba was an alcaldía mayor, now in Veracruz state. Leocadia Gertrudis López, a Spaniard who acted as Lucía's sponsor in the wedding, confirmed that Lucía ran away "because of the bad treatment (*malos tratos*) of her mother-in-law."

73. AGN, Inq., vol. 1192, fs. 1–85. Although María was born of Spanish parents, she was orphaned at four months and raised in the convent of Santa Clara in Mexico City. At fourteen she went to live with a sister and in 1772, a year later, married the mestizo José Antonio Santos. José was from San Juan Teotihuacán and a farmer (labrador) in nearby Tepexpan. As José was a man of humble standing, María had not gained much by marrying him. However, as an orphan she did not have the economic leverage to do better. Whatever the logic of the match, it was an unhappy one.

74. María ran away to Mexico City and served sister Gertrudis Gil in the convent of San Lorenzo. Five months later, however, three aunts of her husband, José Antonio Santos, saw María on the street, took her to the priest of Santa Catalina, and notified José. José came and brought María back to Tepexpan to resume married life.

75. Davis, *Society and Culture*, pp. 124–51, especially pp. 145 and 313n37.

76. AGN, Inq., vol. 1128.

77. Her mother was probably a widow, for nothing is said of her father.

78. In Mexico don Joseph married a second time, in 1772, and the Inquisition arrested and tried him for bigamy. To the inquisitors in 1774 he told a more embellished story than the brief summary in the text suggests. He apparently hoped they would accept it as justification for the abandonment of doña Francisca. The day of the wedding, he said, "a *compañero* and friend said, 'what have you done, man? This woman is a descendant of Jews.'" For good measure, don Joseph added, the same friend "after some years" told him that doña Francisca had died. The

inquisitors were not impressed. They found don Joseph guilty and sentenced him to abjure a light suspicion of heresy (abjure de levi), to receive two hundred lashes, and to serve in an African presidio (to be determined by the Supreme Council of the Inquisition in Madrid) for six years.

79. AGN, Inq., vol. 1139, fs. 82–186.

80. AGN, Inq., vol. 1279, exp. 13, fs. 1–99. The quotation comes from his autobiographical statement.

81. Structural factors that moderated treatment, according to Davis, were common economic cause, sexual dependence, concern for children, and "shared religious interest." Davis, *Society and Culture*, p. 145.

82. Behar, "Sex and Sin," pp. 34–54, especially 41, 46, and 52n; Calvo tabulates for the region of Guadalajara that women accounted for 89 percent of the users of magical remedies and that men made up 81 percent of the targets of these remedies. Overwhelmingly, then, the behavior has a setting and logic connected with gender. Calvo, *Poder*, pp. 208–25.

83. AGN, Inq., vol. 137, exp. 5.

84. She also gave birth to two children during this time.

85. Although the courts were lenient with men who murdered their wives or lovers, as Lipsett-Rivera and Pescador have shown. Sonya Lipsett-Rivera, "La violencia dentro de la familia formal e informal," unpublished paper, Coloquio Familia y vida privada en la historia de Iberoamérica, May 3–4, 1993, Mexico City; Juan Javier Pescador, "Uxoricidas-indultados: Justicia, familia y patriarcado en el México central, 1770–1820," unpublished paper, Coloquio Familia y vida privada en la historia de Iberoamérica, May 3–4, 1993, Mexico City.

86. Lipsett-Rivera found two cases, both very late (1790 and 1800), in which wives murdered their husbands by poisoning them. Both at the time had other lovers, who supported their action: the one directly by providing the herb; the other psychologically, by demonstrating a more kindly behavior that contrasted with her husband's beatings. Lipsett-Rivera, "La violencia," pp. 19–20.

87. María did not indicate how she knew he thought her dead. Presumably she spoke later to a neighbor who had got this from Domingo himself, as he was leaving.

88. This point is developed in more detail in Boyer, "Women," pp. 237–270.

89. Corella, *Prática de el confessionario*, p. 62.

90. Ibid., pp. 65–66. In his commentary Corella cites Tiraquel, who says that a husband may not strike his wife under any circumstances. But he counters this with three other authorities. Juggling authorities, of course, constituted a 'proof.' But more importantly for our purposes, it illustrates a range of opinion from which Corella and others writing books of application might choose. In spite of variations in both the theoretical and applied literature, I assume that applied moral theology as represented in the confessional manuals does not stray far from consensus on fundamentals, for example the assumption of patriarchal authority in the family. The important principle here, however, was that "in a Christian society it was the

priests alone who were qualified to pronounce upon the bond that brought society into being, to pronounce on the faith." Walter Ullmann, *Medieval Political Thought* (Baltimore: Penguin, 1975), p. 81.

91. Secular law followed a parallel path, allowing husbands to administer "moderate physical punishment" but, at the same time, called "wife beating" a crime. Arrom, *The Women*, p. 72.

92. AGN, Inq., vol. 1292, exp. 7, fs. 1–101. In going she also left her son with his grandfather (her father-in-law).

93. The courts, and probably wives and acquaintances, considered drunkenness a mitigating circumstance, but "drinking was not," as Taylor stresses, "accepted as a license to kill." Taylor, *Drinking*, p. 104; Giraud, "La reacción social," p. 332.

94. "In almost all cases of crime against single women," Socolow points out in her study of women and crime in late colonial Buenos Aires, "the female victim was usually presumed both by the court and the social norms to have deserved the injury." Susan Migden Socolow, "Women and Crime: Buenos Aires, 1757–97," in Lyman L. Johnson, ed., *The Problem of Order in Changing Societies: Essays on Crime and Policing in Argentina and Uruguay, 1750–1940* (Albuquerque: University of New Mexico Press, 1990), p. 10.

95. Giraud, "La reacción social," p. 329.

96. AGN, Inq., vol. 441, exp. 2, fs. 356r–411v.

97. In about half of the cases of wife murder studied by Lipsett-Rivera, someone tried to intervene, but in only three of fourteen instances of the murder of a lover did anyone try to stop the violence. If 'outsiders' were reluctant to intervene in these extreme cases, one would think they would be even more likely to hang back in cases of less-serious beatings. Lippsett-Rivera, "La violencia," p. 15.

98. AGN, Inq., vol. 1180, fs. 14–98. The household also included Juan's brother Antonio García, a "farmer," and his wife, María de la Concepción de los Reyes, who had been padrinos of Juan and Rosa's marriage.

99. Taylor, *Drinking*, pp. 83–97, 153. Later when Rosa ran away with another man, Juan pursued with intent to kill.

100. AGN, Inq., vol. 1214.

101. María lived with Raymundo for five months, until Ramón returned and took her to Guanajuato with him. Six years later she took up with Raymundo once again (in the meantime he had married), this time for nine months. All of this remains hazy and ill-defined, because references to this period of María's life in the file are brief and not mentioned in sequence. What is clear, however, is that Ramón treated María badly, and on at least two occasions she used Raymundo as a way to escape him.

102. AGN, Inq., vol. 29, exp. 11, fs. 102–412.

103. This is from Juan's testimony of November 1566.

104. AGN, Inq., vol. 1156, exp. 13, fs. 309ff. In the same statement, he points more directly to his reason for separating from Ignacia after a six-year marriage

(1764–70). "At the end of 1770 he separated from her because of the 'annoyances of imprisonment' because his brother-in-law Marcos de la Cruz had him arrested for 20 pesos that he owed him."

105. The circumstance that the liaison was blatant may have caused Ignacia some loss of face, but it also had a consolation. Its notoriety meant that it could not evolve into a permanent household, as did another one later. Later Miguel, living with his mistress Francisca Mendoza, an Indian, on an hacienda in the district of Huasca (probably Guzcacasaloya, a subcabecera of Atotonilco el Grande, five leagues or so north of Pachuca; Gerhard, *A Guide*, p. 337), faced the ultimatum of a local priest who, with the hacienda administrator, told Miguel that he must separate or marry. Fearful that he would be imprisoned or whipped for this illicit relationship, a usual practice of this priest, Miguel married a second time.

106. Ruth Behar, "Sexual Witchcraft, Colonialism, and Women's Powers," in Lavrin, ed., *Sexuality and Marriage*, p. 183.

107. AGN, Inq., vol. 796, exp. 52, fs. 506–14.

108. She described his visits as follows: "The first time he came with his brother and stayed a few days. The second and third times were last May when she was sick. He came by and she complained to him with tears that she was poor and destitute. But he had only come to pick up a hat that he had left the last time he was in Mexico City. She didn't see him again until last Thursday afternoon [June 1722] when he came with his uncle, both on horseback, and stayed until Saturday. He slept at the house every night but took his meals outside and then the Inquisition arrested him."

109. AGN, Inq., vol. 1156.

110. AGN, Inq., vol. 964, exp. 4, fs. 211–302.

111. AGN, Inq., vol. 91, exp. 5.

112. He had sponsored the child of Gómez and Francisca at baptism.

113. Parry, summarizing the *Recopilación de Leyes de Indias*, notes that applicants obtained the title *escribano real* or *escribano real de las Indias* by proving, with notarized depositions, "Old Christianity," *limpieza de sangre*, honesty, and professional competence." Normally, this documentation would be "submitted to the audiencia in whose district the applicant proposed to practise," and if all was in order that body issued a provisional title to be confirmed by the crown. J. H. Parry, *The Sale of Public Office in the Spanish Indies under the Hapsburgs*, Ibero-Americana 37 (Berkeley and Los Angeles: University of California Press, 1953), p. 6. In Gómez's case the dowry had funded his trip to Madrid where he obtained his position.

114. Villafuerte García, "Casar y compadrar," p. 66.

115. AGN, Inq., vol. 1073.

116. AGN, Inq., vol. 130.

117. Yet as Socolow found and we shall see below, married women willingly engaged in sexual relations sometimes. And more clearly than I have found, Socolow finds husbands tolerating adultery, probably because they "were either

ashamed or afraid to file charges with the local judge." Socolow, "Women and Crime," p. 12.

118. AGN, Inq., vol. 526, exp. 2, fs. 37–151.

119. AGN, Inq., vol. 370, exp. 3, fs. 307–20.

120. Based on the Jesuit hacienda La Sieneguilla, Francisco was returning from Mexico City, where he had gone in the service of Father Pedro Sánchez of the society.

121. AGN, Inq., vol. 1341.

122. AGN, Inq., vol. 548, exp. 5.

123. AGN, Inq., vol. 332, exp. 7.

124. The hacienda, called La Magdalena, was located next to the pueblo of Santiago Tlacotepec (Cuautla Amilpas?).

125. AGN, Inq., vol. 972, exp. 1.

126. AGN, Inq., vol. 547, exp. 6.

127. Gerónimo Guerra, a Canary Islander, also believed that his wife, Catalina Pérez, "a Cuban Indian," was unfaithful, but he did not explain why. Gerónimo abandoned her in 1582, after eight years of "living badly married (*mal casado*) and discontented." The problem: "He knew full well . . . that none of the children that his wife had borne were his but of others." AGN, Inq., vol. 135, exp. 6.

128. AGN, Inq., vol. 272, exp. 1, and vol. 262, exp. 6.

129. AGN, Inq., vol. 548, exp. 4.

130. Shorter, *The Making of the Modern Family*, p. 57.

131. AGN, Inq., vol. 1194, exp. 1, fs. 1–102. José and Inés both were classified as castas.

132. AGN, Inq., vol. 1089, exp. 1, fs. 1–108.

133. Andrés served as a cowherd on Hacienda de las Prietas, near Ixtlahuacan (Metepec).

134. Bárbara's departure with Bernadino broke, at least for the time being, two marriages. In spite of efforts to apprehend her and Bernadino for concubinage (officials arrested them within two weeks), they escaped their detention and stayed together for at least a year.

135. AGN, Inq., vol. 942, fs. 1–100. The incident took place in 1740 or so, after five or six years of married life in San Juan Zacatepec.

136. AGN, Inq., vol. 1277, exp. 11, fs. 1–60.

137. AGN, Inq., vol. 547, exp. 8.

138. Testifying in 1706 Hypólita said that she stayed a year; Matías said that it had been two months.

139. "Por ser tan orrorosa de condición." His appearance had indeed suffered some degeneration, to judge by the more clinical description of the notary of the Inquisition: "a small, thin man; his face dark, long, and withered; his beard grayish with a moustache; a scar in the middle of his forehead; dark eyes; the lower teeth rotten, the upper [ones] missing."

140. AGN, Inq., vol. 262, exp. 3.

141. The notary describes Mariana as *"una India muy ladina,* resident in barrio Santa María la Redonda in the house of the Spaniard Lucía de Monroy, age 26."

142. AGN, Inq., vol. 308, fs. 99rff.

143. AGN, Inq., vol. 548, exp. 3.

144. AGN, Inq., vol. 136, exp. 10.

145. This was Agustín's second marriage. His first, in 1561, was to Cazilda Alonso, who died in 1570.

146. AGN, Inq., vol. 381, exp. 7.

147. At this point Nicolás owed his debt to Sierra who, to indenture his labor for the specified time, gave a lump sum to Sicher to clear the amount Nicolás owed. We do not know why Sierra 'subleased' Nicolás to Caro, although it probably represented only a short-term assignment.

148. Richard Boyer, *La gran inundación: Vida y sociedad en la ciudad de México (1629–1638),* trans. Antonieta Sánchez Mejorada (Mexico City: Secretaría de Educación Pública, 1975), pp. 31–66.

149. AGN, Inq., vol. 135, exp. 3.

150. Information about Antonio comes from the testimony of Diego de Valdez, a ship's carpenter, in a deposition of 1581.

151. Antonio said this to Juan de Xojeca, who was interviewing Antonio at San Juan de Ulúa on behalf of the Inquisition. Xojeca relayed his summary of the conversation in a letter received in Mexico City on July 6, 1583.

152. A comparable husband-wife division of labor was that of Miguel Avila and Manuela Hernández, fruit dealers in Tulancingo. We know about it because in 1737 their two children, Francisco and Juana María, were padrinos of the marriage celebrated between the mestizo Nicolás Arauz and the Indian María Rosa. Later, testifying to confirm the marriage in a bigamy trial, they mention as asides the work of their parents. Juana María explained that "her father is a muleteer and her mother a fruit dealer in the plaza of this pueblo [Tulancingo]"; Nicolás Arauz said that "[they] worked together, he going to Guachinango [about twenty miles] once a week for fruit and she selling it in Tulancingo." AGN, Inq., vol. 1139, fs. 82–186.

153. AGN, Inq., vol. 657, exp. 3, fs. 300–23.

154. Note his exegesis of her words as if she meant them literally. Surely he would have understood her metaphorical meaning all along, as the form of the insult would have been common. I suspect that he is speaking rather woodenly to the Inquisitors here, because he associates the tribunal with the search for Judaizers.

155. AGN, Inq., vol. 794, exp. 24, fs. 226–322.

156. Thompson, *Thomas Gage's Travels,* pp. 68–69. A circumstantial point, the timing of María's pregnancy, also supports the supposition. Testifying in 1736, María said that she had a daughter who was born "three or four months after marrying" Joseph Francisco de Chavarría in 1721, a young mulatto coachman, shoemaker, and all-purpose laborer. María's mother had been against Joseph Francisco's suit, but don Joseph talked her into giving her consent. Joseph Francisco's

autobiographical statement of December 1736 corroborates the timing, saying that he had an illicit friendship with María Micaela for a month, and then a little more than two months later he married her. Don Joseph's longer association with María and the fact that he urged her mother to allow the marriage point to his paternity. Moreover the level at which don Joseph sponsored the marriage (he made his coach available and, at his house, hosted the celebration) suggests a level of patronage more indicative of master and mistress than master and servant.

157. And also went with them when they moved to Encarnación Street and later to La Cruz del Factor. Encarnación, running east-west, was four blocks north of the plaza mayor; Cruz del Factor refers to the second of two streets called del Factor, because in the small plaza formed by the intersection of it and La Canoa there was a fountain, at the spout of which stood a cross. José María Marroqui, *La Ciudad de México*, 2d ed. (Mexico City: Jesús Medina, 1969) 2:401–5.

158. Joseph left with a troupe of actors heading for Zacatecas.

159. AGN, Inq., vol. 374, exp. 11, fs. 146ff.

160. I have been influenced here by the useful general orientation in James C. Scott, *Domination and the Arts of Resistance: Hidden Transcripts* (New Haven and London: Yale University Press, 1990), pp. 1–16.

CHAPTER FIVE

1. As opposed to the view that 'shaping' incidents into stories leaves us no mimetic view of them. Bigamy trials can be seen as analogous to criminal trial proceedings of the Florentine Public Health Magistracy in Calvi's depiction of them as 'theater' played out between judge and defendant. Calvi, *Histories of a Plague Year*, p. 56.

2. Attending to "how narratives are put together" can provide evidence about tellers and their audience and therefore the society in which they are embedded. Davis, *Fiction in the Archives*, pp. 4–6.

3. Consider, for example, Bernal Díaz's well-known account of the Spaniards' visit to the Huitzilopochli pyramid. "Before we had climbed a single step the great Montezuma ordered six papas and two chieftains to descend from the top—where he was making his sacrifices—to accompany our captain. And as he climbed the steps which were 114 in number, they tried to take his arms and help him in the ascent, as they helped their lord Montezuma, thinking that Cortés would tire but he would not let them come near." Bernal Díaz del Castillo, *Historia de la conquista de Nueva España*, intro. and notes by Joaquín Ramírez Cabañas (Mexico City: Editorial Porrua, 1970), p. 173. In addition to detail (114 steps, Cortés's would-be escorts of six papas and two chieftains), one is also struck by a firm sense of sequence ("*before* we had climbed a single step") and of his 'making sense' of the motivation for Montezuma's ordering the escort for Cortés ("thinking that Cortés would tire"). Compare the kind of detail in Díaz's narrative with the more dissociated datum of women's declarations of their ages when applying to marry in

late-eighteenth-century León. Here Brading and Wu found that specificity shades into stylization: "for some reason 18 and 20 were more favoured than 17 and 19. For the older bride 25 was attractive. At the younger limit both 15 and 16 were acceptable." David Brading and Celia Wu, "Population Growth and Crisis: León, 1720–1816," *Journal of Latin American Studies* 5 (1973):13.

4. After Aristotle, verbal "imitations" of specific events, that is *history*, can be opposed to those of "typical" events, that is philosophy. The first requires the specific and the concrete, the second abstracts the former into patterns. Frye, *Anatomy of Criticism*, pp. 82–83.

5. See Kenneth Burke's way of getting at motives by treating "language and thought primarily as modes of action," which he calls "dramatism." Burke, *A Grammar of Motives*, p. xxii.

6. François Chevalier, "New Perspectives and New Focuses on Latin American Research," *Newsletter* [Conference on Latin American History] 21(1)(April 1985):14.

7. AGN, Inq., vol. 308, fs. 140–140v.

8. There is nothing in this file other than the denunciation itself. Given that Meléndez still resided in Antequera, one would have expected further inquiries and possibly his arrest. It is possible that he ran off before he could be detained— possibly to Havana. Additional documentation might have been lost, or may be extant in another file.

9. AGN, Inq., vol. 136, exp. 10. The quotation below comes from a letter, and Antonio therefore uses direct speech.

10. See above for some analysis of Hoz's counteraccusation that Cuellar was not to be trusted because he was a personal enemy.

11. AGN, Inq., vol. 308.

12. Years later, when the affidavit was taken, pieces of testimony such as González's had become linked to the external significance of the inquisitorial inquiry, which was trying to establish the existence of a bona fide marriage.

13. AGN, Inq., vol. 137, exp. 5.

14. AGN, Inq., vol. 595, exp. 20, fs. 456–538.

15. The hacienda is described by Matías as "seven leagues from Guatemala City, next to a village called Excuitan [Escuintla?]."

16. The mention of several sugar haciendas in Las Amilpas might make it seem to be near Cuautla, but Matías' account of his going there only a week later while "*discurriendo*" with his goods makes it more logical to place it in or near his usual orbit in the Soconusco area. Alcedo has an entry under Amilpas as "two volcanoes in the province of Guatemala in New Spain, near the mountains of Soconusco." G. A. Thompson, *The Geographical and Historical Dictionary of America and the West Indies* . . . (New York: Burt Franklin, 1970) 1:49.

17. Given that Matías knew immediately that Sebastián was the alleged escapee, he could have reported him to the authorities. He did not, however, and neither did he immediately relay this information to Domingo, who found it out from don

Antonio de Aguilar's sons. Both men were concerned to verify the accusation before they took the matter further.

18. AGN, Inq., vol. 1088, fs. 211–74.

19. Locals commonly scrutinized strangers, and the need for this was embedded in legislation or custom. Receptions combined a watchful welcome fueled by curiosity and the eagerness for news from the outside, but with the awareness that a newcomer might disrupt the community. An ordinance for São Paulo in 1831 reflects the latter: "No one may give lodging or rent a house to a person unknown in this municipality for more than twenty-four hours without his first being presented to the cognizant Justice of the Peace and obtaining from him a declaration of his entry, and only with this document may he be given residence." Quoted in Richard M. Morse, *From Community to Metropolis: A Biography of São Paulo, Brazil*, new and enlarged ed. (New York: Octagon Books, 1974), p. 34.

20. AGN, Inq., vol. 526, exp. 2, fs. 37–151.

21. AGN, Inq., vol. 1305, exp. 2, fs. 1–86.

22. AGN, Inq., vol. 610, exp. 11, fs. 233–384.

23. Barbola's civil status was single (*soltera*) but not virginal (*doncella*).

24. The question appears as direct speech and in familiar voice: "¿No te acuerdas deste mulato y quando se casó?"

25. AGN, Inq., vol. 1194, exp. 1, fs. 1–102.

26. From the context of the document, Puesto de Coyotes (an estancia?) would have been near Armadillo, a pueblo in the jurisdiction of San Luis Potosí (twenty-five miles or so to the northeast), now in San Luis Potosí state.

27. The pro forma dimension of the exchange is evident in that Pedro had just seen José's wife. Possibly he knew that he had more up-to-date knowledge of her than José himself! Another reading is possible, therefore: that Pedro asked the question ironically, to discomfit José.

28. AGN, Inq., vol. 1192, fs. 1–85.

29. According to Aguirre Beltrán, one of the main tasks of the Inquisition was to remain "alert and vigilent to prevent the small conquistador group from being absorbed and dominated by the ideas of the great conquered mass and of the enslaved population." Gonzalo Aguirre Beltrán, *Medicina y magia: El proceso de aculturación en la estructura colonial* (Mexico City: Instituto Nacional Indigenista, 1963), p. 78.

30. Calvo suggests that Indian magic was "one of the few forms of revenge they could use against their oppressors." Calvo, *Poder, religión y sociedad*, p. 211. Alberro differentiates between "empirical" and "destructive" witchcraft and suggests that the former (to gain lovers, find lost objects, etc.) was more common than the latter (to maim, kill, or ruin someone). The witches of Celaya early in the seventeenth century were without exception "despised" (*despreciadas*), but at the same time they were respected for their 'services' to the community and were therefore treated with deference. Alberro, *Inquisición y sociedad*, pp. 303, 310.

31. AGN, Inq., vol. 1199, exp. 29, fs. 214–62.

32. AGN, Inq., vol. 1128. With this obsession don Joseph fits the profile of many men of the era, dating at least from the early seventeenth century, who tried to find hidden treasure or rich mines by consulting shamens or witches. Alberro, *Inquisición y sociedad*, p. 299.

33. Aguirre Beltrán (*Medicina y magia*) documents a number of cases; Alberro, *Inquisición y sociedad*, pp. 183–84, although her entire chapter (pp. 283–341) is essential reading.

34. AGN, Inq., vol. 1128.

35. See John Beard Haviland, *Gossip, Reputation, and Knowledge in Zinacantán* (Chicago and London: University of Chicago Press, 1977), pp. 68–90, for a rare contemporary study that strikes me as analogous to my concern in this chapter. As for content see especially his table 2 (p. 74), in which many marriage-related categories can be recombined to become overwhelmingly the dominant topic of gossip in Zinacantán.

36. AGN, Inq., vol. 312, exp. 73, fs. 428–93.

37. Antonio reported this to Anna, he said, because earlier, on mentioning the same news to the coachman Juan Bautista (of Puebla), Juan had told him that Juan Francisco (according to Anna) was married in Cádiz. She became a kind of clearing house for pulling the fragments of the story into a coherent whole.

38. Antonio added to this that Luis de Morales and his son Diego, his relatives no doubt, presently in Puebla but residents of Oaxaca, would be able to confirm the marriage in Oaxaca, because of their "knowledge of the said city." Luis, called an *obrajero*, owned or at least had an interest in a textile factory in Oaxaca. My guess is that it produced silk cloth that was marketed by his kinsman Antonio in Puebla and also possibly in Mexico City.

39. AGN, Inq., vol. 1156.

40. AGN, Inq., vol. 594, exp. 9, fs. 534–619.

41. Dias de la Cueva acted as "interpreter of indigenous peoples of this province." However, Sebastián de la Cruz, a young man who served him and who also called himself an interpreter, may have been the source of his knowledge of Indian languages. Sebastián's background and early life with his Indian mother is documented in this proceso, whereas Dias' is not.

42. Apparently he had not known before this moment that Juan Ruiz was his father.

43. Probably she would have meant clarification of her status and regaining control of her property. The notary, as indicated by my translation, records her plea to Juan as direct speech.

44. Thompson, *Thomas Gage's Travels*, pp. 45–46.

45. AGN. Inq., vol. 525, exp. 51.

46. AGN, Inq., vol. 548, exp. 4.

47. Almost certainly Joseph Hidalgo, owner of the biscuit factory, and Miguel Hidalgo, owner of the mule teams, were related and in some sort of partnership: Joseph manufacturing hardtack for sea voyages, Miguel transporting it to Veracruz.

48. AGN, Inq., vol. 1138, fs. 211–341.

49. They married in 1734, lived together five years, and had two children.

50. AGN, Inq., vol. 310, exp. 7.

51. The uncle was Christóbal's eponym and the head of the cathedral chapter in Seville.

52. The reported conversation comes from don Francisco's testimony of July 12, 1616. Note that the notary recorded it as direct speech.

53. Christóbal was about ten years older than don Francisco.

54. I infer the last because Antonio did not even know Ojeda's Christian name.

55. Fray Juan was guardian of the Franciscan monastery and, as calificador, judged whether suspicious behavior implied heresy.

56. AGN, Inq., vol. 36, exp. 11, fs. 500–575.

57. This patronizing stance has a parallel in the "disdainful" attitude of inquisitors and commissioners to reports of witches and witchcraft. In the words of a former alcalde of Celaya in 1614, these had to do with "plática común y de vulgo (no inclinándose a creerlo)." Cited in Alberro, *Inquisición y sociedad*, p. 294.

58. AGN, Inq., vol. 136, exp. 10.

59. Agustín affected an hidalgo style, although he was penniless. Cuellar had counted on more generosity and seems to have assumed that Agustín had not been forthcoming because of ill will rather than penury.

60. AGN, Inq., vol. 138, exp. 5.

61. Later they would rearrest him but on the basis of more evidence, and he would confess that the charge had been true.

62. AGN, Inq., vol. 24, exp. 3, fs. 109–126v, 143–155.

63. It could not have been quite so public, for the woman was left unnamed to prevent complications should her husband find that she was so charged.

64. Men in the Indies without their wives were legally supposed to return within three years. Guillermo F. Margadant, "La familia en el derecho novohispano," in Gonzalbo, *Familias novohispanas*, p. 45.

65. AGN, Inq., vol. 25, exp. 4 and 5.

66. AGN, Inq., vol. 441, exp. 2, fs. 356–411v.

67. AGN, Inq., vol. 25, exp. 4 and 5.

68. AGN, Inq., vol. 657, exp. 1, fs. 125–75. As well as having more weight as sources of information, the rich and well-born were more likely to get away with rude remarks, irreverent opinions, and rebellious acts. Alberro, *Inquisición y sociedad*, pp. 383–98.

69. AGN, Inq., vol. 819, exp. 8, fs. 21–60.

70. AGN, Inq., vol. 523, fs. 131–257.

71. AGN, Inq., vol. 595, exp. 20, fs. 456–538.

72. On the general principle as applied to "witnesses most likely to gain credence from a Spanish court," see Woodrow Borah, *Justice by Insurance: The General Indian Court and the Legal Aides of the Half-Real* (Berkeley and Los Angeles: University of California Press, 1983), p. 242. See also Karen Spalding, "Social Climb-

ers: Changing Patterns of Mobility among the Indians of Colonial Peru," HAHR 50(4) (November 1970):646.

73. AGN, Inq., vol. 608, exp. 3, fs. 216–99.

74. AGN, Inq., vol. 332, exp. 7.

75. The combination of being both a woman and an Indian would have put Juana at the lowest rung of credibility within the Spanish judicial system. Giraud, "La reacción social," pp. 329, 332.

76. AGN, Inq., vol. 606, exp. 10 and 11, fs. 578–613.

77. The Spanish word is *fierro*, which could have been chains, branding irons, plowshares, or other iron implements.

78. As might be expected, Spaniards had few problems in accepting 'good' news borne by Indians as true. The "mestizoed Spaniard" (*español amestizado*) Isidro del Castillo married a second time, he said, because of a report that reached him in the town of Tumba while he was en route to Mexico City to sell straw. "He heard from different Indians of San Andrés [jurisdiction of Chalco, now in the federal district] that his wife and stepfather had died." Perhaps this in itself would not have led to a second marriage, except that shortly afterward a priest of Chalco arrested Isidro for living in concubinage and told him that he had to marry. So in this tight spot, he did, with no evident concern that the report had come from Indians. AGN, Inq., vol. 814, exp. 4, fs. 390–482.

Similarly Laureano de la Cruz, after a long separation (six to eight years?) from his wife, received word from "Juan Manuel, an Indian with a mule team who was carrying sugar" that his wife had died. He added, however, that he "didn't believe it completely." Yet as with the report from San Andrés, it had come directly from his wife's home town. A kind of calculated probability, pushed by the fact that such news would have been personally convenient, was the basis for accepting it as true. AGN, Inq., vol. 1277, fs. 1–111.

79. AGN, Inq., vol. 605, exp. 2, fs. 189–278.

80. AGN, Inq., vol. 137, exp. 9.

81. AGN, Inq., vol. 308, fs. 99ff.

82. Perhaps the only ones willing to risk withholding evidence of bigamy from the Inquisition, as we saw above, were blood or fictive relatives of a bigamist. In March 1701, for example, Pedro Guerrero of Tescuco admitted that he had remained silent to protect his compadre, Joseph el Gachupín. AGN, Inq., vol. 544, exp. 23, fs. 463–81.

83. AGN, Inq., vol. 108, exp. 4, fs. 291–92.

84. AGN, Inq., vol. 1139, fs. 82–186.

85. AGN, Inq., vol. 134, exp. 8.

86. Christóbal sent Diego de Pastrana and Francisco de Castillo, the first a man with his surname, the second with that of the godfather. Not only do we see relatives approaching relatives for information, therefore, but also that the Castillos, the Pastranas, and the Ojedas were all dealing in silk and based both in Puebla and Mexico City as family connections intermeshed with professional ones.

87. AGN, Inq., vol. 134, exp. 3.

88. Diego, at that point, described himself as a forty-two-year-old fruit dealer and vecino of Mexico City.

89. The sentence was pronounced on March 6, 1575.

90. AGN, Inq., vol. 815, fs. 456–573.

91. So María remembered his homecoming, in her denunciation of him a year or so later.

92. Such covert methods would not have surprised the inquisitors. At night they frequently arranged for "nocturnal spying" outside prison doors so that notaries could record conversations when prisoners spoke less guardedly. They kept this procedural irregularity a secret from the Suprema. Alberro, *Inquisición y sociedad*, p. 235.

93. AGN, Inq., vol. 381, exp. 7. He was found out in August 1634, when some lads from the obraje told him that in the market they had run into a black woman who was looking for him and who said she was his mother-in-law. They were scandalized because they knew him to be married to a woman in the obraje.

94. AGN, Inq., vol. 23, exp. 8, fs. 69–153.

95. AGN, Inq., vol. 1231, exp. 9, fs. 171–287. José had been living for four years in the pueblo of Parangaricutiro, seventeen leagues or so west of Pátzquaro, in the bishopric of Valladolid.

96. AGN, Inq., vol. 136, exp. 3. Catalina Gómez, age thirty-four, was a widow (probably a recent one) and came to the Indies to live with her sister (unnamed) and brother-in-law, Claudio de Arziniega, in Mexico City.

97. It is puzzling that Juan does not know González's Christian name, given their friendship. Juan was fourteen years younger than González, having left Toledo when he was fifteen and González twenty-nine. Is it possible that as a youth he addressed him in other terms?

98. AGN, Inq., vol. 797, fs. 234–354. Juan declared that he was twenty-seven in 1741, which would make the year of his birth four to six years before this marriage.

99. He said "1708 or 1710," but the parish register dates the marriage to April 18, 1707.

100. Joseph's birth year works out to be about 1686.

101. Pedro died in the hospital in Mérida, probably in 1741, before having an audience with the inquisitors. In Spain Juana died in July of the same year, after living for six years in the hospital of San Juan de Letrán in Bexar de la Frontera.

102. AGN, Inq., vol. 317, exp. 1. From Diego's testimony to the inquisitors on June 10, 1615.

103. Yet it seems puzzling that Diego, Antonio's denouncer, would also help him avoid arrest. Here is his account: "Last night Antonio Pinero embarked in a small boat for the town of Campeche because he knew and understood that this charge against him was pending and the witness, with Luis Díaz, helped Antonio set sail and begin his trip."

104. AGN, Inq., vol. 1066, exp. 4.

105. AGN, Inq., vol. 543, exp. 11, fs. 141–75.

106. This part of the conversation, as reported by Manuel and recorded by the notary, is written as follows: "tenga Vd. que no soy Bartolomé que no soy esa persona." The formal, even stiff phrasing (assuming the notary's accurate transcription) implies at the very least Bartolomé's attempt to distance himself from his old acquaintance, accompanied by the tension of a possible unmasking of his assumed identity. Note too its style: polite, correct, formal, distant, and used by a 'stranger' (one evidently superior in calidad) to address an inferior.

107. See the relevant section in chapter 3 for more on this aspect of the case.

108. David Brading, for purposes of a different discussion, has characterized European settlement in comparable terms, "as a network of urban knots connected by the fine lines of commercial credit and family relation." David A. Brading, "Government and Elite in Late Colonial Mexico," HAHR 53(3) (August 1973): 394.

109. Taylor, Drinking, p. 67. Noting the extreme amounts of alcohol consumed in Mexico City, Taylor judges that "an unknown but surely significant part of the liquor was consumed by the tens of thousands of rural people who flocked to the city for periods of a few days or weeks at a time." Many have discussed the centrality of Mexico City in the life of New Spain. See, for example, Lockhart, "Capital and Province," pp. 99–123, especially 109; Leslie Lewis, "In Mexico City's Shadow: Some Aspects of Economic Activity and Social Processes in Texcoco, 1570–1620," in Altman and Lockhart, eds., Provinces of Early Mexico, pp. 125–53; John M. Tutino, "Provincial Spaniards, Indian Towns, and Haciendas: Interrelated Agrarian Sectors in the Valleys of Mexico and Toluca, 1750–1810," in Altman and Lockhart, Provinces of Early Mexico, pp. 177–94. In Richard Boyer, "Mexico in the Seventeenth Century: Transition of a Colonial Society," HAHR 57(3)(August 1977):455–78, I focus on a period when the metropolis was dominant in spite of considerable regional self-definition and autonomy. Population figures for late-eighteenth-century Mexico City, compiled by Keith Davies, can be found in Richard Boyer and Keith Davies, Urbanization in 19th Century Latin America: Statistics and Sources (Los Angeles: UCLA Latin American Center, 1973), p. 41; Kicza, Colonial Entrepreneurs, pp. 1–5. For some figures from the seventeenth century, see Boyer, La gran inundación, pp. 31–32 and 56–66. For the sixteenth century, see Gibson, The Aztecs, pp. 377–81.

110. AGN, Inq., vol. 308, fs. 140–140v.

111. AGN, Inq., vol. 1102, exp. 1, fs. 1–130.

112. AGN, Inq., vol. 1279, exp. 13, fs. 1–99.

113. AGN, Inq., vol. 794, exp. 24, fs. 226–322.

114. AGN, Inq., vol. 1139, fs. 187–287.

115. In fact the understanding must have been merely an oral one, for Orchate

apparently failed to make provision for her freedom in his will. Instead she became the property of his widow. Yet her promised freedom loomed large in the marriage negotiations with Nicolás, for both María and her mother said that official confirmation would be only a formality.

116. Note that Nicolás got the name and address of a suitable notary and then searched him out. This means that he did not simply wander around blindly and engage the services of the first notary he ran into.

117. The file does not specify his exact relationship to the deceased, but I assume a close one.

118. María and Nicolas give us a glimpse of provincials in Mexico City who visit for administrative or judicial purposes. A notion of how frequently such visits occurred from small and distant places is suggested by the visits of delegations from Indian villages to the capital for hearings before the General Indian Court. Resolution of a given litigation frequently required many visits over a period of years. Borah, *Justice by Insurance*, especially the cases he summarizes, pp. 120–226.

119. AGN, Inq., vol. 1341. Gerhard, after Bishop Mota y Escobar, characterizes the port early in the seventeenth century as "a colony of Greek fishermen intermarried with Negroes," and in the eighteenth, as populated mostly by mulattoes. Gerhard, *A Guide*, pp. 361–62.

120. Probably the epidemic of 1736–39. Gerhard, *A Guide*, p. 182.

121. There is no indication that Ramírez saw a discrepancy between this and Magdalena's letter stating that he himself had caused her death by stabbing. The original presumption, perhaps, was that the knife had not finished María off immediately but only after infection and "fevers" had done their work.

122. Acceptable proof of a spouse's death would consist of notarized transcriptions of an entry in a parish register. In practice, as we have seen throughout, people relied on the word of compatriots, muleteers, and other travelers, and on news sent in letters.

123. Yet how to explain the actual message that María had died? No answer can be given, but we can cite the equally improbable instance of Francisco Noguerol de Ulloa's two sisters, both nuns, falsely sending him 'news' that his wife died. Their ploy, part of an attempt to bring him home so he could comfort his elderly mother before she died, was based on the assumption that he would not return as long as his wife was alive. Cook and Cook, *Good Faith*, pp. 102–4.

124. AGN, Inq., vol. 1062, exp. 2.

125. Chiautla and Piastla both had alcaldes mayores during the colonial period, the second a dual seating with Acatlán. They lie in the border zone of the states of Puebla and Guererro. Gerhard, *A Guide*, pp. 42–44, 108–9.

126. AGN, Inq., vol. 308, fs. 110–11.

127. This file is as interesting as it is fragmentary. There is no indication that it went beyond Hernández's initial denunciation. One of the letters is inserted in the file (fol. 111). A substantive problem that cannot be resolved with the documen-

tation is that Rodríguez appears to have resided in Sombrerete for five years or so, and the baby obviously was conceived in January 1613. Hernández, I think, mistook his friend in Sombrerete for the Rodríguez of the letters. Others with similar suspicions often did more checking before going to the Inquisition.

128. AGN, Inq., vol. 256, exp. 5.

129. AGN, Inq., vol. 1192, fs. 1–85.

130. That Hypólita de Alcántara (born ca. 1666 in Mexico City) avoided her husband, Matías, even while observing him in Mexico City, also demonstrates that anonymity was possible. She knew, for example, when he went to live in his parent's house near the Alameda, and also when he moved to Puebla with a cohort in his craft, the embroiderer Mateo. As Hypólita avoided Matías, he, after his release from the obraje, searched for her (*por muchas y varias diligencias*) in a little drama of hide-and-seek that lasted about a year and a half. AGN, Inq., vol. 547, exp. 8.

131. Huntington Library-12-HM35106-Pt. 2.

132. The date of Rivera's trial was 1603, only two years after the mining camp was settled. He may have been among the first to arrive at a time of rapid settlement of the area, for Vázquez de Espinosa reports 120 vecinos and many transients there in 1604. Gerhard, *The North Frontier*, pp. 192–95.

133. AGN, Inq., vol. 1180, fs. 14–98.

134. AGN, Inq., vol. 1013. He attained the rank of corporal or sergeant, it seems, for he was a "squad leader" (*cabo de escuadra*). His first appearance before the inquisitors is dated October 3, 1760.

135. AGN, Inq., vol. 310, exp. 3.

136. AGN, Inq., vol. 23, exp. 10, fs. 166–226.

137. AGN, Inq., vol. 1277, fs. 1–111.

138. AGN, Inq., vol. 824, exp. 12, fs. 74–197.

139. AGN, Inq., vol. 610, exp. 11, fs. 233–384. I discuss this case in more detail in Richard Boyer, "Slavery and the Inquisition in New Spain: A Note on the 'Closed System' Thesis of Stanley Elkins," in Jeffrey Cole, ed., *The Church and Society in Latin American History* (New Orleans: Tulane University Latin American Center, 1984), pp. 125–37.

140. AGN, Inq., vol. 972, exp. 1.

141. AGN, Inq., vol. 699.

142. It is possible that a group of confidence men specializing in preparing forged testimony centered in Veracruz. Havana, like Veracruz, was a vital point of contact with Spain, as we can see in two examples. Francisco de Riberos received news there "from people of his home that his mother was dead," a message that just as easily could have reached him in Veracruz (AGN, Inq., vol. 325, exp. 6). In another case Pedro García Bullones, already in New Spain in 1536, tried to get his wife, Isabel Rodríguez, to join him (AGN, Inq., vol. 22, exp. 2). At least once he sent for her and later also returned to Spain, to bring her to the Indies. En route for a second attempt to collect her, Pedro ran into a compatriot in Havana, who told him she had died.

143. In Riberos's case, cited in the previous note, from Conde, four leagues from Oporto.

144. AGN, Inq., vol. 23, exp. 5, fs. 23–29.

145. AGN, Inq., vol. 526, exp. 7, fs. 380–98. See the reference to other cases involving similar inquiries from Seville in chapter 4.

146. AGN, Inq., vol. 135, exp. 1.

147. AGN, Inq., vol. 1246.

CONCLUSION

1. Paso y Troncoso, *Epistolario* 7:248.

2. Paso y Troncoso, *Epistolario* 11:144.

3. Jiménez Rueda, *Don Pedro Moya de Contreras*, p. 49.

4. The Seminar on the History of Mentalities and Religion in Colonial Mexico goes further. After Althusser, they hypothesize "the Church as the ideological apparatus of the dominant state." They seem to mean by this that church teachings conflate to the interests of the dominant classes who controlled the state, a supposed connection I have commented on elsewhere. My concern here is the more modest one of showing some examples of the mentality of ordinary people, or in different terms, some results of the so-called imposition of church ideology. The term *imposition* might seem more appropriately applied to Jews and native people than to those who had been born into and indoctrinated in Christian ideology for generations. However, Christianity was not static, and in early modern times, particularly in the post-Tridentine period, the church made a number of encroachments on popular culture, to exert more control over the lives of people. Sergio Ortega Noriega, "Seminario de historia de las mentalidades," pp. 100–18; Richard Boyer, "Escribiendo la historia," pp. 119–37.

5. AGN, Inq., vol. 1242, exp. 19, fs. 262–316.

6. AGN, Inq., vol. 1266, exp. 8, fs. 246r–311v.

7. Ricard, *Spiritual Conquest*, pp. 102–3.

8. AGN, Inq., vol. 1089, exp. 1, fs. 1–108.

9. AGN, Inq., vol. 1279, exp. 13, fs. 1–99.

10. AGN, Inq., vol. 441, exp. 2, fs. 356–411v.

11. AGN, Inq., vol. 24, exp. 6, fs. 157–249.

12. Later in his statement, Alonso says something a little different about Juan's practice of hearing the mass: "He knows that Juan López hears mass in the three churches every Friday that he is in the city."

13. AGN, Inq., vol. 1292, exp. 7, fs. 1–101.

14. AGN, Inq., vol. 605, exp. 2, fs. 189–278. It seems that Pedro is calling himself a "*miserable*" in the juridical sense, perhaps hoping to put himself under special jurisdiction as "weak and wretched," thereby to be granted the special procedures reserved for such people. Borah, *Justice by Insurance*, pp. 11–12; Lyle N. McAlister, *Spain and Portugal in the New World, 1492–1700* (Minneapolis:

University of Minnesota Press, 1984), pp. 395–96; Spalding, "Social Climbers," p. 646.

15. C. H. Haring, *The Spanish Empire in America* (New York: Harcourt, Brace & World, 1947), pp. 267–68. The *cruzada*, or the sale of indulgences, was actually a tax disguised as a charity. Introduced during the Reconquest, it was authorized by the popes to fund the expansion of Christianity against the infidel and, although collected by religious officials, went into the royal treasury. Of course purchasers also benefited, in that indulgences reduced temporal punishments for sins levied at the time of sacramental absolution.

16. AGN, Inq., vol. 1246.

17. AGN, Inq., vol. 1194, exp. 1, fs. 1–102.

18. AGN, Inq., vol. 23, exp. 10, fs. 166–226.

19. The clear sequence also serves to underscore his good faith in not marrying a second time until after hearing of his wife's death.

20. AGN, Inq., vol. 606, exp. 10 and 11, fs. 578–613.

21. Surprisingly Esquival himself seemed unsure of what to do, and referred Francisco to another priest named Soriano, who told Francisco to go to the Holy Office and confess his sin, "because [as Pedro remembered] if your first wife is still alive clearly you cannot marry a second time when you are a faithful Christian Catholic."

22. AGN, Inq., vol. 1066, exp. 4, fs. 168–76.

23. AGN, Inq., vol. 317, exp. 1.

24. AGN, Inq., vol. 921, exp. 29.

25. AGN, Inq., vol. 922, exp. 1.

26. AGN, Inq., vol. 548, exp. 4.

27. Which he dated as "the year that the fleet of the black vomit, as it was called because so many were sick, arrived at Vera Cruz."

28. Contrition was distinguished from attrition (the mere fear of punishment), which "destroys the efficacy of the sacrament." Donald J. Wilcox, *In Search of God and Self: Renaissance and Reformation Thought* (Boston: Houghton Mifflin, 1975), p. 259. Pedro and Juan, in their internal struggle with contrition and attrition, suggest considerable internalization of ideals connected with the sacrament of penance.

29. AGN, Inq., vol. 796, exp. 52, fs. 506–14.

30. Missing in this file is the judgment and sentencing, so we do not know how successful Miguel's defense was. From the way it was proceeding to this point, I think it unlikely that it had much effect. For a more elaborate case detailing how a "streetwise" woman presented herself to the Inquisition as a simple innocent, see Richard L. Kagan, *Lucrecia's Dreams: Politics and Prophecy in Sixteenth-Century Spain* (Berkeley, Los Angeles, Oxford: University of California Press, 1990), especially pp. 32, 138, 144.

31. AGN, Inq., vol. 1277, fs. 1–111.

32. In fact death always lay close by and ready to strike, with or without warning. Almost any sickness or injury could prove fatal, and the afflicted often seemed

more likely to die than to survive. The Spaniard Vicente Valles, for example, assumed that his wife had probably died, although the last news he had of her was only that she had fallen ill. It had come, he explained in his "self-denunciation" of March 1760, in 1759, after eleven years of marriage and the birth of five children, in a letter she sent from Madrid "in someone else's hand for she does not know how to write" and reported her as "very sick with stomach pains" and six months passed and he did not hear any more, whether she was dead or alive, so he married again. AGN, Inq., vol. 1066.

From Oaxaca Ana Hernández had made this same assumption about her husband in Toledo. The issue came up in 1555, when she was charged with bigamy and witnesses testified that he was alive. Authorities ordered her to return to him, but she delayed, thinking it seems, that the longer she waited the more likely he would be dead. By December 1560 she was arguing that he was probably dead "because he is, as he was when she married him, a very old man and also sick." After failing to locate him (she sent letters and 10 pesos with Alexo Rodríguez, who was traveling to Spain and Toledo), she presumed that if old age had not killed him, then 1557, the "year of pestilence in Toledo when many died of hunger," surely would have finished him off. AGN, Inq., vol. 36, exp. 10, fs. 402ff. Without direct information to work with, Vicente and Ana worked with probabilities. Ill health, aging, epidemics, famine (all combined in Ana's case) pointed to the likelihood of death.

More difficult and more fearsome were deaths unaccompanied by advance signs. In 1620 the Spaniard Hernando de Rosas, a man apparently in good health then in his midforties, embarked for New Spain from Manila but failed to survive the crossing. AGN, Inq., vol. 333, exp. 29. "Today, January 20, 1621, while sailing for New Spain [wrote Pedro Pérez de Arteaga, scribe of the galleon San Andrés], I saw Hernando de Rosas, a passenger of this ship, die of natural causes of a sickness that God gave him and thus I saw his body thrown into the sea."

Not that men and women in their forties were not showing signs of aging. Above we saw forty-two-year-old Matías Cortés with a "withered" face, scarred forehead, and teeth either missing or "rotten." AGN, Inq., vol. 547, exp. 8. At thirty-nine Joseph Muñoz de Sanabria's four prominent arrow scars on his right leg were a reminder of his close call in a skirmish with Indians in Nuevo León, twenty years before. AGN, Inq., vol. 815, exp. 1, fs. 1–133. Even minor problems were notable, because they could become major. Juan de Xojeca, investigating Alonso Sánchez Navarro for the Inquisition, expected to identify him, at least in part, by a cyst on his forehead. AGN, Inq., vol. 135, exp. 3. Juan noted that the cyst was gone, but in clinical detail explained why he supposed it recently removed: "Above the left eyebrow in the temple is a scar as large as the first joint of the index finger and because it is not deep or accompanied by bruising and has healed well, it appears that the cut was made with a sharp instrument in order to remove the cyst."

33. AGN, Inq., vol. 333, exp. 29.

34. AGN, Inq., vol. 441, exp. 2, fs. 356–411v. And before she became sick, "she

heard the mass every day at Santa Teresa, and for the past two years she has always confessed; the last time that she took communion was in her house while she was sick in bed." Five days later a doctor reported that Mariana "had a miscarriage ten days ago and with the humidity of her cell is suffering from attacks of tumors in her neck." On that same day she complained of "aching in her bones and some tumors in her neck." Nearly four months later, on July 6, she again asked the inquisitors to consider her medical condition, complaining that she was "very sick and dying because she has chill in her bones that does not let her sleep at night and often causes her to faint." Doctor don Diego Osorio agreed that she was in "manifest danger of dying," and because of this the inquisitors finally acted, ordering that "because of the continuous dampness and water in the said cells which cannot be dried out now because it is the rainy season, [Mariana] be moved with her maid to the apartment or room where the jailer and his wife live."

Don Diego was to monitor her condition daily. A month later, Mariana said she was still suffering fainting spells and again asked the judges to speed their deliberations. They came to a decision on September 2, almost exactly six months after Mariana's arrest, absolving her on the grounds that her second marriage had been entered into in good faith, on the reasonable assumption that her first husband was dead. For more on the dampness of the Inquisition cells, see Alberro, *Inquisición y sociedad*, p. 223.

35. AGN, Inq., vol. 1214, exp. 11, fs. 126–245.

36. AGN, Inq., vol. 608, exp. 3, fs. 216–99.

37. AGN, Inq., vol. 1277, exp. 10, fs. 1–35.

38. AGN, Inq., vol. 922, exp. 1.

39. AGN, Inq., vol. 548, exp. 4. For a discussion and sample of these tragic results of the confinement of imprisonment by the Inquisition (a product of boredom, isolation, interminable imprisonments, and unbearable psychological pressure), see Alberro, *Inquisición y sociedad*, pp. 252–60.

40. AGN, Inq., vol. 595, exp. 20, fs. 456–538.

41. D. A. Brading, "Tridentine Catholicism and Enlightened Despotism in Bourbon Mexico," *Journal of Latin American Studies* 15(1)(1983):22. Lockhart also reminds us that "some important features of the social organization of Spanish America did not change perceptibly during the 300 years of the colonial period." James Lockhart, "Social Organization and Social Change in Colonial Spanish America," in Leslie Bethell, ed., *The Cambridge History of Latin America* (Cambridge: Cambridge University Press, 1984) 2:266.

Bibliography

Archival and Manuscript Sources

AGN. *Archivo General de la Nación, Mexico City*

Ramo Inquisición: vols. 22; 23; 24; 25; 26; 29; 36; 90; 91; 108; 134; 135; 136; 137; 138; 250; 256; .261; 262; 272; 308; 310; 312; 317; 325; 332; 333; 347; 370; 374; 381; 399; 441; 466; 508; 523; 524; 524; 525; 526; 543; 544; 547; 548; 563; 580; 586; 592; 594; 595; 605; 606; 608; 610; 642; 648; 657; 699; 790; 794; 796; 797; 814; 815; 816; 819; 820; 824; 834; 918; 919; 921; 922; 933; 942; 964; 969; 972; 978; 1013; 1062; 1066; 1073; 1088; 1089; 1102; 1104; 1128; 1138; 1139; 1145; 1156; 1161; 1166; 1180; 1192; 1194; 1199; 1207; 1214; 1231; 1234; 1242; 1246; 1258; 1266; 1275; 1277; 1277; 1279; 1292; 1301; 1305; 1336; 1341; 1364; 1371; 1387.

The Huntington Library

HM 35106-Pt. 2; HM 35159.

Books and Articles

Aguirre Beltrán, Gonzalo. *Medicina y magia: el proceso de aculturación en la estructura colonial.* Mexico City: Instituto Nacional Indigenista, 1963.

Alberro, Solange. "Beatriz de Padilla: Mistress and Mother." In *Struggle and Survival,* ed. Sweet and Nash, pp. 247–56.

————. *Inquisición y Sociedad en México, 1571–1700.* Mexico City: Fondo de Cultura Económica, 1988.

————. "Juan de Morga and Gertrudis de Escobar: Rebellious Slaves." In *Struggle and Survival,* eds. Sweet and Nash, pp. 165–88.

————. *La Actividad del Santo Oficio de la Inquisición en Nueva España 1571–1700.* Mexico City: Instituto Nacional de Antropología e Historia, 1981.

Alonso Romero, María Paz. *El Proceso Penal en Castilla (siglos XIII–XVIII)*. Salamanca: Ediciones de la Universidad de Salamanca, 1982.

Altman, Ida. *Emigrants and Society: Extremadura and Spanish America in the Sixteenth Century*. Berkeley and Los Angeles: University of California Press, 1989.

Altman, Ida, and James Lockhart, eds. *Provinces of Early Mexico: Variants of Spanish American Regional Evolution*. Los Angeles: UCLA Latin American Center Publications, 1976.

Archivo General de la Nación, México. *Catálogo del Ramo Inquisición* (1). Revisado y corregido por Guillermina Ramírez Montes. Serie: Guías y Catálogos 42. Mexico City: Departamento de Publicaciones del Archivo General de la Nación, 1979.

Arrom, Silvia Marina. *La muger mexicana ante el divorcio ecclesiástico, 1800–1850*. Mexico City: Secretaría de Educación Pública, 1976.

_____. *The Women of Mexico City, 1790–1857*. Stanford: Stanford University Press, 1985.

Aufderheide, Patricia. "True Confessions: The Inquisition and Social Attitudes in Brazil at the Turn of the XVII Century." *Luso-Brazilian Review* 10 (2) (Winter 1973): 208–240.

Bazant, Jan. *Cinco Haciendas Mexicanas: Tres siglos de vida rural en San Luis Potosí (1600–1910)*. México City: El Colegio de México, 1975.

Behar, Ruth. "Sex and Sin, Witchcraft and the Devil in Late-Colonial Mexico." *American Ethnologist* 14 (1) (February 1987): 34–54.

_____. "Sexual Witchcraft, Colonialism, and Women's Powers." In *Sexuality and Marriage*, ed. Lavrin: pp. 178–206.

Benavente, Olivia. "La biginia/bigamia en México." *Fem: Publicación feminista trimestral* 2 (April–June 1978): 64–65.

Bennassar, Bartolomé ed. *L'Inquisition espagnole du XVᵉ—XIXᵉ Siècle*. Paris: Hachette, 1979.

Bocanegra, Mathias de. *Jews and the Inquisition of Mexico 1649*. Trans. Seymour B. Liebman. Lawrence, Kansas: Coronado Press, 1974.

Borah, Woodrow, coord. *El gobierno provincial en la Nueva España, 1570–1787*. Mexico City: Universidad Nacional Autónoma de México, 1985.

_____. *Justice by Insurance: The General Indian Court of Colonial Mexico and the Legal Aides of the Half-Real*. Berkeley and Los Angeles: University of California Press, 1983.

_____. *Price Trends of Royal Tribute Commodities in Nueva Galicia, 1557–1598*. Ibero-Americana: 55. Berkeley, Los Angeles, Oxford: University of California Publications, 1992.

Borah, Woodrow, and Sherburne F. Cook. "Marriage and Legitimacy in Mexican Culture: Mexico and California." *California Law Review* 54 (1966): 946–997.

Bossy, John. "The Counter-Reformation and the People of Catholic Europe." *Past and Present* 47 (May 1970): 51–70.

_____. "The Mass as a Social Institution," *Past and Present* 100 (August 1983): 29–61.

Bourdieu, Pierre "Marriage Strategies as Strategies of Social Reproduction. In *Family and Society*, ed. Forster and Ranum, pp. 117–144.

Boyer, Richard. "Absolutism versus Corporatism in New Spain: The Administration of the Marquis de Gelves, 1621–1624." *International History Review*, 4 (4) (November 1982): 475–503.

_____. "Escribiendo la historia de la religión y mentalidades en Nueva España." In *Familia y Sexualidad en Nueva España*, Seminario de historia de las mentalidades, pp. 119–137.

_____. "Juan Vázquez, Muleteer of Seventeenth-Century Mexico." *The Americas* 37 (1981): 421–443.

_____. *La gran inundación: vida y sociedad en la ciudad de México (1629–1638)*. Tran. Antonieta Sánchez Mejorada. Mexico City: Secretaría de Educación Pública, 1975.

_____. "The Inquisitor, the Witness, and the Historian: the Document as Discourse." Unpublished paper, meeting of Canadian Association of Hispanists, Carleton University, Ottawa, Ontario, May 31, 1993.

_____. "Mexico in the Seventeenth Century: Transition of a Colonial Society." *Hispanic American Historical Review* 57 (3) (August 1977): 455–478.

_____. "Slavery and the Inquisition in New Spain: A Note on the 'Closed System' Thesis of Stanley Elkins." In *The Church and Society in Latin American History*, ed. Jeffrey Cole. New Orleans: Tulane University Latin American Center, 1984, pp. 125–137.

_____. "Women, La Mala Vida, and the Politics of Marriage." In *Sexuality and Marriage*, ed. Lavrin, pp. 252–286.

Boyer, Richard, and Keith Davies. *Urbanization in 19th Century Latin America: Statistics and Sources*. Los Angeles: UCLA Latin American Center, 1973.

Boyle, Leonard. "Montaillou Revisited: Mentalité and Methodology." In *Pathways to Medieval Peasants. Papers in Medieval Studies*, ed. J. A. Raftis (Toronto: Pontifical Institute of Mediaeval Studies, 1981), 2: 119–140.

Brading, D. A. "Government and Elite in Late Colonial Mexico." *Hispanic American Historical Review* 53 (3) (August 1973): 389–414.

_____. *The Origins of Mexican Nationalism*. University of Cambridge: Centre of Latin American Studies, 1985.

_____. "Tridentine Catholicism and Enlightened Despotism in Bourbon Mexico." *Journal of Latin American Studies* 15 (1) (1983): 1–22.

Brading, D. A., and Celia Wu. "Population Growth and Crisis: León, 1720–1816." *Journal of Latin American Studies* 5 (1973): 1–36.

Braudel, Fernand. *The Wheels of Commerce: Civilization and Capitalism, 15th–18th*

Century. Trans. Siân Reynolds. 3 vols. New York: Harper and Row, 1981–84.

Brundage, James A. "Sexual Equality in Medieval Canon Law." In *Medieval Women and the Sources of Medieval History*, ed. Joel T. Rosenthal. Athens and London: University of Georgia Press, 1990, pp. 66–79.

Burguière, André. "La historia de la familia en Francia: Problemas y recientes aproximaciones." In *Familia y sexualidad*, Seminario de Historia de las Mentalidades, pp. 15–35.

————. "Le rituel du mariage en France: Pratiques ecclésiastiques et pratiques populaires (XVIII siècle)." *Annales: Economies, Sociétés, Civilisations* 33 (3) (May–June 1978): 637–649.

Burke, Kenneth. *A Grammar of Motives*. Berkeley, Los Angeles, London: University of California Press, 1969 [1945].

————. *Language as Symbolic Action*. Berkeley, Los Angeles, London: University of California Press, 1966.

Calvi, Giulia. *Histories of a Plague Year: The Social and the Imaginary in Baroque Florence*. Trans. Dario Biocca and Bryant T. Ragan, Jr. Berkeley and Los Angeles: University of California Press, 1989.

Calvo, Thomas. "Matrimonio, iglesia y sociedad en el occidente de México: Zamora (siglos XVII a XIX)." In *Familias Novohispanas*, coord. Gonzalbo, pp. 101–108.

————. *Poder, religión y sociedad en la Guadalajara del siglo XVII*. Mexico City: Centre d'études Mexicaines et Centraméricaines/H. Ayuntamiento de Guadalajara, 1992.

————. "The Warmth of the Hearth: Seventeenth-Century Guadalajara Families." In *Sexuality and Marriage*, ed. Lavrin, pp. 287–312.

Castañeda, Carmen. "La formación de la pareja y el matrimonio." In *Familias novohispanas*, coord. Gonzalbo A., pp. 73–90.

Castro Gutiérrez, Felipe. *La extinción de la Artesanía Gremial*. Mexico City: Universidad Nacional Autónoma de México, 1986.

Cervantes, Miguel de. *Six Exemplary Novels*. Trans. Harriet de Onís. New York: Barron's Educational Series, 1961, pp. 163–201.

————. "La fuerza de la sangre." In *Spanish Stories/Cuentos Españoles*, ed. Angel Flores. New York: Bantam, 1960, pp. 64–91.

Chaunu, Huguette, and Pierre Chaunu. *Séville et l'Atlantique (1504–1650)*. 5 vols. Paris: Librairie Armand Colin, 1955–56.

Chaunu, Pierre. "Inquisition et vie quotidienne dans l'Amérique Espagnole au XVIIe siècle." *Annales Economies, Sociétés, Civilixzations* 11 (2) (1956): 228–236.

Chevalier, François. "New Perspectives and New Focuses on Latin American Research." *Newsletter* [Conference on Latin American History] 21 (1) (April 1985): 13–16.

Chomsky, Noam. "A Cartesian View of Language Structure." In *Noam Chomsky: *Language and Politics*, ed. C. P. Otero. Montreal and New York: Black Rose Books, 1968, pp. 100–115.

Cline, S. L. *Colonial Culhuacan, 1580–1600: A Social History of an Aztec Town.* Albuquerque: University of New Mexico Press, 1986.

Cobb, Richard. *Death in Paris, 1795–1801.* Oxford: Oxford University Press, 1978.

Cohen, Elizabeth S., and Thomas V. Cohen. "Camilla the Go-between: The Politics of Gender in a Roman Household (1559)." *Continuity and Change* 4 (1) (1989): 53–77.

Contreras, Jaime. "Las adecuaciones estructurales en la Península." In *Historia de la Inquisición en España y América*, pp. 754–59.

———. "Aldermen and Judaizers: Cryptojudaism, Counter-Reformation, and Local Power. In *Culture and Control*, ed. Cruz and Perry, pp. 93–123.

Contretas, Jaime, and Jean Pierre Dedieu. "Geografía de la Inquisición española: la formación de los distritos, 1470–1820." *Hispania* 40 (1980): 40–42.

Contretas, Jaime, and Gustav Henningsen. "Forty-Four Thousand Cases of the Spanish Inquisition (1540–1700): Analysis of a Historical Data Bank." In *The Inquisition*, ed. Henningsen and Tedeschi, pp. 100–129.

Cook, Alexandra Parma, and David Noble Cook. *Good Faith and Truthful Ignorance: A Case of Transatlantic Bigamy.* Durham and London: Duke University Press, 1991.

Corella, P Fr. Iayme de. *Práctica de el confessonario y explicación de las 65 Proposiciones . . .* [Valencia: Imprenta de Iaume de Bordazar, 1689].

Cortés Jácome, María Elena. "El grupo familiar de los negros y mulatos: Discurso y comportamientos según los archivos inquisitoriales, siglos XVI–XVIII." Thesis for the title of Licenciado en historia, Facultad de Filosofía y Letras, Universidad Nacional Autónoma de México, 1984.

Cott, Nancy F. "Divorce and the Changing Status of Women in Eighteenth-Century Massachusetts." *William and Mary Quarterly*, 3d ser., 33 (1976): 586–614.

Cruz, Anne. J. "La bella malmaridada: Lessons for the Good Wife." In *Culture and Control*, ed. Cruz and Perry, pp. 145–170.

Cruz, Anne J., and Mary Elizabeth Perry, eds. *Culture and Control in Counter-Reformation Spain.* Minneapolis: University of Minnesota Press, 1992.

Davis, Natalie Zemon. "Les conteurs de Montaillou." *Annales: Economies, Sociétés, Civilisations* 34 (1) (1979): 61–73.

———. *Fiction in the Archives: Pardon Tales and their Tellers in Sixteenth-Century France.* Stanford: Stanford University Press, 1987.

———. *Society and Culture in Early Modern France.* Stanford: Stanford University Press, 1975.

Dealy, Glen Caudill. *The Latin Americans: Spirit and Ethos*. Boulder: Westview Press, 1992.

Dedieu, Jean Pierre. *L'Administration de la Foi: L'Inquisition de Tolède (XVIe–XVIIIe Siècle*. Madrid: Casa de Velázquez, 1989.

_____. "The Archives of the Holy Office of Toledo as a Source for Historical Anthropology." Tran. E. W. Monter. In *The Inquisition*, ed. Henningsen and Tedeschi, pp. 158–189.

_____. "'Christianization' in New Castile: Catechism: Communion, Mass, and Confirmation in the Toledo Archbishopric, 1540–1650." In *Culture and Control*, ed. Cruz and Perry, pp. 1–24.

_____. "The Inquisition and Popular Culture in New Castile." In *Inquisition and Society*, ed. and tran. Haliczer, pp. 129–146.

_____. "L'Inquisition et le Droit: Analyse Formelle de la Procédure Inquisitoriale en Cause de Foi." *Mélanges de la Casa de Velázquez* 23 (1987): 227–251.

_____. "Le Modèle Sexuel: La Défense du Mariage Chrétien." In *L'Inquisition Espagnole XVᵉ–XIXᵉ Siècle*, ed. Bennassar, pp. 313–338.

Delumeau, Jean. *Sin and Fear: The Emergence of a Western Guilt Culture, 13th–18th Centuries*. Tran. Eric Nicholson. New York: St. Martin's Press, 1990.

Díaz del Castillo, Bernal. *Historia de la conquista de Nueva España*. Intro. and notes by Joaquín Ramírez Cabañas. Mexico City: Editorial Porrua, 1970.

Diccionario de la lengua Castellana. 7th ed. Madrid: La Academia Española, 1832.

Diccionario Universal de Historia y de Geografía. 7 vols. Madrid: D. Francisco de Paula Mellado, 1846–48.

Dillard, Heath. *Daughters of the Reconquest: Women in Castilian Town Society, 1100–1300*. Cambridge: Cambridge University Press, 1984.

Domínguez Ortiz, Antonio. *The Golden Age of Spain, 1516–1659*. Tran. James Casey. New York: Basic Books, 1971.

Donahue, Jr., Charles. "The Canon Law on the Formation of Marriage and Social Practice in the Later Middle Ages." *Journal of Family History* 8 (2) (Summer 1983): 144–158.

Donovan, J., trans. *The Catechism of the Council of Trent*. Dublin: Richard Coyne; London: Keating and Browne, 1829.

Duvernoy, Jean. *Inquisition à Pamiers: Interrogatoires de Jacques Fournier, 1318–1325 choisis, traduits du texte latin et présentés par . . .* [Toulouse]: Editions Edouard Privat, 1966.

Elliott, J. H. *Europe Divided 1559–1598*. Glasgow: Fontana/Collins, 1968.

Enciso Rojas, Dolores. "El delito de bigamia y el Tribunal del Santo Oficio de la Inquisición en Nueva España, siglo XVIII." Thesis for the title Licenciado en Historia, Universidad Nacional Autónoma de México, 1983.

Farriss, Nancy. *Maya Society Under Colonial Rule: The Collective Enterprise of Survival*. Princeton: Princeton University Press, 1984.

Fernández del Castillo, Bernardo Pérez. *Historia de la escribanía en la Nueva España y del notariado en México*. Mexico City: Editorial Porrua, 1988.
Forster, Robert, and Orest Ranum, eds. *Family and Society: Selecti ns from the Annales: Economies, Sociétés, Civilisations*. Trans. Elborg Forster and Patricia M. Ranum. Baltimore and London: Johns Hopkins University Press, 1976.
"Foro de Ideas," *Excelsior* (7 de Mayo de 1993): I: 1–4.
Foucault, Michel. *The History of Sexuality. Vol. 1: An Introduction*. Tran. Robert Hurley. New York: Random House, 1978.
Frye, Northrop. *Anatomy of Criticism: Four Essays*. Princeton: Princeton University Press, 1957.
Fuson. Robert H, trans. *The Log of Christopher Columbus*. Camden, Me.: International Marine Publishing Company, 1987.
Gaibrois, M. Ballesteros. "Los fondos inquisitoriales americanísticos." In *Historia de la Inquisición*, 1:90–135.
García, Francisco San Pedro. "La Reforma del Concilio de Trento en la diócesis de Coria." *Hispania Sacra* 10 (2ª semestre 1957): 273–99.
García, Genaro, ed. *Autos de fé de la Inquisición de México con extractos de sus causas 1646–1648*. Mexico City: La viuda de C. Bouret, 1910.
Genovese, Eugene D. *Roll, Jordan, Roll: The World the Slaves Made*. New York: Vintage Books, 1976.
Gerhard, Peter. *A Guide to the Historical Geography of New Spain*. Cambridge: Cambridge University Press, 1972.
———. *The North Frontier of New Spain*. Princeton: Princeton University Press, 1982.
Gibson, Charles. *The Aztecs under Spanish Rule: A History of the Indians of the Valley of Mexico, 1519–1810*. Stanford: Stanford University Press, 1964.
———. *Tlaxcala in the Sixteenth Century*. Stanford: Stanford University Press, 1967 [1952].
Ginzburg, Carlo. *The Cheese and the Worms: The Cosmos of a Sixteenth-Century Miller*. Trans. John Tedeschi and Anne Tedeschi. Baltimore: Johns Hopkins University Press, 1980.
———. *Clues, Myths, and the Historical Method*. Trans. John Tedeschi and Anne C. Tedeschi. Baltimore and London: Johns Hopkins University Press, 1989.
———. "Clues: Roots of an Evidential Paradigm," in *Clues*, Ginzburg, pp. 96–125.
Giraud, François. "De las problemáticas europeas al caso novohispano: Apuntes para una historia de la familia mexicana." In *Familia y sexualidad*, Seminario de Historia de las Mentalidades, pp. 56–80.
———. "La reacción social ante la violación: Del discurso a la práctica (Nueva España, siglo XVIII)." In *El Placer de Pecar*, Seminario de Historia de las Mentalidades, pp. 295–352.

Glowinski, Michal. "Document as Novel." *New Literary History* 18 (2) (Winter 1987): 385–401.

Gonzalbo Aizpuru, Pilar, coordinator. *Familias Novohispanas: Siglos XVI al XIX.* Mexico City: El Colegio de México, 1991.

———. *Las mujeres en la Nueva España: Educación y vida cotidiana.* Mexico City: El Colegio de México, 1987.

———. "La ortodoxia imposible: Doctrina y prática social en el campo novo-hispano." In *La ciudad y el campo,* ed. Sánchez, Van Young, and von Wobeser, 2: 857–66.

González, Jorge R. "El delito de solicitación en el obispado de Puebla durante el siglo XVIII." Thesis, Escuela Nacional de Antropología e Historia, INAH, Mexico City, 1982.

Gottlieb, Beatrice. "The Meaning of Clandestine Marriage." In *Family and Sexuality,* ed. Wheaton and Hareven, pp. 49–83.

Goubert, Pierre. *The Ancien Régime: French Society, 1600–1750.* Trans. Steve Cox. New York: Harper and Row, 1973.

Greenleaf, Richard E. "The Archivo Provisional de la Inquisición (México): A Descriptive Checklist." *The Americas* 31 (2) (October 1974): 206–11.

———. "The Great Visitas of the Mexican Holy Office 1645–1669," *The Americas* 44 (4) (April 1988): 399–420.

———. *Inquisición y sociedad en el México colonial.* Madrid: J. Porrua Turanzas, 1985.

———. "The Inquisition Brotherhood: Cofradía de San Pedro Martir of Colonial Mexico." *The Americas* 40 (2) (October 1983): 171–207.

———. *The Mexican Inquisition of the Sixteenth Century.* Albuquerque: University of New Mexico Press, 1969.

———. "The Mexican Inquisition and the Indians: Sources for the Ethno-historian." *The Americas* 34 (3) (January 1978): 315–337.

———. *Zumárraga and the Mexican Inquisition 1536–1543.* Washington, D.C.: Academy of American Franciscan History, 1962.

Gruzinski, Serge. *La Colonisation de l'Imaginaire: Sociétés Indigènes et Occidentalisation dans le Mexique Espagnol XVIe–XVIIIe siècle.* Paris: Editions Gallimard, 1988.

———. "Confesión, alianza y sexualidad entre los Indios de Nueva España. Introducción al estudio de los confesionarios en lenguas indígenas." In *El placer,* Seminario de Historia de las Mentalidades, pp. 169–215.

———. "La memoria mutilada: construcción del pasado y mecanismos de la memoria en un grupo otomí de la mitad del siglo XVII." In *La memoria y el olvido,* Seminario de Historia de las Mentalidades, pp. 33–46.

———. *Man-Gods in the Mexican Highlands.* Tran. Eileen Corrigan. Stanford.: Stanford University Press, 1989.

———. Gutiérrez, Ramon A. "From Honor to Love: Transformations of the Meaning of Sexuality in Colonial New Mexico." In *Kinship Ideology and*

Practice in Latin America, ed. Raymond T. Smith. Chapel Hill and London: University of North Carolina Press, 1984, pp. 237–263.

_____. "Honor Ideology, Marriage Negotiation, and Class-Gender Domination in New Mexico, 1690–1848." *Latin American Perspectives* 12 (Winter 1985): 81–104.

_____. *When Jesus Came, the Corn Mothers Went Away: Marriage, Sexuality, and Power in New Mexico, 1500–1846*. Stanford: Stanford University Press, 1991.

Hadley, Phillip L. *Minería y sociedad en el centro minero de Santa Eulalia, Chihuahua (1709–1750)*. Trans. Roberto Gómez Coroza. Mexico City: Fondo de Cultura Económica, 1979.

Haliczer, Stephen, ed. and trans. *Inquisition and Society in Early Modern Europe*. London and Sydney: Croom Helm, 1987.

Haring, C. H. *The Spanish Empire in America*. New York and Burlingame: Harcourt, Brace and World, 1947.

Haviland, John Beard. *Gossip, Reputation, and Knowledge in Zinacantán*. Chicago and London: University of Chicago Press, 1977.

Henningsen, Gustav. "The Archives and the Historiography of the Spanish Inquisition," In *The Inquisition*, ed. Henningsen and Tedeschi, pp. 54–78.

_____. "El Banco de datos: Las relaciones de causas de la Inquisición española (1550–1700)." *Boletín de la Real Academia de la Historia* 174 (1977): 547–70.

_____. *The Witches' Advocate: Basque Witchcraft and the Spanish Inquisition (1609–1614)*. Reno: University of Nevada Press, 1980.

Henningsen, Gustav, and John Tedeschi, eds. *The Inquisition in Early Modern Europe: Studies on Sources and Methods*. Dekalb, Ill.: Northern Illinois University Press, 1986.

Historia de la Inquisición en España y América, I: El conocimiento científico y el proceso histórico de la Institución (1478–1834). Directed by Joaquín Pérez Villanueva and Bartolomé Escandell Bonet. Madrid: Biblioteca de Autores Cristianos/Centro de Estudios Inquisitoriales, 1984.

Hoberman, Louisa Schell. *Mexico's Merchant Elite, 1590–1660: Silver, State, and Society*. Durham and London: Duke University Press, 1991.

Hordes, Stanley M. "The Crypto-Jewish Community of New Spain, 1620–1649: A Collective Biography." Ph.D diss., Tulane University, 1980.

_____. "The Inquisition as Economic and Political Agent: The Campaign of the Mexican Holy Office against the Crypto-Jews in the Mid-Seventeenth Century." *The Americas* 39 (1982): 23–38.

A. Huerga. "La implantación del Santo Oficio en México." In *Historia de la Inquisición*, 1: 724–30.

_____. "El Tribunal de México en la época de Felipe II." In *Historia de la Inquisición*, 1: 937–69.

Icaza, Francisco A. de, compiler. *Conquistadores y pobladores de Nueva España: Diccionario autobiográfico sacado de los textos originales*. 2 vols. Biblioteca de

Facsímiles Mexicanos. Guadalajara: Edmundo Aviña Levy, 1969 [Madrid, 1923].

Jiménez Rueda, Julio. *Don Pedro Moya de Contreras: Primer Inquisidor de México.* Mexico City: Ediciones Xochitl, 1944.

Kagan, Richard L. *Lucrecia's Dreams: Politics and Prophecy in Sixteenth-Century Spain.* Berkeley, Los Angeles, Oxford: University of California Press, 1990.

Kaminsky, Howard. "From Mentalité to Mentality: The Implications of a Novelty." In *The Middle Period in Latin America: Values and Attitudes in the 17th–19th Centuries,* ed. Szuchman. Boulder & London: Lynne Rienner Publishers, 1989: pp. 19–31.

Kicza, John E. *Colonial Entrepreneurs: Families and Business in Bourbon Mexico City.* Albuquerque: University of New Mexico Press, 1983.

Klor de Alva, J. Jorge. "Sin and Confession among the Colonial Nahuas: The Confessional as a Tool for Domination." In *La ciudad y el campo,* ed. Sánchez, Van Young, and von Wobeser, 1: 91–101.

Lanning, John Tate. *The Royal Protomedicato: The Regulation of the Medical Profession in the Spanish Empire.* Ed. John Jay Tepaske. Durham: Duke University Press, 1985.

Laslett, Peter. *The World We Have Lost.* London: Methuen and Company, 1965 [1970].

Lautman, Françoise. "Differences or Changes in Family Organization." In *Family and Society,* ed. Forster and Ranum, pp. 251–261.

Lavrin, Asunción. "Introduction: The Scenario, the Actors, and the Issues." In *Sexuality and Marriage,* ed. Lavrin, pp. 1–43.

_____. "Sexuality in Colonial Mexico: A Church Dilemma." In *Sexuality and Marriage,* ed. Lavrin, pp. 47–92.

_____, ed. *Sexuality and Marriage in Colonial Latin America.* Lincoln: University of Nebraska Press, 1989.

Lavrin, Asunción, and Couturier, Edith. "Dowries and Wills: A View of Women's Socioeconomic Role in Colonial Guadalajara and Puebla, 1640–1790." *Hispanic American Historical Review* 59 (2) (May 1979): 280–304.

Lea, Henry Charles. *A History of the Inquisition of Spain.* 4 vols. New York: AMS Press, 1966 [1906–07].

Le Goff, Jacques. *The Birth of Purgatory.* Trans. Arthur Goldhammer. Chicago: University of Chicago Press, 1981.

Leonard, Irving A. *Baroque Times in Old Mexico: Seventeenth-Century Persons, Places, and Practices.* Ann Arbor: University of Michigan Press, 1959.

Le Roy Ladurie, Emmanuel. *Montaillou: The Promised Land of Error.* Trans. Barbara Bray. New York: George Braziller, 1978.

Levillier, Roberto. *Nueva crónica de la conquista del Tucumán.* 3 vols. Madrid: Sucesores de Rivadeneyra, 1927–31.

Lewis, Leslie. "In Mexico City's Shadow: Some Aspects of Economic Activity and Social Processes in Texcoco, 1570–1620." In *Provinces of Early Mexico*, ed. Altman and Lockhart, pp. 125–153.

Liebman, Seymour B. "The Great Conspiracy in New Spain." *The Americas* 30 (1973): 13–81.

―――. *The Jews in New Spain: Faith, Flame, and the Inquisition*. Coral Gables: University of Miami Press, 1970.

Lipsett-Rivera, Sonya. "La violencia dentro de la familia formal e informal." Paper prepared for the Conference Familia y vida privada en la historia de Iberoamérica, May 3–4, 1993, Mexico City.

Lockhart, James. "Capital and Province, Spaniard and Indian: The Example of Late Sixteenth-Century Toluca." In *Provinces of Early Mexico*, ed. Altman and Lockhart, pp. 99–123.

―――. *Nahuas and Spaniards: Postconquest Central Mexican History and Philology*. Stanford: Stanford University Press, 1991.

―――. Review of *Reliving the Past: The Worlds of Social History*, ed. Olivier Zunz. *Hispanic American Historical Review* 67 (3) (August 1987): 499–501.

―――. "Social Organization and Social Change in Colonial Spanish America." In *The Cambridge History of Latin America*, ed. Leslie Bethell. 2 vols. Cambridge: Cambridge University Press, 1984, II: 263–319.

―――. "Spaniards Among Indians: Toluca in the Late Sixteenth Century." In *Nahuas and Spaniards*, Lockhart, pp. 202–42.

―――. *Spanish Peru, 1532–1560: A Colonial Society*. Madison: University of Wisconsin Press, 1968.

Lockhart, James, and Enrique Otte. *Letters and People of the Spanish Indies: The Sixteenth Century*. London: Cambridge University Press, 1976.

López Austin, Alfredo. "La construcción de la memoria." In *La memoria y el olvido*, Seminario de Historia de las Mentalidades, pp. 75–79.

López Lara, Ramón, ed. *El obispado de Michoacán en el siglo XVII: Informe inédito de beneficios, pueblos y lenguas* (Colección "Estudios Michoacanos," 3). Morelia: Fimax Publicistas, 1973.

Lynch, John. *Spain under the Habsburgs*. 2 vols. Oxford: Basil Blackwell, 1964.

Macleod, Murdo J. "Ethnic Relations and Indian Society in the Province of Guatemala, ca. 1620–ca. 1800." In *Spaniards and Indians*, ed. Macleod and Wasserstrom, pp. 189–214.

―――. *Spanish Central America: A Socioeconomic History, 1520–1720*. Berkeley: University of California Press, 1973.

Macleod, Murdo J, and Robert Wasserstrom, eds. *Spaniards and Indians in Southeastern Mesoamerica: Essays on the History of Ethnic Relations*. Lincoln and London: University of Nebraska Press, 1983.

Malvido, Elsa. "Algunos aportes de los estudios de demografía histórica al estudio de la familia en la época colonial de México." In *Familia y sexualidad*, Seminario de Historia de las Mentalidades, pp. 81–99.

Margadant, Guillermo F. "La familia en el derecho novohispano." In *Familias novohispanas*, coord. Gonzalbo A., pp. 27–56.

Marroqui, José María. *La Ciudad de México*. 3 vols. 2d ed. Mexico City: Jesús Medina, 1969.

Martínez-Alier, Verena. Marriage, *Class and Colour in Nineteenth-Century Cuba: A Study of Racial Attitudes and Sexual Values in a Slave Society*. 2d ed. Ann Arbor: University of Michigan Press, 1989.

McAlister, Lyle N. *Spain and Portugal in the New World, 1492–1700*. Minneapolis: University of Minnesota Press, 1984.

McCaa, Robert. "Calidad, Class, and Marriage in Colonial Mexico: The Case of Parral, 1788–90," *Hispanic American Historical Review* 64 (3) (August 1984): 477–501.

_____. "Gustos de los padres, inclinaciones de los novios y reglas de una feria nupcial colonial: Parral, 1770–1814." *Historia Mexicana*, 40 (4) (1991): 579–614.

_____. "Marriageways: Courtship, Coupling, Cohabitation and Matrimony in Mexico and Spain, 1500–1900." Paper prepared for the Conference Familia y Vida Privada en la historia de Iberoamérica, May 3–4, 1993, Mexico City.

Medina, José Toribio. *Historia del Tribunal del Santo Oficio de la Inquisición en México*. 2d. ed., ampliada por Julio Jiménez Rueda. Mexico City: Ediciones Fuente Cultural, 1952.

Monteserin, M. Jiménez. "Léxico inquisitorial." In *Historia de la Inquisición en España y América*, 1:184–217.

Morgan, Edmund S. *American Slavery, American Freedom: The Ordeal of Colonial Virginia*. New York: W. W. Norton and Company, 1975.

Morin, Claude. *Santa Ines Zacatelco (1646–1812)*. Mexico City: Instituto Nacional de Antropología e Historia, 1973.

Morse, Richard M. From *Community to Metropolis: A Biography of São Paulo, Brazil*. New and enlarged ed. New York: Octagon Books, 1974.

Mosse, G. L. "Changes in Religious Thought." In *The New Cambridge Modern History*, vol. 4: *The Decline of Spain and the Thirty Years War, 1609–48/59*, ed J.P. Cooper. Cambridge: Cambridge University Press, 1970, pp. 169–201.

Muir, Edward, and Guido Ruggiero, eds. *Microhistory and the Lost Peoples of Europe*. Trans. Eren Branch. Baltimore and London: Johns Hopkins University Press, 1991.

Muriel, Josefina. "La transmisión cultural en la familia criolla novohispana." In *Familias novohispanas*, coord. Gonzalbo, pp. 109–122.

Nalle, Sara. "Religion and Reform in a Spanish Diocese: Cuenca, 1545–1650." Ph.D. diss., Johns Hopkins University, 1983.

Nazarri, Muriel. "Parents and Daughters: Change in the Practice of Dowry in

São Paulo (1600–1770)." *Hispanic American Historical Review* 70 (4) (November 1990): 639–65.

O'Gorman, Edmundo, Director. *Guía de las actas de cabildo de la ciudad de México, siglo XVI.* Mexico City: Fondo de Cultura Económica, 1970.

Ortega Noriega, Sergio. "Introducción a la Historia de las Mentalidades. Aspectos metodológicos." *Estudios de Historia Novohispana* 8 (Mexico City: UNAM, 1985): 127–138.

_____. "Seminario de historia de las mentalidades y religión en México colonial." In *Familia y Sexualidad en Nueva España*, Seminario de Historia de las Mentalidades, pp. 100–18.

_____, ed. *De la santidad a la perversión o de porqué se cumplía la ley de Dios en la sociedad novohispana.* Mexico City: Grijalbo, 1986.

Parry, J. H. *The Sale of Public Office in the Spanish Indies under the Hapsburgs.* Ibero-Americana 37. Berkeley and Los Angeles: University of California Press, 1953.

Paso y Troncoso, Francisco del, compiler. *Epistolario de Nueva España, 1505–1818.* 16 vols. Mexico City: Antigua Librería Robredo de José Porrúa e Hijos, 1939–42.

Pastor, Rodolfo. "El repartimiento de mercancías y los alcaldes mayores novohispanos: un systema de explotación, de sus orígenes a la crisis de 1810." In *El gobierno provincial*, ed. Borah, pp. 201–236.

Perry, Mary Elizabeth. *Gender and Disorder in Early Modern Seville.* Princeton: Princeton University Press, 1990.

Pescador, Juan Javier. *De bautizados a fieles difuntos: Familia y mentalidades en una parroquia urbana: Santa Catarina de México, 1568–1820.* Mexico City: El Colegio de México, 1992.

_____. "Uxoricidas-Indultados: Justicia, Familia y Patriarcado en el México Central, 1770–1820." Paper prepared for the Conference Familia y vida privada en la historia de Iberoamérica, May 3–4, 1993, Mexico City.

Peters, Edward. *Inquisition.* Berkeley and Los Angeles: University of California Press, 1989.

Porras Munoz, Guillermo. *El gobierno de la cuidad de México en el siglo XVI.* Mexico City: Universidad Nacional Autónoma de México, 1982.

_____. *Iglesia y estado en Nueva Vizcaya (1562–1821).* Mexico City: Universidad Nacional Autónoma de México, 1980.

Reyes G., Cayetano. "Expósitos e hidalgos, la polarización social de la Nueva España." *Boletín del Archivo General de la Nación*, ser.3, 5 (2) (16) (April–June 1981):3–5.

Ricard, Robert. *The Spiritual Conquest of Mexico.* Trans. Lesley Byrd Simpson. Berkeley, Los Angeles, London: University of California Press, 1966.

Rosaldo, Renato. "From the Door of His Tent: The Fieldworker and the Inquisitor." In *Writing Culture: The Poetics and Politics of Ethnography*, ed.

James Clifford and George E. Marcus, Berkeley and Los Angeles: University of California Press, 1986, pp. 77–97.

Ruiz Gaytán F., Beatriz. "Un grupo trabajador importante no incluido en la historia laboral mexicana (trabajadoras domésticas)." In *El trabajo y los trabajadores en la historia de México*, comp. Elsa Cecilia Frost, Michael C. Meyer and Josefina Zoraida Vásquez. Mexico City and Tucson: El Colegio de México and University of Arizona Press, 1979, pp. 419–55.

Samuel, Raphael. "Reading the Signs." *History Workshop* 32 (Autumn 1991): 88–109.

Sánchez, Ricardo, Eric Van Young, and Gisela von Wobeser, eds. *La ciudad y el campo en la historia de México: Memoria de la VII Reunión de Historiadores Mexicanos y Norteamericanos*. 2 vols. Mexico City: Universidad Nacional Autónoma de México, 1992.

Santamaría, Francisco J. *Diccionario de Mejicanismos*. Mexico City: Editorial Porrua, 1959.

Sarrión Mora, Adelina. "El médico y la sociedad rural del siglo XVII: El proceso inquisitorial de Francisco Martínez Casas." In *Inquisición Española: Nuevas Aproximaciones*, ed. Jaime Contreras. Madrid: Centro de Estudios Inquisitoriales, 1987, pp. 297–321.

Scardaville, Michael C. "Alcohol Abuse and Tavern Reform in Late Colonial Mexico City." *Hispanic American Historical Review* 60:4 (November 1980): 643–71.

———. "Crime and the Urban Poor: Mexico City in the Late Colonial Period." Ph.D. Diss., University of Florida, 1977.

Scott, James C. *Domination and the Arts of Resistance: Hidden Transcripts*. New Haven and London: Yale University Press, 1990.

Seed, Patricia. "Marriage Promises and the Value of a Woman's Testimony in Colonial Mexico." *Signs* 13 (2) (Winter 1988): 253–76.

———. *To Love, Honor, and Obey in Colonial Mexico: Conflicts Over Marriage Choice, 1574–1821*. Stanford: Stanford University Press, 1988.

Seminario de Historia de las Mentalidades. *Del Dicho al hecho . . . : Transgresiones y pautas culturales en la Nueva España*. Mexico City: Instituto Nacional de Antropología e Historia, 1989.

———. *Familia y sexualidad en Nueva España*. Mexico City: Fondo de Cultura Económica, 1982.

———. *Introducción a la historia de las mentalidades*. Cuadernos de trabajo, no. 24. Mexico City: Instituto Nacional de Antropología e Historia, 1979.

———. *La memoria y el olvido: Segundo simposio de historia de las mentalidades*. Mexico City: Instituto Nacional de Antropología e Historia-SEP Cultura, 1985.

———. *El placer de pecar y el afán de normar*. Mexico City: Editorial Joaquín Mortiz, 1987.

_____. *Seis ensayos sobre el discurso colonial relativo a la comunidad doméstica.* Cuadernos de trabajo, no. 35. Mexico City: Instituto Nacional de Antropología e Historia, 1980.

Shorter, Edward. *The Making of the Modern Family.* New York: Basic Books, 1975.

Simpson, Lesley Byrd. *Many Mexicos.* 4th rev. ed. Berkeley and Los Angeles: University of California Press, 1966.

Socolow, Susan M. "Acceptable Partners: Marriage Choice in Colonial Argentina, 1778–1810." In *Sexuality and Marriage*, ed. Lavrin, pp. 209–46.

_____. "Women and Crime: Buenos Aires, 1757–97." In *The Problem of Order in Changing Societies: Essays on Crime and Policing in Argentina and Uruguay, 1750–1940*, ed. Lyman L. Johnson. Albuquerque: University of New Mexico Press, 1990, pp. 1–18.

Spalding, Karen. "Social Climbers: Changing Patterns of Mobility among the Indians of Colonial Peru." *Hispanic American Historical Review* 50 (4) (November 1970): 645–64.

Suárez Fernández, L. "Los antecedentes medievales de la Institución." In *Historia de la Inquisición*, I:249–67.

Swann, Michael M. Tierra Adentro: Settlement and Society in Colonial Durango. Boulder: Westview Press, 1982.

Tambs, Lewis A. "The Inquisition in Eighteenth-Century Mexico," *The Americas* 22 (2) (October 1965): 167–181.

Taylor, William B. *Drinking, Homicide, and Rebellion in Colonial Mexican Villages.* Stanford: Stanford University Press, 1979.

Tedeschi, John. "Preliminary Observations on Writing a History of the Roman Inquisition." In *Continuity and Discontinuity in Church History*, ed. F. Forrester Church and Timothy George. Leiden: E. J. Brill, 1979, pp. 232–249.

Thompson, E. P. "Patrician Society, Plebeian Culture." *Journal of Social History* 7 (1) (Fall 1973): 382–405.

Thompson, G. A. *The Geographical and Historical Dictionary of America and the West Indies . . .* 5 vols. New York: Burt Franklin 1970 [Reprint ed.].

Thompson, J. Eric S, ed. *Thomas Gage's Travels in the New World.* Norman: University of Oklahoma Press, 1958.

Todorov, Tzvetan. *The Conquest of America.* Trans. Richard Howard. New York: Harper and Row, 1987.

Tutino, John M. From *Insurrection to Revolution in Mexico: Social Bases of Agrarian Violence, 1750–1940.* Princeton: Princeton University Press, 1988.

_____. "Provincial Spaniards, Indian Towns, and Haciendas: Interrelated Agrarian Sectors in the Valleys of Mexico and Toluca, 1750–1810." In *Provinces of Early Mexico*, ed. Altman and Lockhart, pp. 177–194.

Twinam, Ann. "Honor, Sexuality, and Illegitimacy in Colonial Spanish America." In *Sexuality and Marriage*, ed. Lavrin, pp. 118–55.

Ullmann, Walter. *Medieval Political Thought*. Baltimore: Penguin, 1975.

Van Oss, Adriaan C. *Catholic Colonialism: A Parish History of Guatemala, 1524–1821*. Cambridge: Cambridge University Press, 1986.

Van Young, Eric. "The Cuautla Lazarus: Double Subjectives in Reading Texts on Popular Collective Action." *Colonial Latin American Review* 2 (1–2) (1993): 3–26.

———. "Millennium on the northern marches: the mad messiah of Durango and popular rebellion in Mexico, 1800–1850." *Comparative Studies in Society and History* 28 (1986): 385–413.

Villafuerte García, María de Lourdes. "Casar y compadrar cada uno con su igual: casos de oposición al matrimonio de la ciudad de México, 1628–1634." In *Del dicho*, Seminario de Historia de las Mentalidades, pp. 59–76.

Viqueira Albán, Juan Pero. *¿Relajados o reprimidos? Diversiones públicas y vida social en la ciudad de México durante el Siglo de las Luces*. Mexico City: Fondo de Cultura Económica, 1987.

Wakefield, Walter L. Heresy, *Crusade and Inquisition in Southern France, 1100–1250*. Berkeley and Los Angeles: University of California Press, 1974.

Wheaton, Robert. "Introduction: Recent Trends in the Historical Study of the French Family." In *Family and Sexuality*, ed. Wheaton and Hareven, pp. 3–26.

Wheaton, Robert, and Tamara K. Hareven, eds. *Family and Sexuality in French History*. Philadelphia: University of Pennsylvania Press, 1980.

White, Deborah Gray. *Ar'nt I a Woman? Female Slaves in the Plantation South*. New York: Norton, 1985.

Wilcox, Donald J. *In Search of God and Self: Renaissance and Reformation Thought*. Boston: Houghton Mifflin, 1975.

Zorita, Alonso de. *Life and Labor in Ancient Mexico: The Brief and Summary Relation of the Lords of New Spain*. Trans. and with an intro. by Benjamin Keen. New Brunswick, New Jersey: Rutgers University Press, 1963.

Index

About the Book and the Author

LIVES OF THE BIGAMISTS
Marriage, Family, and Community in Colonial Mexico
Richard Boyer

✛ THIS FASCINATING EXAMINATION of bigamy in colonial Mexico reveals for the first time the lives, routines, and networks of ordinary people. The author, drawing from his close reading of Inquisition files, situates these people in the web of daily life: in families as they grow up and in communities as they learn the ways of society. And with vivid glimpses of courtship, loss of virginity, marriage, adultery, abusive treatment, and failed marriage, he also follows them in their private lives. Throughout he views private intersecting with public life in the play of paternalist and deferential mannerisms, which both hid and smoothed inequities within the social order.

In their campaign to root out bigamy, the Inquisition relied on people to denounce one another. How they went about this reveals that gossip and curiosity sustained a surer and swifter system of communications than we might have imagined.

The many pieces of stories recounted here convey emotions and reactions rarely preserved from past centuries. From a young child enduring abuse and rape by relatives to the wily suitor who tricks a father with a tale of lost loot stored in a robber's cave to elope with his daughter, throughout this volume we hear the voices of hitherto invisible people.

"A distinguished book."—Professor William B. Taylor

Richard Boyer is a professor of history at Simon Fraser University and the author of a book on seventeenth century Mexico City as well as a number of articles on colonial Mexico.